The
Politics
of
Aristotle

The
Politics
of
Aristotle

Translated, *with* introduction,
analysis, *and* notes, *by*
Peter L. Phillips Simpson

The University of North Carolina Press *Chapel Hill and London*

Library of Congress Cataloging-in-Publication Data

Aristotle.

[Politics. English]

The Politics of Aristotle / translated, with
introduction, analysis, and notes, by Peter L. Phillips
Simpson.

p.   cm.

Includes bibliographical references and index.

ISBN 0-8078-2327-9 (cloth : alk. paper). —
ISBN 0-8078-4637-6 (pbk. : alk. paper)

1. Political science—Early works to 1800.   I. Simpson,
Peter L. Phillips, 1951- .

JC71.A41S47   1997

320'.01'1—dc20   96-30395

                                                      CIP

01 00 99 98 97   5 4 3 2 1

To the pupils and teachers
of Kingswood School,
Bath, England,
where I was first introduced
to the delights of Greek.

Contents

Acknowledgments

I have incurred many debts, extending back over many years, in the process of thinking about Aristotle's *Politics* and in preparing this translation of it. By far my greatest debt is due to Paul Rahe. Not only did he first put into my mind the idea of doing this translation, but he was unstinting in his encouragement, advice, and criticism at every subsequent stage. The number of errors from which he has saved me and the number of improvements into which he has persuaded me can hardly be calculated. Doubtless he would wish he had conquered more of my stubbornness and saved me from more of the errors that remain and persuaded me into more of the improvements that are lacking. Perhaps, however, he will be satisfied to have achieved as much as he did. Certainly, the merits that the translation now has are due in no small part to his untiring kindness and friendship.

There are other friends and colleagues, and students too, who at various stages and in various ways have given me advice about how to understand and translate Aristotle's *Politics*. This advice I have not always taken, to be sure, but I have always been forced to think it through and, if I disagreed with it, to work out my reasons for doing so and carefully weigh those reasons against the countervailing advice. Since the respective contributions of these friends, colleagues, and students are not now clearly distinguishable in my mind, I will content myself with listing them alphabetically. However, one of them should be singled out first. Robert Talisse read the entire manuscript just before it was due to go to the Press for printing and, apart from other helpful suggestions, gave advice that enabled me to settle my mind on one particular and important point of translation. Others I should mention include Günter Bien, Robert Chiles, Diskin Clay, Ian Crombie, George Forrest, Dieter Harlfinger, Karl-Joachim Hölkeskamp, George Kennedy, Richard Kennington, Carnes Lord, Fred D. Miller Jr., Larry Nachman, Carlo Natali, Martin Ostwald, Pierre Pellegrin, Michael Rohr, Eckart Schütrumpf, Jacob Stern, and Zeph Stewart. I would also like to give a special word of thanks to the anonymous reader for the University of North Carolina Press, who gave several valuable criticisms and suggestions. None of these gentlemen, of course, is responsible for any errors remaining.

I have had the privilege of teaching Aristotle's *Politics* several times over the past fifteen years, at University College Dublin, at the Catholic University of America, at the Graduate School of the City University of New

York, and at the International Academy for Philosophy in the Principality of Liechtenstein. I would like to thank all my students at each of these places who, in various and sometimes unknowing ways, helped to improve and clarify my thinking. I would also like to thank all my colleagues at the same places, as well as those at the College of Staten Island of the City University of New York, for support and encouragement of a more general but no less necessary kind.

While working on Aristotle's *Politics*, and on the translation in particular, I received much assistance in the form of grants, fellowships, and study leaves. I must thank first of all the College of Staten Island of the City University of New York for granting me a special study leave while I was still a junior faculty member and a further sabbatical leave some years later to finish this work. In addition I must thank the Professional Staffs Congress of the same university for supporting me with summer travel grants and fellowships over a period of some six years and in particular for providing a handsome subvention to the University of North Carolina Press to help defray the costs of publication.

I must thank, too, the Center for Hellenic Studies in Washington, D.C., where I spent a delightful year in 1991–92. Zeph Stewart and his engaging wife Diana were splendid hosts—all the more splendid, perhaps, because it was Zeph's last year as director and the two of them evidently wanted to make it one of his very best. In this, as far as I was concerned, they succeeded admirably. I would also like to offer thanks to the senior fellows for appointing me to a junior fellowship; to all the staff of the Center, who each performed their respective jobs with much efficiency and grace; and, last but not least, to the other junior fellows in my year, who, with or without spouses and children, all contributed to the restful atmosphere and collegial scholarship of the place: Mary Whitlock Blundell, Carlo Brillante, Diana Delia, Christopher Faraone, Karl-Joachim Hölkeskamp, Lisa Kallet-Marx, Andrei Rossius.

During my sabbatical leave, the Earhart Foundation in Ann Arbor, Michigan, awarded me a substantial fellowship that enabled me to devote the entire academic year to this project. Without the Foundation's assistance I might not have been sufficiently freed from financial necessities to give myself fully to research and writing. I remain most grateful, therefore, to the Trustees of the Earhart Foundation for their generosity in this regard.

The concluding stages of my study for, and writing of, the translation were completed in Rome and Athens. I am grateful to the American University of Rome, the American Academy in Rome, the American School of Classical Studies at Athens, and the Australian Archaeological Institute at Athens for their help and support. Those among their staffs and fellows with whom I had most direct contact are remembered with much gratitude and affection. A special debt of thanks is additionally owed to the staff of the University of North Carolina Press, in particular to Lewis Bateman, Katherine Malin, and Ron Maner, for all the hard work and care they devoted to bringing this work to publication.

I would like to end these acknowledgments, however, by expressing my thanks not to any who were directly involved in this particular exercise in translating Greek but rather to those who first taught me how to read and translate any Greek at all. I mean my teachers at Kingswood School in Bath, England, where I received what I still consider to be the most precious part of my school education, a thorough grounding in the classics. The learning of the Greek and Latin languages, history, and literature has suffered much eclipse on both sides of the Atlantic even, indeed, since I was a boy. I consider myself fortunate that enough of it was still there in my younger days, and at Kingswood School in particular, that I could still be initiated into the mysteries, and by such able, caring, and patient teachers. To Michael Bishop, Desmond Brown, Alec Dakin, John Gardner, and George Hubbuck I give my heartfelt thanks. I hope this translation will not make them ashamed to acknowledge me for one of their pupils.

May 1996
New York City

Introduction

The following translation of Aristotle's *Politics* has been written with a view to my commentary on the same work, contained in a companion volume. Since the commentary is a philosophical one, the translation has been written to facilitate as much as possible comprehension of the philosophical sense. As a result, the translation is distinctive in several important respects, most notably in its division of the text, its accompanying headings and summaries, and new translations of certain difficult sentences. Also distinctive are the way it reconceptualizes the unity of the text and changes the order of the books and the way it locates the *Politics* in the context of the *Nicomachean Ethics*.

Division and Interpretation of the Text

Since antiquity, the Greek text of the *Politics* has been divided into books and chapters, and though these divisions are doubtless not Aristotle's, they do on the whole mark the logical articulations of his argument. However, there are some cases where the chapters (though not the books) obscure rather than reveal these articulations; in addition, these chapters lack divisions into paragraphs. Editors and translators must determine the paragraph divisions themselves. Moreover, they also must provide punctuation and sentence divisions, for the ancients used little in the way of punctuation marks. While in most cases the right punctuation is obvious from the Greek itself (from the grammar and the particles), sometimes it is not, and sentences admit of more than one division and more than one sense. For the most part, of course, the context itself makes clear what the right division and the right sense are. Sometimes, however, it does not; sometimes too what seems clear to one editor or translator does not seem so to others. In such cases, therefore, editors and translators are obliged to reach their own judgment about what the logic and sense of Aristotle's argument require. In other words, editors and translators are obliged to become, however minimally, commentators as well. For my part, I have chosen to become a commentator altogether, by providing a separate and philosophical commentary in addition to the translation. Moreover, because, in the course of writing the commentary, I have come to a number of novel interpretations of Aristotle's argument, these novel interpretations are necessarily reflected in novel divisions in the translation (as for instance in the first two chapters of what is book 4 of my translation) and also in novel translations (as for instance at 1254b23–24, 1291a31–33, and 1300a38–b1).[1]

In addition, I have gone further and have not merely introduced new divisions and translations where necessary, but have marked the whole text by inserting throughout it headings and summaries for what I take to be the main divisions of Aristotle's argument. These headings and summaries are, it must be stressed, all my own additions and do not translate anything in the text. Such a practice of providing headings and summaries is not, to be sure, a novel one, since some other translators and commentators have done the same; but it is a controversial one, for it can seem that in this way one is intervening too much in the text and imposing an interpretation on it instead of allowing readers to interpret for themselves. I admit the difficulty here, but there is an opposite difficulty: that the translated text, if left bare and uncommented, can seem so obscure as to be impenetrable, especially to the uninstructed reader. Such obscurity is the more likely in the case of Aristotle, who can be extraordinarily brief and elliptical. The translator is therefore left with the alternatives of either letting readers flounder about or aiding them to an interpretation through the translation itself. Of course any translator is already interpreting to some extent, above all through the vocabulary one chooses and the divisions and punctuation one adopts. But in the case of Aristotle much more by way of interpretation is required if his writing is to be rendered sufficiently intelligible. The best way to provide this something more is, I contend, to intersperse the translation with appropriate headings and summaries. In this way readers can be alerted in advance as to what comes next and how it fits in with what has gone before, while at the same time not having an interpretation imposed on them willy-nilly. The interpretation is expressed in the headings and summaries, not embedded in the translation proper, so that readers are always able to test the interpretation against the translation and see if it really is a fair one.

In this way, indeed, one can steer a mean between two main styles of translation, the literal and the paraphrastic.[2] The paraphrastic style, as its name implies, renders the original not by translating word for word but by paraphrase, so that the sense is conveyed but not necessarily the precise words. One can, instead, be rather loose with respect to words and omit and add as one thinks fit. One thus gains the advantage of being able to

---

1. Throughout this translation and its accompanying analytical outline, text passages are identified by Bekker numbers, which reference the edition of Aristotle's works published by the Berlin Academy (1831–70). For example, the passage identified as 1.4.1253b23 is found in book 1, chapter 4, page 1253, column b, line 23.

2. See Saunders (1986: 216).

produce a translation that is immediately readable and also contains within itself sufficient indications of the structure and direction of the argument as to prevent readers becoming confused and lost. The corresponding disadvantage, of course, is not merely that such a translation is inaccurate as to precise words and details but, more seriously, that it hides its interpretation within itself and does not give readers the wherewithal to judge the accuracy of this interpretation or to form an alternative interpretation of their own. The literal style of translation, by contrast, has the advantage that it can be very accurate as to precise words and details and thus, because it does not hide an interpretation within itself (or does so as little as possible), can leave readers free to reach their own interpretations. Its corresponding disadvantage, however, as already noted, is that the translation can become so hard to read and leave the text so impenetrable that readers are not so much free to form their own judgments as incapable of doing so.

It would be unfair to say that any of the currently available translations is altogether of one style or the other, but they do all tend, some markedly so, toward this or that extreme. However, one can avoid having to choose between these styles, or at any rate avoid having to choose between their respective advantages and disadvantages, by producing a translation that is literal or tends to that extreme (without, however, being so literal as to cease to be readable English) while providing at the same time, through separate headings and summaries, all the indications of structure and argument that an uninstructed reader will need. Such a combination is what I have attempted to achieve in the following translation. What the translation may still unavoidably lack, by way of accuracy on the one hand or intelligibility on the other, can be suitably supplied, I hope, by the commentary.

In drawing a distinction between translation and interpretation, I do not wish to imply that a translation is not also in some ways an interpretation. For, as already noted, a translator must at least choose what vocabulary to use, and such choice necessarily involves interpretation. I merely wish to draw attention to the fact that interpretation is a manifold task and that a given translation can undertake more or less of this task. Specifically, it can go beyond the finding of equivalents for the words and sentences of the original language to the inclusion also of some exposition of structure and argument—through paraphrase, for instance, or through headings and summaries, or through editorial additions in the text, or in some other way. One cannot separate the former task from the task of translating, but one can so separate the latter task, and it is the latter I particularly have in mind when I speak of interpretation and of its distinction from translation.

On the other hand, I do not wish to give any support to the idea that an interpretation, or even a translation to the extent it too has to interpret, is always in some ways an imposition on the text or a distortion and falsification of it. For, on the contrary, interpretations can be either correct or incorrect and they can be so only because they do, or do not, uncover the meaning that is already present in the text.[3] A false interpretation is indeed an imposition and a distortion, but a true one is not. I have tried everywhere to give a true interpretation, but that I have tried does not guarantee that I have succeeded. Readers must perforce use their own minds to judge the accuracy of what I have said. But I have done what I could, whether in the translation itself or in the commentary, to make such judging possible.

Unity and Order of the Text

That the *Politics* is the work of Aristotle is not a matter for doubt. What is doubted is whether it forms a single and coherent whole, planned by Aristotle as such, or whether instead it is a composite of disparate parts that were originally written at different times, on different assumptions and for different reasons, and that were put together, in a not very convincing manner, by some editor. The general state of scholarly opinion on this question may be said to be as follows: there are first those scholars who say that the *Politics* is not a coherent whole either in doctrine or form; there are second those who say it is a coherent whole in doctrine but not in form; and there are those who say it is a coherent whole in both doctrine and form.[4]

The first group argue for their view on the ground that the *Politics* contains many contradictions and incoherences, both within and between books, and that these are incompatible with the *Politics* being a complete whole as opposed to an ill-assorted amalgam. The second group agree that there are incoherences but counter that these are in the form only and do not extend to the doctrine, or extend only to certain details of the doctrine and not to its substance. The third group also agree that there are incoherences in the form but counter that these are apparent, not real, and that be-

---

3. The theory, espoused by some, that words and texts do not have meanings of themselves but that the meaning is always created by the reader in the act of reading, can hardly be sustained. For, first, unless words had meanings of themselves they could never be used by an author to convey anything, or anything definite, to the author's readers, and so could never be used by proponents of this theory to state the theory. Second, any words used to state the theory would, according to the theory itself, mean whatever the reader made them mean while reading them, including, if the reader chose, the opposite of the theory. Third, the proponents of the theory could never say that such a reader had misunderstood the theory. For they could only say this if they said that the reader had taken the words stating the theory to mean something other than what they do really mean. But if these words do really mean something independently of what the reader takes them to mean, then words can, after all, have a meaning independently or by themselves, which is contrary to the theory.

4. Representative of the first group are Jaeger (1923) and Schütrumpf (1991); of the second, Barker (1946), Johnson (1990), Mulgan (1977), and Newman (1887); of the third, Lord (1982, 1984) and Nichols (1992).

neath this appearance the whole is coherent in both doctrine and form. For they say that Aristotle deliberately gave the appearance of formal disunity for rhetorical and pedagogical reasons since what he wanted to say he did not say openly, in the manner modern readers expect, but hid it behind a certain veil of obscurity so as to deter one class of readers and attract another.

My own view is that none of these groups is correct and that the *Politics* is a formal and doctrinal unity without even apparent incoherence.[5] I do not, indeed, maintain that this unity is luminous at a first or cursory reading, but I do maintain that it is really there and that it can eventually become luminous. The divisions, headings, and summaries of the following translation, along with the analytical outline, are designed to make that unity luminous, and sufficiently so that it can be understood even on a first reading. Any puzzles or difficulties that remain should be resolved by the commentary, or the commentary should enable readers to resolve them for themselves. For this reason it is not necessary for me to undertake an express refutation of the other views about the unity of the *Politics* (though I do say much by way of refutation in the commentary, as opportunity offers). All these other views share a common assumption, namely that there are disunities and incoherences in the *Politics* of the sort claimed (doctrinal or formal, real or apparent). So if there are in fact no such disunities or incoherences, and if it can be shown that there are none, then all these other views collapse together, and it is not necessary to do anything further to refute them. Therefore, since I claim to have shown precisely this in the following translation, I can refer the reader there directly and dispense with further discussion of the matter. The reader should, however, keep particularly in view the analytical outline, for it provides a visible schema of how I suppose the whole *Politics* breaks down into its parts and how these parts come together to form a steady and logical progression of argument from beginning to end.

There is, nevertheless, one question related to the unity of the *Politics* that does need discussing here, and that is the question of the arrangement or ordering of the books. For I have, in opposition to all currently available translations, put these books in an order other than the order they have in the surviving manuscripts, and I need to explain and justify this decision. The view that the manuscript ordering of the books of the *Politics* is wrong used to be common among scholars and, indeed, is reflected in several past translations and editions.[6] It is also the opinion of one contemporary translator (even though he forbore to carry it through into his translation).[7] The

5. In this regard I am perhaps closest to Miller (1995: 24, 183–90) among modern scholars.
6. As in the editions of Newman (1887) and Susemihl and Hicks (1894) and the translation of Welldon (1883).
7. Lord (1984: 16).

view is that books 7 and 8 of the manuscripts have been displaced (whether because of an editor or of some mechanical accident in the process of transmission) and should properly come between books 3 and 4.

The fundamental evidence for this view is that what Aristotle says at the end of book 3 that he is going to do next he does not in fact do next but only later in books 7 and 8. This anomaly or oddity is easy to see and cannot have escaped anyone's notice; but caution, perhaps, and a just conservatism induced people to leave the text alone. It was not until 1577 that Scaino da Salo first openly argued for a change in the ordering of the books. Scaino was very conscious of the boldness of his proceeding and took great pains to prove that he was not so much changing the order of the books as putting them back into the order originally intended by Aristotle. His arguments were comprehensive and, though not all of equal weight, constituted a convincing case. Unfortunately, his work was largely ignored until it was enthusiastically taken up by Barthélemy Saint-Hilaire some 250 years later. Thereafter, the view that the ordering of the books should be changed became dominant until the work of Jaeger, first published in 1923, caused it to wane.

Jaeger recognized as much as anyone the oddity in the manuscript ordering of the books, but he gave a different account of it. Aristotle's own thinking, reasoned Jaeger, had undergone development from an early and idealistic stage, represented in particular by books 7 and 8, to a later and more realistic stage represented in particular by books 4 to 6. The *Politics* as we now have it, he argued, was never a coherent whole; it consists instead of disparate and incompatible elements belonging to different stages of intellectual development that were never intended by Aristotle to constitute a single work. Therefore, he concluded, the sort of problems that induced Scaino to reorder the books are genuine problems and genuinely there, but they could never be solved or removed by such reordering, for they sprang from incoherences in the content and not in the form only.

Jaeger's work itself, however, is full of problems of its own, from arbitrary assumptions to straight errors,[8] and has itself now fallen out of favor. Besides, the thesis on which it rests, that the *Politics* as we have it is not a doctrinal and formal unity, can be shown to be false. Scaino's contention, therefore, must be reconsidered and accepted or rejected on its own terms. There is, however, a complication that must be considered and set aside first. For among those scholars who agreed that books 7 and 8 should come between books 3 and 4, there were some, including Saint-Hilaire himself, who thought that book 6 should also come before book 5 (thus giving the order

8. Barker (1946: xxxvii–xlvi), Bodéus (1993: 1–2), Grene (1963: chapter 1), Lachterman (1990), Lord (1981: 468–70; 1984: 14–17), Miller (1995: 23–24), Pellegrin (1987), Rowe (1977), Simpson (1993).

1, 2, 3, 7, 8, 4, 6, 5). Their reasoning was based on a passage where Aristotle is speaking of the questions he is going to examine (4.2.1289b20-26). The second to last of these questions is how to set up the several regimes and the last is how regimes are destroyed and preserved. This last question is manifestly dealt with in book 5 but the other appears to be dealt with in book 6, and so in an order contrary to that allotted to it. The solution seemed to be, therefore, to reorder these books too and place 6 before 5. This solution, however, causes more problems than it solves, for it brings one into direct conflict with passages in book 6 that expressly speak of book 5 as having already preceded (6.1.1316b31-36, 1317a37-38; 6.4.1319b4-6, 6.5.1319b37-1320a4). Saint-Hilaire and others therefore had to expunge these passages as later interpolations. But this is a desperate remedy.

Scaino himself, who also agreed that book 6 contained Aristotle's answer to the second to last question in 4.2, had a simpler and neater solution. He left book 6 as and where it was and simply transposed a few words in 4.2 itself so that the question of how regimes are destroyed and preserved was made to come before the question about how to set up regimes.[9] This solution is less drastic than the other, and to that extent preferable, but it still requires tampering with the text. A solution that is better still is to note that the whole problem is anyway a false one. For Aristotle makes clear at the beginning of book 6 that that book is an addendum to his discussion of the questions set out in the program at the end of 4.2 and is not the original discussion. The original discussion of the question about how to set up regimes comes earlier, in 4.14-16, and so before book 5, as he said.

The question of reordering, then, concerns only whether to put books 7 and 8 between books 3 and 4. The main arguments for doing so are philological and based simply on Aristotle's own words, not on any theory about what order he ought, a priori, to have followed.[10] The first is the argument already mentioned, that Aristotle says at the end of book 3 (chapter 18) that he is going to discuss next the best regime and that he also specifies that books 7 and 8 are that discussion (7.1.1323a14-21, 7.4.1325b33-38, 7.13.1331b24-26). So these words indicate he intended book 7 to follow book 3. The second argument reinforces the first, for the words that end 3.18 (1288b5-6) are almost literally the same as those that begin 7.1 (1323a14-15) and are certainly the same in thought. The third argument is that Aristotle says in book 4 that the discussion of the best regime has already preceded (4.2.1289a30-35, 4.3.1290a1-3, 4.7.1293b1-7, and by implication at 4.8.1293b22-27; note also the close verbal parallel between 4.7.1293b3-5 and 7.9.1328b37-39). But this

---

9. Scaino (1577: 30-31).

10. They escape, therefore, the problems about arguments based on such a priori theory noted by Pellegrin (1987).

discussion is, he says (as just noted), found in books 7 and 8. So these words too indicate that he intended book 7 to follow book 3.

The above arguments are the more convincing for relying, as they do, on Aristotle's express words. They should be considered decisive.[11] That they are not so considered is largely because of arguments on the other side that seem to bring the matter back into doubt. These arguments, however, all have ready answers. The first and strongest of them is that the outline for the *Politics* laid down at *Ethics* 10.9.1181b15–23 seems to say that the discussion of the best regime, or books 7 and 8, is to come last. But in fact it can be shown that that outline says the opposite and that, properly interpreted, it requires 7 and 8 to be transposed between 3 and 4 and not left where they are (I point to the evidence for these claims in the notes to the translation). A second argument is that the best regime of books 7 and 8 is not the best regime spoken of in book 3, so to transpose the books does not solve the problem posed by the end of 3. But this interpretation of books 7 and 8 is not convincing and anyway conflicts with the words of Aristotle in book 7, as noted above. A third argument is that there is a reference in 7 (about "the other regimes" at 4.1325b34) that seems to be to book 4 as if 4 had preceded. However, this reference is better understood as being to the discussions in book 2. A fourth argument is that book 4 refers back to 3 as if 3, and not 7 and 8, had just preceded. But in fact the references in 4 show only that 3 has preceded and not that it has *just* preceded. A fifth argument is that there seems to be a reference in 7 (about the names for certain kinds of office, at 12.1331b6–15) back to 6.8. But there is no reason to suppose any reference at all here, or no reason to suppose the reference is *back* to 6.8 rather than *forward* to 6.8.

The conclusion to draw, then, is that books 7 and 8 were intended by Aristotle to come between books 3 and 4 and so should be put back there. Accordingly, that is what I have done in the following translation. Still, in deference to the manuscript order (which is the order predominantly followed by scholars and commentators and by most current translations and editions), I number the books after book 3, albeit at the risk of some awkwardness, with two numbers: the first for their correct order and the second (in parentheses) for their manuscript order—that is, 1, 2, 3, 4(7), 5(8), 6(4), 7(5), 8(6).[12]

11. It is worth noting that Jaeger considered them decisive (1934: 268). At any rate he agreed that books 7 and 8 were originally intended by Aristotle to follow 3. He claimed only that this intention belonged to an earlier stage in Aristotle's thinking and could not be used to help make sense of the books of the *Politics* as we now have them.

12. In this I follow the example of Newman (1887).

The Context of the *Politics*

It is a common assumption that to understand a work one has to understand its context. This assumption is, however, ambiguous, for context itself is ambiguous. Generally, context is taken to mean historical context or the time and place of the work's composition and the life and times of the author. Such historical placing of a work is often thought to be especially important in the case of the *Politics*, which is not only full of references to historical events but also seems to be about a historical phenomenon, the ancient Greek *polis*. But to make this supposition and to lay it down as a prerequisite for understanding what Aristotle says is to beg the question against him. The *Politics*, according to Aristotle himself, is not about a historical phenomenon, nor is it about a Greek phenomenon. It is about a natural phenomenon which, if prominent in ancient Greece, could in principle exist in any place and at any time and which, moreover, is necessary at every place and at every time if human beings are to attain happiness.

Our modern opinions about history, however, and about its dominance over human life and thought, make us think that there is no such thing as nature in the sense of something prior to history and independent of it. On the contrary, in our current view, nature is something posterior and itself a product of history. So we tend to smile at those, like Aristotle, who believe in an independent nature as we tend to smile at the naïveté of small children. Could we set aside our opinions for a moment, or at least suppose that they need not be as obviously true as we suppose them to be, we should instead look at Aristotle and his *Politics* with something like shocked astonishment. Really? The *polis* is natural and necessary for happiness? And we, who lack the *polis*, are living unnatural lives and are deprived of happiness? How can this be, and how can our leaders be so careless and indifferent about something so important?

I will not, however, try to settle here this dispute between our modern preference for history and Aristotle's preference for nature. Neither will I assume the modern preference in advance. For that, as I said, would beg the question against Aristotle. I wish at least to give Aristotle the chance to have his say. So I propose to say nothing about the historical context of the *Politics*. I have, nevertheless, appended to the translation historical notes about the events Aristotle refers to in the course of his exposition,[13] but I have done so more to satisfy curiosity than to aid understanding. For although Aristotle refers to these events to illustrate his argument, the argument itself, as I have just remarked, is about nature and not about history (save insofar as

13. All dates given in these notes are therefore B.C. and not A.D.

history reveals and displays nature). One should note, indeed, in this regard that in order to understand Aristotle's argument we do not need to know anything more about these events than he himself tells us, even though what he tells us is sometimes only a name. A case in point is the "affair at Andros," used to illustrate the venality of the ephors at Sparta (2.9.1270b11–13). We do not know what event Aristotle is referring to or even a single one of the details, yet our ignorance has not hindered us in the least from understanding what he is saying or arguing. Indeed, scholars are guided in their conjectures about this affair at Andros by their understanding of what Aristotle says, not guided in their understanding of what Aristotle says by their conjectures about the affair.

But context, as I said, is ambiguous, and besides historical context there is also philosophical context, knowledge of which *is* necessary for understanding the *Politics*. Philosophical context, though, is also ambiguous and can mean the remote and general context or the immediate and particular context. The remote and general context is Aristotle's philosophical writings as a whole, especially, perhaps, his *Physics* and *Metaphysics*, which contain his systematic exposition of certain fundamental terms common to every science—as, above all, *physis* or "nature."[14] But knowing this context, though valuable for situating the *Politics* with respect to the other parts of philosophy, does not seem to be as valuable for understanding the *Politics* itself. At any rate, as I try to show in the commentary and as may be evident to some extent from the summaries in the translation, one can make sense of Aristotle's arguments without having to refer expressly to any of these other writings; and, significantly, Aristotle himself does not so refer.

He does, however, refer, and refer often, to one of his other works, namely the *Ethics*. Indeed he considers the *Ethics* already to be politics, or political science (*Ethics* 1.2–3), and does not understand what it studies to be separate from what the *Politics* studies. Repeated reminders of the political character of the *Ethics* are found throughout that work. Notable in this regard, in fact, is its very last chapter, which is, and is clearly meant to be, an introduction or transition to the study of cities and regimes proper—that is, to the study that is contained in the *Politics*. However, controversy has arisen among scholars on this point. Some believe that the introduction to the study of regimes at the end of the *Ethics* is not an introduction to the *Politics* as we now have it and moreover that the *Ethics* referred to in the *Politics* is not the *Nicomachean Ethics*, in which alone this introduction occurs, but rather the *Eudemian Ethics*.[15] I myself am convinced that this view is mistaken and ar-

---

14. This remote context of the *Politics* is discussed at some length by Kamp (1985).

15. Lord (1984: 19–21). The view that the *Ethics* referred to in the *Politics* is the *Eudemian* and not the *Nicomachean* is based largely on the references to the *Ethics* in *Politics* 4(7).13.

gue to that effect in the commentary, though I have also added enough in the notes at the relevant points of the translation to indicate my general line of argument.

But at all events, if the *Politics* does, as I maintain, refer to and presuppose the *Nicomachean Ethics*, it is this work alone among Aristotle's writings that serves as the immediate and particular context of the *Politics*. A knowledge of it, therefore, and especially of its concluding chapter, is necessary for an understanding of the *Politics*. Accordingly, I have placed, as aid and instruction to the reader, a translation of that last chapter before the translation of the eight books of the *Politics*. It forms the proper context, and the only indispensable context, for reading and understanding the *Politics*.

The Greek text of the *Politics* that I have used for the translation is that of Dreizehnter, which is the most recent and is based on a more complete review of the available manuscripts than previous editions. It is, however, not without its flaws,[16] and I have often departed from it (as I indicate in the notes at the relevant points). I have almost always done so when it departs from the manuscripts, and indeed on certain occasions I have had to depart from it for several lines together. On those occasions I have gone back to the text of Newman. For the translation of the last chapter of the *Ethics* I have used the text of Bywater. In writing my translation I have benefited much from the translations of others, notably those of Barker and Lord, but also those of Jowett, Welldon, and Sinclair/Saunders.

Key Terms

One of the most important decisions a translator can make, and a decision in which one's own understanding of the text comes especially into play, is what vocabulary to use, above all for the key terms of the original. For this reason and because the vocabulary used has no small effect on how readers understand and interpret what they read, I ought to say something about my own decisions in this regard. The main disputes about vocabulary center on the key word *polis* and the words derived from it, such as *politeia* and *politikos*. These disputes concern, for instance, whether to translate *polis* as "city" or "state" or even "city-state," *politeia* as "polity" or "regime" or "constitution," *politikos* as "politician" or "statesman." It would be desirable to find a set of English words that were similarly related to each other as the original Greek words are. But while it is possible to do this with respect to certain pairs (as "city" and "citizen" for *polis* and *politēs*, "state" and "statesman" for *polis* and *politikos*, "polity" and "politician" for *politeia* and *politikos*), it is not possible to do this for all of them together.

16. See the review by Schneider (1973).

One could, of course, abandon the attempt to find translations and merely transliterate the Greek words instead. But this seems a counsel of despair and, moreover, runs the risk of giving a false impression. For it runs the risk of giving the impression that Aristotle is talking about things or phenomena that are peculiarly Greek, which can be referred to only by using Greek terms, and thus is talking about things that are transient and relative to a particular period of human history, not about things that are timeless and relative to universal human nature. But, as I noted earlier, Aristotle supposes himself throughout to be talking of human nature and not of human history (except in relation to human nature) and indeed gives express arguments to this effect (as when he argues that humans are by nature political animals, in 1.2). Perhaps Aristotle is wrong in this regard, but we ought to try to avoid giving this impression in advance or before his arguments have been duly weighed. Likewise, we ought to try to avoid stating these arguments using words that, because they are transliterations and not translations, suggest the falsity of the arguments they are being used to convey. Transliterations, or even neologisms, might, indeed, be forced on us if our own language and experience proved to be so impoverished or so different that we possessed no word to do the necessary translating. But we ought not to reach that conclusion too quickly or lightly, and certainly not before we have gone through all the resources available to us and still failed to come up with a defensible translation. These resources include, one should stress, not only the words and their senses prevalent in current speech but also any words and senses that, even though less used, are still available in our linguistic heritage (provided they have not become so obsolete as to sound outlandish).

The translator, then, must confront, not bypass, the problem of translating the words of Aristotle's Greek and must strive to find acceptable equivalents for these words, or for as many of them as possible, and especially for the key or important words. In my view, such equivalents can be found; indeed, most of them already exist somewhere or other in the well-established tradition of translating Aristotle into English. Therefore, my choices of words are for the most part not new, but follow one or another of the several already well-trodden paths. The particular path, or rather combination of paths, that I have chosen to follow takes its beginning from the conviction that it is a mistake to translate *polis* as "state."[17] For, first, the word "state" is typically used in speaking of nations, and a nation is not a *polis*. Even if the state is the only modern entity that exercises anything like the control once exercised by the *polis*, it is nevertheless a corruption and not an extension of the *polis*. For it is not at all the sort of community that Aristotle has in mind

17. A view also argued by Berti (in Gigon and Fischer 1988: 90) and by Jaffa (in Strauss and Cropsey 1972: 65–67); cf. Barker (1946: lxiii–lxiv).

when he speaks of the *polis*. The *polis* is that community which responds to the natural desire of human beings to perfect themselves in happy and noble living and which exists by nature in order to realize that goal (1.2, 3.9). It therefore has to be small, or small enough that the citizens can know each others' character and rule with a view to each others' character (4(7).4). It also has to be small enough to be capable of receiving a common political arrangement or a single *politeia*, for a *polis* is identified by its *politeia* (3.3). But the state is far too big to have a single *politeia* and too big to allow its citizens to know character and to rule with a view to character. The state, indeed, is as big as it is partly to ensure that rule is not exercised with a view to character but that such matters are left to individual choice.

Second, the state does not signify a community or a common way of life. It is understood rather in terms of force, for the state proper is typically defined as that which has a monopoly of legitimate coercion. But the *polis* is first and foremost a community. It does, to be sure, exercise control over other communities and has the power to coerce them, but it is still itself a community or a sharing together in a common life. The state, by contrast, stands over against community (for it stands over against society, which is the locus in modern states of community and sharing of life together).[18] A sign of this is that we can talk of a given community as *our* community or as something *we* all share together, and so we can also talk of loving and caring for our community and even of dying for it. By contrast we do not talk, or do not talk happily, of a state as *our* state or of loving and dying for the state.[19]

If *polis*, therefore, does not mean state, neither can it mean city-state (which would imply that the *polis* is a certain kind of state). The option left, then, is to translate *polis* as "city." But this option too is problematic because modern cities are also large (as large, in certain cases, as some modern states) and are just as incapable of ruling with a view to character. But there is this difference: "city," unlike "state," signifies a community, a sign of which

18. See Miller (1995: 19–20, 358–61) and Mulgan (1977: 16–17). Both Miller and Mulgan accuse Aristotle of equivocation for using *polis* sometimes to mean state and sometimes to mean society. But what this supposed equivocation really shows is not that Aristotle uses *polis* with two different meanings but that he uses it with one meaning that cuts across the division we now draw between state and society. *Polis* does not signify state or society but something that is both and neither at the same time, just as do our terms "country" or "fatherland" when we speak, for instance, of dying for country or fatherland. *Polis* is not an illegitimate fusion of state and society but a third thing altogether, and the real question between Aristotle on the one hand and Miller and Mulgan on the other is whether the single notion of *polis* or the double notion of state and society gives one a truer understanding of political phenomena. To say that *polis* is a fusion of the other two notions begs this question against Aristotle.

19. "Society" will hardly do as a translation of *polis*, for though society carries with it some of the warmth associated with community, it does not carry with it any sense of political organization and rule (for that is said rather to belong to the state). *Polis*, however, does very much carry this sense.

is that we can talk of love of our city and even of fighting and dying for our city.[20] Moreover, "city" is a name still in standard use for referring to what Aristotle would call *poleis*—for example, the medieval Italian republics like Venice and Florence. It is also the standard name, outside translations of the *Politics* at any rate, for referring to ancient Athens or Sparta or Thebes or any other ancient Greek *polis*. Indeed the neologism "city-state" helps to confirm this. The fact that we soften "state" with "city" when speaking of ancient *poleis* shows that "city" is the name for expressing that characteristic of ancient *poleis* that makes them different from states as we now speak of states.

But if *polis* must, therefore, be translated as "city" and not as "state" or "city-state," then this will naturally lead to the translation of *politēs* as "citizen" (even though we use this term for members of nations and states too) but away from the translation of *politikos* as "statesman." True, "statesman" does tend to mean someone with the sort of wisdom, prudence, and care for the common good that Aristotle understands by the true *politikos*, whereas "politician" often means someone who is rather low and devious and concerned to exploit rule for private advantage. But even though "politician" can mean this, it does so with the implication that politicians should not be so low and devious and that those who are have somehow failed in their duty and have given their profession, which in itself is something noble, a bad name. In this way, indeed, "politician" is a rather good word to use to translate *politikos*, because the same was true of *politikos* in Aristotle's day. Both words properly mean someone noble and public-spirited, but both have derogatory connotations because of the bad example of actual politicians.[21]

Translating *polis* as "city" does not, however, determine anything about how to translate *politeia*. Nevertheless, good reasons can be given for not translating it as "constitution." For a constitution is a set of rules (written or unwritten), and though *politeia* includes rules (as the laws that determine the offices), it means above all the people, or the parts of the city—whether the poor, the rich, or the virtuous—who are actually in control. It signifies a body of rulers, in other words, and not a set of rules.[22] Hence Aristotle identifies the *politeia* with the *politeuma* and means by *politeuma* the ruling body or, we might even say, the ruling class (3.6.1278b8–15). *Politeia* is therefore closer to what we mean by the establishment than to what we mean by

---

20. Such "fighting" and "dying" typically manifest themselves nowadays at sporting events among fans of teams from rival cities, and then only in the form of high passions and opposing shouts and cheers, when one side is elated at victory and the other dashed by defeat. But these passions can also drive fans into fights and brawls (during which some have died), which shows that even modern cities are still capable of exciting the sort of intense affection and loyalty also excited by what we call fatherland or country, but not by what we call state.

21. See Miller (1995: 13 n.21).

22. See Mulgan (1977: 56) and Susemihl and Hicks (1894: 365–66).

the constitution. Indeed, one could not trouble to translate *politeia* at all but transliterate it as "polity," for polity has become a respectable English word that signifies manner of rule. If I prefer to translate it instead as "regime," this is in part because regime is already much in favor as a translation of *politeia*, but mainly because regime conveys, as polity does not, the idea of a way of life (we speak, for instance, of athletes following a regime, or a regimen, and mean thereby a whole pattern of life that they are to follow for a certain period). *Politeia*, by signifying the ruling body, signifies the way of life of the city, since the ruling body necessarily imposes on the whole city, by its ruling, its own vision of happiness and of the best way to live (2.11.1273a37-b1, 4(7).8.1328a35-b2). True, Aristotle also refers to the *politeia* as the kind of composition of the city (3.3.1276b1-11) and also says it is the way cities arrange (*taxis*) their offices (6(4).1.1289a15-18), both of which passages may suggest that by *politeia* he means something of a more institutional character. But a closer look at the contexts shows otherwise. For what Aristotle means in the first passage is how the inhabitants of the city are "composed" with respect to having, or not having, shares in rule. The inhabitants who do have shares, and so are citizens, are the *politeia*. In the second passage, since the "arrangement," or *taxis*, in question is the arrangement of the offices, it means which of the inhabitants of the city are so arranged as to share in the offices. So in both cases the *politeia* means the arrangement or composition of people with respect to rule; hence it means, first and foremost, the ruling body and the way of living or distinctive character of that ruling body. Such a sense is captured by the word "regime" but not by the word "constitution."

Aristotle also uses *politeia* to mean a particular species or kind of regime, for which "polity" has in fact become a standard translation and the translation I also adopt. But, of course, if one thus translates *politeia* in its general sense as "regime" and in its specific sense as "polity," one is giving to Aristotle's text a greater precision than he himself chose to give it, and there is a case, adopted by some translators, for using the same word to translate *politeia* in both of its senses. Nevertheless, if Aristotle, more in deference to common usage than to philosophical accuracy (*Ethics* 8.10.1160a33-35), uses the same word with two senses, the senses themselves are perfectly distinct. Consequently, with a view to the commentary—where, for the purposes of exposition, my focus is naturally on the difference of sense rather than on the sameness of word—I have preferred to employ in the translation a difference of word too.

In addition to the terms based on the root word *polis*, there are other important terms that Aristotle uses and about which I ought to say something here. Translations adopted for *kurios* include "authority," "sovereign," "supreme," "decisive," and others of the sort. Something can be said for all these suggestions, of course, but I have decided to depart from the practice of other translators and to use the word "control" instead. I have found "control" easier to handle than other words in rendering the various ways Aristotle uses *kurios* and its cognates; and "control" does, in addition, include the ideas expressed by these other words. For instance, those who are in control of the city or regime must also be those who are sovereign, supreme, and decisive, for what they say and think must be the final determinant of what the city does and what the regime is like. Further, while "control" can also express the idea of authority, it need merely express the idea of effective power, power that in fact dominates whether or not it has any right or legitimacy so to do. "Authority," by contrast, tends to carry with it the idea of right or legitimacy as well as power. But Aristotle uses *kurios* in such a way that it need not mean legitimate power but only effective power. Tyranny, for instance, is never legitimate or just for Aristotle, yet he does not hesitate to speak of the tyrant as *kurios* while he is tyrant. There is an element, if you like, of brute realism in Aristotle's use of *kurios* that the word "authority" can obscure.[23]

The word *kalos* has the fundamental meaning of beautiful, but beautiful in the sense of the full range of beautiful things, not just bodily ones, including in particular beautiful souls, characters, laws, and regimes. Thus it carries a sense that can also, and perhaps better, be expressed in English by the word "noble." I have chosen, in fact, to translate *kalos* usually as "noble" and as "beautiful" only where the context seems to require a reference to bodily beauty in particular.[24] Aristotle is very free in his use of *kalos* and employs it in places where we would more naturally employ the tamer and different words "well" or "fine" or "correct." But it is not insignificant, I think, that Aristotle uses *kalos*. For there are other words at his disposal, which he does in fact also use, that literally mean "well" or "fine" or "correct," and yet he prefers so often to use *kalos* instead. The prime reason for this is, no doubt, that one of Aristotle's theses, as fundamental to the *Ethics* as to the *Politics*, is that only the noble is ultimately well and correct and good and that anything that is not noble is not really well or correct or good. Thus, unnatural though it may initially sound to our ears, I have forced the English to say "noble" when Aristotle says *kalos*, so that this fact is itself forced on the reader's attention.

Ergon and its cognates I have generally translated as "work," which is its fundamental meaning, whether by work is meant the thing produced

23. I have occasionally retained "authority" or a form thereof when "control" makes less sense, as for instance when Aristotle speaks of the *kurios* ("authoritative") meaning of something.

24. Note that I have translated *kalokagathos*, literally "noble and good," as "gentleman," for a gentleman is someone who, in the root sense of that word, is noble and good.

or done or the producing or doing itself.[25] I have retained "work" even in places where it has the sense of, and would more traditionally be translated as, "function." The reason I have done so is because "work" expresses what is decisive in the idea of function. For the function of a thing is the typical work of that thing, what it is designed by nature or art to do and in which it realizes best what it is. So since "work" is what is doing the work, so to speak, in the idea of function, I thought it better to retain "work" as the translation for *ergon* throughout. *Ergon* is related, especially in the sense of function, to *telos*, which I have translated variously as "end" or "goal," for a thing's *ergon* or function is that in which it perfects and completes itself, that in which it realizes its end or goal. The cognates of *telos* I have generally translated as "complete" or "perfect" or some derivative.

Dēmos and its cognates I have translated using "populace," "popular," and so forth. I have avoided translating *dēmos* as "people" or "the people" for two reasons. First, the word "people" has proved indispensable for many other uses, especially for providing a substantive in English where the Greek dispenses with one (for instance, where Greek is content with "some" or "many," English can require "some people" or "many people"). Second, when we say "the people" in a political context in English, we do not typically mean what *dēmos* means in Greek. For by "the people" we typically mean all those who live in or are citizens of a given city or state. But the *dēmos* are only a part of the people in this sense, for they are simply the mass of the free poor. So they are rather what we mean by the phrase "the common people." In fact, while the word "populace" can mean the population in general of a given place, its first meaning is this one of the common people. So provided readers keep these facts in mind, they will find "the populace" a better and less misleading translation for *dēmos* than "the people."

So much may be said in explanation of my translations of some of the more important words of the *Politics*. For my translations of other words, see the glossary.

Works Cited

This list of sources contains only those referred to in the introduction. A more comprehensive bibliography appears in the commentary.

Barker, Sir Ernest. 1946. *The Politics of Aristotle*. Oxford: Oxford University Press.
Bodéus, Richard. 1982. *Le Philosophe et la Cité*. Paris: Les Belles Lettres. English

---

25. I have occasionally translated *ergon* as "facts" when the context required this. But "fact" too refers back to the same idea, for it comes from *factum*, which is Latin for a thing done or made.

translation: *The Political Dimensions of Aristotle's* Ethics. Trans. Jan E. Garrett. Albany: State University of New York, 1993.

Bywater, Ingram. 1894. *Aristotelis Ethica Nicomachea*. Oxford: Clarendon Press.

Dreizehnter, Alois. 1970. *Aristoteles' Politica*. Munich: Wilhelm Fink.

Gigon, Olof, and Michael W. Fischer, eds. 1988. *Antike Rechts- und Sozialphilosophie*. New York: Peter Lang.

Grene, Marjorie. 1963. *A Portrait of Aristotle*. Chicago: University of Chicago Press.

Jaeger, Werner W. 1923. *Aristoteles. Grundlegung einer Geschichte seiner Entwicklung*. Berlin: Weidmann. English translation: *Aristotle. Fundamentals of the History of His Development*. Trans. Richard R. Robinson. Oxford: Clarendon Press, 1934.

Johnson, Curtis N. 1990. *Aristotle's Theory of the State*. New York: St. Martin's Press.

Jowett, Benjamin. 1885. *The Politics of Aristotle*. 2 vols. Oxford: Clarendon Press.

Kamp, Andreas. 1985. *Die politische Philosophie des Aristoteles und ihre metaphysischen Grundlagen*. Freiburg: Alber.

Keyt, David, and Fred D. Miller Jr., eds. 1991. *A Companion to Aristotle's Politics*. Oxford: Blackwell.

Lachterman, David. 1990. "Did Aristotle Develop? Reflections on Jaeger's Thesis." *Revue de Philosophie Ancienne* 8: 3–40.

Lord, Carnes. 1981. "The Character and Composition of Aristotle's *Politics*." *Political Theory* 9: 459–78.

———. 1982. *Education and Culture in the Political Thought of Aristotle*. Ithaca: Cornell University Press.

———. 1984. *Aristotle. The Politics*. Chicago: University of Chicago Press.

Miller, Fred D., Jr. 1995. *Nature, Justice and Rights in Aristotle's Politics*. Oxford: Clarendon Press.

Mulgan, Richard. 1977. *Aristotle's Political Theory*. Oxford: Clarendon Press.

Newman, William L. 1887–1902. *The Politics of Aristotle*. 4 vols. Oxford: Clarendon Press.

Nichols, Mary P. 1992. *Citizens and Statesmen: A Study of Aristotle's Politics*. Lanham, Md.: Rowman and Littlefield.

Pellegrin, Pierre. 1987. "La Politique d'Aristote: Unité et Fractures." *Revue Philosophique de la France et de l'Etranger* 177: 129–59.

Rowe, Christopher J. 1977. "Aims and Methods in Aristotle's *Politics*." *Classical Quarterly* 27: 159–72. Rev. ed. in Keyt and Miller, cited above.

Saint-Hilaire, Barthélemy. 1848. *La Politique d'Aristote*. 2d ed. Paris.

Saunders, Trevor, J. 1986. Review of Lord's Translation of the *Politics*. *Classical Review* 36: 216–19.

Scaino da Salo. 1577. *In Octo Aristotelis Libros qui Extant de Republica Quaestiones*. Rome.

Schneider, Bernd. 1973. Review of Dreizehnter's *Aristoteles' Politica*. *Gnomon* 45: 336–45.

Schütrumpf, Eckart. 1991. *Aristoteles. Politik*. 2 vols. Berlin: Akadamie Verlag.

Simpson, Peter L. P. 1993. Review of Schütrumpf's *Aristoteles. Politik*. *American Journal of Philology* 114: 320–23.

Sinclair, Thomas A. 1962. *Aristotle. The Politics*. Harmondsworth, England: Penguin. Rev. ed. by Trevor J. Saunders, 1981.

Strauss, Leo, and Joseph Cropsey, eds. 1972. *History of Political Philosophy*. Chicago: Rand MacNally.

Susemihl, Franz, and Robert D. Hicks, eds. 1894. *The Politics of Aristotle*. London: MacMillan.

Welldon, James E. C. 1883. *The Politics of Aristotle*. London: Macmillan.

Glossary

I have included here only the more significant of the words Aristotle uses in the *Politics*; cognates are not included unless some special sense needed noting. Some remarks in the entries below are repeated in the notes to the translation at relevant points. Consult also the index.

agathos: good.
agora: public square, market(place).
akolastos: intemperate.
akrasia: weakness of will. Refers to the condition of knowing what to do but failing to do it because one is overcome by passion.
allagē: exchange.
andreia: courage.
aporia: difficulty; neediness. Literally, it means lack of a way or means of achieving something, and hence difficulty in the case of thinking and neediness in the case of making a living. The needy are the *aporoi*.
archē: rule, office; beginning; principle.
architektōn: ruling craftsman. Root of our word "architect," it means a master craftsman who is not just an expert at his craft (*technē*) but who also rules (*archē*) or directs other craftsman working under him.
archōn: ruler, officeholder.
aretē: virtue.
aristokratia: aristocracy (literally, rule of the best).
ascholia: occupation (literally, lack of leisure, from *scholē*).
atelēs: incomplete (literally, not having reached the end, *telos*).
autarkeia: self-sufficiency.

banausos: mechanic, vulgar mechanic. It literally means someone who works using fire, but it has a wider reference, along with a derogatory connotation, to artisans or craftsmen generally.
basileia: kingship.
bios: way of life.
boulē: council.
bouleuesthai: to deliberate.

charientes: the refined (literally, those who are specially graced or favored).

chorēgia: equipment. Literally, it refers to the things needed to equip a chorus properly for the dramatic festivals at Athens, but thence it naturally comes to mean the supply of resources needed to undertake actions generally.

chrēmata: commodities, money. Aristotle calls *chrēmata* "all things whose worth is measured in money" (*Ethics* 4.1.1119b26–27), hence commodities or merchandise. By a natural extension, the word comes to mean also the money that measures commodities.

chrēmatistikē: business. The art of acquiring *chrēmata*.

deilia: cowardice.

dēmagōgos: demagogue (literally, a leader of the *dēmos*).

dēmiourgos: craftsman (literally, someone who works for the *dēmos*).

dēmokratia: democracy (rule of the *dēmos*).

dēmos: the populace, the mass of the free poor.

despotēs: master (of slaves). Root of our word "despot."

diagōgē: cultured pursuits. Literally, it means a way of passing one's time or life, but Aristotle always uses it to mean a cultured way of doing this.

dianoia: thought (in the sense both of what is thought and of the faculty that does the thinking). From the same root as *nous*.

dikaios: just.

dikaiosunē: justice, the virtue of justice.

dikastēs: juror.

dikē: right; lawsuit, court case. Root of the preceding three Greek words.

doulos: slave.

drachmē: drachma (a denomination of Greek money and the average daily wage).

dunamis: power, force; capacity, capability, ability (especially, in these last cases, when referring to one of the arts or sciences).

dunasteia: dynasty (literally, a power group; the name for the extreme or tyrannical form of oligarchy).

eidos: a kind (in the sense of a species or form of something).

ekklēsia: the public assembly (especially in a democracy). It gives us our word "ecclesiastical" and so on.

eleutheriotēs: liberality.

eleutheros: liberal, free.

epieikēs: decent.

epimeleia: care.

ergon: work.

ethnos: nation. It gives us our word "ethnic."

ethos: habit, custom.

ēthos: character. It gives us our word "ethics."

eudaimonia: happiness. Literally, it means having a good *daimōn* or genius guiding one's lot in life.

eugeneia: good birth. The well-born are the *eugeneis*.

eunomia: good state of law. *Eunomia* was something of a code word in ancient Greece for the arrangement of things at Sparta, since the Spartans claimed (though without much justification, according to Aristotle) to have *eunomia*. One of their poets, Tyrtaeus, wrote a poem with that title. "To be well legislated" translates the verbal cognate *eunomeisthai*.

euporia: prosperity, being well-off. The well-off are the *euporoi*.

euthunai: audit or examination of accounts. Refers to the practice of examining the accounts and conduct of outgoing officeholders to ensure they have not abused office.

genos: family; class; race.

gnōrimoi: the notables.

hexis: habit (in the sense of a disposition of soul; used especially of the virtues).

homoioi: similars; the Peers (in Sparta).

hopla: arms, weapons, heavy arms.

hoplitikon: armed force, heavy armed force. The hoplites, *hoplitai*, were the heavy armed infantry of ancient Greece, but *hoplitikon* can refer to an armed force generally and need not always mean the hoplite force.

kalokagathos: gentleman (literally someone noble and good).

kalos: beautiful, noble.

kapēlikē: trading, the art of trading.

karteria: steadfast endurance.

katharsis: purification. A particular effect of certain kinds of music (see 5(8).7). Gives us our word "catharsis."

koinōnia: community. Derived from *koinos* ("common"), it means a community in the literal sense of sharing in common.

kosmos: adornment, ordered adornment. It gives us our words "cosmos" (the ordered adornment that the array of the whole universe displays) and "cosmetics" (which are a form of adornment).

ktēma: possession, possessions.

ktēsis: property.

ktētikē: the science of property.

kurios: control, someone in control; authority.

leitourgia: public service. It literally means working for the people, the *laos*, and gives us our word "liturgy," as *laos* gives us our word "laity."

logos: reasoned word, reasoned speech, argument, discussion, reason. The primary meaning is "word," but from this the other meanings naturally derive—as, for example, the thought signified by the word, the thing of which the thought is a thought, the faculty of reason by which we think and speak. It is generally rendered as "reason" in the translation but sometimes as "word" or "discussion" or "argument" where the context requires some reference to the activity or expression of reason. It gives us our word "logic" and the suffix "-logy." Note that *aitia* is also sometimes translated as reason, but only when reason means the cause of something.

megalopsuchia: magnanimity (literally, greatness of soul).

meson: the mean; the middle.

metablētikē: of exchange, the art of exchange.

metabolē: change (of regime), revolution.

metrios: measure, measured.

metriotēs: measuredness.

mna: mina (a denomination of Greek money equivalent to 100 drachmas).

monarchos: monarch. It literally means one who rules (*archē*) alone (*monos*) and is used indifferently of kings and tyrants and household managers.

mousikē: music. It literally means "the art of the muses" and hence refers to artistic and literary accomplishments generally, not just to what we now call music. Nevertheless, it can also mean music in our sense.

nomos: law.

nomothetēs: legislator.

nous: intellect.

obolos: obol (a denomination of Greek money equivalent to one-sixth of a drachma).

ochlos: crowd (a rather derogatory term for a mass of people).

oikonomia: household management. It comes from *oikos*, meaning a household, and *nomos* (law), and gives us our word "economy."

oligarchia: oligarchy (literally, rule of the few, but in fact rule of the rich).

pambasileia: total kingship (someone who rules alone as king, *basileus*, with control over everything, *panta*).

pathēma: feeling.

pathētikos: passionate.

pathos: passion (this and the preceding two words come from *paschein*, meaning to suffer or be affected).

penia: poverty. The poor are the *penētes*.
philosophia: philosophy. Literally, love (*philia*) of wisdom (*sophia*).
phronēsis: prudence.
phusis: nature. Gives us our words "physics," "physical," and so on.
plēthos: multitude, the multitude.
ploutos: riches, wealth. The rich are the *plousioi*.
polis: city. It is at the root of the following five Greek words and gives us our
     words "politics," "political," and so on.
politeia: regime; polity.
politeuma: ruling body.
politēs: citizen.
politikē: political science.
politikos: politician, political; proper to a polity.
praktikos: practical.
praxis: action, activity, deed, act.
prohairesis: (deliberate) choice.
psuchē: soul. Gives us our word "psychic" and so on.

scholē: leisure, school (which is derived from *scholē*).
sophisma: sophism.
sophistēs: sophist.
sōphrosunē: moderation.
spoudaios: serious. As applied to men or laws or cities, as it often is, this word
     signifies instances of each that are serious about being what they are. So a
     spoudaios man is someone who is serious about being a man, or someone
     who takes being a man seriously enough to acquire the virtues proper to
     a man. Likewise, *spoudaios* laws are laws that are serious in being laws,
     or laws that the legislator has laid down with sufficient seriousness as to
     make them do what laws are supposed to do, namely lead the citizens
     toward virtue.
stasis: faction, factional strife.
sunesis: understanding (one of the parts of prudence or *phronēsis*).
sussitia: common messes (where citizens regularly met to take their meals
     together).

talanton: talent (a denomination of Greek money equivalent to sixty minas).
taxis: arrangement (especially of the offices in the regime). It literally means
     the drawing up of men in line for battle.
technē: art, skill, craft. Gives us our words "technology," "technique," and
     so on.
technitēs: artisan.
teleios: complete, perfect (derived from *telos*).

telos: end, goal.

theōrein: to study.

theōretikos: contemplative.

theōria: study; viewing. *Theōrein*, from which *theōria* comes, literally means "to gaze at," and so can be used of spectators or viewers. It comes to mean "study" by transference to the gazing, as it were, of the intellect. It gives us our words "theory," "theoretical," and so on.

thēs: laborer (also, one of the four classes set up by Solon at Athens).

thumos: spirit, spiritedness.

timē: honor (especially the honors of office).

turannis: tyranny

zōē: life.

Analytical Outline of the *Politics*

Book Four: The Best Regime

Book Five: Education in the Best Regime

The
Politics
of
Aristotle

Introduction

to the *Politics*

Nicomachean

Ethics 10.9

CHAPTER 9

The Incompleteness of the Ethics. *The project of the* Ethics *is incomplete because the end in practical matters is to become virtuous, not to know about virtue, and words can achieve this only among the young who are already in love with the noble, not among the many who follow their passions and have no notion of the noble.*

1179a33 If then, enough has been said in outline both about these matters[1] and about the virtues, as also about friendship and pleasure,[2] are we to suppose that we have reached the end of our chosen project? Or is it the case that, as is said, where matters of practice are concerned, the end does not lie in studying and recognizing each thing but rather in doing it? Indeed not even in the case of virtue is knowing it enough, but we have to try to get it and use it[3]—or is there some other way of becoming good?

1179b4 Now if reasoned words[4] were sufficient by themselves to make us decent, they would, to follow a remark of Theognis,[5] justly carry off many

---

1. Namely the two kinds of happiness, practical and theoretical, just discussed in 10.6–8; cf. 6.1176a30–32.

2. The virtues have been discussed in books 2 to 7, friendship in books 8 to 9, and pleasure in book 10.1–5.

3. Cf. 2.2.1103b26–31, 2.4.1105b9–18.

4. The Greek is *logos*, which has a wide but naturally related group of meanings ranging from its primary one of word, to the thought signified by the word, to the thing of which the thought is a thought, to the faculty of reason by which we think and reason, and hence also to discussion and argument. It will generally be rendered as "reason" in this translation but sometimes also as "reasoned words," as here, or as "discussion" or "argument," where the context requires some reference to the activity or expression of reason.

5. *Elegies* 432–34.

and great rewards, and the thing to do would be to provide them.[6] But, as it is, words seem to have the strength to incite and urge on those of the young who are generous and to get a well-bred character and one truly in love with the noble to be possessed by virtue; but they appear incapable of inciting the many toward becoming gentlemen.[7] For the many naturally obey the rule of fear, not of shame, and shun what is base not because it is ugly but because it is punished. Living by passion as they do, they pursue their own pleasures and whatever will bring these pleasures about, fleeing the contrary pains; but of the noble and the truly pleasant they do not even have the notion, since they have never tasted it. How could reasoned words reform such people? For it is not possible, or not easy, to replace by reason what has long since become fixed in the character.

The Need for Legislation. *We become good through nature and habituation and teaching, but nature is not in our control and teaching works only where the hearer's soul has been rightly habituated beforehand. For the many, right habituation requires being brought up in the right way from youth and being coerced to behave the same way throughout life. Such discipline is the work of reason backed up by force, and this is found in the law, because law has the necessary force and its force is less resented than is personal coercion.*

1179b18 We should perhaps be well pleased if, with everything present that seems to make us decent, we might get a share of virtue. Now, some suppose that it is by nature that we become good, others that it is by habituation, and others by teaching. What belongs to nature is clearly not up to us but comes to those who are truly fortunate as a result of causes that are divine. Reason and teaching by no means prevail in everyone's case; instead, there is need that the hearer's soul, like earth about to nourish the seed, be worked over in its habits beforehand so as to enjoy and hate in a noble way. For anyone living by passion would neither listen to words of restraint nor even understand them, and how is it possible to change by persuasion someone whose condition is like that? Passion, as a general rule, does not seem to yield to reason but to force. So one's character must already be somehow akin to virtue, in love with the noble and annoyed at the ugly.

1179b31 To get the right guidance toward virtue from one's youth is hard unless one has been brought up under the right laws, for the many, especially when young, do not find it pleasant to live a life of moderation and steadfast endurance. That is why the way one is brought up and what one pursues must be arranged by law, since these pursuits will not be painful

6. The "them" is ambiguous and could refer to words or rewards, or perhaps both.
7. The Greek is *kalokagathia*, a combination of the words for noble or beautiful (*kalos*) and good (*agathos*).

once they have become habitual. But perhaps it is not sufficient to have the right upbringing and care when we are young; rather, because we need to practice these pursuits and get used to them also when we have become men, we would need laws for that too and, indeed, speaking generally, for the whole of our life. For the many obey the rule of necessity rather than of reason, of punishment rather than of nobility. Hence some [8] think that those who are laying down laws should, on the one hand, encourage and incite to virtue by appeal to the noble, on the grounds that any who have been decently prepared in their habits will pay heed, but should, on the other hand, impose punishment and retribution on the disobedient and those whose nature is rather deficient, while altogether banishing the incurable. For, they say, the decent person who is living with an eye for the noble will obey the rule of reason, but someone base, who longs for pleasure, must be chastised with pain like a beast of burden. That is why they also say that the pains must be such as directly oppose the longed-for pleasures.

1180a14 If therefore, as was said, anyone going to be good must be brought up and habituated nobly and must live out his life in decent pursuits in the same way, doing nothing base either with or against his will, then this result will be achieved by those whose way of life is guided by a certain intellect and right arrangement of things that has force behind it. Now there is no force or compulsion in a father's command, nor indeed in that of any one man as a general rule, unless he is a king or someone of the sort. But law does have the power to compel, and law is reasoned speech that proceeds from prudence and intellect of some sort. Also, human beings who oppose people's urges are resented even if they are correct in what they are doing, but the law's laying down of what is decent is not oppressive.

The Need for Legislators. *Most cities do not make it one of their responsibilities to take care of education in virtue, so one should do what one can in the household instead. But to do this requires becoming a legislator and skilled in legislation, for one must lay down for the household the sort of laws that should be laid down for the city. It does not matter that laws in a household are unwritten and concern few people, for this does not matter in other arts either; nor does it matter that a common care for education can be inferior to private care, for the same skill is still required in both cases, as it is also in other arts.*

1180a24 Only in the city of the Spartans, along with a few others, does the legislator seem to have taken care about how people are brought up and what things they pursue. In most cities these matters are neglected, and each lives as he wishes, giving sacred law, in Cyclops' fashion, to his wife and chil-

---

8. Perhaps a reference to Plato *Laws* 4.718c–723d.

dren.[9] So while it would be best if the care became a common one and were correctly managed and if doing this were a possibility,[10] yet, in the absence of common care, it would seem proper for each individually to promote the virtue of his children and friends, or at least to make that his choice. But, from what has been said, it would seem that one would be better able to do this if one became a legislator. For while common cares clearly become common through the laws, they become decent through serious[11] laws.

1180a35 Whether the laws are written or unwritten would not seem to make any difference, nor whether they are used to educate one person or many, just as this seems to make no difference either in the case of music or gymnastics or any other pursuit. For as in cities what prevails is the accepted customs and character, so in households what prevails is a father's words and habits, and all the more so given that he is their kin and does them kindnesses, for already by their nature his children have a fondness for him and are well disposed to obey.

1180b7 Further, education that is adapted to the individual is superior to education that is common, just as in the case of medicine. For while, as a general truth, staying calm and refraining from food are beneficial to a patient in a fever, to this particular patient they might not be. Also, an expert in boxing might not impose the same way of fighting on everyone. Indeed greater accuracy would seem to be achieved in the case of individuals if the care were private, for then each would more often get the aid that befits him. Still, the care of individuals would seem best done by a doctor or a gymnast or anyone else who knows in universal terms what benefits everyone or benefits those of this sort (for sciences are said to be, and are, of what is common). Of course, nothing, perhaps, prevents even a person who has no science but who has, by experience, accurately observed what happens in any particular case from caring nobly for some individual, just as there are those who seem to be, for themselves, the best doctor but are incapable of giving any aid to someone else. Nevertheless, perhaps, it would seem that at least the one who wanted to become skilled in an art or study should pro-

9. An implicit reference to Homer *Odyssey* 9.114–15. The Greek word for sacred law is *themis*, which signifies law or right along with a sense of the awe that belongs to what is primary and unwritten (Themis personified was a goddess).

10. I leave the Greek as it stands and do not move this phrase, as some editors recommend, to follow "promote the virtue of his children and friends" with the meaning "and be able to do this."

11. The Greek word is *spoudaios*. A *spoudaios* man is someone who is serious about being a man, or someone who takes being a man sufficiently seriously to acquire the virtues proper to a man. Likewise, *spoudaios* laws are laws that are serious in being laws, or laws that the legislator has taken seriously enough to design them to do what laws are supposed to do, namely lead the citizens toward virtue.

ceed on to the universal and, as far as possible, get to know that (for it was said that sciences concern the universal). And perhaps likewise someone who wanted to make others, many or a few, better by his care should, if it is by laws that we become good, try to become a legislator. For to put whoever is set before one into noble condition is not something that just anyone can do, but only, if at all, he who has the science, just as is the case with medicine and anything else that requires care and prudence of some sort.

How to Become a Legislator: The Need for the *Politics*. *There are two who profess expertise in politics and legislation: sophists, who do not practice, and politicians, who do. Politicians manifestly cannot teach the art, because if they could, they would already have done so; the sophists cannot either, because they have no idea what it is, equating it with rhetoric or with the mere collecting of laws and not with correct judgment. But correct judgment cannot be acquired in this way, as medicine shows. So since legislation has been left unexamined by others, we must undertake the study of laws and regimes ourselves.*

1180b28 Should we then, after this, examine whence and how one might become skilled in legislation? Is it, as in other cases, from the experts, the experts in politics (since legislation seems to be part of politics), or do things appear not to be the same in politics as in the other sciences and abilities? For in the latter it is manifestly the same people who pass on the ability and exercise it themselves—as doctors, for instance, and painters. By contrast, the sophists proclaim that they teach politics, but none of them practices it. Rather those engaged in politics do that, and they seem to do it by some power or experience rather than by thought. For they are conspicuous in not writing or speaking about such things (though that would be nobler perhaps than making speeches for law courts and assembly) and in not having made politicians out of their own sons or any other of their friends. But one would have reasonably expected them to do this if they were capable of it, since they could have left behind nothing better for their cities, nor could they have chosen anything better for themselves, or indeed for those dearest to them, than such an ability. Experience does, indeed, seem to make no little contribution (otherwise familiarity with politics would not have made them politicians), so for those who desire to know about politics there does seem to be need of experience in addition.

1181a12 But those sophists who proclaim that they teach politics seem to be a very long way from doing so, for they have no knowledge at all of what sort of thing it is or of what sort of matters it deals with. Otherwise, they would not have put it on the same level as rhetoric, or on a worse one, nor would they think it easy for anyone to legislate who had made a collection of well-reputed laws. For they suppose it to be a matter of selecting the best ones—as if the selection did not need understanding and as if reaching a correct judgment were not, as it is in music, the most important thing. For it is those who have experience of any particular thing who can judge correctly the works it produces and by what means and in what way these are brought to completion and what harmonizes with what. As for those without the experience, it is sufficient if, as in painting, they can tell whether the work has been done well or badly.[12] But laws seem to be the works produced by politics. So how then could laws make one a legislator or enable one to judge which of them were best? People do not even become doctors from books, although doctors try, at any rate, to state not only the treatments but also, by distinguishing the conditions, how to cure and treat each patient. These books do seem to be of some help to the experienced, but they are useless for those who lack the knowledge. Perhaps, then, collections of laws and regimes would be of service to those who know how to study and judge what is in a noble condition or its opposite and what fits with whom.[13] But those who do not have this habit would not, except by chance, exercise a noble judgment when going through such collections, though their understanding with respect to them might improve.

1181b12 Therefore, since the subject of legislation has been left unexamined by those who were before us, perhaps it is better for us to investigate it ourselves instead, and indeed to investigate regimes generally, so that the philosophy of human affairs might, as far as is in our power, reach completion. **1181b15** So first let us try to consider if anything was nobly said by our predecessors on any particular matter,[14] then from the collected regimes[15] try to study what sort of things preserve and destroy cities and what sort of things preserve and destroy each regime[16]—that is, for what reasons some

---

12. Cf. *Politics* 3.11, in particular 1281b38–1282a23. The "understanding" Aristotle is talking about is *sunesis*, on which see *Ethics* 6.10.

13. Or "what fits with what"; the Greek is indeterminate and could mean either.

14. *Politics* 2.

15. Usually thought to be the collection of 158 actual regimes made by Aristotle and his school (and of which only the treatment of Athens survives in other than fragments and epitomes), but it could also be the collection of regimes actually contained in the *Politics* itself (in books 3, 4(7), 5(8), and 6(4)).

16. Usually taken to be a reference to *Politics* 7(5), but that book is only about what preserves and destroys regimes. Cities, by contrast, must be preserved and destroyed by these regimes themselves (a city will realize its goal of good life, and so be preserved, if its regime is good and not otherwise, *Politics* 3.6–7). So presumably Aristotle is referring here, first, to his treatment of correct and deviant regimes in *Politics* 3, 4(7), 5(8), 6(4), and then, second, to his treatment of what preserves and destroys regimes in 7(5).

of them are nobly governed and others the opposite. For when we have studied these things, we might perhaps get more of an overall view of what sort of regime is best and how each is arranged and with what laws and customs.[17] So let us begin our discussion.

17. Usually taken to be a reference to the treatment of the simply best regime in *Politics* 4(7) and 5(8). But Aristotle is speaking of all regimes, not just the simply best, and of the overall view one can take once the things just mentioned have been studied. Therefore, he would seem to be speaking of what the reader can do after having finished reading the *Politics*, rather than of anything he himself does in the writing of it.

Book 1

The Primacy
of the City

CHAPTER 1

The Primacy of the City. *The city, like any community, aims at some good, but the city is the controlling community and so must aim at the most controlling good of all. It is an error, therefore, to suppose that rule over the city differs in degree and not in kind from rule over other and lesser communities. This will be evident if the city is divided and examined in its parts.*

1252a1 Since we see that every city is some sort of community[1] and that every community gets established with some good in view (for everyone does everything for the sake of what they think good), it is clear that, while all communities have some good that they are aiming at, the community that has the most control of all and that embraces all the others is doing this most of all and is aiming at the most controlling of goods. This community is the city as it is called, the community that is political.

1252a7 Consequently all those who think that a politician, a royal ruler, a household manager, and a master over slaves are the same are not speaking nobly.[2] For they suppose that these rulers do not differ in kind but only in the number of subjects ruled over. For instance, they think that if someone rules over a few people, he is a master; if over more than a few, a household

---

1. The Greek is *koinōnia*, a derivative of *koinos* ("common"), and so means a community in the literal sense of sharing in common.

2. Those whom Aristotle is criticizing here may conceivably be the Stranger in Plato's *Statesman* (258e8–259d1) and Socrates in Xenophon's *Memorabilia* (3.4). But there are nameless others mentioned elsewhere in the *Politics* who would fall under the same criticism, as those who identify political rule with despotic rule (4(7).2.1324b32–34, 8(6).2.1317b11–16), those who identify political rule with that part of household management concerned with making money (1.9.1258a2–14, 1.11.1259a33–36), those who identify royal rule with despotic rule (3.16), and those who identify household management with despotic rule (1.2.1252b5–7, 8(6).8.1323a5–6).

manager; if over even more still, a politician or royal ruler, adopting the view that there is no difference between a large household and a small city. As for the politician and royal ruler, they say that the latter has control all by himself and that the former, on the basis of the principles of this sort of science, alternates between ruling and being ruled. But these opinions are not true, as will become clear if we carry out our investigation in the usual way.[3] For as in other cases the composite whole must be divided up into its incomposite parts (for these are the smallest parts of the whole), so if we also look at what the city is made up of, we will get a better view of its parts too, both as to how they differ from each other and as to whether it is possible to get some grasp proper to art of each of the rulers just mentioned.

CHAPTER 2

The City and Its Parts

The Household. *The first communities are the two natural ones of (i) husband and wife for generation and (ii) master and slave for survival. These two together form the household. Households exist for the needs of the day. Villages spring from households, above all through the generation of children and grandchildren, and exist for needs beyond the day.*

1252a24 If one were to see how things develop naturally from the beginning, one would, in this as in other matters, get the noblest view of them. First, then, it is necessary that those who cannot exist without each other couple together, as female and male on the one hand for the sake of generation (and this not from deliberate choice, but because, like the other animals and plants, they have a natural desire to leave behind something else like themselves), and as ruler by nature and ruled on the other on account of preservation. For that which has the capacity to see ahead with its thought is by nature ruler and master, and that which has the capacity to carry out with its body what the other has seen is by nature ruled and slave. That is why the same thing benefits both master and slave.

1252a34 By nature, of course, female and slave are distinct. For nature makes nothing in the niggardly way that bronze workers make the Delphic knife;[4] on the contrary, she makes one thing for one thing. For it is when instruments are made to serve only one work and not many that they are

---

3. The analytic and synthetic method of dividing a whole into its parts and then seeing how the whole is formed from the parts. This method is discussed in *Physics* 1.1, and is found throughout Aristotle's writings.

4. Evidently a knife designed to perform several disparate functions and not one alone.

most nobly finished off. Among the barbarians, however, the female is in the same position as the slave. But that is because there is nothing among the barbarians with the natural capacity to rule, and their community is that of male and female slave. Therefore "it is reasonable for Greeks to rule barbarians," say the poets,[5] supposing that to be a barbarian and to be a slave are by nature the same thing.

1252b9 From the two communities just mentioned the household first came to be, so Hesiod spoke correctly when he composed the line: "first a house, a wife, and an ox for ploughing,"[6] because as far as the poor are concerned, an ox takes the place of a slave. The household, then, is by nature a community set up for the needs of every day, whose members Charondas calls "fellows of the same bread" and Epimenides the Cretan "fellows of the same manger."[7]

1252b15 But as soon as several households have come together into a community for other than the needs of the day, then there is a village. By nature, in fact, the village seems to be principally an offshoot[8] of the household, namely the children and the children of children, those whom some call "fellows of the same milk." That is also why cities used to be ruled by kings in the beginning, just as is still the case among the nations today, because those who came together into cities were living under kings. For in every household the eldest is king, and as a result the offshoots of the household were ruled in the same way because of their common descent. And this is what Homer says: "each one gave sacred law to children and wives."[9] For they were scattered about, and that is how they had their dwellings in ancient times. It is also for this same reason that everyone says the gods are ruled monarchically, because they themselves used to be ruled like that in times gone by or are still so ruled today; just as human beings make the form of the gods look like themselves, so they do the same with the way the gods live.

The City. The completion of household and village is the city, which is for the sake of good life and not life alone. Thus, (i) the city is natural because the households it completes are natural; (ii) human beings are by nature political for this same reason and also because they alone have speech; (iii) the city is prior to individuals and makes

5. Euripides, *Iphigenia in Aulis* 1400.

6. *Works and Days* 405.

7. Charondas was a lawgiver from Catana in Sicily. He is mentioned again in 2.12 and 6(4).11 and 13. Epimenides of Crete is said to have written on the Cretan regime (Diogenes Laertius 1.109–15).

8. The word is literally "from the household" (*apoikia*) and is the standard Greek term for colony. The village could accordingly be described as a sort of community of "households from the household."

9. *Odyssey* 9.114–15, the same quotation about the Cyclops that Aristotle has implicitly referred to just before in the *Ethics* 10.9.1180a26–29.

them to be what they are; (iv) the drive to the city is natural, but he who sets up a
city is responsible for things of very great goodness, because justice, which makes men
best, belongs to the city.

1252b27 When the community made up of several villages is complete, it is
then a city, possessing the limit of every self-sufficiency, practically speaking;
and though it originates for the sake of staying alive, it exists for the sake of
living well.

1252b30 Consequently, every city exists by nature, if, that is, the first communities also do. For the city is the goal of those communities and nature
is a goal, since we say that a thing's nature is the sort of thing it is when its
generation has reached its goal (as in the case of a human being, a horse, or
a house). Further, that for the sake of which something exists — that is, its
goal — is best, and self-sufficiency is both a goal and best.

1253a1 So it is manifest that the city is among the things that exist by nature,
that a human being is by nature a political animal, and that anyone who is
cityless by nature and not by chance is either of a depraved sort or better
than a human being. He is like the one reproached by Homer as "without
clan, without sacred law, without hearth." [10] For someone who is like this by
nature is at the same time eager for war, after the manner of a solitary piece
in draughts.

1253a7 It is clear, then, that a human being is more of a political animal than
is any bee or than are any of those animals that live in herds. For nature, as
we say, makes nothing in vain, and humans are the only animals who possess reasoned speech.[11] Voice, of course, serves to indicate what is painful
and pleasant; that is why it is also found in the other animals, because their
nature has reached the point where they can perceive what is painful and
pleasant and express these to each other. But speech serves to make plain
what is advantageous and harmful and so also what is just and unjust. For it
is a peculiarity of humans, in contrast to the other animals, to have perception of good and bad, just and unjust, and the like; and community in these
things makes a household and a city.

1253a18 In addition, the city is by nature prior to the household and to
each one of us taken singly. For the whole is necessarily prior to the part.
For instance, there will be neither foot nor hand when the whole body has
been destroyed (except equivocally, as when one speaks of a foot or hand
made of stone), for such a foot or hand will have been ruined. Everything is
defined by its work and by its power, so that a foot and hand in such a condition should no longer be said to be the same thing (except equivocally). It

10. *Iliad* 9.63.
11. The Greek is *logos*.

is clear, then, that the city exists by nature and that it has priority over the individual. For if no individual is self-sufficient when isolated, he will be like all other parts in relation to their whole. But anyone who lacks the capacity to share in community, or has no need to because of his self-sufficiency, is no part of the city and as a result is either a beast or a god.

1253a29 By nature, then, the drive for such a community exists in everyone; but the first to set one up is responsible for things of very great goodness. For as human beings are the best of all animals when perfected, so they are the worst when divorced from law and right. The reason is that injustice is most difficult to deal with when furnished with weapons, and the weapons a human being has are meant by nature to go along with prudence and virtue, but it is only too possible to turn them to contrary uses. Consequently, if a human being lacks virtue, he is a most unholy and savage thing, and when it comes to sex and food, the worst. But justice is something political, for right is the arrangement of a political community, and right is discrimination of what is just.[12]

CHAPTER 3

Household Management and Its Parts. *The household is composed of husband and wife, father and child, master and slave; and household management is divided into the management of these three relations. There is also a question about a possible fourth part of household management, namely business. Each of these parts requires investigation, and first comes mastery and slavery, both so as to see what slaves are for and to get a better understanding of mastery and slavery than is provided by current conceptions.*

1253b1 Since it is manifest what parts the city is made up of, it is necessary first to speak of household management (for every city is made up of households). The parts of household management are the parts that the household itself is made up of, and these are, in the case of the complete household, free persons and slaves. But as we have to begin by examining each thing in its smallest parts,[13] and as the first and smallest parts of the household are master and slave, husband and wife, and father and child, our investigation must focus on these three and on what they are and should be like. These three are the science of mastery, of marrying (for the being yoked together of woman and man has no name), and of child-getting (for this too lacks a

---

12. The Greek word for right here is *dikē*, and *dikē* is what lies at the root (etymologically and really) of the other two words, *dikaion* (just) and *dikaiosunē* (justice). Justice is the virtue of doing what is just and the just is the right; cf. *Ethics* 5.

13. The method stated at the end of 1.1.

name of its own).[14] Let these three, then, be as we say. But there is a certain part that to some seems to be household management and to others a very great part of it, and we shall have to study how things stand with respect to it (I mean what is called business).[15]

1253b14 First, however, let us speak about master and slave, with these two aims in view: to see what relates to the use slaves are needed for and to see if we cannot get hold of some knowledge about master and slave that is superior to current conceptions. For, as we said at the beginning,[16] some think that mastery is a sort of science and that household management, mastery, and political and royal rule are all the same science. But others think that to be a master is against nature, for they say it is by law that one person is a slave and another a master, whereas by nature there is no difference at all. Hence, they say the thing is also not just, because it is a matter of force.

CHAPTER 4

Slavery

The Definition of the Slave. *Property is part of the household and property is the multitude of tools that household management, like any art, needs to complete its work, namely life. Among these, the slave is property as a living tool, needed as an assistant to work other tools, and he is a tool for doing, not for making, since life is doing and not making. Property is also what belongs wholly to another, so the slave belongs wholly to another. Accordingly, the slave by nature is a human being who is by nature the possession of another as a tool for purposes of doing or action.*

1253b23 Since property is a part of the household and the science of property is a part of household management (for without necessities, neither life nor good life are possible); and since just as the determinate arts must have their proper tools if they are to complete their work, so too does the household manager; and since tools are either lifeless or living—as the pilot's rudder, for instance, is a lifeless tool, but his lookout man on the prow is a

14. Aristotle gropes for words in these cases because while the word for the rule of a master, *despotikē*, expresses his meaning well enough, the words he uses for the other two kinds of rule, *gamikē* and *teknopoiētikē* (not *patrikē* or "paternal management" as Dreizehnter has it), do not. The first properly expresses the idea of getting married but not also of being married, the second the idea of getting children but not also of rearing children.

15. The Greek word for business is *chrēmatistikē*, the art of acquiring *chrēmata*, and *chrēmata* are "all things whose worth is measured in money" (*Ethics* 4.1.1119b26–27), that is, commodities or merchandise. But the word also sometimes means, by a natural extension, the money that measures commodities.

16. In 1.1.

living one (for an assistant, as far as the arts are concerned, has the form of a tool)—accordingly a possession is a tool for the purposes of life, property is a multitude of such tools, and the slave is a living possession. Also, every assistant is, as it were, a tool for tools. For suppose that each tool could complete its work either by being told to do so or because it perceived what was to be done in advance, as they relate of those of Daedalus or of the tripods of Hephaestus, which the poet says "entered the divine assembly self moved." [17] If shuttles could thus do their weaving by themselves or if picks could thus play the cithara,[18] ruling craftsmen[19] would have no need of assistants nor masters of slaves.

1254a1 The tools mentioned are for making something, but a possession is for doing something (we get something else out of a shuttle besides the use of it, but from clothing or a bed we get the use only). In addition, since making and doing are different in kind and since both need tools, the same difference must be found in the tools as well. But a way of life is doing, not making. Consequently, the slave is an assistant in matters that concern doing.

1254a8 We speak of a possession in the same way that we speak of a part. A part is not only part of something else but also wholly belongs to that something else, and the same is true of a possession. Consequently, the master is only master of the slave but does not belong to him, while the slave is not only slave of the master but wholly belongs to him as well.

1254a13 What the nature and power of a slave are is clear from these considerations. For anyone who, while a human being, does not by nature belong to himself but to another is by nature a slave, and he is a human being belonging to another who, while being human,[20] is a possession, and a possession in the sense of a tool that is separate[21] and for doing something.

17. Homer *Iliad* 18.376. Daedalus was a sculptor whose statues were so lifelike they seemed actually to move.

18. The cithara was a kind of stringed instrument, like a lute.

19. The Greek word is *architektōn* (which gives us our word "architect") and literally means a ruling (*archi*) craftsman (*tektōn*), a craftsman who is not just an expert at his craft (a master craftsman) but who also directs other craftsman working under him.

20. Reading *anthrōpos* ("human being"), a variant in some manuscripts, instead of *doulos* ("slave") as in other manuscripts and Dreizehnter. This other reading would give the sense ". . . who, being a slave, is a possession . . . ."

21. Separate from his master unlike the hand of 1.2.1253a20–25, which is not physically separate but must remain attached to the whole.

CHAPTER 5

Slave and Master by Nature

First Proof. *The question whether anyone is by nature a slave can be answered both by reason and also by appeal to what actually occurs. For, as regards what actually occurs, ruling and being ruled are something necessary and beneficial; some things are separated into ruler and ruled at generation; rulers and ruled come in several forms; and rule over better subjects is better. For ruler and ruled appear in every composite whole. Examples are the political rule of intellect over appetite and of male over female and the despotic rule of soul over body and of humans over animals. So any human beings related to others as body to soul or as animal to human are slaves by nature, and such are those whose best work is the use of the body.*

1254a17 The next thing to investigate is whether or not anyone is by nature like this and whether serving as a slave is better and just for anyone or whether instead all slavery is against nature. But it is not hard to study by reason what the answer is, nor to learn it from what actually occurs. For ruling and being ruled are not only necessary but beneficial, and in the case of some things a separation of them into ruler and ruled occurs immediately at generation. There are many kinds of rulers and ruled, and rule over better subjects is always better (as rule over a human is better than over an animal), since from better materials a better work is completed, and when one thing rules and another is ruled, there is always some work they have.

1254a28 For in everything that is fashioned into a common unity from the combination of several parts, whether the parts be continuous or discrete, a ruling and a ruled part are apparent, and this inheres in living things from the whole of nature. For rule exists even in lifeless things, as in the case of harmony—though that is a rather extraneous topic of investigation. The living animal, however, is composed first of soul and body, where by nature the former is the ruler and the latter the ruled. But what is natural must be looked for in things whose disposition accords with nature, not in things that have been corrupted. Hence we must look at that human being who has the best disposition both in body and soul, since what is natural will be clear in him. For in those who are depraved or in a depraved condition the body often seems to dominate the soul because their condition is base and against nature.

1254b2 But it is, as we say, first possible in the living animal to study both despotic and political rule, for the soul rules the body with despotic rule and the intellect rules appetite with political or royal rule. Here it is manifestly natural and beneficial for the body to be ruled by the soul and for the passionate part of the soul to be ruled by the intellect (the part that possesses reason). But all of them are damaged together if rule is shared equally or reversed. The same holds true of human beings with respect to the other animals. The tame animals are better in nature than the wild ones, and it is better for the former all to be ruled by humans because thus they are preserved. In addition, the relation of the male to the female is by nature that of better to worse and ruler to ruled.

1254b14 Things must also hold in the same way for all human beings. Thus, all those who are as widely separated from others as are soul and body or human and beast—and that is the condition of those whose work is the use of the body and from whom such work is the best that there is—are slaves by nature. For them, it is better to be ruled over by a master, if indeed it is also better in the case of the things just mentioned.[22]

Second Proof. *The same result follows from reason, that the slave by definition belongs to another. Those whose best work is the use of the body do not have reason themselves (and so belong to another), but they can perceive it and be of assistance after the manner of animals (and so are living tools). This condition is a condition of soul, but nature also tries to duplicate it in the body. All would concede slavery and mastery to the inferior and superior in body; much more justly should they do so to the inferior and superior in soul.*

1254b20 For the slave by nature is someone who has the power of belonging to another (which is why in fact he does belong to another) and who shares reason sufficiently to perceive it but not to have it. For the other animals give of their assistance without perceiving by reason but rather by what they feel.[23] Also, the need we have of the two is very much the same, since bodily help in the supply of necessities comes from both slaves and tame animals alike.

1254b27 Now, nature wishes to make a difference also in the bodies of free and slave, with those of the latter being strong for necessary uses and those of the former being erect and useless for such working but useful for a political way of life (a life that is divided between the needs of war and peace).[24]

22. The body and animals, for which, as just stated, despotic rule by the soul or by humans is better.

23. There is some dispute about the Greek here, and translators tend to take it as meaning that the other animals do not perceive or follow reason but rather follow their feelings or passions. But such translations treat the text as drawing a distinction between slaves and animals, whereas Aristotle has just likened the two to each other and should be continuing the likeness here. The translation I offer is meant to overcome this difficulty. It differs from other translations in taking *hypēretei* absolutely and in its primary sense of "give assistance" (picking up on the word for assistant, *hypēretēs*, in the last chapter), not in its other sense of "follow" or "obey" and as governing "feelings" (*pathēmasin*).

24. Cf. 4(7).14.1333a30–b5.

Often, however, the opposite happens, and some have the bodies of the free while others have the souls. But however that may be, it is manifest that if some people were to develop bodies like the statues of the gods, everyone would say that those left behind deserved to be their slaves. So if this holds true in the case of bodies, it would be much more just to draw the distinction in the case of souls. But nobility of soul is not so easy to see as nobility of body.

1254b39 It is manifest then that by nature some are free and others slaves and that service as a slave is for the latter both beneficial and just.

CHAPTER 6

Slave and Master by Law

Against Those Who Altogether Condemn Slavery. *Those who condemn slavery as unjust are right up to a point, because there is also slavery by the law of conquest. But those versed in the laws say it is terrible if what is forced into submission is to become slave of the stronger. Among the wise some agree with them and some do not, but the wise allow, contrary to those versed in the laws, that mastery by conquerors who are superior in virtue is just.*

1255a3 It is not hard to see that those who have contrary opinions are right up to a point, for "slave" and "slavish service" have two meanings and there is "slave" and "slavish service" by law as well.[25] The law in question is a certain agreement by which what is conquered in war is said to belong to the conquerors. Now, many of those versed in the laws bring against this principle of justice a writ of illegality, as they would against an orator in the assembly.[26] Their supposition is that it is a terrible thing if what is forced into submission is to become the slave and subject of what has the capacity to use force or is stronger in power.

1255a11 There are some also among the wise who hold this view, though others of them think differently. The cause of the dispute, and what makes their arguments overlap, is that when virtue gets hold of equipment,[27] it has a special capacity to use force, and also the conqueror always excels in some

---

25. That is, as well as by nature.

26. In the popular assembly at Athens a writ of illegality (*graphē paranomōn*) could be brought against anyone who proposed a law contrary to established law. The phrase "principle of justice" translates *to dikaion* ("the just") in the Greek, which Aristotle seems to use several times in this passage to refer to the law in question.

27. The Greek is *chorēgia* and refers to the things needed to equip a chorus properly for the dramatic festivals at Athens. Hence it comes also to refer to the supply of resources and means needed to undertake actions generally.

form of goodness. Consequently, the force seems not to be without virtue and the dispute seems to turn only on the principle of justice itself. For, on this account, some think the principle is kindness, while others think it is this, that rule by the stronger is just.[28] At any rate, when these arguments are set aside, the other arguments—that the better in virtue ought not to rule and be master—are neither strong nor convincing.

Against Those Who Altogether Approve of Slavery. Those who hold the contrary position—that is, that all slavery by law is just—have to deny this when they admit that since those are not slaves who do not deserve to be slaves, it cannot be the case that all rule by conquest is just. Their attempt to instead confine slavery to barbarians and freedom to themselves as the well-born is really to look for the slave and free by nature. But to suppose that those born to the good are always good ignores nature's failures.

1255a21 Some take their stand wholly by a sort of justice, as they suppose (for the law is something just), and lay down slavery in war as just but then at once deny it. For it is possible for the rule arising from war[29] not to be just, and no one would say that he who did not deserve to be a slave really was a slave. Otherwise, those reputed to be the most well born will be slaves and descended from slaves if captured and sold. Consequently, they do not wish to give the name of slave to such persons but only to barbarians.

1255a29 Yet in so doing they are looking precisely for the slave by nature that we started with, for they have to say that some are slaves everywhere and others nowhere. It is the same with good birth. For they think of themselves as possessing good birth not just among themselves but everywhere, while they think of the barbarians as possessing good birth only in their own home, thus adopting the view that one of the two is, simply speaking, well-born and free, while the other is not. As Theodectes' Helen puts it: "Who would think it meet to address me as servant, sprung as I am from divine roots on both sides?"[30] But to say this sort of thing is to give a definition of slave and free, good birth and low birth, in terms of virtue and vice since it is to claim that the good are born from the good in the same way that

28. I punctuate the Greek thus: *auto touto, dikaion to* ("it is this, that . . . is just"), not *auto touto dikaion, to* ("this itself is just, rule . . .") with Dreizehnter.

29. Most translate this as "the beginning of wars" (the Greek *arche* can mean either beginning or rule). But that the beginning of certain wars might be unjust is not what accounts for the possibility that some of those conquered might not deserve to be enslaved. For even if a war began justly, the conqueror could not justly enslave the conquered unless they were already and independently slaves by nature. Besides, what is relevant to Aristotle's argument is not how wars begin but how they end, namely what one does with the conquered after one has won rule over them.

30. Frag. 3 Nauck. Theodectes was a tragic poet of the fourth century.

humans are born from humans or beasts from beasts. While nature has such a desire, she is, however, seldom able to realize it.

Summary. *The dispute about slavery has some justification, because the enslaved and the free by law need not always be slave and free by nature. But sometimes they are, and in such cases slavery is beneficial and just and involves a form of friendship, though the reverse is true otherwise.*

1255b4 So it is clear that the dispute about slavery has some reason behind it and that some slaves are not by nature slaves and some free are not by nature free. It is also clear that in other cases a natural distinction does obtain, where it is beneficial and just for the one to be slave and the other master. Here the first should be ruled by the second with the rule for which the second is naturally fitted, namely mastery. But if mastery is exercised badly, it is not beneficial to either of them, for part and whole, body and soul, are benefited by the same thing and the slave is a part of his master as a sort of living but separate part of his body. Consequently, a certain mutual benefit and friendship exist between master and slave when they deserve by nature to be master and slave, but the opposite happens when their relationship is not like this but is by law and forced.

CHAPTER 7

Mastery as Rule and as Science. *Mastery is not the same as the other kinds of rule, nor is it a kind of science, for master and slave differ by character of soul, not by knowledge. Nevertheless, there are sciences proper to the master and to the slave. The science of possessing slaves, by war and hunting, is a different science.*

1255b16 The above conclusions also make it evident that despotic rule and political rule are not the same thing, and that not all of the kinds of rule are the same as each other, contrary to what some say.[31] For political rule is by nature rule over the free, while despotic rule is rule over slaves; and household management is monarchical (for every household is ruled monarchically), while political rule is rule over free and equals.
1255b20 Now the master is not said to be a master because of any science he has but because he is of a certain character, and likewise with slave and free. But there can be sciences characteristic of both master and slave. The science characteristic of the latter would be the sort that someone used to teach in Syracuse, where he would instruct houseboys in their regular round

31. Those criticized in 1.1.

of chores for a fee. But there could be teaching in more than these sorts of things, as in cookery and other such services. For work differs from work, with some enjoying more honor and others being more necessary; as the proverb has it: "slave goes before slave and master before master."[32] Now such kinds of science are all characteristic of the slave, but the master's science is the science of using slaves. For the master is not a master in getting possession of slaves but in using them. There is nothing grand or dignified about this science, for what the slave must know how to make, that the master must know how to command. Consequently, all those who have the ability not to suffer the ill of it themselves give the honor instead to a steward while they themselves engage in politics or philosophy.

1255b37 The science of property is different from both these sciences,[33] that is to say the just form of it, which is a certain science of war or hunting. So let this be our determination about slave and master.

CHAPTER 8

Property

The Questions about Business. *There is a question whether business is the same as the science of household management or a part of or an assistant to it. That it is not the same is evident because business provides and the science of household management uses. The dispute is whether business is a part of this science or different from it.*

1256a1 But since the slave was a part of property, let us go on to study the whole of property and business in general according to our usual method.[34] First, then, someone might raise the difficulty whether business is the same as the science of household management or some part of or assistant to it; and if it is an assistant, whether it is in the same way as making shuttles is an assistant to weaving or as bronze working is an assistant to making statues. For these do not assist in the same way; the first provides the tools and the second the material. By material I mean the underlying stuff from which the work is made, as wool in the case of weaving and bronze in the case of making statues. Now, it is clear that the science of household management is not the same as business, since it belongs to the latter to provide and to the former to use. For what will be the science that will use the things of the household if not the science of household management? But it is matter

32. Philemon frag. 54 Kock.
33. The sciences characteristic of master and of slave, respectively.
34. See 1.1.

for dispute whether business is some part of the science of household management or is a kind different from it.

The Science of Property and Household Management. *The job of the expert in business is to study the sources of property. As property has many parts, the first question is whether the care of food is part of business. Food and the other necessities of life are provided by nature, for (i) animal and human ways of life are naturally differentiated according to their ways of acquiring such necessities, and (ii) nature gives such property to grown animals in the same as way as she gives it to the young at first generation. So plants and animals are given by nature as property for human beings, and the science of such property must be part of the science of household management. This property is true wealth because it is limited with a view to good life, and true wealth is limited, as are the tools of any art.*

1256a15 For if it belongs to the businessman to think out where commodities and property will come from, and if property and wealth contain many parts, then the first thing for dispute is whether the science of farming, and generally the care and property of food, is a part of business[35] or is some class different from it.

1256a19 But there are many kinds of food and hence many ways of life among animals and humans. For it is not possible to live without food and consequently differences of food have differentiated the animals' ways of life. For among wild animals some live in herds and others live scattered about, in whichever way is advantageous to them for food because of the fact that some eat animals, others crops, and others everything. So nature has distinguished their ways of life with a view to their ease in the getting of these kinds of food. And since the same thing is not by nature pleasant to all but differs as they differ, so the ways of life among animal eaters themselves, and among plant eaters, diverge from each other.

1256a29 It is similar with human beings, for their ways of life differ a great deal. The most idle are nomads, whose food comes to them from tame animals without effort as they take their leisure, though as their flocks must change from place to place in pursuit of pasture, they are also compelled to follow along as if farming a living farm. Other humans live from hunting, and different groups from different kinds of hunting. So some, for example, live from piracy, others from fishing (that is, all those who dwell next to lakes, marshes, rivers, or a sea suitable for fish), and others from hunting birds and wild beasts. But the largest class of human beings lives from the land and cultivated crops. So many, then, are more or less the human ways

---

35. Reading *chrēmatistikēs* ("business") with the manuscripts instead of *oikonomikēs* ("household management") with Dreizehnter.

of life, or at least those of them that have their work in what is spontaneously grown and do not provide food through exchange and trading. They are the nomadic, the piratical, the fishing, the hunting, and the farming ways of life. But there are some who live pleasantly by mixing these ways, supplying the way of life that is most wanting[36] by adding to it another where it happens to be lacking in self-sufficiency. For example, some combine the nomadic and the piratical ways of life and others the farming and the hunting ways of life, and they spend each of their days, just as the others do, as need might require of them.

1256b7 Property of this sort has manifestly been given by nature herself to all animals—in the same way when they are grown as immediately at their first coming to be. For even at generation's very beginning some animals produce all the food their offspring need until they can get it for themselves, as do, for instance, those that produce grubs or eggs. On the other hand, animals that give birth to live young carry food for their offspring in themselves for a certain time—I mean the natural stuff we call milk. Consequently, it is similarly clear that in the case of things that have grown, we must suppose plants to be for the sake of animals and animals for the sake of humans, the tame ones for use and food and the wild ones, or most of them at any rate, for food and other kinds of help, so that clothing and other tools may be got from them. If nature, therefore, makes nothing either incomplete or in vain, then she has necessarily made all these things for the sake of human beings, and hence the art of war will also by nature be a science of property in a way. For the art of hunting is a part of it, and this art has to be used against wild animals and those human beings who, though unwilling to be ruled, are naturally fit for it, as this war is by nature just.

1256b26 So, one kind of the science of property is naturally part of the science of household management, and this property must either be present or the science must provide it so that it is present. It consists in a store of things necessary for life and useful to the community of city or household. And true wealth at any rate would seem to be made up of these things. For self-sufficiency in this sort of property with a view to good life is not unlimited, contrary to what Solon says in the line: "to wealth no limit has been laid down for human beings."[37] For such a limit has been laid down, just as it has in the case of the other arts. No tool of any art is without limit in either quantity or size, and wealth is a multitude of tools for the arts of ruling household and city.

36. I read *endeestaton* with the manuscripts, not *endeesteron* ("more wanting") with Drei-zehnter.
37. Frag. 1.71 Diehl.

1256b37 It is clear, then, that and why there is by nature a certain science of property for managers of the household and for politicians.

CHAPTER 9

The Two Kinds of Business

The Science of Property and Exchange. *There is another kind of science of property that is especially and justly called business. It is what gives rise to the idea that wealth has no limit, and it is often confused with the first science of property. However, though close, it is different from it. Property admits of a double use, its proper use and its use in being exchanged for something else; and the art of exchange initially arose because humans naturally have a surplus in some things and a deficiency in others. As a way of securing self-sufficiency outside the household such exchange is neither against nature nor a kind of what is especially called business.*

1256b40 But there is another class of science of property, which people above all call business and which it is just to call business, and because of which it does seem that there is no limit to wealth and property. Many think it to be one and the same with that just described, on account of the closeness between them. But it is neither the same as it nor far removed. The first exists by nature, while this other does not but rather comes about through a certain sort of experience and art.

1257a5 Let us take our beginning from the fact that every piece of property has a double use. Both are uses of the thing as such, though not in the same way, but one is a use proper to the thing and the other is not—as, for instance, the wearing of a shoe and the exchanging of it. Both are uses of the shoe, because the one who exchanges a shoe for money or food with someone who needs a shoe uses the shoe as a shoe but not in its proper use. For it did not come to be for the sake of exchange. The same holds of other pieces of property as well. For the art of exchange concerns all of them, having taken its beginning initially from what accords with nature, that in some things human beings have more than is sufficient and in others less. Hence it is clear that the art of trading does not by nature belong to business, for people needed to practice exchange only so far as was sufficient for them. So it is manifest that in the first community, the household, there is no need of exchange; that occurs only when the community has become more numerous. For those in a household would share all the same things in common, but those in separate ones would share many things from others as well, and they would have to give and receive in exchange as their needs required. This still happens among barbarian nations, for they exchange useful things for useful things and no further—for instance, giving wine and receiving grain, and so on with other things of the same sort. This art of exchange is neither against nature nor is it any kind of business since it was only for completing the self-sufficiency that accords with nature.

The Emergence from Exchange of Another Kind of Business. *To facilitate natural exchange, money is invented, and with the invention of money comes the possibility of using exchange to increase money and not to sustain natural sufficiency. This is what people usually call "business," this second and trading kind of business, and it explains the opinions people have about wealth and business. But the intrinsic uselessness of money shows there must be another kind of business, namely the household kind from the last chapter. The two kinds differ in that the trading kind does not produce property, is all about money, and has no limit to its wealth. People nevertheless confuse the two, because both use property in exchange. The ends of each, however, are different.*

1257a30 But business arose, conformably to reason, from this art. For when, through importing what they lacked and exporting what they had in abundance, people got their help from more foreign sources, the use of money was of necessity provided; for not all things that are naturally needed are easy to carry about. Hence, people came to an agreement of that sort, namely for the purposes of exchange, to give and take from each other something which, being itself something useful, was easily adaptable to the needs of life—such as iron, silver, and anything else of the sort. At first this was determined simply by size and weight, but eventually they stamped it with a mark so as to release themselves from measuring it, since the mark stood as an indication of how much there was. So once money had been provided, there arose from necessary exchange the other kind of business, the trading kind. It perhaps existed at first in a simple manner but soon became, through experience, more of an art, to see from what sources and how to make most profit through the activity of exchange.

1257b5 That is why business seems to be about money above all and its work the ability to study where a multitude of commodities will come from. For this business seems to be productive of wealth or commodities, and a quantity of money is also often set down as wealth, on account of business and the art of trading having this as their concern. But again at other times money seems to be a nonsense and altogether a thing of law[38] and by nature nothing, because if its users change the currency, the original one is not worth anything nor useful at all with a view to necessities, and someone who is rich in money will often be lacking in necessary food. Yet it is a

38. There is a pun in the Greek here, for money is *nomisma* and law is *nomos*.

strange thing for that to be wealth which one can abound in and still starve to death, like that fellow Midas[39] in the fable when, because of the insatiability of his prayer, everything placed beside him changed to gold.

1257b17 Hence people seek a different definition of wealth and of business, and do so rightly. For natural business and wealth are different, and this latter business is proper to household management but the other is proper to trading, not being productive of commodities in any way except by exchange of commodities. And it seems to be about money, for money is the element and limit of the exchange. And the wealth that comes from this business is indeed without limit. For the medical art is without limit with respect to being healthy and all arts are without limit with respect to their end (for the end is above all what they want to produce). But they do have a limit with respect to what is for the sake of the end, because the end is the limit for all of them. So, in like manner, there is no limit to the end of business either, and its end is the sort of wealth just mentioned or property in commodities. But to the science of household management, which is not business, there is a limit; for that is not the work of the science of household management.

1257b32 That is why it appears on the one hand that all wealth must have a limit and yet why on the other hand we see the opposite happening in fact. For all those engaged in business increase money without limit. The reason is the closeness between them. For the two uses of business,[40] being of the same thing, overlap, since property has the same use in both cases[41] but not in the same respect: while of the one use, something else is the end; of the other, the end is increase. As a result, it seems to some that increase is the work of the science of household management, and they end up thinking they must either preserve or increase their substance of money without limit.

Reason for Its Emergence. *People are disposed to think that the end of business is increase and to confuse the two kinds of business because they are more serious about life than about good life, or because they identify good life with bodily enjoyments. And if they cannot get what they want through business itself, they pervert everything else into business instead.*

39. A mythical king of Phrygia who prayed that everything he touched should turn to gold and who, of course, found his food turned to gold too.

40. Reading *hekatera* with the manuscripts and taking it with *chrēsis* ("the two uses"). If *hekateras* is read with Dreizehnter, it will have to be taken with *tēs chrēmatistikēs* to mean "the use of the two kinds of business."

41. Reading *chrēseōs ktēsis* ("property has the same use") with the manuscripts, rather than *ktēseōs chrēsis* ("the use is of the same property") with Dreizehnter. I take the point to be that property is used for exchange in both cases, but in one case for natural sufficiency and in the other for sheer increase.

1257b40 The reason for this disposition of theirs is that they are serious about living but not about living well, and so since their desire for that is infinite, they desire also an infinite amount of the things that produce it. Even those who apply themselves to living well seek what conduces to bodily enjoyments, so since this also seems to exist in property, all their pursuits focus on the practice of business. And that is how the other kind of business came to be. For as their enjoyment is found in excess, they seek what produces the excess they enjoy. If they cannot provide this excess through business, they try to provide it through some other cause, using each of their capabilities in a way that does not accord with nature. For the work of courage is not to produce commodities but boldness. Nor is this the work of generalship or of medicine either, but rather victory is in the first case and health in the second. But they make all of them into businesses, supposing this to be the end and that everything must answer to the end.[42]

1258a14 Such, then, is our discussion of business: both about the unnecessary kind and what it is and for what reason we are in need of it,[43] and also about the necessary kind—that it is different from the other and is by nature proper to household management, being concerned with food, and which, unlike the other, is not infinite but has a limit.

CHAPTER 10

Business as Part of Household Management. *An analogy with weaving suggests that the household manager's job does not include the getting of property but only the using of it. An analogy with medicine suggests the same thing. But, in fact, medicine is in a way part of the household manager's job, and so in the same way is business (the household manager must ensure that what medicine prescribes for health and what business prescribes for property are both carried out), though medicine and business are, as such, assistants and not parts of household management. At any rate this is true of the first or household kind of business; it is not true of the trading, kind which is blameworthy and contrary to nature. Even less is it true of usury, which, as making money out of money, is most contrary to nature.*

1258a19 The difficulty raised from the beginning[44] is also clear, namely whether business belongs to the household manager and politician or whether it does not but property must be to hand (for just as political sci-

---

42. Aristotle may have the Spartans, among others, in mind here; cf. 2.9.1271b7–10 and 4(7).15.1334a40–b5.

43. Strictly speaking, we are not in need of it. But a reason could make us in need of it, namely the reason that we care more about life or bodily pleasure than living well.

44. 1.8.1256a13–14.

ence does not produce human beings but makes use of them after taking them from nature, so also must nature, land or sea or something else, give food) and it befits the household manager to dispose properly what comes from these sources. For it does not belong to the weaving art to make the wool but to use it and to recognize what sort is serviceable and fitting and what sort is poor and unfitting. For one might also raise the difficulty as to why business should be part of household management while medicine is not, even though those in the household must be healthy just as they must live or do anything else that is necessary. But since it is in one way the concern of the household manager and the ruler also to see about health while in another way this concern is not theirs but the doctor's, so likewise it is in one way the concern of the household manager to see about commodities and in another way not his concern but the concern of the assistant science. **1258a34** Property should above all, as was said earlier,[45] be present by nature. For it is nature's work to provide food to what has been born, since everything finds food in the residue of what it is born from. That is why, according to nature, business is for everyone from crops and animals. But business is twofold, as we said, one being proper to trading and the other to household management. The latter is necessary and praiseworthy but the one proper to exchange is justly blamed, since it is not according to nature but is a taking from each other. Hence, most reasonably is the art of usury hated, because it gets its property from money itself and not from what money was supplied for. Money came into being for the sake of exchange, but interest just makes the money itself increase. That is how interest got its name, for offspring are like the parents that gave them birth, and interest is money born of money.[46] Consequently, among business practices this is most of all contrary to nature.

CHAPTER 11

The Practice of Business. *There are several parts to the use or practice of business, both of the most proper kind of business and of the kind that is exchange. There is also a third kind of business lying between these two, which itself has several parts. All these parts differ in profitability and worth, but how best to carry them out can be discovered from existing books and from making collections of stories about success-ful business practices, as with the stories about monopoly associated with Thales and others. Such knowledge can be useful for political as well as household rulers.*

45. 1.8.1256b7–22.
46. The Greek for interest is *tokos*, which literally means offspring.

1258b9 Having sufficiently determined what concerns knowledge we must next go through what concerns use. Study of all such things has something liberal about it, but to be actually experienced in them belongs to necessity. **1258b12** The useful parts of business are the following: being experienced in livestock and what sorts are most profitable where and how—as, for instance, what sort of property is most profitable in the case of horses or cattle or sheep, and similarly of the other animals (for one must be experienced in how they compare in profitability both with respect to each other and with respect to particular places, for some thrive here and others there); next, being experienced in farming, both of grain and fruits, and in the keeping of bees and other animals, fish and fowl, from which one can derive some help. These, then, are the parts and first elements of business in its most proper sense.

1258b21 Of the business that is exchange the largest part is mercantile activity, and of this there are three parts: provisioning a ship, carrying goods, and putting them up for sale (these differ one from the other by offering greater security or greater returns). The second part of this kind of business is lending money at interest, and the third is wage labor. Of wage labor, there is the sort involving the vulgar arts and the sort involving those who have no skill but are useful with their bodies only.

1258b27 A third kind of business lies between this second one and the first, for it has in it some part of the business according to nature and some part of the business proper to exchange. It deals with things that come from the earth or with unfruitful but useful things growing in the earth—as, for example, logging and all kinds of mining. Mining has by now come to include many class-divisions, for the things mined from the earth are of many kinds.

1258b33 The account of each of these things so far has been given in general terms, and while it would be useful with a view to actual working to speak of them in detail one by one, spending time on this matter would be crude. The most craftsmanlike of these works are those in which chance plays the least role, the most mechanical [47] are those that damage the body most, the most slavish are those in which the body is most used, and the most low-born are those where there is least need of virtue in addition. But since writings on these matters exist, such as those by Chares of Paros and Apollodorus of Lemnos [48] on the farming of grain and crops and those by others similarly on other subjects, let him whose care it is use these for his study. Also, scattered stories about the ways in which some people have

47. The Greek word is *banausos*, which literally means someone who works by fire, but it has a general reference, along with a derogatory connotation, to all artisans or craftsmen engaged in bodily work.

48. Apollodorus is cited in the agricultural writings of Varro and Pliny, but Chares (or Charetides) is otherwise unknown.

been successful in business should be collected, for all these ways are useful for those who honor business.

1259a6 There is, for example, the achievement of Thales of Miletus.[49] For what he thought up was a business scheme, but it is associated with his name because of his wisdom, though it happens to be something general. They say that when he was being reproached, because of his poverty, with the uselessness of philosophy, he noticed from his study of the stars that there was going to be a good olive harvest. So while it was still winter, he got possession of a little money and put a deposit on all the olive presses in Miletus and Chios, paying out a small sum because no one was bidding against him. Then when the harvest season came and many presses were suddenly in demand all at once, he rented them out on whatever terms he chose and collected a great deal of money. Thus he showed that it is easy for philosophers to get rich if they want to, but that that is not what they have a serious interest in.

1259a18 Such, then, is how they say Thales gave proof of his wisdom, but, as we said, this sort of business scheme, getting a monopoly for oneself if one can, is a general one. Hence some cities also use this means of raising funds when they are short: they secure a monopoly on goods for sale. In Sicily there was a man who used some money deposited with him to buy up all the iron from the foundries, and then when the dealers arrived from their shops, he was the only one selling it. He did not raise the price very much and yet he added a hundred talents[50] to his original fifty. When Dionysius learned about it, he ordered the man to take his money and leave Syracuse on the grounds that he had made a discovery detrimental to Dionysius' own affairs.[51] Nevertheless, Thales' insight and this man's were the same, for both contrived to get a monopoly for themselves.

1259a33 It is useful also for political rulers to know about these things, for many cities have need of business practices and suchlike revenues, just as households do, only more so. Hence, some politicians even focus all their political activity on these matters alone.

---

49. The reputed founder of philosophy. He lived in the late sixth and early fifth centuries.

50. A talent was worth sixty minas and a mina was worth 100 drachmas. The drachma was the average daily wage.

51. There were two tyrants of Syracuse by the name of Dionysius: Dionysius I (405–367) and Dionysius II (367–344). It is not clear to which one Aristotle is referring to. On the tyrannical practice of getting rid of potential rivals, see 3.14.1284a27–36 and 7(5).11.1313a34–41.

CHAPTER 12

Husband and Wife, Father and Child. *The remaining two parts of the household also illustrate different kinds of rule: the male rules the female politically and the father rules the child royally, and while both are rule over the free, the first is rule over a free and equal and the second is rule over the free and unequal.*

1259a37 Since there were three parts to the science of household management, the first being the science of mastery over slaves, which has already been treated, and the others being paternal science and matrimonial science, [we must now speak of these last two. These are different in kind both from the first and from each other],⁵² for rule over wife and children is rule over free in both cases, but not in the same way: rule over wife is political and over children royal. For by nature the male is more fitted for leading than the female, unless he is in some way constituted contrary to nature; in addition, the older and complete is more fitted for leading than the younger and incomplete.

1259b4 Now, in most cases of political rule the ruler and ruled alternate with each other, for they wish by their nature to stand on equal ground and to differ in nothing. Nevertheless, when one is ruling and the other being ruled, the one ruling seeks to be different in outward form, manner of address, and honors, as in Amasis' story about his footpan.⁵³ But that is the condition in which the male always stands with respect to the female.

1259b10 Rule over children is royal, for the begetter is ruler both by virtue of affection and of age, which is a kind of royal rule. Hence Homer speaks nobly when he addresses as "father of men and gods" Zeus who is king of them all. For a king must differ in nature but be the same in family, and that is how the older relates to the younger and the begetter to his child.

CHAPTER 13

Virtue as the Overall Concern of Household Management

Virtue in the Parts of the Household. *The concern of household management is with human beings and their virtue more than with property, and with free human*

---

52. There seems to be a lacuna in the Greek here. The square brackets contain what I take to be the sense.

53. Amasis, a king of Egypt of lowly origin, had his golden footpan made into a statue of a god, which the Egyptians then worshipped. Footpan and statue were thus the same stuff but different in outward form, and so is it also with equals when they alternate between ruling and being ruled.

beings more than with slaves. Difficulties as to whether and how virtue can exist in slaves, and in the ruled generally, as well as in rulers, point to the fact that their several virtues are specifically different. This is confirmed by reference to the differences between the souls of the ruler and the several kinds of the ruled. Thus all have the virtues, but there is one courage of the ruler and a different courage for each of the ruled, and so on.

1259b18 It is manifest, then, that household management is more serious about human beings than about property in lifeless things, about the virtue of the former than about the virtue of property (which we call wealth), and about the virtue of the free than about the virtue of slaves.

1259b21 Now one might first raise a difficulty about slaves, whether besides their virtues as tools and servants they have any virtue of a more honorable sort—such as moderation, courage, justice, and the other like habits—or whether they have none besides the bodily forms of assistance they give. Difficulties arise on both sides of the question. For if slaves do have such other virtues, then how will they differ from the free? Yet if they do not, it is strange, since they are human beings and have a share in reason. Just about the same question can be asked about wife and child. Do they too have virtues, and must the wife be moderate, courageous, and just, and can a child be intemperate and moderate or not? In fact, what is required here is an investigation about natural ruler and ruled in general and about whether their virtue is the same or different. For if both must have a share in the qualities of a gentleman, why should the one rule and the other be ruled once and for all? They certainly cannot differ by more and less, since ruling and being ruled differ in kind while more and less do not. But if one of them is to have virtue and the other not, it would be astonishing. For if the ruler is not going to be moderate and just, how will he rule nobly? And if the ruled is not going to be, how will he be ruled nobly? For he will not do anything of what is required if he is intemperate and cowardly.

1260a2 It is manifest, then, that both must have a share in virtue but that there must be differences in the virtue, just as there are differences also among those who are by nature ruled. Consideration of the soul leads us directly to this result.[54] For ruler and ruled exist by nature in the soul, and we say that the virtue of each of these is different, as the virtue of the part that has reason and of the part that does not.[55] So it is clear that the same must hold also in other cases. Consequently, most rulers and ruled are by nature so. For the free rules the slave in one way, the male the female in another, and the man the child in another. In all of them the parts of the soul exist but

54. Cf. 1.5.1254a34–b9.
55. *Ethics* 1.13.1103a3–10.

exist differently. For the slave does not have the element of deliberation at all; the female has it, but it is not in control; the child has it, but it is incomplete. **1260a14** So one must suppose that the same differentiation is also to be found in the virtues of character, and that they must all share in them, though not in the same way but only as much as is required for the work of each. Hence the ruler must have complete virtue of character, for the work belongs simply to the ruling craftsman, and reason is a ruling craftsman. But each of the others must have as much as falls to their share. Consequently, it is clear that all of them must have virtue of character but that a woman's and a man's moderation are not the same, nor are their courage or justice (contrary to what Socrates thought),[56] but the one is ruling courage and the other assisting courage, and so on with the other virtues.

1260a24 The point is clear if we look at them more closely one by one. For those who speak in general terms deceive themselves when they say that virtue is a good condition of soul, or acting rightly, or something else of the sort. Those who, like Gorgias,[57] count off the virtues speak much better than those who give such definitions.[58] Therefore we must think about everyone in the same way that the poet spoke about woman in the line "silence brings adornment to a woman"[59]—something, however, that is not true of a man. So in the case of the child, since he is incomplete, his virtue does not belong to him in relation to himself but in relation to his end and his leader. The same holds of the slave with respect to his master.

How to Secure Virtue in the Household. *The slave needs minimal virtue, which he must be taught by his master, for the slave is sharing in his master's life, unlike artisans who are slaves only when working for someone, have need of virtue only at those times, and do not have their existence by nature. The master, therefore, should reason with slaves and not just give them commands. As for wife and children, their education in virtue must be carried out with a view to the city, and hence must be left for the discussion of regimes, which commences, as regards the best regime, in the next book.*

1260a33 We set it down that the slave's usefulness was with respect to necessities,[60] so it is clear that he needs little virtue, just enough to prevent him being deficient in his work through intemperance or cowardice. But one might raise the difficulty, if that is true, whether artisans also will need to have virtue, for they are often deficient in their work. The case is very dif-

56. Cf. Plato *Meno* 72d4–73c5.
57. A famous sophist of the fifth century from Leontini in Sicily.
58. Cf. Plato *Meno* 71c5–72d1.
59. Sophocles *Ajax* 293. The word for "adornment" is *kosmos*, a name also for the ordered array of the whole universe, or the "cosmos," from which our word "cosmetic" derives.
60. 1.4 and 5 above.

ferent, surely? For the slave shares his master's life, but the artisan is more remote and has as much of virtue as he has of slavery (for the artisan mechanic has a separated slavery). Also, while the slave exists by nature, no shoemaker does nor does any other artisan. Manifestly, therefore, must it be the master who is the cause of such virtue in his slave, not the one who has the master's science of instructing slaves in their work.[61] Hence, those do not speak nobly who deprive slaves of reasoned speech and tell us only to give commands to them.[62] Slaves must be reasoned with even more than children. But let such be our determination of these matters.

1260b8 About man and woman, children and father, and about the virtue of each of them and their intercourse with each other, and what is noble in this regard and what is not, and how to pursue the good and avoid the bad—all these things must be broached in our discussion of regimes.[63] For since any household is part of a city and these are parts of a household, and since the virtue of the part must look to the virtue of the whole, the education of children and women must be undertaken with an eye to the regime, at least so it must be if having children and women who are serious makes a difference to having a serious city. But it must make a difference, for women are half the free and from children come those who share in the regime.

1260b20 So since we have finished our determination of these matters and since the others must be spoken of elsewhere, let us set aside our present discussion as complete and make another beginning. First, let us examine those who have expressed views about the best regime.

61. For this distinction, see 1.7 above.
62. Possibly a reference to Plato *Laws* 777e4–6.
63. The discussion of regimes begins with the next book (this first book has instead been about the city). The topics mentioned here are picked up again from book 4(7).15 onward to the end of book 5(8), but are dealt with incompletely, as book 5(8) itself is incomplete.

Book 2

Regimes Said by
Others to Be Best

CHAPTER 1

Reason and Order of the Examination. *A study of the best regime requires an examination of regimes praised by others, both to make evident what is right and useful in these other regimes and to prevent our search for some better regime from giving the impression of sophistry. The natural beginning is to be found by asking whether the citizens should share everything in common or not; this question leads directly to Plato's* Republic.

1260b27 Since our chosen project is to study which political community is the best of all for those who can live as much as possible according to prayer,[1] we must examine other regimes too, both those in use in cities said to be well legislated and those that may have been spoken of by anyone and seem to be in a noble condition. Our aim is to see what is right and useful in them and, in addition, to prevent our search for something other than these regimes from looking as if we just wanted to play the sophist. Rather we would have it appear that we are undertaking this enquiry only because the regimes now to hand are not in a noble condition.

1260b36 A beginning must first be made, a beginning that is the natural one for this investigation. For the citizens must all share either everything in common, or nothing, or some things and not others. Now it is clear that sharing nothing in common is impossible: a regime is a kind of community, and the first necessity is to share the place in common, for one city has one place and citizens are those who share one city. The question rather is this: if the city is to be nobly managed, is it better to share all of the things that can be shared or better to share some of them and not others? For the

---

1. "According to prayer" (*kat' euchēn*) is a literal translation of Aristotle's standard way of referring to the best regime. It is meant to convey the thought that the best regime is the regime that has all the advantages one would pray for (4(7).4.1325b35–39).

citizens could share children, wives, and possessions with each other, as in Plato's *Republic*, where Socrates says all these should be common.[2] So is it better to have them arranged as they are now or as the law written in the *Republic* would have it?

CHAPTER 2

The Regime of Plato's *Republic*

Common Wives and Children. *Common wives pose many problems and three in particular: (i) that the purpose for which such legislation is said to be necessary does not follow from the arguments; (ii) that the end of unity proposed for the city is impossible in the way it is talked about; (iii) that it is not qualified.*

1261a10 There are, indeed, both many other problems with making wives common to everyone and the problem that the purpose for which Socrates says such legislation is needed is not obviously what results from his arguments. Further, the end that he says the city should have, as he in fact talks about it, is impossible, and as to how it is to be qualified he gives no determination.[3] I am talking about the supposition that it is best for the city to be to the greatest extent all one, for that is the supposition Socrates adopts.[4]

Failure to Qualify the Fundamental Supposition about Unity. *Socrates' supposition of unity is faulty in two ways. First, it has the consequence of destroying the city by reducing it to a single individual; and what destroys a thing is not best for it. Distinctions must be drawn, specifically between unity of similars, as in an alliance, and unity of dissimilars, as in a city; in this latter case, unity must be understood in terms of reciprocal equality, not unqualified unity. Second, what is less unified is more self-sufficient (as the city is more self-sufficient than the household). Since self-sufficiency is better, less unity must be better for the city rather than more.*

1261a15 It is clear, however, that as a city advances and becomes more of a unity, it will cease to exist. For a city is in its nature a certain multitude, but as it becomes more of a unity, it will shrink to a household from a city and to a single human being from a household (for we would say a household was more of a unity than a city and an individual more than a household).

---

2. *Republic* 461d5–465e3.

3. These problems appear to be discussed in reverse order: the first, that the purpose does not result from the arguments, in chapter 4; the second, that the end as talked about is impossible, in chapter 3; the third, that this end is not qualified, here in chapter 2.

4. A reference to the result of the discussion Socrates has with Glaucon in *Republic* 462a2–d7.

Consequently, no one should do this even if he could, for he will do away with the city.

1261a22 A city is made up not only of many human beings but also of human beings who differ in kind. No city comes into existence from those who are all alike, for a city is not an alliance. An alliance gets its usefulness from its numbers even if they are all of the same kind, for the nature of an alliance is to provide the sort of help that a greater weight does when it presses down the scales. It is in this sort of way that a city also differs from a nation (when people are not scattered about in villages but confederated like the Arcadians),⁵ and the parts from which a city must become a unity differ in kind. Hence, it is reciprocal equality that saves cities, as was said before in the *Ethics*.⁶

1261a32 The same reciprocation is necessary even among those who are free and equal, for they cannot all rule at once but only by yearly intervals or by some other arrangement or timing. In this way they all get to rule, just as all would get to be shoemakers and carpenters if they kept changing places and did not always remain one or the other. But since remaining one or the other is better in the case of the affairs of the political community as well, clearly the same persons should, if possible, always rule. However, when permanent rule is not possible, because all are equal in nature, and when it is also just that all share in rule (whether ruling is something good or base), then an imitation of permanent rule is achieved if equals yield to each other in turn and are, when out of office, all alike.⁷ For as they rule and are ruled in turn, they become, as it were, different persons (and the same happens when one office is held by one person and another by another). So it is clear from these considerations that the city is not by nature a unity in the way some say it is, and that what is said to be the greatest good for cities does away with cities; yet the good of each thing surely preserves it.

1261b10 It is also manifest in another way that seeking to unify the city too much is not better. For a household is more self-sufficient than an individual and a city more self-sufficient than a household, and a city tends at any rate to come into existence just when the community that the multitude forms has achieved self-sufficiency. So if what is more self-sufficient is more choice-worthy, then what is less a unity is more choiceworthy than what is more a unity.

---

5. Aristotle's meaning seems to be that even a nation so far united as to form a confederacy (like the Arcadians in the northern Peloponnese, but unlike many barbarian nations, which were little more than scattered villages) is not a city but at most a military alliance.

6. *Ethics* 5.5, especially 1132b33–1133a5.

7. The Greek of this passage is corrupt, and a variety of emendations and translations is possible. The general sense, however, is not in doubt.

CHAPTER 3

Unity as Appealed to in the Proof of Unity Is Impossible

The Word "All." *The city is not proved to be a unity by the argument about "all saying mine and not mine together," for (i) this argument is fallacious in equivocating over different senses of the word "all," and (ii) what belongs thus to all in common is least cared for.*

1261b16 Yet even if this is best, that the community is united to the greatest extent, the fact that it is so united does not appear to be proved by the argument about all saying mine and not mine together (for Socrates thinks this a sign of the city's being completely one).[8] For "all" has a double meaning. If it is taken in the sense of each separately, perhaps more of what Socrates wants would be realized. For then each will address the same boy as his son and the same woman as his wife and so on with property and everything else that happens to him. But as it is, that is not how those who have wives and children in common will speak. All will indeed speak, but not in the sense of each separately (and the same holds of property too, which they will all call their own but not in the sense of each separately).

1261b27 Clearly then, there is a paralogism in the use of the term "all." For, because of their double sense, "all" and "both" are both odd and even and generate contentious syllogisms in argument.[9] Hence, all saying the same is in one sense noble but impossible, while in the other sense there is nothing of likemindedness in it.

1261b32 In addition, the phrase is damaging in another way, for what belongs in common to the most people gets the least care. People care most about what is their own and less about what is common, or only as much as it touches them. For, among other things, they are more neglectful of what is common because they think someone else is looking after it, as happens, for instance, in domestic chores, where many servants sometimes give worse assistance than fewer would. So each of the citizens has a thousand

---

8. Aristotle is referring especially to *Republic* 464a1–b7. Here Socrates argues that if all in the city have everything in common, including children and wives, they will together all say "mine" and "not mine" of the same things and not of different things. This will be sufficient indication of the unity of the city.

9. Or one could translate: "because of the double sense, 'all' and 'both' and 'odd' and 'even' generate . . . ." But Aristotle is presumably not saying that "odd" and "even" have a double sense, but that "all" and "both" do when predicated of two or more odd and even numbers. So all or both of three and five are both odd and even because they are odd separately and even together (together they make eight). A syllogism is contentious if its aim is apparent victory (*Sophistical Refutations* 11.171b31–33), as would be the victory if one used the above example to argue that three and five were both separately odd and even.

sons, not in the sense that they are his, but in the sense that any one of them is likewise the son of anyone else; hence, they will all likewise neglect them.

The Word "Mine." There are two problems with the word "mine": (i) the word "mine" will be used disjunctively and without any assurance of truth, which is worse than the nondisjunctive way "mine" is standardly used now; (ii) all will not in fact say mine and not mine together, since some will conjecture enough to say mine and not mine separately.

1262a1 Further, each says "mine" of anyone among the citizens who is doing well, or badly,[10] in the sense of what fraction he happens to be of the whole number; for example, he says "mine or so-and-so's" and mentions in this way each of the thousand, or however many the city is composed of. Even then he speaks in doubt, for it is not clear who has had a child born to him or whether the child, once born, survived.[11] Yet is this way of calling the same child "mine" as practiced by each of two or ten thousand better than the way they say "mine" in cities now? For now the same person is addressed by one as his son, by another as his brother, by another as his cousin, and so on according to other names of blood or marital relationship, whether of one's own marriage first or also of some relative's; in addition, someone else addresses the same person as his clansman or tribesman. For it is better to be someone's own cousin than to be a son in the way just described.

1262a14 But be that as it may, it will not be possible to prevent some from suspecting who their brothers, children, fathers, and mothers are. For they will inevitably trust to conclusions about each other on the basis of the similarities that exist between parents and children. That such happens in fact is asserted by some of those who have spent time traveling round the world. For they say that some inhabitants of upper Libya have wives in common and yet distinguish the children according to similarities to their fathers. There are also some women, and some females among other animals, such as horses and cattle, that have a strong natural tendency to produce offspring like their sires, as did the mare in Pharsalus called the Just.

CHAPTER 4

The Result Is the Opposite of That Intended. Having wives and children in common will lead to the opposite of what Socrates intends: (i) it will lead to worse violent crimes; (ii) it passes over the impropriety of sexual relations between fathers and sons

10. A reference to *Republic* 463e3–5.
11. No one is supposed to know if they have begotten children or whether the rulers allowed the offspring to survive (*Republic* 459d7–460d7)

and brothers; (iii) it is directed to the wrong class; (iv) it will weaken the ties of love;
(v) the envisaged transfers of children from class to class cannot be done so as to pre-
serve the necessary secrecy; (vi) these transfers will also be occasion for worse physical
and sexual crimes.

1262a25 Those who establish this sort of community will also not find it easy to avoid such difficulties as assault, voluntary and involuntary manslaughter, fighting, and slander.[12] It is unholy to commit any of these against fathers or mothers or near relations (as opposed to outsiders). But such things must happen even more often among those who do not know their relatives than among those who do, and when they do happen, the latter will be able to perform the customary expiations while the former will not.
1262a32 It is also strange to make sons common and then to deny lovers[13] only sexual intercourse but to permit them to love and engage in other practices which, between father and son or brother and brother, are the most improper of all, as indeed is love by itself. It is just as strange to deny sexual intercourse for no other reason than that the pleasure generated is too strong but to regard it as of no consequence that the lovers are father and son or brothers.[14]
1262a40 Common wives and children among the farmers would seem to be more useful than among the guardians,[15] for there will be less friendship where wives and children are common, and that is how the ruled should be if they are to be obedient and not engage in subversion.
1262b3 Generally, in fact, from such a law must result the opposite of what correctly enacted laws should bring about and the opposite of the purpose for which Socrates thinks it necessary so to arrange matters about children and wives.[16] For we suppose friendship to be a very great good for cities, since in this way they will least split into factions; moreover, Socrates praises the unity of the city most of all, which seems to be (and is asserted by him to be) the work of friendship. So, for example, in the discourses on love we see Aristophanes saying about lovers that, because of their great affection, they desire "to grow together" and to become both one from being two.[17] Now the result in this particular case must be that either one or both lovers is destroyed, but in Socrates' city the result must be that friendship gets watered down, because of the sort of community that exists there—that is, because

12. An implicit reference to *Republic* 464d7–e7.
13. Male homosexual lovers.
14. *Republic* 468b9–c4, and 403a4–c2 with 461b9–e4.
15. The city of the *Republic* is divided into a producing class (farmers in particular) and a warrior and ruling class (the guardians).
16. Cf. the opening words of 2.2.1261a11–12.
17. Plato *Symposium* 191a5–8, 192d5–e9.

father least addresses son, and son father, as "mine." For as a great deal of water added to a little wine makes the mixture imperceptible, so the same happens here with the relationships of father, son, and so on, because in such a city it is inevitable that a father take very little thought for his sons, or a son for his father, or brothers for each other. The reason is that there are two things in particular that make human beings care and love: what is one's own and what is dear, neither of which can exist among those who govern themselves after this fashion.

1262b24 But there is also much confusion about how the children, when born, will be transferred from the ranks of the farmers and artisans to those of the guardians or vice versa;[18] and those who do the giving and receiving must know who has been given to whom.

1262b29 Further, what was mentioned earlier[19] (I mean assaults, love affairs, and murders) must happen more often in these cases. For those given to the other citizens will no longer call the guardians their brothers, children, fathers, and mothers, nor will those given to the guardians thus address the other citizens, so as to avoid, on grounds of kinship, committing any such crimes against them.

1262b35 Let such then be our discussion of the community of children and wives.

CHAPTER 5

Common Property. *The question of common property needs to be considered separately from the issue of common wives and children. Of the several possible arrangements, common possession involves many difficulties, but private possessions with common use (as secured by virtue) will combine the best in both, as is already the case in some cities. Moreover, to possess something as our own affords us, through natural love of self and love of others, very great pleasure.*

1262b37 The next thing to examine is property and how those who are going to be governed by the best regime ought to arrange it. Is property to be common or not? One may well examine this question quite apart from legislation about children and wives. I mean, even if children and wives are held separately, as is now universally the case, one can still ask whether it is better for possessions and their use to be common. For instance, land could be held separately, but the crops could be brought to a common store and

---

18. Socrates allowed for children born to one class to be transferred to another class if they turned out really to belong to that other class (*Republic* 415a1–d2).

19. At the beginning of the chapter: 1262a25–27.

consumed in common, as some nations in fact do. Or the opposite could happen, with land common and farmed in common but the crops divided for private use, and this kind of community also is said to exist among some barbarians. Or both land and crops could be common.

1263a8 Now, if the farmers were of another class, arrangements about property would be different and easier, but if the citizens do the toiling themselves, this matter of possessions would be a source of much discontent. For if the citizens are not equal but unequal in the enjoyments they take and the work they do, accusations against those who enjoy or take a lot but toil little will necessarily arise from those who toil more but take less. Generally speaking, it is a hard thing to live and share together in any human matter, but especially in matters of this sort, as is clear from fellow travelers sharing a journey together. For most of them, pretty much, split up over quarrels about small and everyday matters. Moreover, we quarrel most with those servants whom we use most for daily chores. Common possessions, then, are beset with these and the like difficulties.

1263a22 The way matters are now, however, would, if adorned[20] by character and an arrangement of correct laws, be much superior: it would have the good from both—I mean the good from having possessions in common and the good from keeping them private. For possessions must in a way be common but as a general rule private, because when the care of them is apportioned out, it will not be a cause of complaints but rather will lead to greater improvements, as each applies himself to his own, while, when it comes to use, virtue will ensure that, according to the proverb, "the things of friends are common."

1263a30 Written outlines to this effect can already be found in some cities, so the thing is not impossible. In fact, in nobly managed cities especially some of the elements are in existence, while the rest might be introduced. For in such cities each has his private property but makes some of it useful to friends, and some of it he treats as common. In Sparta, for instance, they use each other's slaves as if they were their own, and likewise their horses and dogs, and when journeying in the country they take whatever they need from the fields. Clearly, then, it is better for possessions to be private and to be made common in use. But ensuring that the citizens have the necessary character is the private work of the legislator.

1263a40 Further, it is beyond telling what a difference is made in respect of pleasure by regarding something as one's own. For it is not in vain that each one of us loves himself; on the contrary it is something natural. Self love is, of course, rightly blamed but to love oneself is not self love; rather self

20. The root of the Greek word here is *kosmos*.

love is loving oneself more than one ought, as also in the case of the money lover, since nearly all of us have a love for these sorts of things.

1263b5 Moreover, helping and doing favors for friends, strangers, and companions is a thing most pleasant, and it requires private property.

Communism in General. Socrates' scheme of communism as a whole (i) diminishes the virtues, (ii) persuades by a fair but deceitful appearance, (iii) has a false notion of unity, (iv) ignores the long experience of past time, (v) would be overturned in practice.

1263b7 Those who make the city too much of a unity are not only deprived of these pleasures but, in addition, they also manifestly do away with works of two virtues, by which I mean moderation as regards women (for keeping away, through moderation, from a woman who is another's is a noble work) and liberality as regards possessions (for no one will be able to show his liberality nor do any liberal act since the work of liberality exists in the way one uses one's possessions).

1263b15 This kind of legislation has, indeed, a fair appearance and might seem full of love for humankind. Anyone who hears of it accepts it gladly, thinking that a marvelous friendship of everyone for everyone will result, especially when the charge is also made that what is to blame for the evils now existent in regimes is that property is not common (I mean such evils as mutually hostile lawsuits about contracts, convictions for perjury, and flattery of the rich).[21] None of these evils, however, comes about through lack of communism but through depravity, since we see that precisely those who possess and share things in common differ far more with each other than those who hold their substance separately. The problem is that those we see disagreeing over what they share in common are few in comparison with the many whose possessions are private. Moreover, justice requires one to say not only how many evils but also how many goods those who share together will be deprived of. Their life, in fact, seems altogether impossible.

1263b27 The reason why Socrates was misled is, one must think, the incorrectness of his supposition. Both the household and the city must, of course, in some sense be a unity, but not in every sense. For as a city progresses in this direction, it will in one way cease to be a city and in another way be a worse city as it comes close to not being a city, rather like what would happen if one reduced a many-voiced harmony to unison or rhythm to a single beat. Things being as they are, however, a city, since it is a multitude, as was said before,[22] must be made one and common through its education. So it is strange, at any rate for someone who intends to introduce educa-

---

21. An implicit reference to Plato *Republic* 464d7–465d1.
22. 2.2.1261a18.

tion and supposes that thereby the city will be serious, to think he can set things straight by means of such devices and not by means of customs, philosophy, and laws like the common messes used by the legislators in Sparta and Crete to establish community of possessions.

1264a1 One must not forget this fact either, that there is need to pay attention to the great amount of time and the many years gone by in which it could not have escaped notice whether this condition was a noble one. For pretty well everything has been discovered, but some things have not been brought together and other things people know about but do not use.

1264a5 Matters would, however, become particularly clear if one saw such a community actually being set up. For it will not be possible to create the city without dividing and separating its parts, some into common messes, others into clans and tribes. As a consequence, nothing would get legislated other than a prohibition on farming for the guardians, something that the Spartans attempt to do even now.

The Regime as a Whole

Subjects. *As regards the largest class in the regime, the farmers and artisans, Socrates has not determined whether they should have common wives, children, and property or not. But whichever of the several possibilities one chooses, insuperable difficulties arise.*

1264a11 Furthermore, as to what the regime will be like for those who are members of it, Socrates has not said, nor is it easy to say. Yet pretty well the mass of the city, at any rate, is that of the other citizens about whom nothing has been determined, as to whether the farmers should have common possessions or each one his private share, and also whether their wives and children should be common or private.[23]

1264a17 Suppose, then, that they are all to have everything common in the same way. How will they differ from the guardians? Or what will they gain from putting up with their rule? Or what will they be told to make them put up with it, except the sort of sophistry practiced by the Cretans? For the Cretans allow their slaves the same as themselves in other things and withhold only gymnastic exercises and the possession of arms.

1264a22 But if, on the contrary, the other citizens have the sort of things they have in other cities, how will the whole community be arranged? Two cities must necessarily be formed in the one, and cities opposed to each other

---

23. Aristotle's emphasis is not on a failure by Socrates to say whether the farmers *will* have common property, wives, and children (it seems clear from the *Republic* that Socrates means them not to have these things in common), but on his failure to say whether they *should*. He is not criticizing Socrates' failure to decide the question but his failure to give reasons for the decision.

at that. For he puts the guardians on the one side as a sort of occupying garrison, with the farmers, artisans, and the rest on the other side as the citizens.[24]

1264a27 There will also exist among them all the accusations, lawsuits, and other evils that he says are found in cities. Yet Socrates goes on to say that, because of the education, they will not need many regulations—as about conduct in the city, the market, and the like[25]—when in fact he gives that education only to the guardians.

1264a32 Further, he gives the farmers control over their possessions and has them pay a tax.[26] But in that case they are much more likely to be intractable and full of high thoughts than are the helots and serfs and slaves that some have today.[27]

1264a36 Let that be as it may, however, for whether these things must be the same or not, nothing at any rate has been decided about them, nor about the related matters of what regime, education, and laws the farmers are to have. And what their character will be like from the point of view of preserving the community of the guardians is not easy to find out, nor indeed is it a matter of little consequence.

1264a40 So suppose he makes the wives common but the possessions private. Who then will manage the household in the way their menfolk manage things in the fields? This same question would arise if the farmers' possessions as well as their wives were common. It is strange also to take an analogy from wild animals to show that women should undertake the same pursuits as men when in fact there is no household management among animals.[28]

Rulers. As regards rulers, there are two difficulties to note: (i) the rulers are always the same; (ii) the legislator does not intend their happiness.

1264b6 The way Socrates sets up the rulers is unsafe, for he has the same persons always ruling, which is a cause of faction even among those who possess no special merit, or at any rate among men who are spirited and warlike. That it is necessary for Socrates to make the same persons rulers is manifest, for the gold from god is not mixed at one time in the souls of some and at another time in the souls of others but in the same ones all the

---

24. *Republic* 415d6–417b9, 419a1–420c7, 543a1–c3.

25. *Republic* 425b10–427a7.

26. The portion of their produce that they give to the guardians (*Republic* 416d7–e3).

27. "Serfs" (*penestai*) was the standard name for the serfs of Thessaly, as "helots" was for those of Sparta.

28. Socrates uses an analogy from dogs (*Republic* 451d4–9). Aristotle omits to consider the fourth possibility, that wives are private but possessions common, perhaps because this combination is manifestly impossible. Private families cannot but necessitate private possessions, as a private house at least.

time. Gold, he says, is mixed in some immediately at birth, silver in others, and bronze and iron in those who are going to be farmers and artisans.[29]

1264b15 Further he takes happiness away from the guardians and says it is the whole city the legislator must make happy.[30] But the whole city cannot be happy unless most or all or some of its parts are happy. Being happy is not the same sort of thing as a number being even. Evenness can belong to the whole without belonging to any of the parts,[31] whereas happiness cannot. If the guardians are not happy, however, who else can be? For it certainly cannot be the artisans, at any rate, nor the multitude of vulgar mechanics.

1264b24 These are the difficulties, then, that beset the regime Socrates has spoken about, and there are others of no less consequence.

CHAPTER 6

The Regime of Plato's *Laws*

From the Regime of the Republic *to That of the* Laws. *The regime of the* Laws *also deserves treatment as being similar to that of the* Republic, *for a comparison shows that, despite differences, the two are very close.*

1264b26 Rather similar too is the case of the *Laws*, which was written later, so we had better conduct some brief examination of the regime there also. For even in the *Republic* Socrates came to determinations about altogether few things with respect to what the condition of the community of wives and children should be like, and about property and the arrangement of the regime. For he divides the multitude of the inhabitants into two parts, the farmers and the warriors, and from the latter he makes a third part that deliberates and judges. As to whether the farmers and artisans share in any office or not, and as to whether they should[32] possess arms and go along to war or not, Socrates has decided nothing. He does, however, think that the women should go along to war and share in the same education as the guardians.[33] But as for the rest, he has filled his discourse with extraneous matter, as about what the education of the guardians should be like.

1265a1 The greatest part of the *Laws* happens to be laws, and he[34] has de-

---

29. *Republic* 414b8–415c7.
30. *Republic* 420b3–421c6.
31. Seven and five, for instance, are odd, but the whole they make, twelve, is even.
32. Notice the "should" again. Aristotle is not complaining that Socrates has made no decision (Socrates does indicate that the farmers will not go to war, *Republic* 374b6–d6), but that he has not given adequate reasons for the decision.
33. *Republic* 451d1–452a5.
34. The reference of this "he" would seem to be Socrates, but the Athenian Stranger, not

termined little about the regime. Also though he wishes this regime to be one that cities have more in common with,[35] little by little he brings it round again toward the other. For apart from the community of wives and property, the other things he attributes to both regimes are the same. For even the education is the same, as is also refraining from necessary work and the common messes, save that in this regime he says there should be common messes for the women as well and that the number of those who bear arms is to be 5,000, whereas there it was 1,000.[36]

Presuppositions of the Regime. *As regards the presuppositions of the regime, the following difficulties arise: (i) the amount of land required to sustain 5,000 in idleness will be far too large; (ii) the laws should be made taking into account also the neighboring territory; (iii) the measure given for property is too vague as well as incomplete; (iv) property should not be limited without also limiting childbirth; (v) how the rulers will differ from the ruled is not explained; (vi) if increase in other possessions is allowed beyond a certain point it should be allowed in land too; (vii) managing two households instead of one is too difficult.*

1265a10 Now all the discourses of Socrates have something about them that is extraordinary, exquisite, original, and probing, but that they should be noble in every regard is perhaps too much to expect. So, for instance, take this multitude just mentioned — one must not be blind to the fact that it will require the territory of Babylon or some other one of unlimited extent to feed 5,000 in idleness and along with them another crowd, many times as large, of women and attendants. Suppositions should, indeed, be made according to prayer but not any that are impossible.[37]

1265a18 It is said that the legislator should look to two things when laying down laws: the territory and the human beings.[38] It would also be a noble thing to lay them down with a view to the neighboring territories, especially if the city is supposed to lead a political and not a solitary way of life.

Socrates, is the main interlocutor in the *Laws*. Elsewhere in this chapter, however, Aristotle is careful not to name the speaker but uses instead phrases like "it is said" or "in the *Laws*." Therefore, perhaps he intends the reference of "he" to be vague but with a suggestion that the Stranger is a thin disguise for Socrates.

35. *Laws* 739a1–e5.

36. Women were included in the common messes for men in the *Republic* (458c6–d3), whereas in the *Laws* they would have their own separate ones (806e2–4). Common messes were where the citizens regularly met to take their meals together, their point being to strengthen, by regular association, the bonds of friendship and unity. The number of those who bear arms, allows Socrates in an aside, could be a mere 1,000 in the *Republic* (423a8), but they are said to be exactly 5,040, not a round 5,000, in the *Laws* (737e1–738b1, 753b4–756b6). However, Aristotle is speaking broadly, and nothing in his criticism hangs on the imprecision.

37. Cf. *Laws* 709a1–d6, 742e1–4.

38. Not said in so many words in the *Laws* but implied by 704a1–708d7.

For then the arms it uses for war must not only be such as are useful in its own territory but on foreign terrain as well. However, if one rejects such a way of life, whether for oneself alone or for the city in common, it is none-theless necessary to be fearsome to one's enemies, both as they enter one's territory and also as they leave it.[39]

1265a28 As regards the amount of property, one should consider whether it is not better to define it differently by defining it more clearly. For he says that there should be as much as is required to live moderately,[40] which is like saying "as is required to live well," for the phrase is too general. In addition, it is possible to live moderately but wretchedly. A better definition would be "as is required to live moderately and liberally." For the second without the first could accompany luxury and the first without the second could accom-pany hardship. At all events, since these are the only choiceworthy habits that have to do with the use of one's substance (one cannot, for instance, use one's substance mildly or bravely but only moderately and liberally), it is the exercise of them[41] that the use of property must consequently require.

1265a38 It is strange, too, that while he makes possessions equal, he does not arrange anything about the number of the citizens but leaves the produc-tion of children without limit. The idea is that no matter how many children are born, the childlessness of some couples will ensure that the number of citizens remains more or less constant, because such is what now seems to happen in cities.[42] But there is not the same need for accuracy in cities now as in the *Laws*. For in cities now no one goes without, because properties can be divided up for any number, but in the *Laws* properties are indivis-ible, and any who are left out, whether few or many, must of necessity have nothing. One would think it necessary instead to set a limit on reproduction rather than on property, so that children are not produced above a certain number (a number which, of course, will have to be calculated keeping in mind the chances that some of those born will die and that others will be childless). But to let the matter alone, as is done in most cities, must nec-essarily cause poverty among the citizens, and poverty brings about faction and villainy. Pheidon of Corinth, in fact, one of the most ancient legislators, thought it necessary that the households and the number of citizens remain the same even if to begin with all had lots that were unequal in size.[43] But

---

39. On the debate, implicit here, about the rival merits of a city leading a life involving an active role in foreign affairs or keeping itself isolated by itself, see 4(7).1–3.

40. *Laws* 737d1–2.

41. Reading *chrēseis* ("the exercise of them") with the manuscripts, not *hexeis* with Drei-zehnter, which would give the sense: "since these are the only choiceworthy habits . . . it is these habits that . . ."

42. *Laws* 740b1–741a5.

43. Nothing is otherwise known about this Pheidon.

in the *Laws* it is the opposite. As to our own view about how these things might be better arranged, it must be given later.[44]

1265b18 What concerns the rulers is also left out from the *Laws*—I mean how they will differ from the ruled. For he says that the condition of rulers with respect to the ruled must be as warp and woof, which are made of different wools.[45]

1265b21 Since he allows an increase in one's whole substance up to five times the original amount,[46] why should increase in land not be allowed up to a certain point?

1265b24 Further, it is necessary to take a look at whether the division of homesteads is advantageous from the point of view of household management. For to each one he distributed two homesteads that he divided and set apart,[47] but it is difficult to manage two households.

The Regime as a Whole. *As regards the regime as a whole, the following difficulties arise: (i) the regime aims at being a polity, a mean between democracy and oligarchy, but even if this is the regime cities have most in common with, it is not, as is claimed, the second best regime, since the Spartan is supposed by many to be a better mixture, and is better than this regime, which is said to be a mixture of democracy and tyranny, the two worst regimes; (ii) in fact, however, it does not mix any element from tyranny or monarchy at all; (iii) the practice of electing officeholders from a pool of those previously elected will allow domination of the regime by small cliques.*

1265b26 The whole arrangement of the regime aims at being neither democracy nor oligarchy but a mean between the two, which people call polity, for it is made up of those who bear arms.[48] Now if he is establishing this regime as that among the other regimes which cities have most in common with, he has perhaps spoken nobly, but if as the best after the first regime,[49] then not nobly. For perhaps someone might rather commend the regime of the Spartans or some other one of a more aristocratic sort. Now, there are those who say that the best regime must be mixed from all regimes, which is why they praise the regime of the Spartans. For some declare that it is mixed from oligarchy, monarchy, and democracy—calling the kingship a monarchy, the office of senators an oligarchy, and the office of ephors the way things are run democratically (for the ephors are drawn from the populace). Others, however, call the ephorate a tyranny and locate

44. 4(7).10, 16.
45. *Laws* 734e6–735a4.
46. *Laws* 744e3–5.
47. *Laws* 745c3–d2, 775e5–b4.
48. *Laws* 753b4–7, 755e8–756a3.
49. The regime of the *Republic*.

the democratic element of rule in the common messes and the rest of the Spartans' daily life. In the *Laws* it is said that the best regime must be a mixture of a democracy and a tyranny,[50] which one might set down as either altogether not regimes or the worst regimes of all. Therefore, those speak better who make the mixture from more regimes, for that regime which has more regimes in its mixture is better.

1266a5 Next, the regime manifestly does not have anything of monarchy in it, but it is oligarchic and democratic, with a tendency to incline more toward oligarchy. The fact is clear from the way rulers are appointed. Selection by lot from among those previously elected is indeed common to both oligarchy and democracy, but to require those who are better off to attend the assembly, to vote for rulers, and to do whatever else there is of a political nature, while leaving the others free, is a feature of oligarchy. It is also oligarchic to try to draw the majority of rulers from the well-off and the greatest offices from the class with the highest assessments.[51] He also makes the election of the council oligarchic. For all are required to vote, but first from the first class, then again from the second class in equal number, and then from the third class, except that not all are required to vote in the case of electing from the third and fourth classes, and in the case of electing from the fourth class only the first and second classes are required to vote. Then he says that from those so elected an equal number must be designated from each class.[52] So the electors who are from the highest classes and of a better sort will be more numerous, because some of those from the popular sort will not take part in the election, as it is not required of them. That such a regime should not be established from democracy and monarchy is clear from these remarks and from what will be said later when our investigation turns to this sort of regime.[53]

1266a26 As far as election of rulers is concerned, it is dangerous to elect from those already elected.[54] For if even a few in number are willing to band together, the elected will always be the ones whom they want.

1266a28 That, then, is how matters stand concerning the regime of the *Laws*.

50. *Laws* 693d2–701e7.

51. *Laws* 753b4–756e2, 763d4–764a7, 765c1–d3, 766b1–c1, 767c2–768c2.

52. *Laws* 756b7–e8.

53. 6(4).7–9, 11–13.

54. The fact just noted, that those appointed to the council are first elected from the four classes and then others are elected from these again.

CHAPTER 7

The Regime of Phaleas of Chalcedon

Phaleas' Materialism. *Other proposed regimes are nearer existing ones than either of the two just discussed and take their beginning from necessary features of cities. So Phaleas of Chalcedon was the first to focus on property and its arrangement to cure political ills.*

1266a31 There are also other regimes, proposed either by private persons or by philosophers and politicians, but all of them are closer than both the above to the established regimes under which people are actually governed. For no one else proposed the novelties of common children and wives or of messes for women; rather they take their beginning from what is necessary. Some, for instance, think that the greatest thing is to have matters to do with possessions nobly arranged, for they say it is about possessions that everyone creates factions.

1266a39 It was for this reason that Phaleas of Chalcedon[55] first introduced such a policy, for he says that the possessions of the citizens should be equal. He thought this policy would not be hard for cities just being founded but that it would take more work in cities already settled. Nevertheless, he thought a leveling might be very quickly achieved by having the rich give but not receive dowries, and the poor receive but not give them. Plato, in writing the *Laws*, thought it necessary to leave these matters alone up to a certain point, but he denied to any citizen the right to acquire more than five times the smallest amount, as noted earlier.[56]

Criticism of Phaleas. *The problems with Phaleus' regime are these: (i) if possessions are to be limited, childbirth should be too; (ii) equalizing possessions can be of some help, but the equal possessions may themselves be too great or too small; (iii) desires should be leveled, rather than property; (iv) equal education is no answer to this problem but only education of the right sort; (v) faction is caused by inequality of honors as well as inequality of possessions; (vi) people do wrong not only to secure necessities but also to sate desire, where equalizing property can be of no help; (vii) the importance of foreign affairs is ignored; (viii) leveling property will not do much to solve the domestic problem of faction; (ix) only landed property is equalized, not also moveable property; (x) the city Phaleas is instituting could only be a small one.*

1266b8 But proposers of such legislation should not ignore, as they do now ignore, that it is appropriate for those who lay down limits for property to

55. Phaleas is otherwise unknown.
56. 2.6.1265b21–23.

lay down a limit for children as well. For if the number of children exceeds the amount of property, the law is bound to be broken and, law-breaking aside, it is a base thing for many to become poor after having been rich, since it is hard for such people not to initiate revolution.

1266b14 That the leveling of property does indeed have some effect on the political community was evidently recognized even by some in ancient times, as, for instance, in the legislation of Solon.[57] Others also have a law that prevents anyone from acquiring as much land as he might want. In like manner there are laws prohibiting the sale of one's property (as in Locri, where the law forbids it unless some manifest misfortune is shown to have occurred) or laws requiring that the original allotments be preserved intact. The abrogation of a law to this effect in Leucas made the regime overly popular because the result was that the offices were no longer filled by those from the designated assessments.[58] But there can be an equality of possessions that is so great that it causes extravagance or so small that it causes penury. Clearly then, it is not enough for the legislator to make possessions equal; he must aim at the mean.

1266b28 Still, even an arrangement of measured property for all is no use, since desires need leveling more than possessions, and that is not possible without an adequate education under the laws.

1266b31 But perhaps Phaleas would say that that was what he was actually talking about, for he supposes cities need an equality in both things, property and education. Well, then, he ought to say what the education will be. And it is no use it being one and the same, for an education can be one and the same and yet such as to set people on a greedy pursuit of money or honors or both.

1266b38 Furthermore, people fall into factional conflict not only because of inequality in possessions but also because of inequality in honors, though contrariwise in each case: inequality of possessions makes the many revolt, and equality of honors the respectable — whence the verse "in equal honor whether he be good or bad."[59]

1267a2 Human beings, however, not only do wrong because of necessities, for which Phaleas thinks equality of property is the remedy (to prevent cold or hunger driving them to thievery), but also in order to enjoy themselves and not be in a state of longing. For if they have a desire for things above

57. Solon legislated for Athens in about 593 and sought, among other things, to abolish the wide and oppressive property differences existing at the time (*Athēnaiōn Politeia* 6–10, esp. 6). He is discussed more fully in 2.12.1273b35–1274a21.

58. Presumably, eligibility for office went with possession of the original lot, so that as this became reduced in size through partial selling off, the property qualifications for office were necessarily reduced and more of the populace were able to meet them.

59. Homer *Iliad* 9.319.

what they need, they will do wrong as a way of curing it, and indeed not only for this purpose but also if their desire is for the enjoyment of pleasures that are without pain. What then is the remedy for these three?[60] A little property with hard work for the first, and moderation for the second. But as regards the third, if there are some who want to get enjoyment relying on themselves alone, they are not going to find a remedy except in philosophy, for the other pleasures require human beings. The greatest wrongs, at any rate, are committed because of excess and not because of need (tyrants, for instance, are not people trying to avoid the cold). That is why it is killers of tyrants, not killers of thieves, who receive the greatest honors. So we must conclude that Phaleas' style of regime is of help against minor injustices only.

1267a17 Another point is that most of the things he wants to set up are conditions for noble government among the citizens by themselves, but there is the same need in the case of relations with neighbors and foreigners as a whole. Thus, a regime needs to be arranged with a view to military strength, a matter on which he has said nothing. The same holds also of property, for there must be enough of it not only for use within the city but also to meet external dangers. Hence, on the one hand, property ought not to exist in so large a quantity that those who are nearby and stronger will desire it while those who have it will be unable to resist attackers, nor, on the other hand, ought it to be so small that the possessors could not even sustain a war against enemies who are their equals and similars. Now Phaleas failed to fix any limit, but this question of what is the beneficial amount of property cannot be ignored. Perhaps the best limit is that should the stronger wage war, they will be doing so even if the property were not as great as it is and not because the excess of it will bring them profit. Take, for example, the occasion when Autophradates was about to lay siege to Atarneus. Eubulus bade him reflect how long it would take to capture the place, calculating the expense such a time would involve, for he said he was willing already to leave Atarneus for less. These words made Autophradates reconsider and give up the siege.[61]

1267a37 So then, equalizing the possessions of citizens is among ways that are of some benefit for preventing faction, but it is not, to speak truly, one of any great significance. For, among other things, the refined sort would get annoyed on the ground that equality is beneath their dignity, which is

---

60. The three are (i) those who commit wrong to get necessities, (ii) those who commit wrong to satisfy their desire for more than is necessary, (iii) those who commit wrong to enjoy painless pleasures.

61. Atarneus was a fortified city in Asia Minor. Eubulus, a wealthy moneychanger, got control of it in the 350s. The exact date of the attack by the Persian general Autophradates is not known. Eubulus was later succeeded by Hermias, whose niece Aristotle married.

why, as a matter of fact, they are often conspicuous in launching attacks and starting factional strife. In addition, the wickedness of human beings is insatiable. So to begin with an allowance of only two obols is enough, but as soon as this practice has become an ancestral tradition, the demand is always made for more, and so it goes on without limit.[62] For it is the nature of desire to have no limit, and satisfying desire is what the many live for. Ruling over such people[63] is a matter not so much of leveling possessions as of providing for the respectable to be by nature such that they do not want to get more and for the base that they cannot (which can be achieved if they are weaker and not wronged).

1267b9 But Phaleas has not even spoken nobly about the equalizing of possessions. For he equalizes only property in land, but there can also be wealth in slaves and cattle and money; movables too, as they are called, can exist in great supply. So either seek an equality or measured arrangement in all of these, or let them all alone.

1267b13 It is manifest from his legislation that Phaleas is establishing a small city, if, that is, all the artisans are to be public slaves and are not to go toward making up the complement of the city. But if there must be public slaves, it is those engaged in communal works who should be so, as in Epidamnus or as Diophantus once tried to arrange in Athens.[64]

1267b19 As regards Phaleas' regime, then, one should be able to see from this discussion more or less whether he succeeded in speaking nobly in any respect or not.

CHAPTER 8

The Regime of Hippodamus of Miletus

Hippodamus as Man and as Legislator. *Hippodamus, the discoverer of the technique of dividing up cities neatly, sought fame also through his extraordinary personal*

---

62. Aristotle is referring to the practice at Athens of giving out a dole to the people so they could afford to attend public meetings and festivals (there is mention of how demagogues increased these doles in *Athēnaiōn Politeia* 28, 41 with 62). An obol was a sixth of a drachma and a drachma was the average daily wage.

63. Reading *tōn toioutōn archē* ("ruling over such people") with the manuscripts, not *tōn toioutōn apergei* ("keeping them away from such demands") with Dreizehnter.

64. The Greek is disputed here, and variants offered by the manuscripts or editors would give a sense more along the lines of "if those working at common tasks must be public slaves, the system should be like the one at Epidamnus or the one Diophantus tried to introduce at Athens." If such be the reading, we are left in the dark about what the system was, since we have no further information about Epidamnus or Diophantus' proposal. The translation offered in the text avoids this problem at least, but who Diophantus was remains uncertain.

behavior. He was the first layman to make proposals about the best regime. These
proposals are several, and are marked by the division of things into threes.

1267b22 Hippodamus of Miletus, the son of Euryphon,[65] who invented the
dividing up of cities and laid out the street plan for the Peiraeus, was rather
extraordinary also in the rest of his way of life from love of honor, so much
so in fact that he seems to some — with the abundance and lavish adornment of his hair and of his clothing too, which, cheap but warm, was worn
not only in winter but also in summer — to have lived in a pretty extravagant
manner. He wished also to be skilled in writing about the whole of nature
and was the first among those not active in politics to put his hand to saying
something about the best regime.

1267b30 The city he constructed had a multitude of 10,000 divided into
three parts; he made one part the artisans, another the farmers, and a third
the warriors or those who bear arms. He divided the land into three parts —
sacred, public, and private — of which the sacred will be what is customarily
made over to the gods, the common what the warriors will live off, and the
private what will belong to the farmers.

1267b37 He thought there were also only three kinds of law, for the things
with which court cases are concerned are three in number: insolence, injury, and death. He also legislated for one supreme court, to which all cases
not held to have been nobly decided were to be appealed, and this court he
constituted from certain elected senators. He thought that verdicts in jury
courts should not be reached by casting ballots[66] but that each juror should
deposit a tablet on which was written either the verdict if he found for
unqualified condemnation, or nothing at all if he found for unqualified acquittal, or the required distinctions if he found partly for one and partly for
the other. For Hippodamus thought current legislation not in a noble state
because in compelling jurors to judge all one way or all the other, it made
them commit perjury. He laid down a law that those who discover something of advantage to the city should be honored, and one that the children
of those who fall in war should be supported by public funds. He was sup-

---

65. Hippodamus was probably active in Athens in the mid-400s.

66. In ancient Athens, jury courts consisted of several hundred persons (or even several
thousand when, for especially important trials, the popular assembly as a whole sat as a
court). There was no presiding judge, and the jury decided both the guilt and the penalty.
Each juror had two ballots, one for condemnation and the other for acquittal, and cast the
ballot indicating his verdict into an urn, discarding the other one. So, after both defendant
and plaintiff had presented their cases, the jurors first voted on the matter of guilt, and a
simple majority was sufficient either to acquit or condemn. If the defendant was condemned,
he and the plaintiff then proposed rival penalties, on which the jurors voted in the same way.
Plato's *Apology* (about the trial of Socrates) contains a nice illustration of the procedure.

posing that there was no legislation to this effect anywhere else, but in fact this law exists in Athens and in some other cities.

1268a11 All the rulers he had elected by the populace, and he was for making the three parts of the city into the populace. Those elected were to take care of common interests, interests of aliens, and interests of orphans. These, then, are the majority of the laws in Hippodamus' arrangement, and the ones most worthy of notice.

Criticism of Hippodamus

Citizens and Land. The difficulties arising from Hippodamus' views of citizens and land include: (i) the farmers and artisans, lacking arms, will be slaves of the warriors and hostile to the regime; (ii) the warriors will have to be stronger and more numerous, so there is no need for farmers and artisans to share in the regime; (iii) the class of farmers serves no purpose; (iv) the problem of who will farm the common land has no satisfactory solution.

1268a16 The first thing one might have a difficulty about is the division of the mass of citizens, for the artisans and farmers and those who possess arms all share in the regime. But the farmers have no arms and the artisans have neither land nor arms, so they will become slaves pretty much of those who do have arms. That they cannot share in all the offices is inevitable (for generals, guardians of the regime, and practically all the offices with the most control must be drawn from those who have arms). Yet if they do not share in the regime, how can they have a friendly attitude toward it?

1268a25 But then it will be necessary also that those who do have arms be stronger than both the other parts, which is not easy unless they are numerous. And if that is the case, why should the others share in the regime or have control over the appointment of rulers?

1268a29 Furthermore, what use are the farmers to the city? The artisans are necessary, for every city needs artisans, and they can get by living from their art just as they do in other cities. As for the farmers, they would reasonably form part of the city if they were providing food for those with arms, but in fact they have land for themselves and farm it for themselves too.

1268a35 Again, take the common land from which the warriors will get their sustenance. If they themselves are to farm it, the fighting and farming part of the city will not be different, yet that is what the legislator wants. If there are going to be some others to do the job, different both from those farming privately and from the fighters, they will be an extra fourth part of the city, sharing in nothing but alien to the regime. Yet if one were to propose that those farming the private land and the common land be the same, then, first, the amount of crops needed by each to sustain two households[67] from his farming could not be enough, and, second, what is the point in their not at once getting sustenance for themselves and providing it to the warriors from the same land and the same allotments?[68] All these things have much confusion in them.

Jurors. Difficulties regarding jurors include: (i) the jurors are made into arbitrators; (ii) there will be no clear verdict reached; (iii) it is false to say current law forces jurors into perjury.

1268b4 The law about jury verdicts is not in a noble condition either, namely his recommendation that the juror should make distinctions in his judgment (though the charge is stated in simple terms) and so become an arbitrator. Making distinctions is possible enough in an arbitration even when those deciding are many, because they can confer with each other about the verdict. In jury courts, however, this possibility does not exist, and many legislators even arrange for the direct opposite, that the jurors not be able to confer.

1268b11 Next, how can the verdict not be in a state of confusion whenever a juror thinks the defendant ought to pay a fine but not as much as the plaintiff thinks? For the plaintiff wants twenty minas[69] but the juror judges ten, or they each pick larger or smaller figures, and another juror judges five, another four (that is clearly the sort of way they will split up); others again will decide for the whole amount, and yet others for nothing. How then will the votes be counted?

1268b17 Furthermore, no one is compelling a juror who simply acquits or condemns to commit perjury, at any rate provided the charge has been justly stated in a simple way. For the one who acquits does not say that the defendant owes nothing but only that he does not owe the twenty minas. That juror has forsworn, however, who condemns although he thinks the twenty minas are not due.

The Law about Discovering Something of Advantage to the City. Difficulties arising from this law include: (i) it will encourage informers and possibly revolution; (ii) it raises the different question of whether existing laws should always be changed

67. His own, that is, and that of a warrior. The case would be different, of course, if the farmers were slaves, for slaves would not form a separate household but be part of the warrior's own (cf. 4(7).10.1329b36–39, 1330a25–31). Hippodamus, however, wanted the farmers to be a separate, free class.

68. That is, what will be the point in dividing the land into private and common to begin with?

69. A mina was 100 drachmas.

for better ones, for if the answer is no, the proposal should be rejected; (iii) this other question needs to be dealt with expressly, and considerations show that while change is sometimes necessary—because (a) change in other arts and sciences is better, and politics is a science; (b) everyone desires the good, not the ancestral; (c) the first humans were foolish, and it would be foolish to keep to their laws; (d) even written laws should be changed because of changes in particulars—nevertheless, change always needs much caution, because frequent change of law accustoms people to disobedience, the above analogy with the arts is false, and not just any law should be changed by just anyone.

1268b22 As regards honor being due to those who find out something of advantage to the city, such legislation is not safe but only presents a fair appearance on first hearing. For it encourages the activity of informers and may bring with it changes of regime.

1268b25 It raises also another problem and another topic of investigation. For there are some who raise a doubt whether it is harmful or beneficial for cities to change the ancestral laws if a better one comes along. So if changing them is not better (some might introduce, on the grounds of the common good, an abolition of the laws or the regime), it is not easy to give a ready assent to what Hippodamus says.

1268b31 But since we have made mention of the issue, it is perhaps better to give a little more explanation. For, as we said, there is a difficulty here and it might seem that to change the laws is better. At any rate such change has been of advantage in the case of the other kinds of knowledge; medicine, for example, has been changed from the ancestral precepts, as has also gymnastics and in general all the arts and abilities. Consequently, if political science is also to be counted as one of these, then clearly similar things must hold of it. There is evidence to be found, one might claim, in the facts themselves, for the ancient laws are overly simple and barbaric: the Greeks used to go about carrying arms and purchased their wives from each other, and, one supposes, everything else that has been left over from ancient customs is altogether simple-minded. There is, for instance, the law in Cyme about cases of homicide, that if the plaintiff can get together a certain number of witnesses to the crime from his own kin, then the defendant is guilty of the murder.

1269a3 In general, all seek for what is good, not for what is ancestral.

1269a4 It is likely, too, that the first humans, whether they were born from the earth or survived some cataclysm,[70] were like any chance person or

---

70. Aristotle is presumably referring to Greek stories, notably that of Deucalion and Pyrrha, about men being originally born from the earth and surviving from some great flood; see Plato *Statesman* 271a4–c2 and *Laws* 677a1–679e5, and Hesiod *Works and Days* 108–73.

simpletons (as indeed is said of the earthborn). So, accordingly, it would be a strange thing to abide by their opinions.

1269a8 In addition, it is not even better to leave written laws unchanged. Just as it is impossible in the case of the other arts to write down everything accurately, so is it also in the case of political arrangement. For one must write in universal terms, but actions concern particulars.

1269a12 So it is clear from these considerations that some laws sometimes must be changed, though as one looks at the question in another way, much caution would seem to be required. For if the improvement is small and it is a base thing to get accustomed to reckless dissolution of the laws, clearly some faults of legislators and rulers should be let alone: the gain resulting from the change will not be as great as is the harm of getting used to disobeying the rulers.

1269a19 Also, the analogy taken from the arts is false since change in the arts is not the same as change in law. Law has no force of persuasion other than custom, and custom gets established only by long passage of time. Consequently, easy changes from existing laws to other new ones make the power of law weak.

1269a24 Furthermore, even if change in the laws is to be permitted, are all laws in every regime to be changed or not? Can anyone do the changing or only certain persons? These things make a great deal of difference. Let us therefore now give up this investigation; there will be other occasions for it.[71]

CHAPTER 9

The Regime of the Spartans

Slavery. *About the regime of the Spartans and most other regimes, two questions arise: whether the legislation agrees with the best arrangement and whether it all agrees with itself. On the matter of slavery the Spartan system is not best, because the slaves, being indigenous, (i) are prone to revolt and (ii) create problems whether treated well or badly.*

1269a29 About the regime of the Spartans and the Cretan regime, as pretty much about the other regimes as well,[72] two investigations arise: the first, whether anything has been legislated that is nobly or not nobly done in view

---

71. The question is not expressly raised again in the *Politics* as we have it, though it does get discussed in effect in passages about the differences between regimes and the causes of revolution, such as 6(4) and 7(5).

72. The Carthaginian, dealt with in 2.11, and the others touched on in 2.12.

of the best arrangement; the second, whether anything has been legislated that is contrary to the supposition or mode of the regime they actually have. **1269a34** Now, it is agreed that a city that is going to be nobly governed must have leisure from doing necessary things, but to secure a way of getting this is not easy. For the serfs of Thessaly have often attacked the Thessalians, and the helots have done likewise to the Spartans on whose misfortunes they are forever, as it were, lying in wait. Nothing, however, of a similar sort has yet happened in the case of the Cretans,[73] the reason being perhaps that even if neighboring cities are at war, they do not make alliances with serfs in revolt, as it would not be an advantage to them, seeing that they too have a subject population. The neighbors of the Spartans, however — Argives, Messenians, and Arcadians — were all hostile. Among the Thessalians too, there were revolts at the beginning, when they were still fighting with those on their borders — Achaeans, Perrhaibeans, and Magnesians.[74]

1269b7 But it would seem, if nothing else, that the matter of looking after serfs, or the sort of association to have with them, is hard work. For if they are treated leniently, they become insolent and think they deserve equality with those in control over them, and if their life is made harsh, they fall to plotting and hating. So it is clear that those on whom helotage brings such results are not managing to discover the best way of doing things.

Women. *The failure to control the women harms (i) the city's happiness, because women are half the city and if they are in a base condition, so is half the city; and (ii) the aim of the regime, steadfast endurance, because (a) the women live licentiously and (b) this female license makes the regime honor wealth, puts rule into the hands of women, and makes them useless in peace and an impediment in war. This fault goes back to the beginnings of the regime.*

1269b12 Further, their letting things go as regards women is harmful both to the chosen object of the regime and to the happiness of the city. For just as a household has man and woman for parts, so a city also must be supposed to be divided almost equally into the numbers of its men and its women. Consequently, in all cities where what concerns the women is in a base condition, there half the city must be considered without legislation. **1269b19** This is indeed what has happened in Sparta. For the legislator,[75] whose desire was for the whole city to have steadfast endurance, was con-

---

73. Thessalians, Spartans, and Cretans all used subject populations as their serfs.
74. Peoples whom the Thessalians eventually reduced to subjection.
75. Tradition made Lycurgus the legislator of Sparta. His dates, however, and even his existence, are disputed.

spicuous in pursuing it as regards the men but neglected it as regards the women, who live in luxury and with every sort of license.

1269b23 Wealth must, as a consequence, become an object of honor in such a regime, and all the more so if the men are overcome by women, as is usually the case with soldiering and warlike nations (excepting the Celts and any others who have manifestly honored sexual intercourse among males). For the one who first told the story about Ares and Aphrodite seems not to have been unreasonable in pairing them together,[76] since all warring types are conspicuously obsessed by sexual relations either with men or women.

1269b31 That is why the same thing happened to the Spartans and why during their empire the management of many things fell into the hands of women. Yet what is the difference between women ruling and the rulers being ruled by women? For the same results occur.

1269b34 Boldness is not useful in any of the affairs of daily life but only, if at all, in war, and in this respect also the Spartans' women were very harmful, as they proved during the Theban invasion.[77] For, unlike in other cities, they were of no help at all but made more uproar than the enemy.

1269b39 Now, this letting go as regards women seems, reasonably enough, to have come about among the Spartans from the very beginning. For the men spent much time absent from home on campaign fighting in the war against the Argives and again in the war against the Arcadians and Messenians. So when they had leisure, they were presented to the legislator ready prepared by their soldiering way of life (which contains many parts of virtue). As regards the women, however, Lycurgus is said to have tried to subject them to his laws, but when they resisted, he gave up. These then are the causes of what happened and so clearly also of the fault in question.[78] But we are not now considering whom to excuse and whom not to excuse, but what is right and what is not right.

Property. The license of the women also contributes to greed and the concentration of land in few hands, which the laws have made worse by allowing bequests of land, large dowries, and the marrying off of heiresses to anyone; the result was a dearth of citizens and the destruction of the city in a single battle. The first remedy that was tried, recruiting from outside the regime, is a temporary expedient, and the second, to

---

76. Ares, the god of war, was supposed to have had a longstanding love affair with Aphrodite, the goddess of love; see Homer *Odyssey* 8.267–366 and Hesiod *Theogony* 933–37.

77. In the year 369.

78. It is also possible to translate this sentence as "the women, then, are causes of what happened . . ." The Greek simply has *hautai* ("these"), which could be taken as agreeing either with "women" in the previous sentence or with "causes" in this one. Perhaps, however, not very much hangs on the difference, since women remain causes in either translation.

release those who father several sons from military obligations, only contributes to the numbers of the poor.

1270a11 That the state things are in as regards the women is not noble seems not only to introduce a certain impropriety into the regime, as has already been said, but also to contribute to greed. For what one might criticize next after the above observations is the unequal distribution of property. Some Spartans have gained possession of huge amounts of property and others extremely little, and hence the land has fallen into the hands of a few. The laws have also arranged these matters basely. For the legislator made it ignoble to buy or sell the existing land, and correctly so, but then he allowed anyone who wished the right to bequeath it or give it away. Yet the same thing must result in this case as in that. Also, two-fifths of the entire land is in the hands of women, both because many become heiresses and because large dowries are given. Yet it were a better arrangement to have no dowries at all, or small ones, or even ones of measured amount. As things stand, however, it is possible for a father to give an heiress in marriage to anyone he likes, and if he dies before he has done so, the one left behind as guardian can give her to anyone he likes. Therefore, indeed, though the land has the capacity to support 1,500 cavalry and 30,000 heavy armed troops, the actual numbers were not even 1,000. Events themselves made evident how base the arrangements were in this matter, for the city could not bear up under a single blow but was destroyed through its lack of human beings.[79]

1270a34 It is said that under the earlier kings a share in the regime was given out to others, so that there was no lack of human beings, even though they were a long time at war. It is also said that at one point the numbers of Spartiates[80] reached 10,000. But whether these assertions are true or not, it would still be better if it was by means of leveling possessions that the city came to abound in men. The law about child-getting is also an impediment to putting this right. The legislator, wishing to have as many Spartiates as possible, encourages the citizens to have more children, for they have a law that anyone who fathers three sons should be free of military duties and that anyone who fathers four should be free of all taxes. Yet it is clear that if many are born and the land remains divided in the way it is, many must become poor.

Offices

The Ephorate. *The ephorate presents the following difficulties: (i) ephors are in charge of the most important matters but, being chosen from the populace, are some-*

---

79. The battle of Leuctra against the Thebans in 371.
80. The name for full Spartan citizens.

times very poor and so venal; (ii) as the equivalent of tyrants, they force the kings into demagoguery and turn the regime away from aristocracy; (iii) they have the advantage of reconciling the populace to the regime but should not be elected in such a childish way, nor should they decide judicial cases at their own discretion rather than by written rules and laws; (iv) their unrestrained way of life is in conflict with the aim of the regime, and the tension makes them into secret libertines.

1270b6 What concerns the ephorate[81] is also in a base condition. For this office has sole control over the greatest matters, but all its members[82] are drawn from the populace[83] and, as a result, very needy sorts often enter it who, because of their lack of means, are easy to bribe. This fact has been proved on many previous occasions and also recently in the affair at Andros, where some of them, corrupted by money, did all that was in them to destroy the whole city.[84]

1270b13 Also, because the office is excessively great and equivalent to a tyranny, even the kings are compelled to behave like demagogues toward them. So in this respect too they have harmed the regime, by making it a democracy in place of an aristocracy.

1270b17 Admittedly, the board of the ephorate does hold the regime together, since, as the populace share in the greatest office, it keeps them quiet. Hence, whether this result was intended by the legislator[85] or came about by chance, matters there are helped by it. For if any regime is going to survive, all the parts of the city must want it both to exist and to remain as it is. So the kings want this because of their own position of honor, the gentlemen because of the senate[86] (for this office is the reward of virtue), and the populace because of the ephorate since it is set up from them all. But still, though the ephorate should be chosen from all, it should not be chosen in the way they go about it now, which is exceedingly childish.[87]

1270b28 Further, though ephors could be anyone at all, they have control over the most important judicial decisions. Hence, it would be better if they judged not at their own discretion but by written rules and the laws.

1270b31 The ephors' manner of life does not agree with what the city wants, for it is in itself very unrestrained, though in other respects it tends to go too much in the direction of harshness. The consequence is that they can-

---

81. The word *ephoros* ("ephor") literally means "overseer."

82. Reading *pantes* ("all its members") with the manuscripts, rather than *pantos* ("from the whole populace") with Dreizehnter.

83. The Greek word is *dēmos*, the mass of the free poor.

84. Nothing for certain is known about this incident.

85. Probably Theopompus in this case, rather than Lycurgus; see 7(5).11.1313a25–33.

86. The Greek is *gerousia*, which more literally means the council of elders.

87. What this method of election was is unclear.

not endure it but flee the laws in secret and give themselves over to bodily pleasures.

The Senate. Criticisms of the Senate include: (i) even if the senators are virtuous, they should not be in office for life; (ii) they are not in fact virtuous, but corrupted by venality and favoritism; (iii) they should not be left unaudited as they are now; (iv) their manner of election is (a) childish, (b) should not be confined only to those who want the office, and (c) promotes love of honor and the crimes attendant thereon.

1270b35 What concerns the office of senator is also not in a noble condition. For though one might say that the office would be of advantage to the city if senators were decent men and adequately educated in manly goodness, yet even so, giving them control over the greatest matters throughout life is a debatable practice. There is an old age of thought as well as of the body. **1271a1** But given the sort of education they actually have, which is such that even the legislator himself has no confidence in their character as good men, the office is not a safe one. In respect of many matters of common concern its members have been conspicuous in taking bribes and showing favoritism. **1271a5** It would accordingly be better if, contrary to current practice, they were not left to go unaudited.[88] The ephorate might seem in fact to be auditing all the offices, but that is too great a privilege for the ephorate, and the way they actually do it is not how we say audits should be performed.[89] **1271a9** Further, the election they have for senators is decided in a childish way, and it is also not right that anyone who is going to be judged worthy of office should himself have to ask for it. If a man is worthy of office, he should rule whether he wants to or not. But as it is, the legislator is conspicuously doing here what he has done in the rest of the regime as well: he first makes the citizens eager for honor and then uses this fact as the way to elect the senators, for no one would ask to rule who was not in love with honor. Yet human beings commit most voluntary wrongs more or less from love of honor or money.

Kings, Common Messes, and Admirals. Kingship, whether better for cities or not, is not better as it is in Sparta, where persons unworthy even by the legislator's own judgment occupy the office. Common messes, not being provisioned from the common treasury, exclude the poor, and so are not the democratic institution the legislator intended. Admirals are like a third king warring against the other two.

88. It was a common practice, especially at Athens, to perform an audit (*euthunai*) of officials when they left office.

89. The ephorate had an arbitrary power to call the other offices to account, but Aristotle evidently wants a formal and regular procedure, not the exercise of a quasi tyranny.

1271a18 Let us postpone for a later discussion whether it is or is not better for kingship to exist in cities,[90] but at any rate it is not better the way it is now.[91] Rather, each king should be judged on the basis of his own way of life. Yet it is clear that not even the legislator himself thinks he can make them into gentlemen. At any rate he does not trust them as sufficiently good men. Hence the custom on embassies is to send out their enemies with them as fellow ambassadors,[92] and it is thought safety for the city if the kings are engaged in factional disputes with each other.

1271a26 Neither was the matter of the common messes (the so-called "phiditia")[93] nobly legislated by the one who first instituted them. The cost ought rather to be defrayed from common funds, as it is in Crete, but among the Spartans each has to provide for himself, even though some of them are very poor and cannot afford the expense. The result is the opposite of what the legislator intends. He wants the institution of common messes to be democratic, but legislated in the way they are now they are hardly democratic at all. For the very poor do not find it easy to take part in them, yet the ancestral way of determining the regime is precisely that he who cannot pay the fee have no share in it.

1271a37 The law about admirals has been criticized, and rightly, by certain others already: it is a cause of faction, for the office is set up over against the kings, who are generals for life, almost as another kingship.

Supposition of the Regime and Finances. *The supposition of the regime is domination, and only a part of virtue, military virtue, is practiced; as a result, the Spartans are successful when fighting but are destroyed when at leisure, and they prize as better than virtue goods that are subordinate to virtue. The finances are also in a bad state, because the common treasury is always empty, though they are compelled to fight major wars, and they are bad at making themselves pay the necessary taxes.*

1271a41 One might also criticize the supposition of the legislator in the same way that Plato did in the *Laws*.[94] For the whole arrangement of his laws is directed to a part of virtue, military virtue, since such virtue is useful for conquest. The Spartans therefore were able to preserve themselves while at war but were destroyed when possessed of empire because they did not know how to use their leisure nor had they practiced training of any authority greater than that of war. And an error not lesser than this one is that

90. 3.14–17.

91. In Sparta there were two different kingly houses, and both kings were hereditary and ruled for life.

92. That is, to send two of the ephors along with the king.

93. The meaning of this term is unclear, but one suggestion is that it is related to the word for friendship (*philia*).

94. 625c9–631a8.

they think the goods people fight for are won by virtue rather than vice, which is noble, but they suppose that these goods are better than virtue, and that, by contrast, is not noble.

1271b10 The matter of common funds is also basely handled by the Spartiates. For there is nothing in the common treasury even though they are compelled to fight major wars, and they are also bad at paying their taxes since, as most of the land is in the possession of the Spartiates, they do not examine each others' returns. What the legislator has brought about is the reverse of beneficial: the city he has made deficient in money, but individuals he has made lovers of it.

1271b17 Let so much be said about the regime of the Spartans. For these are the things in it that one might most of all criticize.

CHAPTER 10

The Regime of the Cretans

How It Is Like the Regime of the Spartans. *The regime of the Cretans is less polished than that of the Spartans, being the earlier form, which the latter imitated, as stories and the history of the island confirm. The institutions of slavery, messes, ephors, senators, and kings all have their analogues in Crete.*

1271b20 The Cretan regime[95] is rather close to the Spartan and is in some few respects not worse, though in most it is less polished. For as appears and as is also asserted, the Spartan regime is for the most part an imitation of the Cretan, and most things that are ancient are less articulated than later ones. They say that Lycurgus, when he gave up his guardianship of King Charilaus and went abroad, spent most of his time about Crete because of common kinship. For the Lyctians[96] were colonists from Sparta, and those who went to the colony adopted the arrangement of laws existing among the inhabitants there. In fact, to this day these subject peoples are still following these laws exactly as before, believing that Minos[97] was the first to set them up.

1271b32 The island seems to be naturally fitted and nobly situated for Greek empire, since it lies pretty much across the entire sea around which all the Greeks are settled. On the one side it is not far from the Peloponnese and on the other not far from the part of Asia about Triopium and Rhodes. That

95. Not the regime of one particular city in Crete but the kind existing in all or most of them.

96. Lyctus was a city in Crete.

97. A semimythical king of Crete who, after his death, became one of the judges in the underworld.

was also how Minos obtained his maritime empire, bringing some of the islands into subjection and sending settlers to others. At length he attacked Sicily where, in the region of Camicus, he ended his life.

1271b40 The Cretan way of arranging things is analogous to the Spartan. The helots do the farming for the latter, the subject peoples for the former. There are common messes in both places, which at any rate in ancient times the Spartans called by the name of "andria," [98] as in Crete, and not "phiditia" (which again makes it clear that the institution came from Crete). Further, the arrangement of the regime is analogous. The ephors have the same power as the so-called "cosmoi" [99] in Crete, except that the ephors are five in number and the cosmoi ten. The senators in Sparta correspond to those in Crete, where they are called the council. The Cretans once had a kingship, but they abolished it, and leadership in war was taken over by the cosmoi. Everyone shares in the assembly, but it has no control except to confirm by vote the decisions of the senators and cosmoi.

How It Is Better and Worse than the Regime of the Spartans. *In the regime of the Cretans, compared to that of the Spartans, (i) the messes are better arranged, being provisioned from the common stock, and the legislator has secured abstemious habits and a low birth rate; (ii) the cosmoi and senators suffer from the same faults as in Sparta, save that the cosmoi do not serve to reconcile the populace to the regime; (iii) the absence of popular revolts is secured instead by (a) the accident of distance, which keeps the amount of corruption through bribes to a minimum, and (b) the powerful expelling the cosmoi from office and currying favor with the populace, a cure, however, which in effect abolishes the city and makes it easy prey to attackers.*

1272a12 What concerns the messes is in a better condition among the Cretans than among the Spartans, for in Sparta each must contribute a specified per capita amount; otherwise, as already noted, the law forbids him to share in the regime.[100] In Crete, things are done in a more common way, for a part is taken from all the crops harvested, from the cattle on the public land, and from the contributions of the subject peoples and assigned to the gods and public services; and another part is taken for the common messes, so that all—women, children, and men—are fed at the common expense.[101] The legislator held a sparing diet to be a useful thing and philosophized many

98. Men's messes, from *andres* (the Greek for "men").

99. The word is *kosmos*, and so "cosmoi" means something like officers charged with "the adornment" of the regime.

100. 2.9.1271a29–37.

101. Presumably the men, who alone share in the messes, receive enough also to take home for their families.

means to secure it and also to segregate the women, by instituting sexual relations among the males so that the women would not have many children. But whether such sexual relations are a base thing or not can be examined on another occasion.[102]

1272a26 That things to do with the messes are arranged better by the Cretans than by the Spartans is thus clear, but things to do with the cosmoi are worse than they are with the ephors. What is bad in the board of ephors is also bad in the cosmoi, for any chance person can enter the office, but while the ephors are a help to the regime, the cosmoi are not. For since the ephorate is chosen from everyone, the populace share in the regime and so want it to continue, but the cosmoi are chosen only from certain families and not from everyone. The senators, moreover, are elected from those who have been cosmoi, and about these senators one might say the same things as about those who become senators in Sparta: their being left unaudited and serving for life is a greater privilege than they deserve, and their exercising rule by their own discretion and not by written rules is dangerous.

1272a39 The acquiescence of the populace, though they do not share in the regime, is no sign that things have been nobly arranged. For the cosmoi, unlike the ephors, can gain nothing from office, as they live on an island far away from any who might corrupt them with bribes.

1272b1 As regards the cure the Cretans themselves use for this fault in the regime, it is a peculiar one and not political but dynastic.[103] For the cosmoi are often expelled from office either by a conspiracy of their colleagues or of private persons. It is also possible for cosmoi to resign in the middle of their term. But it were better if all these things took place according to law and not human wish, which is no safe standard. Basest of all, however, are the frequent abolitions of cosmoi brought about by the powerful when they do not wish to submit to punishment, from which it is also clear that the Cretan arrangement of things has something of a regime to it but is more of a dynasty. The habit of the powerful is to create rival followings among the populace and their friends, to set up monarchies, and to form factions and fight against each other.

1272b13 Yet what is the difference between such behavior and the city periodically ceasing to exist and the regime dissolving? A city in this condition is in great danger, because those who have the desire to attack it will also

102. No such discussion exists in the *Politics* as we have it, but Aristotle's opinion can perhaps be judged from 4(7).16.1335b38–1336a2.

103. The Greek is *dunasteutikē*. Dynasty (*dunasteia*) is the word used later to describe an extreme oligarchy, where a small group of families exercises arbitrary power after the manner of a tyrant; see 6(4).5.1292b5–10.

be able to. But, as we said, Crete is saved by its position because its distance has acted to keep foreigners out.[104] That is also why the subject peoples put up with the Cretans, while the helots at Sparta often revolt. For the Cretans do not take part in foreign empire, and only recently has war from outside come to the island and made manifest the weakness of its laws.[105]

1272b22 Let us, then, say so much about this regime.

CHAPTER 11

The Regime of the Carthaginians

How It Is Better than the Regime of the Spartans and Cretans. The regime of the Carthaginians is similar to the other two save that it is better in many respects, as the acquiescence of the populace and the absence of faction and tyranny indicate. It has common messes, a board of 104 like the ephors, kings, and a senate; however, the 104 are chosen from men of merit, and the kings are not hereditary but drawn from any family that is outstanding.

1272b24 The Carthaginians also seem to govern themselves nobly and to be extraordinary compared with others in many respects, and in some very close to the Spartans in particular. For these three regimes—the Cretan, the Spartan, and that of the Carthaginians third—are in a way close to each other and very different in most respects from the rest.

1272b29 Many of the Carthaginian arrangements are in a noble condition. A sign that the regime has a tight arrangement is that the populace willingly abide by the way the regime is arranged and that neither any faction worth speaking of nor tyranny has arisen among them. The similarities it has to the Spartan regime are, as counterpart to the phiditia, its club messes, and as counterpart to the ephors, the office of the 104, save that it is not worse. For the ephors are drawn from any chance sort but the Carthaginians choose their 104 according to merit. The kings and senators are analogous to the kings and senators in Sparta, and things are better with respect to the kings, who neither belong to the same family nor to any chance one but are chosen from a family that is outstanding, and by election, not by seniority.[106] For

104. That is, it has the same effect as the practice, notorious at Sparta, of actually expelling foreigners (*xenēlasia*).

105. The event referred to is uncertain but could be the invasions of the Phocian Phalaecus in 345–343 or of the Spartan king Agis in 333. The phrase translated "war from outside" (*polemos xenikos*) can also have the technical meaning of "mercenary war," in which case the reference would be to Phalaecus, who was a mercenary captain.

106. The Greek text is controversial at this point and there may be a lacuna. I follow the manuscripts rather than the conjectural emendations of Dreizehnter.

being set in control of important matters, these kings cause much damage when they are of a mediocre sort, which is what they have already done to the city of the Spartans.

Deviations in the Regime of the Carthaginians

Deviations in General. The deviations from what is best are largely the same in all three regimes, but the deviations of the Carthaginian from its supposition of aristocracy are its leaning too much toward democracy and oligarchy. Democratic elements are the powers of the populace in the assembly; oligarchic are the ways the boards of five are elected, exercise control both in and out of office, and elect the 104; aristocratic elements are that officeholders are elected and do not receive pay, and determine the outcome of all lawsuits.

1273a2 Most criticisms one might make on account of its deviations turn out to be common to all the above mentioned regimes, but as regards criticisms with respect to its supposition of aristocracy and polity, some things incline more toward popular rule and others toward oligarchy.

1273a6 Control over what to lay and what not to lay before the populace belongs to the kings along with the senators, provided they all agree; but if they do not, the populace have control also over this. As regards what they do lay before them, the populace are not only allowed to hear the rulers' opinions but have control over passing decisions as well, and any one of them who likes may speak against any proposal (something that is not permitted in the other two regimes).

1273a13 Oligarchic features are that the boards of five,[107] who are in control of many important matters, elect themselves and also elect the office of the 100, which is the greatest office.[108] They also serve for a longer time than any other office, for they exercise rule both after they have left office and before they have yet entered it.

1273a17 As aristocratic features must be reckoned the fact that officeholders do not receive pay and are not chosen by lot, along with anything else of the sort, and also the fact that the boards of officers decide all lawsuits, instead of some deciding some and others others, as in Sparta.[109]

Particular Oligarchic Deviations. The main deviation is the belief that offices should be chosen with an eye to wealth as well as virtue. But (i) the legislator should ensure that the virtuous have means to be at leisure for rule; (ii) even if wealth is neces-

---

107. It is not known who comprised these boards of five or how they functioned.

108. It is generally supposed that these 100 are the same as the 104 mentioned earlier, but the matter is not clear.

109. Cf. 3.1.1275b9–12.

sary for office, the greatest offices should not be for sale; (iii) the virtuous should at least have means to be at leisure while in office. Another deviation is allowing one person to hold several offices at once. But one work is done best by one man; and having many in office is more political than having few. The remedy they apply for oligarchic deviation, always having some of the populace enrich themselves, is a good one but due to chance.

1273a21 But the arrangement of the Carthaginians deviates most from aristocracy toward oligarchy in respect of a certain thought that the many also agree with. They think rulers should be elected not only in aristocratic fashion but also because of their wealth, for they say that someone who has no means cannot perform nobly in office or be at leisure. So if election on the basis of wealth is oligarchical and election on the basis of virtue aristocratic, then this arrangement by which the Carthaginians, among others, have arranged their regime would be of a third sort.[110] For they elect to office with an eye to both these qualities, above all in the case of the greatest offices, the kings and the generals.

1273a31 This deviation from aristocracy, however, must be regarded as an error on the part of the legislator. For one of the most important matters right from the beginning is to see to it that the best are able to be at leisure and can avoid doing anything unseemly not only when in office but also when out of it.

1273a35 Even if the need for leisure requires one to pay attention also to prosperity when electing to office, still it is a base thing to put the greatest offices, king and general, up for sale. This law makes wealth rather than virtue to be the object of honor, that is, it makes the whole city to be in love with money. For the opinion that those in control have about what is honorable will inevitably be followed in the thinking of the other citizens as well, and a regime in which virtue is not held in highest honor cannot be a firm aristocracy. One can reasonably expect that those who have bought an office will get accustomed to making a profit out of it, since it is by having spent money that they are in office. For if someone respectable but poor is going to want to make a profit, it would be strange if a baser man, already out of pocket, is not going to. That is why those should rule who have the ability to do it best.

1273b6 And if the legislator gives up on making the decent sort prosperous, then at any rate he had better make sure that they have leisure when actually ruling.

1273b8 It would also seem a base thing for the same person to occupy several offices, a thing held in high repute among the Carthaginians. For one

---

110. This seems to be an anticipation of what Aristotle argues later about there being other kinds of aristocracy after the best kind (see 6(4).7.1293b1–21).

man completes one work best, and bringing that about is what the legislator should look to and not bid the same man both play the pipes and be a shoemaker. Accordingly, where the city is not small, it is more political as well as more popular if more take part in the offices, since, as we said,[111] it is more communal and the same things[112] each get completed in a nobler and quicker way. This is clear in armies and navies, for in both of these everyone, so to say, is involved in ruling and being ruled.

1273b18 But though the regime is oligarchical, they have a very good way of escaping the consequences by always sending a part of the populace out to subject cities to get rich.[113] In this way they effect a cure and give stability to the regime. But this is the work of chance, whereas the legislator should be the one responsible for making the citizens free of faction. As it is, if some misfortune happens and the majority of the ruled revolt, there is no cure in the laws for restoring calm.

1273b24 Such then is how things stand with the Spartan, Cretan, and Carthaginian regimes, which are justly esteemed.

CHAPTER 12

Other Legislators

Framers of Regimes. Framers of regimes who did not take part in politics have pretty much been dealt with. Framers who did take part legislated either for their own city or for others. So Solon set up the ancestral democracy for his own city of Athens, whose decline into extreme democracy was due to events not in his control. Zaleucus and Charondas in Sicily and Philolaus in Thebes framed regimes for foreign cities.

1273b27 Of those who spoke in any respect about regimes, some did not take part in politics at all but lived out their lives in a private capacity, about all of whom pretty much everything worth saying has been said. Others by contrast did become legislators, being themselves engaged in politics, either in their own cities or also in certain foreign ones. Of these, some framed laws only while others framed regimes as well, such as Lycurgus and Solon, who established both laws and regimes.

1273b35 Now, we have already spoken about Lycurgus,[114] but as for Solon,

---

111. Possibly a reference to 2.2.1261a39–b6.

112. Reading *tōn autōn* ("the same things") with the manuscripts, not *tōn archōn* ("the offices") with Dreizehnter.

113. It is not clear how those sent out to these subject cities were to make money, whether as colonists with rich allotments of land or by holding lucrative office or in some other way.

114. The discussion of Sparta in 2.9.

some think he was a serious legislator. They say he put an end to an oligarchy that was too extreme and was enslaving the populace and that he set up the ancestral democracy, giving a noble mix to the regime. For, they go on, the council of the Areopagus was oligarchic, the election of offices was aristocratic, and the jury courts were popular. It would seem, however, that the first two, the Areopagus and elections, already existed and that Solon kept them as they were and only gave a place to the populace by having the jury courts set up from everyone.

1274a3 That indeed is why some blame him. They say he destroyed the first two by putting control into the hands of jury courts chosen from all by lot. For when this court became strong, those who flattered it like a tyrant turned the regime toward the present democracy. So Ephialtes and Pericles cut back the Areopagus, Pericles introduced payment for service in the law courts, and each demagogue continued on in this way increasing popular power up to the present democracy.[115] But it does not appear that these events followed Solon's choice but rather fell out by chance. For once the populace had become the cause of the naval empire after the Persian Wars, they waxed arrogant and took to themselves base demagogues, while the decent sort were their political opponents. As for Solon, at any rate, he seems to have given the populace the power that was most necessary (electing to office and auditing the accounts), since without it they would have been enslaved and hostile. All the offices, however, he had drawn from the notables and the well-off: from the Pentacosiomedimnoi; the Zeugitai; and the third class, the so-called order of Hippeis. The fourth class, that of the Thetes, had no share in office at all.[116]

1274a22 Zaleucus was a legislator for the Epizephyrean Locrians and Charondas of Catana for his own city and the other Chalcidic cities in Italy and Sicily. Some try to bring the two together by saying that Onomacritus was the first to become clever at legislation and that, though a Locrian, he was trained in Crete, when he stayed there in connection with his art of divining. Thales became his companion, Lycurgus and Zaleucus were disciples of Thales, and Charondas disciple of Zaleucus. But they say these things without much regard for chronology.[117]

---

115. For the details, see *Athēnaiōn Politeia* 25–28.

116. Solon set up four property classes based on annual income assessed in measures of corn: the *Pentakosiomedimnoi* ("500 measure men") were those with 500 measures or more, the *Zeugitai* ("yoke men," so called because they could keep a yoke of oxen) with 200–300, the *Hippeis* ("knights" or "horsemen") with 300–500, and the *Thētes* ("laborers" or perhaps "villeins") with less than 200, *Athēnaiōn Politeia* 7.

117. Dates of these persons are not certain, but Zaleucus and Thales were probably seventh century, Charondas probably sixth century and likewise Onomacritus, if he is the same as the

1274a31 Philolaus the Corinthian also became a legislator for the Thebans. He was of the family of the Bacchiads[118] but became the lover of the Olympic victor Diocles.[119] When Diocles, from disgust at the sexual passion for him of his own mother, Alcyone, left the city, he went to Thebes and there both of them ended their days. Even now their tombs are still pointed out, being easily visible from each other but one with a view toward Corinthian territory and the other not. The tale is told that they themselves arranged the burials thus, Diocles not having Corinthian territory visible from his mound out of hatred for his mother's passion and Philolaus having it visible from his. **1274b1** That, then, was why they settled in Thebes, but Philolaus gave them laws about childbirth, among other things (those they call the adoptive laws), and that is what is peculiar in his legislation, preserving the number of allotments. From Charondas, there is nothing peculiar save perjury trials (he was the first to introduce denunciations for perjury) and the accuracy of his laws, wherein he is more polished even than contemporary legislators.

Framers of Laws. *There are a number of peculiarities to note in the laws of those who did not engage in politics, Phaleas and Plato. As for those who did and legislated for their own city, Draco is peculiar for the severity of his punishments, Pittacus for his law concerning the drunk, while about Androdamas (who legislated for a foreign city) there is nothing peculiar to note.*

1274b9 What is peculiar to Phaleas is his leveling of property and to Plato the sharing of wives and children and property, and common messes for women. Also peculiar to Plato are the law about drinking, that the sober should preside at drinking parties, and the law about military exercises, that there should be training with both hands, as it ought not to be the case that one hand should be useful and the other useless.[120] **1274b15** There are also laws from Draco[121] but he laid them down for a regime already in existence. There is nothing peculiar to note in these laws save their harshness in the severity of the punishments. Pittacus[122] framed laws but not a regime. His law about the drunk is peculiar: that if they commit an offense, they should pay a greater fine than the sober. The reason was that the drunk commit more outrages than the sober, and Pittacus was look-

---

Orphic soothsayer of that name who was influential under the Peisistratids in Athens. The Thales in question is the Cretan poet, not the philosopher from Miletus mentioned in 1.11.

118. The ruling oligarchic family in Corinth in the sixth century.

119. Nothing else is known of either Philolaus or Diocles beyond what Aristotle says here.

120. *Laws* 671d5–672a4, 794d5–795d5.

121. He produced the first written code for Athens in about 620 (*Athēnaiōn Politeia* 4).

122. Ruler of Mytilene in Lesbos, 589–579. He is mentioned again in 3.14.1285a30–b1.

ing to utility, not the greater forgiveness one should feel toward the drunk.

1274b23 Androdamas of Rhegium[123] was a legislator for the Chalcidians in the region of Thrace, and the laws about murders and heiresses are his. There is however nothing peculiar one might say about them.

1274b26 Let such then be our examination of what concerns regimes, both those in control somewhere and those that certain people have spoken about.

123. Nothing more is known about Androdamas.

Book 3

Definition and
Division of Regime

CHAPTER 1

Definition of City and Citizen

Priority of the Citizen. *To see what a regime is, one must first see what a city is; and to see what a city is, one must first see what a citizen is.*

1274b32 When one is inquiring into regimes and into what each is and is like, pretty much the first subject of inquiry concerns the city, to see what the city is. For as things stand now, there is a dispute about the matter and some say the city did the deed while others say it was not the city but the oligarchy or the tyrant. Also we see that the whole activity of the politician and legislator concern the city. And the regime is a sort of arrangement of those who inhabit the city.

1274b38 But since the city, like any other whole made up of many parts, is something composite, clearly the first thing to seek out is the citizen, for the city is a multitude of citizens.[1] Consequently, our inquiry must be into who is to be called a citizen and what a citizen is, for citizen too is often a subject of dispute: not everyone agrees that the same person is a citizen, since someone who is a citizen in a democracy is often not one in an oligarchy.

Preliminary Definition of Citizen. *The citizen being sought for is someone who is a citizen simply speaking. He can be provisionally defined, after the removal of all those called citizen in some other and qualified sense, as anyone who shares in the office of juror and assemblyman.*

---

1. Cf. the method stated at 1.1.1252a17–21.

1275a5 Now we must set aside those who have come by the designation of citizen in some other way—as by being made-citizens,[2] for example. On the other hand, the citizen is not a citizen because he inhabits a certain place, for resident aliens and slaves also share the dwelling place in common; nor are those citizens who have a share in judicial rights, such as to be able both to sue and be sued in court, since that is also true of partners to treaties (they too enjoy these rights). In fact, it is not everywhere that resident aliens share such rights to the full; they must instead appoint a patron to stand in for them, so that their part in this sort of communal relationship is rather incomplete. Like children not yet enrolled by reason of age and like old men who have been discharged, they must be said to be citizens in a way but not altogether simply so. Instead, the qualification "incomplete" or "overage" or something else of the sort must be added (it does not matter what, because the thing meant is clear). For what we are seeking is the citizen simply speaking, the one against whom no complaint can be made that needs putting right (since one can in fact raise and solve similar difficulties about the disenfranchised and exiles).[3]

1275a22 The citizen simply speaking is defined by nothing else so much as by his having a share in judgment and rule or office. But of offices some are differentiated by time such that it is not permitted at all for the same person to hold them twice, or only to do so after certain intervals. Another holds his office indefinitely, as the juror and member of the assembly. Now perhaps someone might say that those of this latter sort are neither rulers nor do they, on this account, share in office. Yet it would be ridiculous to deny rule to those who have the most control.[4] But let the matter not be an issue: the argument is about a word, for what is common to juror and assemblyman, or what one is to call them both, is nameless. So, for the sake of a definition, let it be called indefinite office. We lay it down, then, that those who share office in this way are citizens. And such, more or less, is the definition of citizen that would most fit all those called citizens.

Precise Definition of Citizen and City. *The preliminary definition, being a definition of things ordered according to prior and posterior, suffers from the defect of not applying strictly to all cases (in some regimes there is no office of assemblyman). However, it can be corrected if it is made to say that a citizen is anyone who shares*

2. Presumably this means something like honorary citizens, or those who have been granted the title of citizen but not all the prerogatives that go with it.

3. The disenfranchised and exiled could be called citizens only with the qualification "deprived" or the like.

4. In democracies, especially of the ultimate sort, supreme control rests with the popular assembly and the jury courts.

in deliberation and judgment generally. Accordingly, a city can be defined as a self-sufficient multitude of citizens in this sense.

1275a34 One must not, however, fail to notice that in the case of things whose underlying notions differ in kind and one notion is primary, another secondary, and so on, either a common element does not exist at all insofar as these things are such or it exists only to a minimal extent. But we see that regimes differ in kind from each other and that some are posterior and some prior, for the incorrect and deviant regimes are necessarily posterior to those that are not incorrect (what we mean by deviant regimes will become manifest later).[5] Consequently, the citizen too must be different in the case of each regime.

1275b5 That is why the citizen as above defined is most of all a citizen in a democracy and may, but need not, be a citizen in the other regimes. For in some regimes there is no populace,[6] nor is there a recognized assembly but only specially summoned meetings, and cases in court are decided by separate groups. So, for example, in Sparta some cases concerning contracts are judged by one ephor and others by another, while cases involving homicide are decided by the senators, and yet other cases are decided perhaps by some other office. The same thing also happens in Carthage, for there certain offices decide all cases.[7]

1275b13 But no matter: the definition of citizen admits of being put right because in these other regimes it is not the holder of indefinite office who is assemblyman and juror but rather someone whose office is determinate (for it is to all or some of these latter that deliberation and judgment, whether about everything or about some things, are given).

1257b17 Who the citizen is, then, is manifest from these considerations. For we can now say that whoever is entitled to share in deliberative or judicial office is a citizen in that particular city, and that a city, to speak simply, is a multitude of such persons adequate for self-sufficiency of life.[8]

CHAPTER 2

Confirmation of the Definitions. *Difficulties that arise about the way citizen is defined in practice, and about the justice of those made citizens after a revolution, confirm that these definitions are the correct ones.*

5. 3.6 and 7.
6. That is, no *dēmos*, or mass of the free poor. No such *dēmos* would exist in a true aristocracy or in Aristotle's best regime of 4(7) and 5(8).
7. See 2.11.1273a19-20.
8. See 1.2.1252b27-30.

1275b22 The definition, however, that gets used in practice is that a citizen is someone born of citizen parents on both sides (and not one only, as the father's or the mother's). Some even look for the same requirement further back, among forebears of two or three or more generations. But when the definition is given in this political and swift way, some raise the difficulty about how that third or fourth generation forebear will be a citizen. So Gorgias of Leontini, partly perhaps by way of raising a difficulty but partly also in irony, said that as mortars are things made by mortar makers, so Larissaeans are things made by official craftsmen, for some of them are Larissa makers.[9] But the difficulty here is a simple one: if the forebears shared in the regime in a way that accords with the definition just stated, then they were citizens (for descent from citizen father and mother could certainly not fit the original inhabitants or founders).

1275b34 More of a difficulty, however, perhaps arises about this next case, the case of those who came to share in the regime after it underwent revolution—for example, those who were made citizens at Athens by Cleisthenes after the expulsion of the tyrants (for he enrolled many foreigners and alien slaves in the tribal registers).[10] But the dispute here is not about which of them is a citizen; it is rather about whether they are justly or unjustly so; though one might raise an additional difficulty even about this—namely whether, on the supposition that the unjust and the false have the same force, someone unjustly a citizen is a citizen. Yet since we see that there are also some unjustly in possession of rule who we admit are ruling, though not justly, and since the citizen is defined by rule of some sort (for the citizen is, as we said, one who shares in such and such rule), then clearly even those unjustly citizens must be admitted to be citizens.

9. Larissa was a town in Thessaly. Gorgias is punning on the Greek word *dēmiourgos*, which means both an artisan or craftsman and a public official (hence my translation "official craftsmen"), and on the fact that "Larissa maker" was, apparently, the title of one of the public officials in Larissa. It may also be that the word Larissaean was the name for a certain kind of pot made at Larissa as well as for a citizen of the place, in which case Gorgias' pun takes on another twist.

10. The tyrants were expelled from Athens in 510 and, in the power struggles among the notables that followed, Cleisthenes successfully used this device of enfranchising new citizens to increase the number of his supporters and so to win out against rivals (*Athēnaiōn Politeia* 20–21).

CHAPTER 3

Resolution of Disputes

As Regards the City. The question of who is justly a citizen is connected with the dispute about whether the city did the deed or not, which in turn is connected with the question of when the city is to be regarded as the same or not. The city is not the same merely because the place or the persons are the same. Its sameness depends rather on whether the regime is the same. But resolving this difficulty about identity does not settle the question about the justice of keeping previous agreements, which requires a separate discussion.

1276a6 The question about the justice or injustice of the matter is connected with the dispute mentioned earlier,[11] for there are those who raise the difficulty about when the city did the deed and when it did not—as, for instance, after a democracy has come into existence in place of an oligarchy or a tyranny. On such occasions some people wish neither to observe existing treaties, since it was the tyrant and not the city that contracted them, nor to do many other things of the same sort. Their thinking is that some regimes exist by force and not for the common benefit. Well, in that case, if some democrats rule after the same fashion, we will have to admit that the deeds of their regime are no more nor less the city's than the deeds of the oligarchy or the tyranny.

1276a17 But this argument is, as it seems, akin to the difficulty about how one is to speak of the city as being the same or as not the same but different. Now, the most obvious way to examine this difficulty is with respect to place and human beings. For take the possibility that the place and the human beings are disjoined such that some live in one place and others in another. Here the difficulty presented must be considered a rather tame one since, given the several senses in which city is used, it can fairly easily be sorted out.[12]

1276a24 Things are similar if one asks, in the case of people inhabiting the same place, when the city is to be considered a single one. Certainly not because it is surrounded by walls, for a single wall could be thrown round the Peloponnese.[13] Babylon is probably of this type, and any city that has the

---

11. 3.1.1274b34–36.

12. Aristotle presumably has in mind such cases as Athens and Megara, where there was a separate port at some distance from the main city and where the population was divided between the two locations. In such cases one can say that politically the city is one (for those in both places together form a single citizen body) while geographically it is two (for this citizen body is divided between two separate locations).

13. The Peloponnese is a large area, and in antiquity it contained innumerable different, and hostile, cities, such as Sparta and Argos.

circumference rather of a nation than a city. At any rate, they say that when Babylon was captured, a part of the city was unaware of the fact for three days.[14] It will be useful, however, to examine this difficulty on another occasion[15] (the size of the city, both as regards numbers and as regards whether it is an advantage to have one or several sites,[16] is something not to be ignored by the politician).

1276a34 But when the same persons are inhabiting the same place, is the city to be called the same as long as the inhabitants remain the same in descent, even though all the time some of them are dying off and others coming to be—just as we are wont to say of rivers and springs that they are the same even though all the time some of the flow is arriving and some streaming away? Or are we to say that the human beings can, for this sort of reason, be the same but the city is a different matter? For since the city is a sort of community, and a community of citizens in a regime, then when the regime becomes other in kind and different, the city too, it would seem, must cease to be the same. At any rate, just as we say that a chorus is different when it is for a comedy and when it is for a tragedy, though the human beings in it are often the same, so in like manner we say of any community or composite that it is different if the kind of composition is different (we say, for example, that a musical mode having the same notes is different if it is now Dorian and now Phrygian). So if that is how things stand, it is manifest that we must look to the regime above all when saying the city is the same. The name to call it could be different or the same regardless of whether the inhabitants are the same or whether they are persons who are altogether different.

1276b13 As to the justice of observing or not observing agreements when the city changes to another regime, that belongs to another discussion.[17]

14. The occasion was probably the capture of Babylon by Cyrus in the sixth century.
15. 4(7).4–6.
16. Reading *hen ē pleiō* with some of the manuscripts, in view of the topic actually discussed by Aristotle later in 4(7).6 (whether a city should have a separate port or not), rather than the *genē pleiō* (whether it is an advantage to have "people of several families") adopted by Dreizehnter.
17. Aristotle does not expressly return to this question anywhere else in the *Politics*, but since he understands justice as the common good (3.12.1282b16–18), his answer would presumably be that previous agreements should be kept if keeping them would serve the common good.

CHAPTER 4

As Regards the Citizen

Virtue of Man and Citizen. *In the case of the citizen, one must consider whether the virtue of man and citizen is the same or not. The citizen is like the sailor in being concerned with a common work, that of preserving the regime (as the sailor's is to preserve the ship); his virtue is therefore relative to the regime.*

1276b16 The next thing to examine after what has just been said is whether the virtue of the good man and of the serious citizen must be regarded as the same or not.[18] But then, if this is indeed a matter in need of examination, it will be necessary first to get some grasp in outline of the virtue of a citizen.[19] **1276b20** We say, therefore, that, like a sailor, a citizen is someone who shares in community with others. And although sailors are unlike in their capacities (for one is a rower, another a helmsman, another a lookout man, and another has some other such title), it is clear both that the most accurate account of their virtue will be peculiar to each, and similarly that there will be some common account that fits them all. For they all have as their work the safety of the voyage (for that is what each of the sailors desires). In like manner, then, the citizens, though being dissimilar to each other, have the safety of the community as their work, and this community is the regime. Hence the virtue of the citizen must be relative to the regime.

That the Virtue of Both Cannot in Every Case Be the Same. *The virtue of both is not always the same, for the following reasons: (i) there are several regimes, so the virtue of the citizen, which is relative to regimes, will be manifold, while that of the man is single; (ii) if no city can be composed of only good men and if all citizens in the best city must be good, then they cannot all be good with the virtue of the good man;*

---

18. Why the virtue of man and citizen should be relevant at this point is not stated, but the following may be suggested. Aristotle is turning now to consider disputes about the citizen. Those, however, who, like the opponents of Cleisthenes, wish to deny citizenship to slaves and aliens appeal to principles of justice. That is, they argue, apparently, that such cannot justly be made citizens because they do not deserve to be citizens, and they do not deserve to be citizens because they are not good men. The dispute, therefore, requires Aristotle to consider what desert for citizenship consists in and how it compares with being a good man—in short, to consider the virtue of man and of citizen. Note also that he uses two words for virtuous man and citizen in this chapter: the regular word for "good" (*agathos*) and another word, *spoudaios*, which means "serious" or perhaps also "serious-minded." A virtuous man or citizen may be called *spoudaios* because he takes being a citizen or a man seriously enough to have acquired the necessary virtues.

19. Getting some grasp of the virtue of a man is presumably not necessary, as that has already been done in the *Ethics*.

(iii) the city is composed of dissimilars, so if all citizens in the best city must be good, they cannot all be good with one and the same virtue.

1276b31 Consequently, if there are several kinds of regime, the complete virtue of the serious citizen clearly cannot be a single one. But the good man we do say is good by reference to a single complete virtue.[20] So it is manifest, therefore, that a citizen can be serious without having acquired the virtue by which a man is serious.

1276b35 But one can, by raising difficulties also in another way, carry over this same discussion to the best regime. For if it is impossible for a city to be composed of only those who are serious but it is necessary for each to do his own work well—that is to say, with virtue—then, since all the citizens cannot be alike, there could not be one virtue for citizen and good man. For the virtue of the serious citizen must be possessed by them all (this is what is necessary to make the city best), but the virtue of the good man cannot be, unless all the citizens in the serious city must necessarily be good men.

1277a5 Again, since the city is composed of dissimilars (I mean that just as the immediate constituents of an animal are soul and body, of the soul reason and appetite, of the household man and woman, of property master and slave, so also in the same way the city is composed both of all these and of other dissimilar kinds in addition), then necessarily the citizens cannot all have one virtue just as neither can the head and file leader in a chorus.[21]

1277a12 That therefore the virtue of man and citizen are not simply the same is manifest from these considerations.

That the Virtue of Both Can in Some Cases Be the Same. *The virtue is the same in the case of the good ruler and politician, who are not only citizens but citizens with the virtue of the good man, namely prudence, as accepted opinions suggest. Other opinions suggest that the good citizen must, in addition to the virtue of ruling, also have the virtue of being ruled. But this must be understood not of despotic rule but only of political rule, where the virtue of ruling politically is acquired through the*

---

20. There is dispute here about the Greek and how to take it. Some translate more along these lines: "the virtue of the serious citizen cannot be a single and complete virtue, but the virtue of the good man is a single virtue, the complete virtue." I follow a variant in the manuscripts and omit *tēn* ("the" in "the complete virtue"), and translate the way I do to bring out the fact that if the citizen's virtue is relative to the regime, then the complete realization of this virtue will be relative to the regime as well, so that citizen virtue will admit of as many complete realizations as there are regimes. By contrast, the virtue of the good man will admit of only one complete realization, namely that relative to human nature.

21. A chorus had one overall head, but each of the files into which it was divided had a leader subordinate to the head. Since the functions of head and leader were different, so would be the virtues or excellences that made each perform their function well.

virtue of being ruled politically. A man is a good citizen if he possesses the virtue of ruling and being ruled, and he is a good man if he possesses the virtue of ruling.

1277a13 But will there then be anyone whose virtue is the same both as serious citizen and as serious man? Well, we say that the serious ruler is good and prudent and that the politician must be prudent.²² Also, some say that the education of a ruler is different right from the start, as is in fact conspicuous from the way the sons of kings are educated in the arts of riding and war. And there is the saying of Euripides "nothing exquisite for me but what the city needs,"²³ the assumption behind which is that there is a certain education for rulers.

1277a20 But if the virtue of good ruler and good man is the same, and if a citizen is also someone who is ruled, then the virtue of man and citizen would not simply be the same (though it would be in the case of a certain citizen), for the virtue of ruler and citizen would not be the same. That is perhaps why Jason²⁴ said he was hungry when he was not being tyrant, because he did not know how to be a private individual. And yet praise is at any rate bestowed on the ability to rule and be ruled, and being able to do both of them nobly seems to be the virtue of a citizen. So if we lay it down that the good man's virtue is the virtue of the ruler but the citizen's includes both, then the two virtues would not be equally praiseworthy.²⁵ Since, therefore, there are these two views—that the ruler and ruled should learn different things and not the same, and that the citizen should know and share both—what follows might now be apparent.

1277a33 For there is a despotic kind of rule, a kind we say concerns necessities, those necessities that the ruler need not know how to produce but rather how to use.²⁶ Knowing the first—I mean being able to do and actually doing servile actions—is quite slavish. But there are, we say, several kinds of slave, since the works they do are several, of which one part is performed by manual workers, those who, as even their name indicates, live from the work of their hands. Among these is included the artisan mechanic, which is why among some in olden times craftsmen did not have any share in rule

22. Reading *politikon* ("politician") with the manuscripts. If one reads the emendation *politēn ouk*, followed by Dreizehnter, the sense is ". . . but that the citizen need not be prudent." The emendation, however, seems unnecessary. Aristotle is just answering his own question by saying, in effect, that the virtue by which the ruler and politician are good makes them to be good men (for prudence is the mark of the good man) and also to be good citizens (for this same prudence is what enables them to do their job in the city well, namely ruling it).

23. Frag. 16 Nauck. Probably words of king Aeolus about the upbringing of his sons.

24. Tyrant of Pherae in Thessaly in the early part of the fourth century.

25. That is, the virtue of being ruled would not be as praiseworthy as the virtue of ruling.

26. Cf. 1.7.

until the ultimate democracy came along. The work performed by those ruled in this way should not be learnt by the good man nor by the politician nor by the good citizen, except in case of need for himself alone (for then it is no longer the case that one is master and another slave).[27]

1277b7 But there is a sort of rule exercised over those who are similar in birth and free. This rule we call political rule, and the ruler must learn it by being ruled, just as one learns to be a cavalry commander by serving under a cavalry commander, or to be general over an army by serving under a general and commanding a regiment and a company. Hence it was nobly said that one cannot rule well without having been ruled. And while virtue in these two cases is different, the good citizen must learn and be able both to be ruled and to rule. This is, in fact, the virtue of a citizen, to know rule over the free from both sides.

1277b16 Indeed, the good man too possesses both. Even if there is a difference in the kind of moderation and justice involved in ruling (for they are also different in the case of someone ruled but free), it is clear that the good man's virtue—justice, for example—would not be single but divided into kinds: one whereby he will rule and another whereby he will be ruled. The difference will be like that between a man's moderation and courage and a woman's. For a man who was courageous in the way a woman is would seem a coward, and a woman who was adorned in speech the way a man is would seem a chatterbox[28] (since it is also the case that household management is different for the two of them, it being his work to acquire and hers to guard). But prudence alone is a virtue proper to the ruler. For all the other virtues would seem necessarily to belong in common to ruler and ruled, but there is no virtue of prudence in the case of someone who is being ruled; he has right opinion instead. For the ruled is like the pipe maker, but the ruler is like the pipe player who uses him.[29]

1277b30 So then, whether the virtue of a good man is the same as that of a serious citizen or different, and how it is the same and how different, is clear from the above.[30]

---

27. Cf. 1.13.1260a39-b1, 4(7).14.1333a3-11, and 5(8).2.1337b15-21.

28. Cf. 1.13.1260a14-31.

29. That is, uses him to make pipes. The pipe player knows, from the nature of his art, what sort of job he needs his instrument to do, and the pipe maker simply has to make pipes to do the job that the player tells him he wants.

30. The virtue is the same because both good man and good citizen possess the virtue of ruling and of being ruled, but it is different because what makes the good man good is ruling virtue alone (ruled virtue he has only because that was the way he acquired ruling virtue), while what makes the good citizen good is both ruled and ruling virtue together.

CHAPTER 5

Citizenship and Virtue of the Vulgar

Preliminary Discussion. *The dispute over whether vulgar mechanics are to count as citizens, raises, in the way it gets posed, no real problem at all. For if they are not citizens, they can still be counted as belonging to the city without being citizens of it; and if they are citizens, then the virtue just described will not belong to every citizen.*

1277b33 A certain difficulty about the citizen still remains.[31] For is the citizen really someone who is entitled to share in rule, or are vulgar mechanics also to be set down as citizens? Well, if these also are to be set down as citizens who have no share in offices, then the kind of virtue just discussed cannot belong to every citizen (for these will then be citizens). But if none of these sort is a citizen, into which part of the city must they each be put, for they are neither resident aliens nor foreigners?

1277b39 Or shall we respond that, from this argument at least, nothing strange follows, because neither slaves nor freedmen are among the groups just mentioned? For the truth is that not everyone without whom a city could not be is to be regarded as a citizen of it, since not even children are citizens in the same way as men are, but the latter are citizens simply and the former only on the basis of a supposition (they are citizens all right, but incomplete ones). So among some in ancient times, vulgar mechanics were slaves or foreigners, which is why many are so still. The best city will not make citizens of mechanics, but if they are citizens, then the virtue of a citizen, which we were just talking about,[32] must not be predicated of every citizen, nor indeed of the free only, but only of those who are released from works of necessity. And as regards these works of necessity, those who perform them for one man are slaves and those who do them for the community are vulgar mechanics and laborers.

Determinative Answer. *The truth is that there are several regimes, and in some of them, as in aristocracies, mechanics and laborers, who are bound to slavish work and are incapable of virtue, could not be citizens, but in others they could be, as in democracies and certain oligarchies. Properly speaking, the citizen is anyone who, whatever the regime may be, is entitled to shares in rule. But only in some regimes would the citizen have the virtue that makes the good man, and then only in his capacity as ruler.*

1278a13 But how things stand in these cases will be manifest if we take the investigation a little further from this point. In fact, the statement already

---

31. 3.1.1275a2–5, 26–28.
32. That is, the virtue of ruling and being ruled discussed in the previous chapter.

given makes the thing clear.³³ For since there are several regimes, there must be several kinds of citizen, and especially of the citizen when he is being ruled. Consequently the vulgar mechanic and the laborer must be citizens in some regime but could not be in certain others—for example, in any regime called an aristocracy and where the honors of office are given in accordance with virtue and merit. For it is impossible to practice the works of virtue while leading the life of a mechanic or laborer.

1278a21 In oligarchies, however, while laborers could not be citizens (for here sharing in office is based on high property assessments), vulgar mechanics could be, since among the wealthy are also many artisans (in Thebes there was a law that anyone who had not kept away from the market for ten years did not share in office). In many regimes the law includes foreigners as well, for certain democracies make the son of a citizen mother a citizen, and many of them do the same for bastards. Nevertheless, since it is from a want of legitimate children that they make citizens of these types (lack of human beings is what drives them so to use the laws), when they have a sufficient crowd to be well-off in this regard, they take away the privilege little by little, first from those born to a slave father or mother and then from those born to citizen mothers, until finally they make citizens only of those born to citizens on both sides.³⁴

1278a34 Therefore, it is clear from these considerations that there are several kinds of citizens and that he is said to be a citizen most of all who shares in the honors of office, as even Homer wrote in the verse "like some vagabond without honor," ³⁵ for one who has no share in honors is indeed like an alien. But where this fact is hidden it is for the sake of deceiving fellow inhabitants.³⁶

1278a40 So whether the virtue by which a good man is also a serious citizen is the same or different is clear from what has been said, because in one city both are the same person, but in another different; and that person is not just anyone but is the politician and the one who exercises control, or is able to exercise control, either by himself or along with others, over the care of common matters.

33. The statement in chapter 1 at 1275b3-20, that who is a citizen differs from regime to regime.

34. Aristotle probably has in mind here what happened in Athens from Cleisthenes to Pericles (*Athēnaiōn Politeia* 26).

35. *Iliad* 9.648.

36. As in the case of the sophism used by the Cretans (2.5.1264a19-22).

CHAPTER 6

Definition and Division of Regime

Definition of Regime. *A regime is the arrangement of a city's ruling offices and especially of its controlling office.*

1278b6 Since these matters have been determined, it is necessary to examine what comes next—namely whether one or several regimes are to be posited, and, if several, which they are, how many in number, and with what distinguishing characteristics.

1278b8 A regime is the way a city is arranged both with respect to its other offices and, above all, with respect to the office that has control over all the rest. For everywhere the ruling body has control in the city, and the ruling body is the regime. I mean, for example, that while in democracies the populace has control, in oligarchies, by contrast, the few have it, and we also say that these have a different regime. We shall speak in the same manner about the other regimes as well.

Division of Regime

First Part of the Division. *Human beings are political animals and desire to live together for its own sake and for the sake of the noble; even life itself is desired because of its nobility. So, such living together nobly is the goal of the city. Also, rule is divided into despotic rule, which is for the benefit of the master who rules, and political rule, which is for the benefit of the ruled. Regimes are correct when the rulers rule the city (which is a community of the free) for the common advantage, and incorrect when they rule for their own advantage alone.*

1278b15 The purpose a city is constituted to serve must first be set down, as must also the number of different kinds of rule there are when it comes to human beings and their sharing life together.

1278b17 Indeed, in the first discourses, where things to do with household management and mastery were determined, it was also stated that by nature human beings are political animals.[37] Hence, even when they are not in need of each others' help, they have no less desire to live together, though it is also true that the common advantage draws them into union insofar as noble living is something they each partake of. So this above all is the end, whether for everyone in common or for each singly. On the other hand, they also come together and maintain the political community for the sake of life alone. For perhaps there is something of the noble even in life taken by

37. I.2.1253a1–18.

itself, unless, in the way it is lived, the hardships are overly excessive. Clearly, most humans put up with a lot of pain and suffering in their effort to cling on to life, as if it contained in itself some natural gladness and sweetness.

1278b30 Dividing the kinds of rule we commonly speak of is also easy, since in our external discourses too[38] we often distinguish between them. For the despotic rule of a master (although in truth the natural slave and natural master have the same advantage) is nevertheless still exercised for the advantage of the master and for that of the slave incidentally (mastery cannot be preserved if the slave is destroyed). Rule over children, on the other hand, and over wife and the household generally, which we call household management, is either for the sake of the ruled or of something common to both. As such, it is for the sake of the ruled—as we see to be the case with the other arts, like medicine and gymnastics—but incidentally it might also be for the sake of the rulers as well. For nothing prevents the physical trainer being himself also sometimes one of the trained, in the same way that the helmsman is also one of the sailors. The trainer or helmsman looks to the good of those he rules, but when he becomes one of them himself as well, he shares incidentally in the assistance he gives. For the latter is a sailor, and the former, though trainer, becomes one of the trained.

1279a8 Hence also in the case of political office, when the city has been set up on the basis of an equality and likeness among the citizens, they think it right to rule by turns. In former times they supposed, according to what was natural, that when someone was taking his turn in performing public service he should look to their good just as they, when ruling previously, had looked to his advantage. But now, on account of the profits they get from the common funds and from office, they want to go on ruling continually, as if they were sick and always being in office made them healthy (for that is perhaps how the sick in such a case would pursue office).[39]

1279a17 So it is manifest that all regimes that look to the common advantage turn out, according to what is simply just, to be correct ones, while those that look only to the advantage of the rulers are mistaken and are all deviations from the correct regimes. For they are despotic, but the city is a community of the free.

---

38. That is, not only earlier on in this treatise (1.5.1254b2–14). What these external discourses were is not clear, but they were probably the dialogues that Aristotle wrote and which seem to have been for more popular consumption outside his school. Unfortunately, only fragments of them now survive.

39. A reference, perhaps, to the tyrant Jason (3.4.1277a24–25).

CHAPTER 7

Second Part of the Division. *The regime is the ruling body and as this must be composed of one or few or many, there will be three correct regimes—kingship, aristocracy, and polity, in which respectively the one, few, or many virtuous rule for the common advantage—and three deviations from these—tyranny, oligarchy, and democracy, in which the one, the well-off, or the needy rule for their own advantage.*

1279a22 With these distinctions in place, the next thing to examine is how many and which the regimes are, first of all as regards those among them that are correct, for the deviations will be manifest once these have been defined. Since regime and ruling body signify the same thing, and since the ruling body is what has control in cities and either one or few or the many must have control, then, whenever the one, the few, or the many rule for the common advantage, the respective regimes must be correct ones. Those, conversely, that are for the private advantage of the one, the few, or the multitude must be deviations (for either participants should not be called citizens or they should share together in the advantage).

1279a32 The regime among monarchies that looks to the common advantage we are accustomed to call kingship, and the regime among those ruled by a few (but more than one) that does the same we call aristocracy (either because the best rule or because they rule with a view to what is best for the city and for those who share it).[40] But when the multitude govern for the common advantage, the regime is called by the name common to all regimes, namely polity.[41] These appellations arise reasonably enough because while it is possible for one or a few to stand out in virtue,[42] it is hard for a larger number to reach perfection in every virtue.[43] They can, however, reach perfection where military virtue in particular is concerned, for that virtue does arise in a multitude. Hence, in this regime, the fighting element and those who possess the arms have the most control.

1279b4 Deviations from these are tyranny from kingship, oligarchy from aristocracy, and democracy from polity. For tyranny is rule by one man for the advantage of himself, oligarchy is for the advantage of the well-off, and democracy is for the advantage of the needy. None of them is for what is profitable in common.

40. Aristocracy means literally "best rule" or "rule of the best."

41. The word translated here as "polity" is the same as the word normally translated as "regime" (*politeia*); see remarks in the introduction, p. xxvii.

42. And so to be, and deserve to be called, the best.

43. Thus, their regime cannot be given a name signifying perfection, nor can it be given a name signifying deviance (for it is not a deviant regime). It can only be given a name that is neutral or signifies simply correctness, which "polity" does.

CHAPTER 8

Confirmation of the Division against Certain Difficulties

First Difficulty: Whether the Deviant Regimes Are Rightly Defined. *There arise certain difficulties about this division, which need investigation. The first concerns whether the deviant regimes are rightly defined as despotic and are rightly distinguished by the number of those who have control in them.*

1279b11 There is need to speak a little more at length about what each of these regimes is, for certain difficulties arise, and when one is treating each subject matter philosophically, not merely with an eye to action, it is proper not to overlook or omit anything but, in each case, to make the truth clear. **1279b15** Tyranny is, as was said, a monarchy that rules the political community despotically like a master; oligarchy does the same when those with possessions have control of the regime; and democracy, on the contrary, does it when those who do not possess a multitude of possessions but are needy have control. The first difficulty concerns the matter of definition. **1279b20** For suppose the majority were well-off and had control of the city, and yet there is a democracy when the multitude is in control. Or again suppose similarly that the needy were fewer than the well-off but were stronger and had control of the regime, and yet there is an oligarchy, they say, when a small number is in control. Then the regimes would appear not to be nobly defined. Even if one were to combine the criteria—fewness with that of being well-off in the one case and numbers with that of neediness in the other—and were accordingly to call the regime oligarchy when the well-off who are few in numbers possess the offices and democracy when the needy who are many do so, still one is only raising another difficulty. For what are we to call the regimes in question, those where the well-off are the majority and the needy a minority but each has control of its own regime—if, that is, no other regime exists besides those just spoken of? [44]

First Part of the Solution: Quantity and Quality in the Definition. *Oligarchy and democracy are not properly differentiated according to the fewness or manyness of the rulers. These are only differences that incidentally, though everywhere, follow the essential differences of wealth and poverty.*

1279b34 Well, what this discussion seems to make clear is that its being the few or many who are in control, the few in oligarchies and the many in democracies, is something incidental, a result of the fact that everywhere the well-off are few and the needy many. That is why the reasons just mentioned

---

44. That is, the six set down in chapter 7.

in fact fail to make a difference. What do differentiate democracy and oligarchy from each other are poverty and wealth; necessarily, wherever rule is exercised on account of wealth, whether by few or many, there is oligarchy, and wherever by the needy, democracy. But, as we said, the former turn out to be few and the latter many, for few get to be well-off but all share in freedom, and these are the reasons they each use to dispute about the regime.

CHAPTER 9

Second Part of the Solution: Despotism in the Definition

That Oligarchic and Democratic Justice Are Partial. *Oligarchy and democracy are deviant regimes because their understanding of justice is partial. Justice does indeed require equality and inequality in the things to be shared, but only in the case of equal and unequal persons. Democrats and oligarchs take equality and inequality partially and suppose that because they are equal or unequal in one thing they are equal or unequal simply. But they fail to say what is most decisive in determining equality and inequality.*

1280a7 First one must grasp what are the defining marks they allege for oligarchy and democracy and what oligarchic and what democratic justice are. For they all get hold of justice of a sort, but only go so far and do not speak of the whole of what is just in the authoritative sense. For instance, justice seems to be equality and it is, but not for all, only for equals; justice also seems to be inequality for in fact it is, but not for all, only for unequals. They, however, dispense with the "for whom" and judge badly.[45] The reason is that their judgment concerns themselves and by and large most people are base judges when it comes to what is their own.

1280a16 Consequently, since what is just is just for certain persons and is divided with respect to the things in the same way as it is for the persons (as was said before in the *Ethics*),[46] they agree about equality in the case of the thing but dispute about it in the case of the persons.[47] They do so mainly

45. They do not dispense with the "for whom" by failing to mention it, for in fact both sides mention the free or the rich as those for whom justice is equality or inequality. Rather they dispense with it by failing to justify or discuss it and by assuming their own view of it instead. Hence both here, and in chapters 12 and 13 below, Aristotle spends much time showing who the "for whom" should really be or in what political equality and inequality properly consist.

46. *Ethics* 5.3. Each person gets an equal or unequal share of the things in proportion to the equality or inequality of his desert.

47. That is, they agree that equal shares should go to equals and unequal shares to unequals, but they disagree about whether they themselves are equal or unequal.

for the reason just given, that they are judging badly about what concerns themselves, but they also suppose that, because they are both speaking up to a point about justice in a sense, they are speaking about justice simply. For the one group think that if they are unequal in some respect—for example, money[48]—they are altogether unequal, while the other group think that if they are equal in some respect—for example, freedom—they are altogether equal. But the thing that has most authority they do not mention.

Why Oligarchic and Democratic Justice Are Partial. *Those who contribute most to the end of the city deserve greater shares. However, if the city existed only for life and not good life, as the oligarchic argument implies, there could be a city of slaves and animals. If it existed as an alliance for defense and commerce, as both the oligarchic and democratic arguments imply, those bound by treaties would be one city, whereas they are not one city and are distinguished from the city by having neither common offices nor the concern for virtue. Were this not so, "city" would just be another name for an alliance, as is manifest from the fact that an alliance having everything cities have, save in not advancing beyond a defensive and commercial contract, is still only an alliance and not a city. Defensive and commercial contracts and the sharing of place and intermarriage are necessary for a city, but in a city, as opposed to an alliance, these become occasions for friendship, and friendship belongs to living well and nobly, not to life alone. So the end of the city is noble life, and those deserve greater shares who contribute most to noble deeds, namely those who are superior in virtue, not those who are equal or superior in freedom or family or wealth.*

1280a25 For suppose people came together and shared in common for the sake of possessions; then they would have as much share in the city as they also had of property, and the oligarchic argument would, as a result, seem a strong one. Certainly it is not just that one who has contributed a single mina to a sum of one hundred minas should have equal shares in that sum, either of the capital or of the proceeds, with one who has contributed all the rest.

1280a31 It is not the case, however, that people come together for the sake of life alone but rather for the sake of living well. Otherwise, there would be a city of slaves and the other animals, whereas in fact there is not, because these share neither in happiness nor in a life lived according to deliberate choice.

1280a34 Nor do people come together for the sake of an alliance to prevent themselves from being wronged by anyone, nor again for purposes of exchange and mutual utility. Otherwise, the Etruscans and Carthaginians and all those who have treaties with each other would be citizens of one

48. Or, more generally, commodities (*chrēmata*).

city. True, they have agreements about imports, treaties about refraining from injustice, and written compacts about military alliance, but there are no offices that they all have in common set up to deal with these matters; instead, each has different ones. Nor are they concerned about what each other's character should be, not even with the aim of preventing anyone subject to the agreements from becoming unjust or acquiring a single depraved habit. They are concerned only that they should not do any wrong to each other. But all those who are concerned about a good state of law concentrate their attention on political virtue and vice, from which it is manifest that the city truly and not verbally so called must make virtue its care.

1280b8 For otherwise the community becomes an alliance that differs only in location from other alliances (those between allies who are far away), and the law becomes a treaty and a guarantor, as Lycophron the sophist[49] said, of each other's rights, but not such as to make the citizens good and just. And that this is how things stand is manifest. For if one were to bring the cities of the Megarians and Corinthians together geographically such that they touched at their walls,[50] still it would not be one city. Nor would it be so even if they intermarried with each other (though this practice is one of the ways of sharing together that is peculiar to cities). The same would be true if there were some who, while having separate dwellings, were nevertheless not at so great a distance that they shared nothing in common but had laws about not doing each other wrong in their commercial dealings (say, if one was a carpenter, another a farmer, another a shoemaker, another something else of the sort, and their number was 10,000). Not even in this case would there yet be a city if they shared nothing else in common besides such things as exchange and alliance. But why ever not? Surely not because of lack of physical proximity in their community. For suppose that, while sharing things in common in this way, they were to join together but everyone used his own household like a city and came to each other's aid only against wrongdoers, as in a defensive alliance. Even then, if one reflected accurately on the case, they would not seem to be a city, so long, that is, as they went on associating in the same way when together as when apart.

1280b29 It is manifest, then, that a city is not a matter of sharing a place in common or for the purpose of not doing each other wrong and for commerce. Rather, while these things must be present if there is to be a city, not even when they all are present is there yet a city, but only when households and families form a community in living well for the sake of a complete and self-sufficient existence. Such life will not be possible, however, unless they

---

49. Little is known about Lycophron, but he may have been a pupil of Gorgias.
50. Corinth and Megara lay not far distant from each other on either side of the Corinthian Isthmus.

do inhabit one and the same location and engage in intermarriage. That is why in cities marriage connections arose, as well as clans and sacrifices and the cultured pursuits [51] involved in living together. Such things are the work of friendship, for the deliberate choice to live together is friendship. The end, then, of the city is living well, but these other things are for the sake of the end, and a city is the community of families and villages in a complete and self-sufficient life, which, we say, is living happily and nobly.

1281a2 So the political community must be set down as existing for the sake of noble deeds and not merely for living together. Hence those who contribute most to such a community have more of a share in the city than those who are equal or greater in freedom or family but unequal in political virtue, or than those who exceed in wealth but are exceeded in virtue. Therefore, that those who dispute about the city all speak of justice in some partial way is manifest from what has been said.

CHAPTER 10

Second Difficulty: Whether Any of the Regimes Is Correct

Statement of the Difficulty. *None of the candidates for having control in the city (and by which the regimes are distinguished) seems satisfactory, since injustice must result in some cases and disenfranchisement in others; and putting the law in control instead raises the same difficulties in another way.*

1281a11 A difficulty arises as to what should be the controlling part of the city, for it is really either the multitude or the rich or the decent or the best one of all or a tyrant. But all of them appear unsatisfactory. How so? Suppose the poor, because they are the majority, divide up the property of the wealthy; is this not unjust? "By Zeus, it seemed justly done to those in control." [52] What else, then, are we to call the ultimate injustice? Or again, if a majority, having got their hands on everything, should distribute the possessions of the few, they are manifestly ruining the city. But virtue assuredly does not ruin what has it, nor is justice destructive of the city. This law, then, clearly cannot be just. In addition, any deeds done by the tyrant must all be just as well, for he uses his superior strength to get his way, just as the multitude do against the rich.

---

51. The Greek is *diagōgē*, a term that figures significantly in the discussion of education in book 5(8).

52. This sentence is in quotes because it is the imagined reply of the democrats to the charge that the many poor are acting unjustly in dividing the property of the rich.

1281a24 But in that case is it just for the minority and the rich to rule? So if these also do the same things and ravage and take away the possessions of the multitude, it will be just? It was just, then, also in the other case. Manifestly, therefore, all these things are base and not just.

1281a28 But should the decent sort rule and have control over everything? In that case, everyone else, not being privileged with political office, will be deprived of honors. For offices, we say, are honors, and when the same people are always ruling, the rest must necessarily be deprived of honors.

1281a32 So is it better for rule to be in the hands of the single most serious man? But this is even more oligarchic, since those deprived of honors are more numerous.

1281a34 Perhaps, however, someone might say that it is a base thing for a human being generally to be in control (at least when he has the passions incident to the soul) and not the law.[53] So if the law is oligarchic or democratic, how will that make any difference as far as the present difficulties are concerned? For what we have just been talking about will happen all the same.

CHAPTER 11

Partial Solution Specific to Polity

Statement and Illustration of the Solution. *It might seem obvious that the many should not be in control rather than the few best, but in fact the many, taken as a whole, might be better than the few best. In such cases they should indeed be in control, but collectively (as over elections and the auditing of offices) and not singly.*

1281a39 About the other cases there will be some discussion later,[54] but the view would seem to be refuted[55] and involved in some difficulty that says the multitude should be in control rather than the few best. Perhaps, however, it might also seem to have truth to it.

1281a42 For the many, each of whom is not a serious man, nevertheless could, when they have come together, be better than those few best—not, indeed, individually but as a whole, just as meals furnished collectively are

53. This may be a reference to Plato *Laws* 713c2–715d6.
54. In chapters 12 and 13.
55. There is some dispute about how to read the text here, and many are inclined to suspect a lacuna or a corruption. I think the Greek can be given an acceptable sense as it stands and I translate accordingly. I take Aristotle to be saying that while this particular view (that the many should rule in place of the few best) seems clearly false and involved in an obvious difficulty (for how could the few best not be better rulers than the many who are not best at all?); nevertheless, it could in some cases be true, namely in the cases he goes on to explain.

better than meals furnished at one person's expense. For each of them, though many, could have a part of virtue and prudence, and just as they could, when joined together in a multitude, become one human being with many feet, hands, and senses, so also could they become one in character and thought. That is why the many are better judges of the works of music and the poets, for one of them judges one part and another another and all of them the whole.

1281b10 Serious men do, however, differ from the many taken singly in this respect, namely that they bring what is scattered about into one, in the same way that the noble are also said to differ from those who are not noble and as artistic paintings are said to differ from the real thing—for at any rate, when each part is taken separately, the eye of this person and some other part of someone else are more noble than the ones in the painting.

1281b15 Now whether this superiority of the many relative to the few serious can exist in the case of any populace and any multitude is unclear, though, by Zeus, it is perhaps clear that it cannot in the case of some of them. Otherwise, the same argument could also be made to fit beasts, and how, practically speaking, do some people differ from beasts? But nothing prevents what has been said from being true of some multitude.

1281b21 Thus one might, by these means, solve the aforementioned difficulty [56] and also the one connected with it, namely over what things the free and the mass of the citizens (all such as are neither rich nor can make even a single claim deriving from virtue) should have control. For if they shared in the greatest offices, it would not be safe, since, on account of their injustice and unwisdom, they would do wrong in some things and go wrong in others. [57] If, on the other hand, they were given no share and had no participation in office, it would be cause for alarm, since the city that has many in it who lack honor and are poor must of necessity be full of enemies.

1281b31 What is left, then, is that they participate in deliberation and judgment, which is why both Solon [58] and certain other legislators arrange for them to elect and audit the rulers but do not let them exercise office singly. For their perception is adequate when they all come together, and when they are combined with the best, they actually help their cities, in the same way that raw food combined with wholesome makes the total amount more useful than a small quantity of the latter would be by itself. In separation, however, each of them lacks the completeness necessary for passing judgment.

---

56. The one mentioned at the beginning of the chapter about how the many could be in control rather than the few best.

57. An example might be the ephorate in Sparta (2.9.1270b6–35).

58. See 2.12.1273b15–21.

Answer to Objections. *The first difficulty with this arrangement is that as in the other arts it is experts who judge and choose experts, so also should it be in judging and choosing rulers. However, the multitude may be an expert in the relevant sense; moreover, in some arts it is not the expert who judges the product but the user, and the user need not possess the art. The second difficulty is that it seems strange to give inferior persons more control than decent ones. But again: the multitude might, as a whole, be superior to the decent few. The first difficulty points to the fact that in these cases well-laid laws should rule. But as laws are relative to the regimes, the question as to which laws these are returns to the question of which regimes are correct.*

1281b38 The first difficulty that confronts such a way of arranging the regime is the following. To judge who has correctly administered a cure for a given disease would seem to be something that belongs to the same person to whom it also belongs to cure and make healthy anyone suffering from that disease—the doctor, in other words. The same would seem to hold of the other sorts of experience and arts. Therefore, just as a doctor must give an account of himself before doctors, so it should be before their peers that others should also give their account. Doctor, of course, includes both the practitioner,[59] the consultant,[60] and anyone educated in the art.[61] For persons of this last sort are in fact found in just about any art, and we allow judgment to the educated no less than to the experts.

1282a7 The same thing, then, would seem to hold also in the case of elections, for choosing rightly is also the work of experts, as choosing a geometrician is the work of experts in geometry and choosing a pilot is that of experts in navigation. For even if some laymen are also involved in the choosing when it comes to certain works and arts, yet they do not have a greater share than the experts. Consequently, by this argument, the multitude ought not to be given control either over the election of officials or over the auditing of accounts.

1282a14 Perhaps, however, not everything here is nobly said. For there is the earlier argument[62] that, provided the multitude are not too slavish, each may be a worse judge than the experts but, when gathered together, they will be better or not worse. Also, in the case of some arts (the ones in which those who do not possess the art can also appreciate the works produced), it is not only the maker who might be the best judge. Appreciating a house, for example, does not just belong to the builder; the one who uses it, namely the household manager, will pass an even better judgment on it. Likewise,

59. The Greek word is *dēmiourgos*, literally "craftsman" or "artisan."
60. The Greek word is *architektonikos* or someone with the quality of the ruling craftsman.
61. Educated in the art but not, presumably, now practicing as a doctor.
62. At the beginning of this chapter.

the pilot judges the rudder better than the carpenter and the dinner guest judges the feast better than the chef.

1282a23 Such, then, is perhaps a sufficient refutation of this difficulty. But there is another connected with it. For it seems strange that inferior types should have control over greater things than the decent. But the auditing of accounts and elections to office are very great things, which in some regimes, as was said, are given over to the populace. For all such matters are in the hands of the assembly, even though those who meet low property qualifications and are of any age are members of it and deliberate and pass judgment, while the treasurers and generals and all who exercise the greatest offices meet high qualifications.

1282a33 But one can in fact also answer this difficulty in the same way, since this practice does perhaps have something correct to it. For it is not the juror or the councilman or the assemblyman who is ruling but the jury court, the council, and the assembly, and each of the aforementioned is a part of these. By part I mean the councilman, the assemblyman, and the juror. Consequently, the multitude justly has control over greater matters, for the populace, the council, and the jury court are composed of many, and the property qualification of all these is higher than that of those who singly or as a small group occupy the great offices.

1282a41 So let our determination of these matters stand thus. But the first mentioned difficulty[63] makes nothing else so manifest as that laws rightly legislated should be in control and that the officeholder, whether he be one or many, should have control over only those things about which the laws—because of the difficulty of giving clear declarations in universal terms about everything—cannot speak with precision.

1282b6 It is not yet clear, however, what rightly legislated laws should be like, and the difficulty stated before remains.[64] For the laws must necessarily be base or serious, just or unjust, like the regimes. Still, this fact, at least, is clear: the laws must be laid down with a view to the regimes. But then, if that is true, clearly laws in accordance with the correct regimes must be just, and those in accordance with the deviant regimes not just.

---

63. The first in this section, about its being the job of the expert to judge experts.
64. At the end of chapter 10 at 1281a34–39.

CHAPTER 12

Complete Solution General to All Regimes

Who May Justly Make Claims to Rule. The end or good in politics is justice or the common advantage. Justice is equal shares for equals, but who is equal and who unequal must not be overlooked. Those superior in any good at all are not thereby unequal, since some goods are manifestly irrelevant. For instance, as regards pipe playing, (i) those equal in the art but superior in other goods do not thereby deserve the better pipes; (ii) those superior in the art but inferior in other goods do still deserve the better pipes; (iii) if the other goods were as much a claim, then all goods would be commensurable. Goods that justly ground claims to shares in office are those relevant to the city: birth and freedom and wealth as regards its existence, virtue as regards its good management.

1282b14 Since the end in every science and art is some good, it will be greatest and most especially good in the science or art that has the most control among them all, and this is the political capability. But the political good is justice, and justice is the common advantage.

1282b18 Everyone is of the view that justice is something equal, and, up to a point anyway, they agree with our philosophical discussions in which ethical questions were determined.[65] For they say that justice is something for someone and that it should be something equal for those who are equal. But what the equality and inequality consist in should not be overlooked,[66] because there is a difficulty here and matter for political philosophy.

1282b23 Someone might perhaps say that, provided people are in all other respects not different but alike, superiority in any good at all requires an unequal distribution of offices, because where the persons differ, so does justice and what they deserve. However, if this be true, then those who excel in color or height or any other good whatever would have the advantage in claims to political rights, and surely the falsehood here is plain to see. The thing is manifest in the case of the other sciences and abilities: pipe players who are equal in the art are not to be given an advantage in pipes just because they are of better family, for they are not going to play the pipes any better. It is the one who is superior in the work who should also get the superior instruments.

1282b34 If what has been said is not yet clear, it will become so if we push the example further. Suppose there is someone who is superior in the art

---

65. Principally *Ethics* 5.4–6.
66. The fault, of course, of those criticized in chapter 9 above.

of pipe playing but is far surpassed in good birth or beauty. Then even if each of these, I mean good birth and beauty, is greater as a good than pipe playing and exceeds pipe playing by a greater proportion than he exceeds in pipe playing, he should still get the superior pipes. Otherwise, superiority in wealth and good birth would have to contribute something to the work, but they contribute nothing.

1283a3 Further, according to the above argument, every good would be commensurable with every other. For suppose a certain size counted as more,[67] then size generally would come into competition with both wealth and freedom.[68] So if this person excels in size more than that person excels in virtue, and if superiority in size generally is of more weight than superiority in virtue, then all goods would be commensurable. For if this much size is better than this much virtue, then clearly that much is equal to it.[69]

1283a9 But as such a result is impossible, it is clear that in politics too people behave reasonably in not basing their disputes about office on any inequality whatever. For if some are slow and others swift, that is no reason for the latter to have more and the former less (gymnastic contests are where such a difference carries off the honors). Rather the dispute must be based on what a city is constituted from. Hence, reasonably do the well-born, the free, and the rich make claims to the honor of office. For both the free and the owners of taxable property are needed, since a city could not be made up entirely of the needy any more than of slaves. But, more to the point, if there is need of these qualities, then there is clearly also need of justice and military virtue,

---

67. That is, more than virtue in the art in its claim to pipes (or more than virtue simply in claims to political office—depending on whether we suppose Aristotle is continuing the example or now directly speaking of claims to rule). I follow the manuscripts here and read *mallon to* ("counted as more"), not the conjectural *sumballoito* (if size "contributed something," that is, to the work of pipe playing) followed by Dreizehnter.

68. In other words, if the good of size could count as more of a claim to pipes than the good of skill or virtue in the art (on the supposition that any good, however irrelevant to the job or end in question, can constitute a claim to something), then any other good, like wealth and freedom, could also count as a claim, and size would find itself competing for the pipes also against wealth, freedom, and the rest.

69. The argument here is elliptical. It can, however, be expanded as follows. If a certain amount of size counts as more of a claim to pipes than a certain amount of virtue or skill in pipe playing, then by reducing the amount of the size one should eventually get to an amount that equals, in its claim to pipes, the original amount of virtue. Hence, size and virtue will be commensurable. Further, supposing also that a certain amount of wealth or freedom counts as more of a claim to pipes than that same amount of virtue, then some lesser amount of both will, in claims to pipes, equal it. Hence they too will be commensurable with virtue. But things equal to a third thing are equal to each other, hence the amount of wealth and freedom equal to the amount of virtue will also equal the amount of size that was equal to it. Consequently, all these goods will be commensurable with each other and with every other good that one allows to make claims to the pipes.

since a city cannot be managed without these either. Without the former, though, a city cannot exist; without the latter it cannot be managed nobly.

CHAPTER 13

Who May Justly Make Claims to Have Control of Rule

Preliminary Discussion. All those who make claims to have control of rule—the wealthy, the free and the well-born, the best, the multitude—seem to have some justice on their side. But the arguments of each, when pushed to their logical conclusion, lead to the difficulty that they overthrow themselves and justify instead the claim of one man alone to be in control.

1283a23 Now, as regards the existence of the city, all or at any rate some of the above would seem to be basing their dispute on correct grounds; but, as regards good life, education and virtue would seem to provide the most just grounds for dispute, as was already said earlier. But as those equal in one thing only should not have an equality in everything, nor those an inequality who are unequal in one thing, all regimes where this occurs must necessarily be deviations. Now, it was also said earlier that everyone in a way disputes justly but that not everyone does so in a way that is simply just.[70]
1283a31 The rich base their dispute on the grounds that they have more of the land, which is something common, and also that they are more trustworthy on the whole when it comes to treaties. The free and the well-born base theirs on the grounds of being close to one another (for those of respectable family are more properly citizens than those of no family, and good birth is held in honor at home by everyone), and also on the grounds that those born of better parents are likely to be better (since what is meant by good birth is virtue of family). For like reason, we will say that virtue also has a just basis for its dispute, since justice, we say, is a communal virtue on which all other virtues must necessarily follow.[71] Moreover, the majority also dispute against the minority, for they are, taken as the majority in contrast with the minority, stronger and wealthier and better.
1283a42 If, then, all of these existed in one city—I mean the good, the wealthy, the well-born, and a political multitude in addition—will the question of who should rule be a matter for dispute or will it not? Of course, the decision of who is to rule in any of the regimes mentioned[72] is not disputed,

70. All the points made in this paragraph were asserted and proved earlier in chapter 9.
71. *Ethics* 5.1.1129b25–30a5.
72. That is, the six regimes described in chapter 7.

since it is by who has control in them that these regimes differ from each other (for instance, by the wealthy in one case, by the men who are serious in another, and so on in each of the rest). But we are investigating how the matter is to be determined when all these are present at the same time.

1283b9 So if those possessed of virtue were altogether few in number, how ought the question to be settled? Or is their fewness to be considered in the light of the work to be done, that is, whether they are capable of managing the city or are so many in number that a city could exist composed of them? But there is a difficulty that confronts all disputants about political honors. For those who claim they deserve rule on the basis of their wealth would seem to be making no just argument, nor likewise would those who do so on the basis of family. For it is clear that if someone was wealthier again than all of them, he should, according to this understanding of justice, rule all of them by himself alone. Similarly, it is clear that someone outstanding in good birth should rule over those who dispute on the basis of freedom. The same thing will perhaps also occur as regards virtue in the case of aristocracies. For if some one man is better than all the others in the ruling body, even though they are serious men, then, on the same principle of justice, he should be in control. So if the multitude too, because they are stronger than the few, should be in control, then, if one or more than one but still a minority are stronger, it is these who ought to be in control rather than the multitude.

The Case for Polity. *The position of those who claim sole rule for themselves, to the exclusion of the multitude, is incorrect, even if their claim is based on virtue. For if the multitude, taken as a whole, turns out to be better than the few best, then the multitude should rule. In such a case, the most correct laws are those that favor the rule of the majority, not just of the few, since the majority are here best and citizens (it is in an aristocracy that the few will alone be best and citizens).*

1283b27 All these considerations seem to make it manifest that the definitions on the basis of which people claim that they themselves deserve to rule while everyone else deserves to be their subjects, are none of them correct. For, in fact, even against those whose claim to deserve control of the ruling body is based on virtue, multitudes would have some argument of justice to make, as they would likewise against those whose claim to deserve it is based on wealth. For nothing prevents the multitude sometimes being better than the few and also wealthier, not as individuals but as a collectivity. **1283b35** Hence this is also how to meet the difficulty that some search out and put in the way. For they raise the difficulty whether the legislator who wants to lay down the most correct laws should, when the case just mentioned occurs, legislate for the advantage of the best or of the majority. But "correct" must be taken in a way that is fair, and taken in this way, "correct" is relative to the advantage of the whole city and to the advantage that is common to the citizens. A citizen generally is one who shares in ruling and being ruled, but as regards each regime, he differs. It is in the best regime that the citizen is the one who has the ability, and makes the choice, to be ruled and to rule with a view to the way of life that accords with virtue.

The Case for Aristocracy and Kingship. *But if one or several individuals are so superior in virtue that they surpass all others, they should not be treated as equals or subjected to law but will be like gods. Other regimes, as democracies and tyrannies in particular, seek to expel those who are excessively superior, and this can up to a point be just, even in correct regimes. But when someone excels in virtue (as opposed to wealth or strength or the like) expulsion would not be correct. Rather, such as these should be accepted gladly as permanent kings in cities.*

1284a3 But if there is a single individual or several individuals (but not enough to make the full complement of a city) so outstanding in the excess of virtue that neither the virtue nor the political power of all the others is commensurable with theirs (if they be several) or his (if he be single), then such should no longer be regarded as part of a city.[73] For they would be wronged if they were thought to deserve equal shares when they are so unequal in virtue and political power. Such would reasonably be like a god among human beings.

1284a11 From this fact it is clear that legislation too must concern those who are equal in birth and power, but that over such as these there can be no law: they themselves are law. For anyone who tried to legislate for them would even be ridiculous, since they would perhaps answer as Antisthenes said the lions did when the hares were making their speech and claiming equal shares for all.[74]

1284a17 This is in fact why cities governed democratically establish ostracism. For these cities most of all seem to make equality their aim and consequently ostracize and remove from the city for determinate periods of time those who through wealth, multitude of friends, or some other political strength seem to have too much power. There is also the story that the Argonauts left Heracles behind for this reason: they say that the Argo herself refused to have him on board with the other sailors because he surpassed them so much. That is also why the censure of those who blame tyranny and the advice Periander gave Thrasybulus cannot be considered

---

73. Rather they are a whole city by themselves—in power and virtue, that is, though not in numbers; cf. 3.17.1288a15–27.

74. "Where are your claws and teeth?" (Aesop *Fables* 241).

to be simply correct. For they say that Periander said nothing to the herald who had been sent to get his advice, but leveled a field of grain by lopping off the ears that overtopped the rest. When the herald, who was ignorant of the reason for what Periander had done, reported the incident, Thrasybulus realized he was to lop off the preeminent men.[75]

1284a33 But this piece of advice is not only of advantage to tyrants, nor do tyrants alone do it. Oligarchies and democracies are in the same position, for ostracism has in its way this same power of cutting down and banishing the preeminent. The same thing, in fact, is done to cities and nations by those who have control of power — as, for example, by the Athenians against the Samians and Chians and Lesbians, for as soon as they had a firm hold on empire, they brought these cities low, contrary to the treaties.[76] The king of the Persians often cut down the Medes and Babylonians and any others who, because they had once possessed empire, had a high opinion of themselves.

1284b3 This problem is a general one for all regimes, including the correct ones. For though the deviant ones do it looking to their private advantage, yet things are the same also for those who look to the common good, as is shown by the example of the other arts and sciences. For no painter would allow an animal to have a foot that exceeded proportions, even if it was surpassing in nobility, nor would a shipbuilder allow the same in the case of the stern or any other part of a ship, nor would a chorus master allow someone to be a member of the chorus who sang louder and more nobly than all the rest. So on this account there is nothing to prevent monarchs from being in harmony with their cities when they perform such actions, provided their rule is helpful to their cities. Hence, as regards generally acknowledged superiorities, the argument about ostracism has a certain political justice to it.

1284b17 It would be better, of course, if the legislator so established the regime to begin with that there was no need of such a cure. Yet if need should arise, then the second best is to try to set things straight with some such corrective device, though that is not what happened in cities. For instead of looking to the advantage of their own regime, they used ostracism for factional purposes. Therefore, that the practice in deviant regimes works to private advantage and is just is manifest, though it is perhaps also manifest that it is not simply just.

1284b25 But in the case of the best regime, there is considerable difficulty not about superiority in the other goods — as strength, wealth, and abun-

75. Periander was tyrant of Corinth (he is mentioned again in 7(5).11.1313a34-37 and 12.1315b24-29), Thrasybulus tyrant of Miletus. Herodotus also records the story (*History* 5.92), but he puts it in the mouth of a Corinthian who makes Thrasybulus give the advice to Periander instead.

76. Aristotle is referring to events during the Athenian naval empire of the fifth century, though it is not clear which specific ones he has in mind.

dance of friends—but if someone arises who is outstanding in virtue. What is to be done? For people would not say that such a one should be expelled and banished, nor, even less, that they should rule over him, for that would be like thinking they deserved to rule over Zeus and divide the offices with him. What is left, then—and it is what seems natural—is that all obey him gladly. Consequently, such as these will be perpetual kings in cities.

CHAPTER 14

Third Difficulty: Whether Kingship Is a Correct Regime

The Kinds of Kingship. *But whether kingship really is good for cities needs to be considered. The kinds of kingship are: (i) that of the Spartans, which is simply a perpetual generalship; (ii) that of the barbarians, which is like a tyranny except it is over willing subjects, hereditary, and according to law; (iii) that of dictatorship, which is an elective tyranny over willing subjects; (iv) that of the heroic ages, which is over willing subjects and with certain delimited powers; (v) that of the total ruler, which is household management of cities and nations and has control over everything.*

1284b35 It would be a noble thing, perhaps, after the above discussion to move on and examine kingship, since we say it is one of the correct regimes. What needs to be examined is whether it is an advantage for a city or country that is going to be nobly managed to be under a kingship or instead to be under some other regime, or whether this is of advantage to some but not to others.

1284b40 First, it is necessary to determine whether there is one class of kingship or whether it has several differentiations. That it does indeed encompass several classes and is not the same manner of rule in all cases is easy to discover. For kingship in the Spartan regime seems to be most especially an instance of kingship according to law. It is not in control of everything but, when a king leaves the territory, he is leader in all that concerns war. In addition, to the kings is given whatever has to do with the gods. This kind of kingship is like an autocratic and perpetual generalship, for it has no control over life and death—except in the case of certain forms of it (such as those of ancient times), by the law of might on military expeditions. Homer makes the matter clear: Agamemnon put up with hearing himself abused in assemblies, but when they went out to fight, he had the control even to kill. At any rate, he says "whom I see apart from the battle . . . there will be no sure escape for him from the dogs and birds, for with me is death." [77] So

77. *Iliad* 2.391–93. The last five words of the quotation are not found in our manuscripts of Homer.

here is one kind of kingship, generalship for life, and it either goes in families or is elected.

1285a16 There is another kind of monarchy besides this one, the sort of kingships that exist among some barbarians. These have power much like that of tyrannies and exist by law and inheritance from ancestors. For the barbarians are by nature more slavish in their character than the Greeks, those in Asia more so than those in Europe, so they submit to despotic rule without complaint. These kingships, then, are tyrannical because despotic, but stable because ancestral and according to law. Their bodyguard is also for the same reason royal and not tyrannical, for kings are protected by the arms of their citizens but tyrants by those of foreigners. The reason is that the former rule according to law and over willing subjects while the latter rule over unwilling ones. As a consequence, kings take a bodyguard from the citizens, but tyrants employ it against them. Here then are two kinds of monarchy.

1285a30 Another kind is the one that used to exist among the ancient Greeks, the sort they call dictators.[78] It is, simply speaking, an elective tyranny and differs from the barbarian kind not because it is not according to law but only because it is not ancestrally inherited. Some possessed this rule for life, others for certain determinate periods and purposes—as, for example, when the Mytilenaeans chose Pittacus to repel the exiles led by Antimenides and the poet Alcaeus. That they elected Pittacus tyrant is shown by Alcaeus in one of his drinking songs, where he reproaches them because "they set up Pittacus, of ill parentage, to be tyrant of their gutless and accursed city, with great praise from the assembled throng."[79] These kingships, then, because tyrannical, are and were despotic but, because elected and over willing subjects, kingly.

1285b3 A fourth kind of royal monarchy is that of the heroic age, which was both voluntary and ancestral according to law. For because the first kings were benefactors of the multitude in the arts or war or because they united them into one or provided them with land, they became kings over willing subjects, and their rule became ancestral among succeeding generations. They were in control of leadership in war and of those sacrifices that did not require a priest. In addition, they were judges in law cases. Some of them did this without swearing an oath, while others did swear (the oath was the lifting up of a scepter). Now, in ancient times the kings ruled continuously over the affairs of the city, of the country, and beyond the borders, but later they themselves gave up some of these powers, while the rest were taken

78. The Greek word is *aisymnētēs*.

79. Frag. 87 Diehl. Mytilene was the main city of the island of Lesbos; the events referred to here took place in about 590.

away by the crowd. The sacrifices alone were left to the kings in other cities but, wherever there was a kingship worth speaking of, it was only leadership in war beyond the borders that the kings retained.

1285b20 These then are the kinds of kingship, being four in number: one is the kingship of the heroic ages, which was over willing subjects and with certain definite powers, since the king was general and judge and had control over affairs to do with the gods; second is the barbarian kind, which is a despotic rule that goes in families and is according to law; third is the one they call a dictatorship, which is an elective tyranny; fourth of these is the Spartan, which is, to speak simply, a perpetual generalship inherited by family. So these four differ in this way from each other.

1285b29 But there is a fifth kind of kingship when a single person has control, like any nation and city, over all common matters, and it is arranged along the lines of household management. For just as household management is a sort of kingship over the household, so this kingship is household management over one or more cities and nations.

CHAPTER 15

Difficulties with Total Kingship

Arguments for Rule of Law Rather Than Rule by One Man. *Only the last kind of kingship is relevant to the present discussion. The difficulties can be approached by asking which is better: rule by the best man or rule by the best laws. The arguments run as follows: (i) if one opts for the best man, because law speaks only of the universal while the best man speaks also of the particulars, yet he must still possess the universal and is moreover beset by passion while the law is not; (ii) if one responds that the best man is at least better at deciding particulars, then one has conceded that he needs universal laws; (iii) he need not in fact be better at deciding particulars, since the multitude could be better than he is and less corruptible, or at least the few of aristocracy could be, provided such a few or multitude can be found (which might now appear no longer to be possible); (iv) if his children succeed him and are as some heirs have been, they will ruin things, and to suppose they will not succeed him is asking too much; (v) he must possess some armed guard to enforce his rule, which is dangerous if he is lawless, though if not, this difficulty can be resolved.*

1285b33 Speaking broadly, then, there are two kinds of kingship to be investigated, this last one and the Spartan. For of the others, most lie between these two and have control over fewer things than total kingship but over more than the Spartan. So the investigation reduces pretty much to two questions: first, whether it is or is not of advantage to cities to have a perpetual generalship (either on the basis of family or by turns); and second, whether it is or is not of advantage to them for one man to have control over everything.

1286a2 Now an investigation into such a generalship has about it more the aspect of law than regime, since the thing could come to exist in any regime. Let us then put this question aside. But the remaining mode of kingship is a kind of regime. Accordingly, this is the mode that needs to be looked into and the difficulties besetting it gone over.

1286a7 A beginning can be made with this question: whether it is an advantage to be ruled by the best man rather than by the best laws. Those who think it is an advantage to be ruled by a king hold the view that the laws speak only of the universal and do not give commands relative to the actual circumstances. Ruling according to written prescriptions is consequently a foolish thing to do in any art. In Egypt, in fact, doctors are permitted, after the fourth day of an illness, to change the treatment, but if they do so before then, it is at their own risk. So, manifestly the best regime cannot be one that is in accordance with written laws.[80] Still, the rulers must, nevertheless, possess the reasoned account of the universal, and, on the whole, what does not have the passionate element added to it is better than that in which it is innate. This element is not present in the law, but of necessity every human soul has it.

1286a20 Yet perhaps someone might respond that a human will instead deliberate more nobly when it comes to particulars. Well, in that case it is clearly necessary for him to be a legislator and for laws to be laid down, though not laws that, since they have to be in control everywhere else, are in control in respects in which they deviate.

1286a24 On the other hand, is it better—as regards what the law cannot judge either altogether or well—that the one best person rule or that everyone should? For as things stand now, it is those in assembly together who pass verdicts, conduct deliberations, and reach decisions, and these decisions, which concern particulars, are decisions that belong to everybody. Now when compared one by one, any given person is perhaps worse, but the city is composed of many and is like a jointly contributed feast, which is nobler than a single and simple one. That is why a crowd can even judge many things better than some one given individual. Further, what is many is more incorruptible: the multitude, like a greater quantity of water, is harder to ruin than a few. A single person's judgment must necessarily be corrupted when he is overcome by anger or some other such passion, but getting everyone in the other case to become angry and go wrong at the

---

80. Aristotle is summarizing here the main argument for kingship found in Plato's *Statesman* 294a10–b6, 295b10–e2, 300c9–d2.

same time takes a lot of doing. Let the multitude in question, however, be the free who are acting in no way against law, except where law is necessarily deficient. This requirement may indeed not be easy to meet where the persons are many. But suppose there were several of them who were good both as men and citizens: would the one person be more incorruptible in ruling or would it instead be those who, though several in number, are all of them good? Is it not clear that it would be the latter? But then, it might be replied, they will fall to factional strife, while the single person is free of faction. To which objection must be posed perhaps, as a counter consideration, that they could be serious of soul just as much as he.

1286b3 So then, if aristocracy is to be regarded as rule by several persons but persons who are all good men, aristocracy would be more worth choosing for cities than kingship (whether the kingship is accompanied by an armed guard or not), provided one could get hold of several men of like quality. That is perhaps why in former ages they used to live under kings, because especially at that time, when the cities they inhabited were small, it was a rare thing to find men very outstanding in virtue; in addition, it was because of their benefactions, which is the work of good men, that kings were established. But when those similar in virtue became many in number, they no longer put up with kings. Instead they sought something communal and established polity.[81] Then they deteriorated and began to use the common funds for business purposes, which, since they made wealth into a thing of honor, is a plausible explanation of how oligarchies arose. The change from oligarchies was, first, into tyrannies and then from tyrannies into democracy, for by concentrating things, through a shameful desire for profit, into fewer and fewer hands, they made the multitude stronger, and the result was that these attacked them and democracies arose. In fact, now that the size of cities has grown bigger, it is perhaps no longer easy for any regime other than democracy to arise.

1286b22 But if one does after all set down kingship as best for cities, how are matters to do with children to be handled? Must the kingship also belong to the family? If so, and if those born are such as some have turned out to be, the results will be harmful. But perhaps the king, though having the control, will not hand things over to his children? That, however, is no longer easy to believe, for the thing is hard and requires greater virtue than human nature admits of.

1286b27 A difficulty arises also about the king's power and whether anyone going to be king must have about him some force by which he can coerce those who are unwilling to obey. How else can he manage his rule? For even if his being in control is lawful and he does nothing to satisfy his own

81. Cf. 6(4).13.1297b16–28.

will against the law, still he must be in possession of some power whereby to protect the laws. Now it is perhaps not difficult to determine what to do with a king like this: force indeed he must have, but a force sufficient only to make him stronger than each singly or than several together, not to make him stronger than the multitude. That is how guards were granted by those in ancient times when they set up someone over the city whom they called dictator or tyrant. Also, when Dionysius asked for a guard, someone counseled the Syracusans to give him one of this sort.

CHAPTER 16

Arguments against Total Kingship. *The arguments against total kingship are these: (i) total kingship, being contrary to the justice of equality, is unnatural and harmful, and law should rule instead; (ii) what the law has to leave undetermined cannot be determined by a human being either, unless he has been first educated by the laws, so law, which, like god, is uncorrupted by passion, should rule; (iii) the analogy with the arts, as medicine, is false, for (a) doctors are not corrupted as politicians are; (b) if they were, written rules would be consulted instead; (c) doctors when sick rely on other doctors, not themselves, just as those seeking justice rely on law; (d) even if persons were preferable to written laws, they are not preferable to laws based on custom; (iv) one man cannot easily manage many things, so partners in rule will be needed sooner or later anyway; (v) if one man should rule because he is better, two men should rule because they will be better still; (vi) the objection to kingship is not that there is no need for humans to rule where law gives out, but that in these cases many and not one should rule, because (a) anyone can rule well when educated by the laws and (b) many ruling together are better than one ruling alone, as reason and the actual practice of monarchs attest.*

1287a1 The discussion has now come to a stand at the king who does everything according to his own will, and an investigation about him must be made. For someone who is called king in subjection to law[82] does not, as we said,[83] constitute a kind of regime, because there can be a perpetual generalship in any regime (as in a democracy or an aristocracy), and there are many who put a single person in control over the management of affairs. Such an office exists at Epidamnus, in fact, and there is a somewhat lesser one at Opus.

1287a8 But as regards total kingship so called (where the king rules in everything according to his own will), it seems to some not even according to

---

82. As the kind of king discussed in the last chapter turned out to be.
83. At the beginning of chapter 15, at 1286a2–5.

nature that one person from among all the citizens, when the city is composed of similars, should be in control. For justice and worth must be by nature the same for those who are by nature similar. Consequently, if the unequal in body are harmed by having equal food and clothing, and if that is how it also is where the honors of office are concerned, then if the equal have what is unequal, the like harm must follow. Hence, what is just is that people exercise rule no more than they are subject to it, and that therefore they rule by turns. But this is already law, for the arrangement is law. Therefore it is preferable that law rule rather than any one of the citizens. And even if, to pursue the same argument, it were better that there be some persons exercising rule, their appointment should be as guardians and servants of the laws. For though there must be some offices, that there should be this one person exercising rule is, they say, not just, at least when all are similar.

1287a23 Then again, whatever the law appears unable to determine could not be discovered by a human being either. Rather the law, having educated rulers for such eventualities, hands over to them, to be managed and decided by their most just opinion,[84] the things it leaves out. It allows them, further, to set things right wherever, as a result of experience, they deem something else to be better than the existing laws. Now, anyone who bids the law to rule seems to bid god and intellect alone to rule, but anyone who bids a human being to rule adds on also the wild beast. For desire is such a beast, and spiritedness perverts rulers even when they are the best of men. Hence law is intellect without appetite.

1287a32 The analogy with the arts, that giving cures according to the book is a base thing and that it is preferable instead to rely on those who possess the art,[85] is false. For friendship does not induce doctors to do things against reason; on the contrary, making the sick healthy is how they earn their pay. But those in political office are accustomed to do many things with an eye to spite and favor—since in fact if patients suspected doctors of being corrupted by enemies to do away with them for profit, they would seek for a cure from written rules instead. Moreover, doctors, when sick, call in other doctors to see them, and trainers, when exercising, call in trainers—the reasoning being that they are not able to judge the truth because they will be judging about themselves and from a state of pain. Hence it is clear that in seeking what is just, they are seeking what is impartial, for that is what the law is. Again, laws based on custom, as opposed to those that are written down, have more control and concern things that have more control, so even if a human being is a more reliable ruler than are written laws, he is not more so than are laws based on custom.

84. These words come from the oath sworn by jurors at Athens.
85. The reference is to chapter 15.1286a11–16.

1287b8 Yet further, it is not easy for one person to oversee many things, so there will need to be many officials appointed in subordination to him. Consequently, what is the difference between having them there right from the start and having one man in this way appoint them?

1287b11 In addition, there is what was said earlier,[86] that if a man who is serious is justly ruler because he is better, then two good men are better than one. That is what is meant by the line "when two go together" and by Agamemnon's prayer "would I had ten such counsellors."[87]

1287b15 Control over some matters, those that law is incapable of determining, is even now exercised by offices, as by the office of juror, for at least as regards those that law can determine, no one disputes that law would be the best rule and judge. But because some things can and some things cannot be embraced under the laws, it is these latter that generate the difficulty and provoke the question whether it is preferable for the best law or the best man to rule (for to legislate about what is matter for deliberation is something impossible). So the counter claim[88] is not that there is no necessity for a human being to be judge in such things, but that the judge should be many and not one alone. For each ruler can judge nobly when educated by the laws. Also it would perhaps seem a strange thing if someone could, when judging with two eyes and ears and acting with two hands and feet, see things better than many can when judging and acting with many, since, as a matter of fact, monarchs even now make for themselves many eyes and ears and hands and feet. For they make joint rulers of those friendly to themselves and their rule. Now if they were not the monarch's friends, they would not do what he chooses. But if they are his friends and friends to his rule—and a friend at any rate is someone equal and similar—then, if he thinks his friends should rule, he is thinking likewise that those should rule who are his equals and similars.

1287b35 These then, more or less, are the arguments asserted by those who dispute against kingship.

CHAPTER 17

Answer to the Difficulties. *The previous arguments hold only of persons who are equal or similar, not of others, for what is by nature just and advantageous is different in the different kinds of rule. Total kingship is naturally appropriate in some conditions, aristocracy and polity in others. Kingship is just in these conditions because*

86. In the third difficulty of chapter 15, at 1286a30–b1.
87. *Iliad* 10.224 and 2.372, respectively.
88. That is, against kingship; the reference is to chapter 15.1286a24–31.

where one man or a family surpasses everyone else in virtue, then justice requires that he and they rule all alone.

1287b36 But while these arguments hold of some persons, perhaps they do not of others. For what is by nature just and advantageous is one thing in the case of despotic rule, another in the case of kingly rule, and another in the case of political rule (the just and advantageous in the case of tyrannical rule, or of any other regime that is a deviation, are not according to nature, for these are against nature). Still, it is at least manifest from what has been said[89] that among those who are equal and similar it is neither advantageous nor just for one man to have control over everything, not even if there are no laws and he himself is law, nor if there are laws and he and they are good or he and they are not good, nor even if he is superior in virtue—unless he is superior in a certain way. What that way is must now be stated.

1288a6 In fact it was, in a way, already stated earlier.[90] First what is fit for kingship must be defined, and what fit for aristocracy and what fit for polity. Fit for kingship is a multitude such that it naturally carries with it a family surpassing in virtue for political leadership; fit for aristocracy is a multitude that naturally carries with it a multitude[91] capable of being ruled with the rule of free persons by those who, on the basis of virtue, are leaders in political rule; fit for polity is a multitude in which there naturally emerges a warlike multitude able to be ruled and rule according to a law that distributes offices by merit to those who are well-off.[92]

1288a15 Whenever it happens, therefore, that either a whole family, or some one man from among the rest, emerges so outstanding in virtue as to exceed the virtue of everyone else, then it is just that this family have the kingship and have control over everything and that he be king. For, as was said earlier, not only does this agree with the justice customarily alleged by those who set up regimes, whether aristocracies or oligarchies or again democracies (for they all[93] think themselves deserving on the basis of some superiority, though not the same superiority); it also accords with the assertion made previously.[94] For to kill or banish or ostracize such a person is surely not appropriate, nor to claim that he deserves to be ruled in part. For the part does

89. In chapter 16 especially.
90. 3.13.1284a2–17.
91. "Multitude" here and in the next clause must be taken in two ways: first to refer to a larger multitude and second to refer to a smaller multitude within the larger one.
92. That is, well-off enough to be able to afford arms; cf. 6(4).13.1297b1–6. In this paragraph I have followed the reading of the manuscripts as given by Newman, not the extensive rearrangements adopted by Dreizehnter.
93. Reading *pantes* with some manuscripts, rather than *pantēi* ("in every respect") with Dreizehnter and others.
94. The references here are to 3.13 generally and to 1284b25–34 in particular.

not by nature surpass the whole, and being the whole is what has happened to someone with an excess so great. Consequently, what is left is for such a one to be obeyed and to have control not in part but simply.

1288a30 Concerning kingship, then, and what its differences are and whether it is of no advantage to cities or whether it is of advantage to some and how, let our determinations stand thus.

CHAPTER 18

Transition to Investigation of the Best Regime. *The best regime is the one managed by the best men, namely kingship and aristocracy. And as virtue of man and citizen is the same in the best regime, finding out how to make men good is the same as finding out how to make them fit for kingship and aristocracy. This topic therefore comes next.*

1288a32 There are, we say, three correct regimes, and of these the best must be that managed by the best persons. Such is the one where either some one man among all or a whole family[95] or a multitude[96] is surpassing in virtue, and where some are able to be ruled and others to rule,[97] with a view to the most choiceworthy life. In the earlier discussions[98] it was also shown that, in the case of the best city, the virtue of man and citizen must be the same. Manifestly, therefore, a man will become serious in the same way and by the same means as a city could be established that is ruled by an aristocracy or a king, and so it will be more or less the same education and the same habits that make a man serious and that make him political and kingly.

1288b2 With these determinations made, it is now necessary to try to speak about the best regime, how it naturally comes to be and gets somehow or other established. Anyone, then, who is going to do this,[99] must conduct the examination that is proper to the subject.

95. The case of kingship.

96. The case of aristocracy. The multitude of polity is too large to be composed of men all of whom are perfect in complete virtue (3.7.1278b39–1279a2).

97. Those able to rule will be mature adults already ruling; those able to be ruled will be younger men still being trained for rule (3.4.1277b7–13).

98. 3.4–5.

99. The Greek says simply "Anyone, then, who is going to . . ." without adding the "do this," which I supply from the previous sentence. Most translators and commentators make no addition and translate the sentence as grammatically incomplete: "Anyone, then, who is going to conduct the examination that is proper to the subject must . . ." There is no need, however, to create this grammatical difficulty, since the sentence can easily be treated as elliptical and the missing sense supplied from the context. That the sentence should indeed be so treated gets support from 6(4).2.1289b20–21, where *ton boulomenon* ("anyone who wants to do so") has to be construed, and is so construed by translators, in the same way as I here construe *ton mellonta* ("anyone who is going to do this").

Book 4

The Best Regime

CHAPTER 1

Preface to the Discussion: The Best Way of Life

That the Life of Virtue Is the Best Life for Everyone. *The best regime is the one in which the citizens live the best life. This is the life of virtue, for (i) of the three kinds of goods, those of the soul, namely the virtues, preserve the other goods and bring more happiness; (ii) the other goods are useful goods and are of limited goodness, but virtues are good without limit; (iii) the best condition of the better thing is better, and virtues are the best condition of the better thing, namely the soul, for the other things are for the sake of the soul and not vice versa; (iv) the god is happy because of the character of his nature, not because of the other goods.*

1323a14 Anyone who is going to conduct the investigation into the best regime that is proper to the subject must first determine what the most choiceworthy way of life is, since if this remains unclear, what the best regime is must also remain unclear. For what is proper to those who govern themselves in the best way is, unless something unreasonable happens, to do the best from what is available to them. Hence, agreement must first be reached on what is for everyone, practically speaking, the most choiceworthy way of life, and then on whether this way of life is the same for all in common as for each separately or whether it is different.

1323a21 Since, therefore, it is our view that much that is adequate has already been said about the best life in our external discourses,[1] we must use those discourses again now. For, to tell the truth, no one would object to one division of goods at least and say that, of the three parts it has—external goods, goods of the body, and goods of the soul—not all of them should be in the possession[2] of the blessed. For no one would call blessed someone

---

1. Probably a reference to Aristotle's lost dialogues; cf. 3.6.1278b31–32.

2. I read *huparchein chrē* with the manuscripts, not *huparchei* ("is in the possession") with Dreizehnter.

who had not an ounce of courage or moderation or justice or prudence but was in fear of flies buzzing about, refrained from no extreme whenever he had a desire to eat or drink, ruined his dearest friends for a mite, and was likewise as senseless and deluded in affairs of thought as a small child or a madman. But while pretty well all would agree to these remarks, they differ when it comes to the question of amount and excess. For they think they have enough virtue provided they have it to some degree or other, but they put no limit to the excess they seek of wealth and money and power and fame and all such things.

1323a38 We, however, will say to them that trustworthy proof on this matter can easily be taken even from the facts themselves. For we see that the virtues are not acquired or retained by means of the external goods but rather the external goods by means of the virtues, and that living happily, whether it exists in enjoyment or virtue or both as far as human beings are concerned, belongs more to those who are adorned to excess in character and thought but observe a measure in their external acquisition of goods than to those who possess a greater amount of these latter than they can use but are deficient in the former.

1323b6 Moreover, the question is also easy to see when examined by reason. For external things have a limit, like any instrument, and everything useful is included among things [3] that in excess must either cause harm or be of no help to their possessors, whereas each of the goods of the soul—if we are to speak of the useful in their case as well as of the noble—must be so much the more useful the more it exists to excess.

1323b13 Generally it is clear, we shall say, that the relation of superiority between the best condition of one thing and the best condition of another corresponds to the distance obtaining between the things of which we say they are the condition. So if the soul is more honorable than property and the body, both simply and relatively to us, then the best conditions of each of these must stand in the corresponding relation. But, further, the other things are by nature to be chosen for the sake of the soul and ought so to be chosen by those of good sense, not the soul for the sake of those other things.

1323b21 So let us agree that each of us has as much of happiness as he has of virtue and prudence and of acting accordingly by taking as witness the god, who is happy indeed but not because of any of the external goods; rather he is happy because of himself and by being in his nature of a certain sort. For this is also the reason that good fortune must be different from happiness, since accident and chance are the cause of goods outside the soul, but no one is just or moderate either by chance or because of chance.

3. Reading *estin* ("is included among") with the manuscripts, not *es ti* ("is for some purpose") with Dreizehnter.

That the Life of Virtue Is the Best Life for the City. The same arguments prove the same conclusion of the city because the terms "virtue" and "happiness" are confessedly the same in the case of both individual and city.

1323b29 Next, and requiring the same arguments, is that a city is happy when it is best or acting nobly. Those who do not do noble things are not acting nobly, but no deed, whether of a man or a city, is noble without virtue and prudence. A city's courage and justice and prudence have the same power and form as do those qualities by participating in which each human being is called just and prudent and moderate.

1323b36 But let these remarks serve as preface to our discussion, for it is not possible not to touch on them nor is it possible to broach all the appropriate arguments (this is work for leisure of another sort). But for now, let so much be laid down: that the best way of life for each separately and for cities in common is the life endowed with a virtue sufficiently equipped that they can take part in the deeds of virtue. As for objectors, if anyone turns out not to be persuaded by what has been said, we must dismiss them for the purpose of the present inquiry and investigate the matter later.[4]

Chapter 2: 1324a5 It remains to say whether the happiness of each single human being is the same as that of a city or not. But this also is manifest, as everyone would agree it was the same. For whoever locates good life for the individual in riches would also bless the whole city if it were rich, and whoever most honors the tyrannical life would say the city that rules over most cities was happiest, and anyone who approves an individual because of his virtue will also say the city is happier the more serious it is.

What the Life of Virtue Is

The Kinds of Virtuous Life. Two investigations remain: whether some can live a better life released from the city than as part of it, and which regime is best. The first is not relevant in a political treatise, and the second raises the question whether the life of practical or philosophical virtue is better.

1324a13 But now the things in need of investigation are these two: first, whether the more choiceworthy way of life is the one that consists in engaging together in politics and sharing a city, or whether it is instead the alien way of life and the life released from the political community; second (regardless of whether sharing a city together is choiceworthy for all or is not choiceworthy for some but only for most), what regime and disposition of the city is to be set down as best. But since this second question, and not that about what is choiceworthy for each individual, is work for political

---

4. Possibly a reference to 4(7).13–15 below.

thought and study, and since this is the investigation we have now chosen, the first question would be outside the work of the present study, but the second one would be its work.

1324a23 Now it is manifest that the best regime must be that arrangement in which anyone might act best and live blessedly. But among those very people who agree that the most choiceworthy way of life is life with virtue, there is a dispute about whether the political and practical way of life is to be chosen or whether instead the life that is released from all externals should be — the contemplative life,[5] for instance, which some say is the only philosophic way to live. For these two kinds of lives (I mean the two of the political and philosophic lives) are, more or less, those that the most ambitious with respect to virtue, both formerly and now as well, have been conspicuous in choosing. It makes no little difference on which side the truth lies, since anyone of good sense, at any rate, must arrange together in view of the best goal both human beings individually and the regime in common.

That the Life of Virtue Is Not Despotic Rule over Neighbors. *Of those who commend the political life, some commend despotic rule over neighbors. But there are several problems with this view: (i) ruling neighbors regardless of justice is not lawful, and so not the work of politics; (ii) nothing of the sort is observed in other arts; (iii) the distinction between those who should be ruled despotically and those who should not is by nature, and only the former should be so ruled and not, as the many think, everyone other than themselves; (iv) a city could be happy with good laws while existing apart by itself, and so would be noble and happy without ruling over anybody.*

1324a35 There are some who think that ruling over one's neighbors involves very great injustice if it is done despotically while if it is done politically, it may involve no injustice but does contain impediments to one's own well-being. There are others whose thinking is virtually the opposite. For they say that the practical and political way of life is the only one fit for a man, since the actions relevant to each virtue are not more the property of private persons than they are of those who undertake common affairs and engage in politics. Such is the opinion of some of them. But others say that a regime in the despotic and tyrannical manner is the only happy one.

1324b3 Among some people, in fact, the defining principle for both laws and regime is ruling despotically over neighbors. Hence it is that though the majority of laws among most peoples are set down in a more or less haphazard manner, yet if anywhere the laws do look to one object, it is at domination that they all aim. So in Sparta and Crete, for instance, the education and the bulk of the laws are arranged pretty much for war. In addition, all nations

---

5. The Greek is *theōrētikos*, which in its cognate verbal form I translate as "study." So one could also translate here as "studious life."

able to seize more for themselves have held just this sort of ability in honor, like the Scythians, Persians, Thracians, and Celts. Among some people, indeed, there are laws to urge them on to this virtue, as in Carthage, where, so it is said, they receive armbands as adornment for all the campaigns they go on. There was also a law once in Macedon that a man who had not killed an enemy wore a halter for a belt, and among the Scythians anyone who had not killed an enemy could not drink the cup as it was passed around at a certain feast. Among the warlike nation of the Iberians, as many obelisks are affixed around a grave as the deceased has slain of enemies. Many other such practices exist elsewhere, enshrined sometimes in laws and sometimes in customs.

1324b22 Yet to anyone willing to look into the matter it would perhaps seem an exceedingly strange thing if the work of the politician was to be able to study how to rule and despotize over neighbors whether they want to be ruled or not. For how could that which is not even lawful be political or characteristic of a legislator? But to rule without regard to whether one is justly or unjustly ruler is not lawful (and it is in fact possible to be conqueror unjustly).

1324b29 What is more, we do not even observe this to be the case in the other sciences, for to secure obedience by persuasion or compulsion from patients on the one hand or from sailors on the other is not the work either of doctor or of helmsman.

1324b32 The many, however, seem to think that political rule is despotic rule, and what they each deny is just or beneficial for themselves they are not ashamed to practice against others. For what they seek in their own case is rule justly exercised, but when it comes to others, they have no care for justice. Yet it would be a strange thing if it were not the case that by nature one thing was fit for despotic rule and another was not.[6] So, if that is how things are, one should not try to rule everyone despotically but only those fit for it, just as one should not try to hunt human beings for a feast or a sacrifice but only what is fit to be hunted for this purpose (and what is so fit is any wild animal that is edible).

1324b41 Yet further, a single city, one governed nobly of course, could be happy all by itself—if indeed it is possible for a city using serious laws to be managed on its own somewhere—and the arrangement of its regime would not be for war nor for dominating over enemies (for let there be no such enemy present).

---

6. See 1.5. There is some dispute as to whether one should read *despozon* ("fit for ruling despotically") with the manuscripts or emend to *desposton* ("fit for being ruled despotically"). I have left the meaning ambiguous in my translation. The sense is not, in fact, much affected either way: if something is fit to rule despotically, there must be something else fit for being ruled despotically, and vice versa.

1325a5 Clearly, then, while all the care taken about war must be considered something noble, it cannot be considered the highest of all ends but rather as for the sake of that end. The serious legislator's part is to see how a city or family or any other community of human beings can partake in good life and in the happiness that is possible for them. There will be differences, of course, in respect of some of the laws that get laid down, and if there are neighbors present, it is the part of the legislator to look to what sort of training must be practiced against what sort of neighbor and how appropriate measures are to be used in each case.[7]

1325a14 But as regards the question of the end toward which to direct the best regime, there will also be occasion later for investigating it properly.[8]

CHAPTER 3

That the Life of Virtue Is Both Practical and Philosophical. *Those who praise the philosophic and political lives are partly right and partly wrong. The former are right to say despotic rule is not grand but wrong to think that all rule is despotic and that happiness is not activity. The latter are right to say happiness is activity but wrong to suppose that only ruling, and not also thinking, is activity. Thinking for its own sake is both activity and more active than external activities, and a life of internal activity can be best for both individuals and cities.*

1325a16 As for those who agree that a life with virtue is the most worth choosing but who disagree about how to exercise it, we must reply to both. For some of them reject political office and are of the opinion that the free person's way of life both is something other than that of a politician and is the one most of all worth choosing. But the others say that this political life itself is best, for they say that anyone who is not doing anything cannot be doing well, and that good activity and happiness are the same.

1325a23 They both speak correctly in some respects but not in others. So the first say, as is indeed true, that the way of life of a free person is better than that of a despot, for there is nothing grand about using a slave qua slave, since giving commands about necessary things has in it nothing noble.[9] But their thinking that all rule is despotic is not correct, for rule over the free differs from rule over slaves no less than that which is free by nature differs from that which is slave by nature (enough was determined about these matters in our initial discussions).[10] Also, their praising inactivity more than

7. Cf. chapters 5, 6, and 11 below.
8. Chapters 13–15.
9. Cf. 1.7.1255b33–37.
10. 1.4–7.

activity is not true, for happiness is action and, further, many noble things reach their goal in the actions of the just and moderate.

1325a34 Someone, however, might suppose, given these determinations, that having control over everyone is best, since in this way one would be in charge of the greatest number of the most noble actions. Consequently, anyone who is able ought not to let his neighbor rule but should deprive him of it, and should take no account, if a father, of his sons, or if sons, of their father, or if a friend, of his friend, but should ignore all this on the grounds that what is best is most worth choosing and that doing well is best.

1325a41 Well, perhaps this argument would be true if those who plunder and use violence will come to possess that which of all things is most choiceworthy. But that they will come to possess it is perhaps impossible, and the supposition laid down is false. For if he[11] does not have as much superiority as a man has over a woman or a father over children or a master over slaves, it could no longer be the case that his actions were noble. So the one who goes wrong here could not later put right all the wrongs against virtue that he has committed. For taking turns is what is noble and just for those who are similar, since taking turns is something similar and equal, whereas what is unequal and dissimilar is, for the equal and similar, against nature, and nothing against nature is noble. Hence it is that if anyone is superior in virtue and in the power to do the best things, to follow him is noble and to obey him just (though power whereby to act must be his as well, not virtue only).

1325b14 But if these arguments are nobly said and happiness is to be set down as acting well, then the practical life would be best both for every city in common and for each individual. The practical life, however, need not be directed toward others, as some think, nor need those thoughts alone be active which are for the sake of what results from acting. Rather much more so are those that are ends in themselves and are kinds of study and thinking for their own sake. For acting well is an end, so some activity is an end, and we also say, even in the case of external actions, that those are most of all acting in the authoritative sense who are, by their thoughts, the ruling craftsmen.

1325b23 But furthermore, neither is it necessary that those cities be inactive which are situated apart by themselves and choose so to live. For action can also take place among the parts, since the parts of a city have many ways in which they are in community with each other (and this could similarly be true also of any single human being). Otherwise, the god and the whole cosmos, which have no actions external to those that are proper to themselves, could scarcely be in a noble condition.

---

11. The "he" here is the person who, according to the supposition just made, rules over everyone and refuses to let them rule.

1325b30 That the same way of life, therefore, must be best both for each human being and for cities and humans in common is manifest.

CHAPTER 4

Presuppositions of the Best Regime

The Amount and Sort of Material. *The best regime requires suitable material if it is to come into existence, just as is the case in other arts. The materials in question are human beings and territory.*

1325b33 Since what has just been said about these matters has been by way of preface and since we studied the other regimes earlier,[12] the first thing to speak of as the beginning of what remains is what sort of things must be presupposed when it comes to the city that is going to be set up according to prayer. For the best regime cannot come to be without a proper amount of equipment. Hence we must, like people in prayer, lay down many suppositions beforehand, though none of them must be impossible.[13]

1325b39 I am speaking, for instance, about the number of citizens and the territory. For just as other craftsmen, as weavers and shipbuilders, need material suitable for their work (since the better this turns out to have been prepared, the more noble, necessarily, is the product that the art can bring about), so also the politician and the legislator need to have their own material available to them and in suitable condition. Of political equipment, there is first the multitude of the human beings, and how many there should be of them and of what sort; and likewise with the territory as well, and how much there should be of this and of what sort.

The Number of Human Beings. *The size of the city is not to be measured by greatness in the sense of largeness of numbers, for (i) greatness has to be understood by reference to capacity to carry out the work, not by quantity; or (ii) if quantity is relevant, it is numbers of those who belong to the city's proper parts that matter, not numbers absolutely. The city has a limit to its size, for (iii) a city with too many people cannot be well legislated, as is evident (a) from the facts and (b) from the argument that nobility and good arrangement are impossible to achieve in a number that exceeds too much; (iv) other things have their limit, lower as well as upper, determined by their nature and power, and so does the city. The limit of size for the city is, there-*

---

12. That is, the other regimes thought to be best that were discussed in book 2 (for the topic now is what regime is best).

13. Cf. 2.6.1265a17–18.

fore, that it be large enough to be self-sufficient but small enough to sustain a regime, that is, small enough for the citizens to be easily surveyed.

1326a8 Most people think that what is proper for the happy city is to be great, which, if true, is asserted in ignorance of what kind of city is great and what kind small. For they judge greatness by the numerical quantity of the inhabitants, whereas one should rather look to power and not to quantity. For a city too has a certain work to do, so the city most able to bring this to completion is the one that should be thought greatest. One would say, for instance, that Hippocrates[14] was greater qua doctor, and not qua human being, than someone who exceeded him in bodily size.

1326a17 Yet even were it necessary to judge this matter by looking to the multitude, one should not do so by reference to any chance multitude (for there must, perhaps, be large numbers of slaves, resident aliens, and foreigners in cities) but to those who form part of the city, that is, who belong to the proper parts from which the city is constituted.[15] For it is superiority in numbers of these that indicates a great city. A city that sends out many vulgar mechanics but few heavy armed troops cannot be great. For a great city is not the same thing as a populous city.

1326a25 Furthermore, the facts themselves at least make this manifest: that it is hard, or perhaps impossible, for a city with too many human beings in it to be well legislated. At least we do not see any city that is held to be nobly governed being lax about its numbers.

1326a29 The same is clear also from proof of reasoned argument. For law is a certain arrangement, and a good state of law must necessarily be good arrangement, but a number that exceeds too much is incapable of receiving arrangement (divine power would be required for that, the sort of power that also holds the whole itself together), since nobility at any rate customarily exists in number and size. Hence also the city whose size is limited by the above stated principle must be the most noble.

1326a35 There is a limit to the size of a city just as there is to everything else — animals, plants, and instruments. For if any one of these is either too small or too large in size, it will not have the power that belongs to it but will sometimes wholly forfeit its nature and sometimes be in a base condition. A ship, for example, that is a few inches long will not be a ship at all, nor one that is two stades long.[16] As it approaches such a size, it will, by smallness on this occasion and largeness on that, ruin the sailing. In like manner, a city

14. Hippocrates of Cos, born about 460, was one of the most noted doctors in the ancient world. The Hippocratic oath is supposed to go back to him.

15. For this distinction, see 4(7).8.

16. A stade is about 600 feet.

that is made up of too few people will not be self-sufficient; but the city is something self-sufficient. Conversely, a city made up of too many will, like a nation, be self-sufficient in necessities, but it will not be a city, because a regime could not easily exist in it. For who will be general of so excessive a multitude, or who will be its herald unless he have the voice of Stentor?[17]

1326b7 Hence the first city to exist is the one that is composed of the first multitude large enough to be self-sufficient with a view to good life in political community. A city that surpasses this one in numbers can, of course, be a greater city, but this process cannot, as we said, go on indefinitely. The limit to how far it can go can easily be seen from the facts. A city's acts are those of its rulers and of its ruled subjects, and the work of the ruler is to command and pass judgment. But with respect to passing judgment on matters of justice and distributing offices according to merit, the citizens must know what each other is like, for where it happens that they do not, these matters of judgment and offices must be in a base condition. For it is not just to decide them in an offhand way, but that is manifestly what happens where there are many people. Further, foreigners and resident aliens could easily get a share in the regime because, given the excessive numbers, escaping detection will not be hard. So it is clear that the best limit for the city is this: the furthest that the excess of numbers for securing a self-sufficient life can go and still be easy to survey.

1326b24 Let such, then, be our discussion of the size of the city.

CHAPTER 5

The Amount and Sort of Territory

Amount and Quality. *The territory must be self-sufficient and large enough to permit the inhabitants to live with leisure in liberality and moderation.*

1326b26 Things are similar also in the case of the territory. For, as regards what sort it is like, everyone would clearly praise the territory that was most self-sufficient, and such a territory must be one that produces everything (for self-sufficiency is having everything to hand and being deficient in nothing). In amount and size it should be large enough that the inhabitants can live a leisured life with liberality and moderation combined. But whether we speak nobly in giving this definition or not must be left for more accurate examination later, when we undertake a general discussion of property and of the prosperity that consists in possessions and say how or in what

---

17. Stentor was one of Homer's warriors and had a proverbially loud voice (*Iliad* 5.785–86).

way things should stand in relation to use itself.[18] For there are many disputes in the investigation of this question that are generated by those who
push things toward one or the other of the extremes in way of life, either to
meanness or to luxury.

Topology and Site of the City

As Regards the Territory. *The territory must be hard for enemies to enter and easy
for citizens to exit and to survey. The site of the city must be such that the territory can
easily be defended from it and goods easily conveyed into it.*

1326b39 The form of the territory is not difficult to see (though there are
things about it where one must also follow the advice of those with military
experience), namely that it must be hard for enemies to enter but easy for
citizens to leave. Further, as we said in the case of the numbers of human
beings, it too must be easy to survey. Being easy to survey means that the
territory is easy to defend.

1327a3 As regards the position of the city, if one is to have it the way one
would pray for, what is appropriate is that it be nobly situated with respect
to both sea and territory. One defining principle of this is what was just
stated, for from the point of view of defensive sallies, it should have access
to every locality. The remaining principle is that it be easy to reach for the
conveyance of crops and of materials for lumbering and for any other such
industries that the territory happens to possess.

CHAPTER 6

As Regards the Sea. *Accessibility to the sea is said to be bad for the city because
of the danger to good legislation from foreigners used to other laws and the danger
to good government from a mass of traders. But the contrary advantages are that the
city will be better defended and more prosperous. The evils can be avoided if the port
is separate and intercourse with it regulated by law, and if marines are dominant over
the naval force and if that force is formed from local farmers.*

1327a11 As for close association with the sea, people dispute a great deal, as
it happens, about whether this is useful or harmful for well-legislated cities.
Letting in foreigners who have been brought up under different laws is said
to be a disadvantage from the point of view of good legislation, as is also
the large population, for from the fact that the sea is being used for exports

---

18. Probably in the lost chapters at the end of book 5(8).

and imports there will, they say, be a multitude of traders around, which is a thing contrary to noble government.[19]

1327a18 But supposing such results did not occur, there is no doubt that it would be better, from the point of view of both safety and prosperity, to have territory and city in close association with the sea. For, as regards bearing up more easily under enemy attack, people must, if they are going to survive, be readily defensible on both elements, land and sea; and as regards damaging the enemy, those who have access to both will be able to do it on one or the other element if they cannot do it on the two of them. As regards provisions that they do not happen to have at home, they will be able to import these while exporting whatever surplus necessities they have.

1327a27 For a city should be a trading center for itself and not for others. Those who make themselves into a marketplace for everyone do so for the sake of the revenue, but a city that is not to engage in such grasping for more should not even possess a trading center of this sort. For even now we see that many lands and cities have ports and harbors naturally well positioned near the city such that these neither form the same town as it nor are too far away, but are dominated by walls and other such fortifications.[20] So it is manifest that the city will enjoy whatever good is to be had from being in community with sea ports, but that it will easily guard against any harm by announcing and defining in its laws who should and who should not have intercourse with each other.

1327a40 As regards naval power, there is no doubt that it is best to have it up to a certain point, for one should be formidable and able to mount a defense by sea as well as by land not only on one's own behalf but also on behalf of some of one's neighbors. As regards the amount and size of this power, one must investigate the way of life of the city, for if its way of life is going to be one of leadership and politics, then it must possess the degree of this power that is commensurate with its activities. But it is not necessary for the city to have the mass of human beings associated with a crowd of seafarers; there is no need to have these as part of the city. For, on the one hand, the marines, who are in control and dominate on voyages, are free and belong to the infantry, and, on the other, if there is a multitude of serfs and farmers on the land, there will necessarily also be an abundance of sailors. We can see this already happening in some places, as in the city of the Heracleots. For they send out many triremes, though they have a city more modest than others in size.

1327b16 Let such then be our distinctions about territory, harbors, cities, and sea, and about naval power.

19. Cf. Plato *Laws* 704d3–705b8.
20. As, for instance, at Athens, Megara, and Corinth.

CHAPTER 7

The Sort of Human Beings. *Divisions in the inhabited world, and in Greece, show that those who share the spirit of the Northerners and the thought of the Asians but lack the deficiencies of each are the best for being led toward virtue. The idea that the city's guardians should be friendly to familiars is correct, for spirit makes friendliness, but not that they should be harsh to strangers, for spirit is harsh rather to wrongdoers, and indeed more so when they are familiars.*

1327b18 About the multitude of citizens, we said already what the limit should be, so now let us speak about what sort of nature they should have. One can, in fact, get a pretty good idea about the matter by looking at those cities among the Greeks that are well reputed and at the way the whole inhabited world is divided up among the nations. For nations in cold regions and in Europe are full of spirit but rather deficient in thought and art. That is why they remain freer but have no regime[21] and cannot rule their neighbors. Nations about Asia are endowed in soul with thought and art but lack spirit. That is why they remain ruled and enslaved. The family of the Greeks, however, is in the middle of these locations, so it shares the character of both. For it is both spirited and endowed with thought. That is why it remains free and best governed and capable, if it chances on a single regime, of ruling everyone.[22]

1327b33 The nations of the Greeks also display the same difference among themselves. For some of them have a one-sided nature, but others are, with respect to both capacities, well mixed. It is manifest, then, that those who are going to be most amenable to being led by the legislator toward virtue must be endowed with thought and spirited in nature.

1327b38 For, to take what some assert should be the qualities of guardians —friendliness toward familiars but savagery toward strangers[23]—it is spirit that generates friendliness, since this is the power of the soul whereby we love. A sign is that spirit is more stirred up against relatives and friends when it thinks it has been slighted than against strangers. Hence, when complaining of his friends, Archilochus appropriately discourses with his spirit: "verily is your torture from your friends."[24] Also, the ruling and free element in

21. The Greek is *apoliteuta*, from *a* ("without") and *politeia* ("regime").

22. Possibly a reference to the peace and alliance imposed on the whole Greek world by Philip of Macedon in 338 and continued by his son Alexander. There may also be a reference back to the alliance achieved, if only fitfully, by all the Greeks against Xerxes during the Persian Wars.

23. Plato *Republic* 375b7–e7.

24. Frag. 67b Diehl. Archilochus was a poet from Paros and flourished about the middle of the seventh century.

everyone comes from this power, for spirit is a ruling and indomitable thing. **1328a8** But that guardians should be harsh toward strangers is not nobly said, since they should not be like this toward anyone. Nor are the magnanimous savage in nature, save toward wrongdoers, though they will, as was said earlier, be more savage toward relatives if they think themselves wronged. That this should be so is reasonable enough. For, in the case of those from whom people suppose a debt of kindness is due, they consider that, in addition to the harm inflicted, they have been deprived of this debt as well. Hence the sayings: "harsh are the wars of brothers" and "those who love to the limit also hate to the limit."[25]

1328a17 Concerning those engaged in politics,[26] then, and how many they should be and of what nature, and again concerning the territory, and how much and of what sort it should be, pretty well everything has been determined. For one should not look to get the same precision from reasoned discussions as from what comes through perception.

CHAPTER 8

The Disposition of the Material

The Classes of Human Beings Necessary to a City. *Of the human beings a city needs, some are not parts of it but only for the sake of it (as are those who are property), and others are parts (as are those who share in the happiness it pursues). They fall into six classes, as determined by the city's several works: farmers, artisans, warriors, the well-off, priests, and decision makers.*

1328a21 Since, as in the case of other things constituted according to nature, the whole composite's parts are not to be identified as those things without which the whole could not be, so clearly neither should everything that must be present in cities be set down as parts of the city nor as the parts of any other community that forms something one in kind. For there must be some one thing that is both common and the same for those who are in community together, whether they are sharing it equally or unequally—for instance, food or an amount of territory or something else of the sort. But when there is something that exists for the sake of another, and this other is the end for the sake of which the first is, then they have nothing in common save by way of making and receiving. I mean, for instance, the relation that any instrument and that craftsmen have to the work produced. For there is

25. Frag. 975 Nauck (Euripides) and 78 (anonymous).
26. That is, the citizens, since it is citizens who share in political rule.

nothing that the house has in common with the builder except that the art of the builder is for the sake of the house.

1328a33 That is why, though cities need property, property is no part of the city. Included among the parts of property are many living things, but the city is a community of similars and is for the sake of the best possible life. Since happiness, however, is best, and since happiness is a perfect exercise and use of virtue, and since it so happens that some people are able to share in this but others slightly or not at all, then clearly that is why there are many kinds and differences to cities and why there are several regimes. For as people each pursue happiness in a different way and by different means, they make different ways of life and regimes for themselves.

1328b2 But it is necessary to examine how many are these very things without which a city could not be, for also included among them, and hence necessarily present, would be what we say are parts of the city. We must, then, get hold of the number of works there are, since this will make the answer clear. So first, food must be present; next, arts (for life needs many instruments); third, arms (for those who share in community must carry arms with them, both as regards their rule, thanks to the disobedient, and as regards any who try to wrong them from without); further, a supply of commodities (so as to have something to meet their own needs and the needs of war); fifth, and primarily, care for the divine, which they call priesthood; and sixth in number, and most necessary of all, judgment about what is advantageous and just in their intercourse with each other.

1328b15 These, then, are the works that practically every city needs. For the city is not any chance multitude but one that, as we say, is self-sufficient for life, and if any one of these happens to be lacking, the community in question cannot be simply self-sufficient. A city, then, must be established in accordance with these works, and so there must be a mass of farmers (to provide the food), artisans, a part to do the fighting, a part that is well-off, priests, and judges to decide what is necessary and advantageous.

CHAPTER 9

The Separation of the Classes from Each Other

Statement and Proof of the Separation. *Whether everyone is to belong to every class or not depends on the regime. In the best regime, the citizens (those capable of sharing its happiness) will not be artisans or farmers; they will be warriors and decision makers, the first when younger and the second when older. They will also be the well-off and, when retired, the priests.*

1328b24 Given these distinctions, we must next examine whether everyone is to take part in all of these works (for the same people could all be farmers and artisans and deliberators and judges), or whether we must suppose different persons for each work mentioned, or whether some of them must of necessity be private and others common. Things are not the same in every regime since, as we said,[27] it is possible for all to share everything or for all not to share everything but for some to share some things and others others. In democracies, for instance, everyone shares everything, but in oligarchies it is the opposite.

1328b33 Our subject of investigation happens to be the best regime, and the best regime is that under which the city might be most happy, and happiness was said earlier[28] to be incapable of existence without virtue. From these facts, then, it manifestly follows that in the city that is most nobly governed and possesses men who are just simply (and not relative to a supposition),[29] the citizens must live no mechanical or commercial way of life. For such ways of life are low-born and opposed to virtue. Nor should those who are going to be citizens be farmers either, since there is need of leisure both for the generation of virtue and for political activity.

1329a2 But since the part that goes to war and the part that deliberates about what is beneficial and decides about what is just are also present in the city and are manifestly most of all parts of it, must these parts also be set down as different or are both to be assigned to the same persons? It is manifest that they must in a way be assigned to the same persons and in a way also to different ones: insofar as each of these two works belongs to a different prime of life and one of them needs prudence and the other power, they must be assigned to different persons; but insofar as it is something impossible that those who are able to apply and block force should always put up with being ruled, to this extent they must be assigned to the same persons (for those who have control of the arms also have control of whether the regime will continue or not). The answer that is left, then, is that our regime must be handed over to both groups, though not at the same time. Instead, just as by nature power exists in the younger and prudence in the older, so making the distribution accord with both is beneficial and just, since it is a division made on the basis of desert.

1329a17 Furthermore, the property too should be associated with these persons, since the citizens must have prosperity and these are the citizens. For the mechanical class has no share in the city, nor any other type that is not

27. Perhaps a reference to 2.1.1260b37–1261a4.
28. 4(7).1.
29. That is, not men who are only just relative to the supposition of some inferior regime, as democracy or oligarchy; cf. 3.4–5 and 6(4).1.

a craftsman of virtue. The point is clear from our supposition. For being happy is something that has to go along with virtue, and a city must not be called happy by looking to some part of it but by looking to all its citizens. It is also manifest that the citizens must possess the property, if the farmers indeed have to be slaves or barbarians or serfs.

1329a27 The part that is left from those enumerated above is the class of priests. But how to arrange them is also manifest. No farmer or mechanic must be set up as a priest, for it is by citizens that gods are fittingly honored. But since the citizen body was divided into two, namely the armed part and the deliberative part, and since it is fitting that those who are worn out with age should give service to the gods and enjoy rest in their company, it is to these that priesthoods should be assigned.

1329a34 The things, then, without which a city cannot be constituted and the number of its parts have been stated. For the presence of farmers and artisans and the whole part of laborers is necessary in cities, but the parts of the city are the armed and deliberative parts. Each of these parts is also distinct from the others, but some always and others by turns.

CHAPTER 10

Confirmation from Ancient Precedents. *The practice of dividing into classes and separating soldiers from farmers, as also that of providing them common messes, are of ancient origin. The same is likely to be true of almost everything, so the legislator should make use of what has already been found out and add only what is still lacking.*

1329a40 It appears to be neither a present nor a recent discovery among philosophers of regimes that the city must be divided up into classes and that the fighting class must be different from the farming class. Things are still like this even today in Egypt and Crete, with Sesostris being, as is said, responsible for such legislation in Egypt and Minos in Crete.[30]

1329b5 The arrangement of messes also seems to be ancient. In Crete they arose under the reign of Minos, while in Italy they are far older. For the chroniclers of those who live there say that a certain Italus became king of Oenotria, that the Oenotrians changed their name and were called Italians after him instead, and that the name Italy was taken by that promontory of Europe that lies between the gulfs of Scylletium and Lametius[31] (which are a half day's journey from each other). They relate, in fact, that this Italus made the Oenotrians, who were nomads, into farmers and, along with laying down other laws for them, first instituted the common messes. Hence

---

30. Cf. 2.10.1271b30–32.
31. On the toe of Italy.

these common messes and some of the laws are still used by certain of those who are descended from him: Opicans inhabited the area toward Etruria and are called, both now and formerly, by the name of Ausonians; and Chonians inhabited the area toward Iapygia and the Ionian Gulf, Siritis so called (the Chonians were also Oenotrians by family).

1329b22 So the arrangement of common messes came from there first, but the separation of the political multitude into classes came from Egypt (for the reign of Sesostris stretches much further back in time than that of Minos). One must, then, suppose that other things too have often been discovered, or rather infinitely often, in the long course of time. For it is likely that need itself was teacher of what was necessary and that, after necessities were supplied, there began, reasonably enough, to be an increase in things directed to superfluity and elegance. Consequently, one must suppose the same holds also of what concerns the regime. A sign that these things are all ancient is given by what has happened in Egypt, for the people there seem the most ancient and yet they have got hold of laws and a political arrangement. So the thing to do is to make adequate use of what has been discovered while trying to find out what is still missing.[32]

The Division of the Territory

With Respect to Farming. *The territory should be divided into common and private and these again into two: the common into one part for the messes and another for the gods, the private so that each citizen has one part near the city and another near the border. The farmers should preferably be slaves of different races and lacking in spirit, with common slaves on common land and private ones on private.*

1329b36 That the territory should belong to those who possess arms and share the regime was said before, as also why those who farm it should be different from them, and how large and of what sort the territory should be.[33] What first needs discussing is how the land is to be divided up, and who and of what quality those should be who farm it, for we say that property should not be a common possession, contrary to what some have said, but it should, following the practice of friends, become common in the way it is used,[34] and no citizen should lack for food. As for the messes, everyone seems to agree that in well-furnished cities it is useful to have them (though why we also go along with this view will be stated later).[35] But these messes

32. These final remarks may be an implicit criticism of Plato and Hippodamus; see 2.2–6, 8, and in particular 2.5.1264a1–6.
33. 4(7).9 and 4(7).5–6.
34. 2.5.1263a22–40.
35. Probably in the lost chapters at the end of book 5(8).

must be shared in common by all the citizens, and it is not easy for the needy, from their private property, both to contribute the required amount and to manage the rest of their household. Common to the whole city are also expenditures relating to the gods.

1330a9 So it is necessary to divide the territory into two parts, one that is common and another that is held privately. Each of these must again be divided into two: the common into one part for services relating to the gods and another for the expense of the common messes, and the private into one part near the borders and another near the city,[36] so that the citizens will share both localities and have two allotments each. For there is equality and justice in this arrangement and more likemindedness with respect to wars against neighbors. Where things are not like this, some think little of hostility against the borders while others worry about it too much and in a way contrary to what is noble. That is why there are laws in some places that those living near the borders should not take part in councils where wars involving them are concerned, because they are deemed incapable, through their private interest, of contributing nobly to the deliberation. So the territory should be thus divided for the aforesaid reasons.

1330a25 As for the farmers, if they are to be as one would pray for, they should preferably be slaves who are neither all of the same race nor spirited[37] (this will make them useful as regards work and safe as regards revolt). Alternatively, they should be barbarian subjects who are similar to the former in nature. The slaves on private lands should belong privately to those who own the property, while those on common lands should be common. But how slaves should be treated, and why it is better for freedom to be held out to all of them as a reward, will be stated later.[38]

CHAPTER 11

With Respect to the Site of the City

Health. *Four things are of importance: health, military activity, political activity, and nobility. Health requires that the city have a site facing east or sheltered from the north wind.*

36. Cf. Plato *Laws* 745c3–d2.
37. Cf. Plato *Laws* 777c6–d2.
38. Probably in the lost chapters at the end of book 5(8). However, we can get some idea of what Aristotle might have said there from *Oeconomica* 1.5, which is an Aristotelian work, if not by Aristotle himself.

1330a34 That the city should, as far as possible, be accessible to the mainland and the sea, and likewise to the whole territory, was said earlier.[39] But as regards its relation to itself, one should pray to get a site for it keeping four things in view.[40] The first, as being a matter of necessity, is health. Those sites are healthier that are inclined toward the dawn and the winds that blow from the sun's rising, but second are those sheltered from the north wind (for they weather the winter better).

Military Action and Nobility. The city should be easy for citizens to exit but difficult for enemies to enter; it should have a healthy location and abundant healthy water to withstand sieges; it should have the fortifications fitting its regime; the town plan should combine regular and irregular divisions to unite nobility with safety; it should have walls, for these provide safety without compromising virtue, and walls that will both be an adornment to the city and answer to military necessities.

1330a41 The remaining things to keep in view are that the city be nobly disposed for political and military action.[41] As regards military action, the city must be easy for the citizens themselves to exit but hard for their opponents to enter or surround. It must have sources of water and springs of its own in abundance, but if not, the construction of large and generous receptacles for rainwater has been found as a way to prevent the supply running short when the territory is cut off by war. Taking care of the citizens' health, since this is a necessity, is a matter of having the site nobly situated in a healthy spot and with a healthy exposure and, secondly, of using healthy sources of water and of not making concern for health something incidental. For what we use most and oftenest for the body contributes most to health, and water and air have an effect of this nature. Hence, where the healthy springs are not all alike or do not exist in abundance, cities of sound mind must separate out water for drinking from water that is for other needs.

1330b17 As regards fortified places, what is advantageous is not alike for every regime. A citadel,[42] for example, fits an oligarchy and a monarchy; a plain fits a democracy; neither fits an aristocracy, but rather several strong forts.

1330b21 Private dwellings are thought to be more pleasantly arranged, and more usefully with a view to other activities, if they are neatly divided in the more recent and Hippodamean fashion,[43] but the opposite fashion, as existed

39. 4(7).5–6 above.
40. There is much doubt about the text and grammar of this sentence, but the sense intended seems clear enough.
41. It may seem that Aristotle mentions here only two factors of the remaining three, but nobility, though it is a factor inseparable from the other two, would seem to be the third.
42. Literally an acropolis, or a single elevated site.
43. See 2.8.1267b22–23.

in ancient times, is preferable from the point of view of safety in war, for then it is hard for foreign garrisons to get out and for attackers to find their way around. So one should adopt both fashions, which is possible enough if one follows farmers and arranges things in "vine clumps," as some call them, and does not neatly divide up the whole city but only certain parts and sections of it.[44] In this way the condition of the city will be a noble one both from the point of safety and from the point of view of ordered adornment.[45]

1330b32 As regards walls, those who say that cities laying claim to virtue should not have them are adopting overly old-fashioned ideas even though they can see that cities with that as their boast are refuted by the facts.[46] Against a similar enemy and one not much superior in size, it can be ignoble to try to save oneself by relying on the fortification of walls. But it also can and does happen that one's attackers are more numerous than human virtue and the virtue to be found in a small number can bear. So if safety is to be had and injury and outrage avoided, the very sure fortification provided by walls must be held to be the defense that is most warlike, especially given the present inventions in missiles and engines for precision siege warfare. For not to think it right to throw walls round cities is like making the territory easy to invade and taking away the mountainous places. It is also like not building walls around private dwellings on the ground that this will make the inhabitants unmanly. Further, one must not forget this fact also: that those who do have walls thrown about their city can use the city in both ways, either as if it had walls and as if it did not, whereas those who do not have walls cannot.

1331a10 But if that is how things are, then not only must walls be thrown around the city, but also care must be taken to see that they are suitable to it, both from the point of view of ordered adornment and from the point of view of military necessities, especially those that are now being brought to light. For just as ways to get more for themselves are a matter of concern to attackers, so are there also inventions that defenders either have made or must look for and use philosophy to think out. For attackers do not even attempt to impose their rule on those who are well prepared.

44. These vine clumps were arranged like the five spots on a die (a quincunx). Aristotle's aim is presumably to have some broad boulevards dividing the city in a regular way but to make the concentrations of dwellings a criss-cross of narrow lanes.

45. The Greek word translated as "ordered adornment" here, and by the same or similar wording in the succeeding pages, is *kosmos* or some cognate thereof.

46. This "refutation by the facts" refers presumably to Sparta (which boasted its lack of walls) and to its invasion by the Thebans in 369. Plato's *Laws* 778d3–779a8 argues against walls.

CHAPTER 12

Political Action and Nobility. *Some messes should be set up in guardhouses about the territory, and others, those for boards of officials, in temples and on a height that fits both virtue and defense; below it should be the free public square, which is reserved for citizens and also has the seniors' gymnasium, while the commercial square must be separate but accessible to land and sea; the priests should have messes near the temples, and the various other officials of town and country should also have theirs near their spheres of control.*

1331a19 Since it is necessary to distribute the multitude of the citizens into messes,[47] and since the walls must possess guardhouses and towers at convenient locations, it is clearly a good idea to set up some of the messes in these guardhouses. That, then, is how these matters may be adorned in orderly fashion.

1331a24 As regards the dwellings given over to the gods and the messes with the most control among the official boards, it is proper that they have a suitable location and the same location (except in the case of temples that are set apart by the law or some pronouncement of the Pythian oracle). Such a location would be one that is both sufficiently conspicuous for the positioning of virtue and is also rather well fortified in relation to the nearby parts of the city.

1331a30 Below this location, it is appropriate to set up the sort of public square that is termed "free" and is called such in Thessaly. This is the one that must be pure from anything set up for sale and which no vulgar mechanic nor farmer nor anyone else of the kind can approach unless he is summoned by the rulers. The location would be well graced if the gymnasium of the older men were also arranged there. For it is appropriate also to divide up this element of ordered adornment according to age and to have some of the rulers pass their time among the young while the older men pass theirs among the rulers (it is presence under the gaze of rulers that above all instills true shame and the fear that belongs to the free).

1331b1 The public square where things are set up for sale should be different from this first one and have a separate location that is easy of access for all the goods sent up from the sea and in from the land.

1331b4 Since the multitude of the city is divided into priests and rulers,[48] it is

---

47. 4(7).10 above.

48. There is dispute about the text at this point. Some wish to add "and soldiers" after "rulers" since soldiers too are proper parts of the city (4(7).9). But perhaps "rulers" can be taken here in a broad sense to include soldiers, since the soldiers will become the rulers as they get older and, even as soldiers, they are exercising subordinate rule while also having control over the defense and preservation of the regime.

appropriate that the priests too have their messes arranged in the vicinity of the temple buildings. As for the official boards whose care is about contracts, the filing of lawsuits, summonses, and other such matters of administration, and also about the management of the public square and the management of the town (as it is called), these should be set up near the square or some common meeting point. Such a place would be near the public square for necessities, for the upper square we have set aside for leisure while this one is for activities that are necessary.

1331b13 This just mentioned arrangement should be imitated in what concerns the territory as well. For there too, for the purpose of keeping guard, the rulers (called foresters by some but field managers by others) should have their guardhouses and messes. Temples should also be distributed over the countryside, some dedicated to gods and others to heroes.

1331b18 But it is pointless to spend time discussing and giving detailed accounts of such matters, for it is not hard to think them through: what is hard is to create them. To speak about them is a work of prayer, but whether they come about is a work of chance. Hence let us, for the present,[49] set aside what further remains on these topics.

CHAPTER 13

The Best Regime Itself

The Goal That the Regime Must Be Capable of Achieving. *If living well is to be achieved, both the goal and the way to it must be laid down properly. The goal is happiness, or the perfect exercise of virtue without qualification, that is, without any impediments from lack of equipment or of the goods of fortune.*

1331b24 What we must speak about instead is the regime itself and from which and what sort of persons the city that is going to be blessed and nobly governed must be made up. The well-being of everyone exists in two things; of these two, one is the right laying down of the goal and end of actions and the other is the finding of the actions that bear on that end. These can be in either harmony or disharmony with each other. For sometimes the goal is nobly laid down, but in their actions people fail to get it; and sometimes they do hit upon everything relevant to the end, but the end they laid down was base. Sometimes they miss out on both—as in medicine, for example, where, on occasion, doctors neither judge nobly what the healthy

---

49. Some further discussion of these matters is given in 8(6).8, but it is not clear if Aristotle means here to be referring ahead to that chapter.

body must be like nor do they hit upon the things that work relative to the defining principle they have presupposed for themselves. In all arts and sciences it is necessary to get a firm grip on both: the end and the actions that are directed to the end.

1331b39 Now it is manifest that everyone desires happiness and to live well, but some have the ability to attain it while others, because of some stroke of fortune or nature, do not (for noble living also requires equipment, though a lesser amount in the case of those in a better condition and a greater amount in the case of those in a worse one). There are others who straight off fail to seek happiness correctly despite having the ability to attain it. But since the object before us is to see the best regime, and since this is the one under which a city would be best governed, and since a city would be best governed under that regime where it can most of all be happy, then clearly we must not ignore what happiness is.

1332a7 We assert, and have so determined it in the *Ethics*[50] (if there is any need of those discussions), that happiness is perfect exercise and use of virtue, and that not conditionally but absolutely. By "conditionally" I am referring to necessities, and by "absolutely" I mean "nobly." Take, for instance, acts of justice. Retributions and punishments that are just spring from virtue, but they are necessitated and possess nobility by way of necessity, for it would be better if there were no need of such things, either in the case of the man or the city. But actions bestowing honors and prosperity are, absolutely speaking, of very high nobility. For the former actions are the choice[51] of an evil of sorts, but the latter actions are the reverse: they are the providers and originators of goods.

1332a19 The serious man would use poverty and disease nobly as well as the other ills of fortune. Blessedness, however, exists in their opposites. For this too was defined in our ethical discussions:[52] that the serious man is such

---

50. The reference is to the extended discussion of what happiness involves in *Nicomachean Ethics* 1.8–11. Some commentators refer also to the *Eudemian Ethics* (2.1.1219a38–b3), but despite certain verbal echoes (which are found also in the *Nicomachean* at 1.8.1098b31–33, 11.1101a14–21, and 13.1102a5–6), the *Eudemian* contains no such discussion as is summarized here.

51. Reading *hairesis* ("choice") with the manuscripts, not the emendation to *anhairesis* ("removal") with Dreizehnter. Punishments can, of course, be regarded as the removal of evil (since they restore the balance of justice), but they can also be regarded as the choice of evil, that is, the evil one inflicts on the criminal as his punishment. Such choice of evil is conditionally noble, that is, on the condition that there is a criminal in need of punishment. Absolutely speaking, one would prefer not to inflict evil on anyone and one chooses to do so here only because it is necessitated by the existence of crime.

52. The thought here, though not the same words, can be found in *Nicomachean Ethics* 1.8 (esp. 1099a11–15) and 3.4. Some stronger verbal similarities can be found at 5.1.1129b1–6, 5.9.1137a26–30, and 9.9.1170a14–16, and also in the *Eudemian Ethics* 7.2.1236b36–1237a3 and 8.15.1248b26–37 and in *Magna Moralia* 2.9.

that, because of his virtue, the things that are simply good are good for him; and, clearly, his use of them must be serious and noble absolutely. That is in fact why human beings think external goods are responsible for happiness, just as if they were to suppose that the lyre rather than the art was responsible for brilliant and noble playing.

That Achieving This Goal Requires Education. *Having the necessary equipment is a work of chance and can only be prayed for. Having the necessary virtue is a work of education and is to be provided by the legislator, at least insofar as education depends on habit and reason and not nature.*

1332a28 So, then, of the things spoken about, some must be present and others must be provided by the legislator. That is why, in respect of those things over which chance has control (and we regard it as having control), we pray that the composition of the city accord with our prayer.[53] That the city be serious is no longer the work of chance but of knowledge and deliberate choice. A city is serious, however, if its citizens, or those who share in the regime, are serious; and in our case all the citizens share in the regime.[54] So what needs investigation is how a man becomes serious.[55] For even though it is possible for all to be serious, but not in the sense that each one individually is so,[56] the latter would be more worth choosing because "all" follows from "each."

1332a38 People become good and serious by means of three things: nature, habit, and reason.[57] For nature must first produce us with the quality of body and soul of a human being and not of some other animal. But it is of no avail, in the case of some things, to be born with them, since habits can alter them. For there are some things that are by nature susceptible, through habits, of change in either direction: to what is worse and to what is better. The other animals live mainly by nature, but some to a small extent by habits also. A human being, however, lives by reason as well (for he alone has reason). Consequently, since humans do many things by reason against habituation and nature if they are persuaded that something else is better, all three of these must harmonize with each other. Now we determined earlier[58] what nature those should have who are going to be amenable to

53. Reading *kat' euchēn* with the manuscripts, not *kata tuchēn* ("accord with chance") with Dreizehnter.

54. As opposed, presumably, to deviant regimes where some of those who ought to have a share are denied it (3.6–7).

55. Cf. 3.18.1288a39–b2.

56. Presumably a reference to the situation in polity when the whole multitude together is virtuous even though each member individually is not (3.11).

57. Cf. *Ethics* 10.9.1179b20–29.

58. 4(7).7 above.

the legislator. What is left is the work of education, for human beings learn some things by habituation and others by listening.

CHAPTER 14

The Education Required

Education Is to Form Both Ruled and Rulers. The political community is divided into rulers and ruled, but as it seldom occurs that any are superior enough always to rule while the others are always to be ruled, all the citizens must be ruled first and rule later, and be educated to be ruled first and to rule later. Education to be ruled is education to be ruled as free, and education to rule is education to be a simply good man.

1332b12 But since every political community is made up of rulers and ruled, the question needs to be investigated whether different persons must be the rulers and the ruled or whether the same ones must be both over a lifetime. For it is clear that the education will also follow in accordance with this distinction.

1332b16 If, then, there were some people as different from others as we think gods and heroes are from human beings, and they were from the very beginning far superior in body and later in soul, so much so that the superiority of the rulers was indisputable and manifest to the ruled, clearly it would be better that once and for all the same persons always rule and the others always get ruled. But since this is not easy to achieve and since things are not as, according to Scylax' report,[59] they are in India, with the kings having so great a superiority over the ruled, it is clear, for many reasons, that everyone must share and share alike and take turns in ruling and being ruled. For fairness is the same thing for those who are alike, and it is difficult for a regime that is constituted contrary to justice to survive. For the ruled will be joined by everyone in the territory who wants to revolt, and it is something impossible that those in the ruling body should be numerous enough to be stronger than all of them.

1332b32 Nevertheless, it is indisputable that the rulers must differ from the ruled. How this is to be achieved then, and how the regime is to be shared, is something the legislator must examine. We spoke about this question earlier,[60] for nature has given the principle for choosing[61] by making what is the same in family to be part younger and part older, for the former of

59. Scylax of Caryanda in Caria traveled to India in the late sixth or early fifth century.
60. 4(7).9.1329a6–17 above.
61. Reading *hairesis* ("choice") with the manuscripts, not *dihaeresis* ("distinction") with Dreizehnter.

whom it is proper to be ruled and for the latter to rule. No one is annoyed if he is ruled because of his age nor does he imagine himself superior, especially as he is going to get back his contribution[62] when he reaches the appropriate age. In a sense, then, the same persons will rule and be ruled, and in a sense different ones. Consequently, the education will also be in a sense the same and in a sense different (for they say that anyone who is going to rule nobly must first be ruled).[63]

1333a3 But rule, as was said in our first discussions,[64] is on the one hand for the sake of the ruler and on the other for the sake of the ruled, the first of which is despotic rule and the second rule over the free. And a difference arises in the case of certain commands that are given, not as regards what is done but as regards what it is done for. That is why, in the case of many works that are considered menial chores, it is noble for the free among the young to do them also. For, in respect of their nobility or lack of it, actions do not differ so much in themselves as in their end and what they are done for.[65]

1333a11 But since we say that the virtue of a citizen—that is, of a ruling citizen—is the same as that of the good man, and that the same person must be ruled first and become ruler later, the concern of the legislator must be to see how the citizens may become good men—that is, by what pursuits they will do so and what the end of the best life is.

Education Must Follow the Division of the Soul

What the Division Is. The soul is divided into a part that has reason, which is itself divided into a practical and contemplative part, and a part that does not have reason but can listen to it. The end is to be found in what is better, and the part that has reason is better and its acts are better. Life too is divided into war and peace, occupation and leisure, and actions into useful and noble; the latter are all better and the end of the former. Legislation must have all these in view but the better more so; education must do likewise.

1333a16 The soul is divided into two parts, of which one part has reason of itself and the other does not have reason of itself but is capable of listening to it. The virtues of these parts we assert to be those by which a man is said to be in any way good.[66] As regards which of these two parts the end

---

62. The Greek is *eranos*, which was a loan or gift for which repayment in some form was expected. Here the idea probably is that as when young they gave the gift of obedience to their elders, so when older themselves they will receive the same gift back again from those who are then their juniors.
63. Cf. 3.4.1277b8–13.
64. 3.4 and 6.
65. Cf. 5(8).2.1337b17–21.
66. *Ethics* 1.13.

is more to be found in, that is a question that those who divide the soul after the manner we say will have no doubt how to answer. For the worse is always for the sake of the better, as is manifest in matters of art and of nature alike. But the part that has reason is better; and this part is divided, following the way we are accustomed to divide it, into two. For as reason is on the one hand practical and on the other hand contemplative,[67] so this part of the soul must also be divided in the same way. Actions too, we will say, are divided analogously; and those of the part that is by nature better must, for anyone capable of attaining all or the two, be more choiceworthy. For the highest attainable is for everyone always what is most worth choosing.

1333a30 There is also a division of life as a whole into occupation and leisure,[68] war and peace; and of things to be done, some are directed to what is necessary and useful and others to what is noble. In their case too the same choice must be made as in the case of the parts of the soul and their respective actions: war is for the sake of peace, occupation for the sake of leisure, necessary and useful things for the sake of noble ones.

1333a37 The politician, then, must look to all these things when legislating in accordance with the parts of the soul and the actions of these parts, but he must look more to those that are better and are ends. He must do the same as well in the case of ways of life and the divisions[69] of action. For while there is need to be capable of engaging in occupation and going to war, there is more need to be capable of living in peace and being at leisure; and while there is need to do necessary and useful actions, there is more need to do noble ones. Consequently, it is toward these goals that the citizens must be educated, both while still children and while in any other age that requires education.

Refutation of the Opposing View. The Greeks thought to be best governed, notably the Spartans, have chosen only some virtues and those they considered to be most useful for empire. This view is false in reason and in fact: (i) if empire is happiest and best, then the Spartans are not happy nor their legislator good, for they have lost empire; (ii) if the Spartans' laws are best and yet they lost what is best by following their laws, the view is ridiculous; (iii) despotic empire is not best because rule over the free is better; (iv) a city is not to be considered happy because it is trained to dominate neighbors, for this (a) promotes domination at home and (b) the same things are best

---

67. See *Ethics* 6.1.1138b35–1139a15. The Greek word here is *theōrētikos*, from *theōrein*, elsewhere translated as "study."

68. The word for "leisure" is *scholē* (which gives us our word "school") and the word for "occupation" is *ascholia*, literally "absence of leisure."

69. Reading *dihaireseis* ("divisions") with the manuscripts not *haireseis* ("choices") with Dreizehnter. Aristotle is referring to what he just said, that actions are divided into those directed to what is necessary and useful and those directed to what is noble.

in private and in common, and exercise for war is not to enslave others but to escape it for oneself, to rule for others' benefit, and to enslave only those who deserve it; (v) the facts themselves prove the same point, as cities devoted to despotic empire came to a bad end when they got it.

1333b5 Those Greeks now held to be governed best, and the legislators who set up their regimes, are not conspicuous for arranging the affairs of the regime toward the best end nor for arranging the laws and education toward all the virtues. Instead, they declined in vulgar fashion toward the virtues they held to be useful and to be of a more grasping sort. Some more recent writers have, in a similar way, also given expression to the same opinion, for in praising the regime of the Spartans, they admire the legislator's goal because he legislated everything toward domination and war,[70] which views are readily refutable by reason and have now been refuted by the facts.

1333b16 For just as most human beings vie for mastery over many others because it brings them much equipment in the goods of fortune, so also Thibron,[71] and all the rest who write about the regime of the Spartans, conspicuously admire its legislator because, as a result of the way they were trained to face dangers, the Spartans ruled over many people. Yet it is clear, since the Spartans do not now have empire at any rate, that they cannot be happy nor can their legislator be good.

1333b23 Moreover, if it was by keeping to his laws, and while having nothing to hinder their acting on them, that they lost noble living, then the view is ridiculous.

1333b26 The supposition about the sort of rule that the legislator must be conspicuous in honoring is not correct either. For rule over free persons is more noble than despotic rule and is more accompanied by virtue.

1333b29 Also, it is not for this reason that one must consider the city happy and praise the legislator—that he trained them for domination so they could rule their neighbors. These things involve great harm, since it is clear that any citizen who can, should try to make it his object to be able to rule over his own city—the very thing the Spartans accuse their king Pausanias of, even though he had the honor of that great office.[72] Not one of such arguments and laws, indeed, is political or helpful or true. For the same things are best both in private and in common, and these must be impressed by the legislator on the souls of human beings; also, exercise for war is not to be practiced in order to enslave those who do not deserve it but so that,

70. Cf. 2.9.1271a41–b10.
71. Little else is known of Thibron.
72. Presumably the Pausanias who tried to become tyrant of Sparta after the Persian Wars, even though he was technically regent rather than king. He is mentioned again in 7(5).1.1301a17–21 and 7(5).7.1307a2–5.

first, they themselves do not become slaves to others, next so that they seek leadership for the aid of the ruled and not for despotism over everybody, and third for mastery over those who deserve to be slaves.

1334a2 But events as well as arguments bear witness that the legislator should give more serious attention to how his legislation about war and about everything else may be arranged for the sake of leisure and peace. For most cities of the sort described are preserved while at war but are destroyed when they have got possession of empire. They lose their temper, like iron, when at peace. The blame lies with the legislator for not having educated them to be able to live at leisure.

CHAPTER 15

What Virtues Education Must Inculcate. *The city needs both the virtues of leisure, which is the end, and those of occupation, in order to secure the end. Courage and steadfastness are virtues of occupation, philosophy a virtue of leisure, moderation and justice virtues of both. The virtues of leisure are more needed, both in order to use good fortune well and in order to be really good and not be exposed as apparently good in war but in peace really slavish. The example of the Spartans is not to be followed, because, like others, they prefer the goods of fortune to those of virtue and pursue only part of virtue, not the whole of it.*

1334a11 Since human beings seem to have the same end both in common and privately, and since the best man and the best regime must have the same standard,[73] it is manifest that the presence of the virtues directed to leisure is required. For, as has often been said, peace is the end of war and leisure the end of occupation. Virtues useful for leisure and cultured activities include both those whose work lies in leisure and those whose work lies in occupation (for in order to have leisure there is need of many necessities). Hence, it becomes the city to be moderate, courageous, and steadfast in endurance, since, as the proverb has it, "there is no leisure for slaves," and those who cannot face dangers bravely are slaves of anybody who attacks them.

1334a22 Courage and steadfast endurance are needed for occupation, philosophy for leisure, and moderation and justice at both times, but more when at peace and leisure. For war compels people to be just and behave moderately, but the enjoyment of good fortune and leisure combined with peace rather make them insolent. A great deal of justice and of moderation, then, is required of those who seem to be doing the best things and who are

73. 4(7).1–3 above.

enjoying—like those "in the isles of the blest," as the poets say[74]—all that brings blessing. For they will be most in need of philosophy and moderation and justice the more they take their leisure amidst the abundance of such goods. It is manifest, then, that the city that is going to be happy and serious must have its share of these virtues. For as it is shameful not to be able to use good things, it is even more so not to be able to use them in leisure but to be revealed as good while occupied and at war and slavish while at peace and leisure.

1334a40 Consequently, it is not after the fashion of the city of the Spartans that one must practice virtue, for they do not differ from others in not having the same view about what the greatest goods are, but in thinking these goods to be the result rather of some sort of virtue. But since [they think] these goods to be greater, and the enjoyment of them to be better than the enjoyment of the virtues, [they practice only the virtue useful for war. That the whole of virtue, however, must be practiced,][75] and for its own sake, is manifest from what has been said. How or by what means this will come about is the thing that needs studying.

The Order of Education. Education in habits should be for the sake of education in reason, because reason is the end of nature, and should come before education in reason, because appetite is in existence before reason develops.

1334b6 We distinguished earlier that there is need of nature, habit, and reason;[76] of these three, the first—what the citizens should be like in their nature—was determined before.[77] What remains is to study whether they must be educated first in reason or in habits, because these must harmonize with each other with the best of harmonies. For it is possible both for reason to have mistaken the best supposition and for habits to have led one similarly away.

1334b12 This fact at any rate is, as in other things, manifest first of all: that generation comes from some beginning and that the end from some beginning is related to another end.[78] But reason and intellect are for us the end

---

74. Hesiod *Works and Days* 170.

75. There seems to be a lacuna in the text at this point. I supply what I take to be the missing sense, using as guide what Aristotle said on this same fault of the Spartans in an earlier passage (2.9.1271a41–b10).

76. 4(7).13.1332a38–b11 above.

77. 4(7).7 above.

78. The sense is that the end of one stage in the process of development is the beginning of another stage and is for a further end still, the final end; hence, the end of generation is the beginning of training in habits, and the end of this is the beginning of training in reason, which is the final end. Alternatively, one could accept the rather attractive suggestion of Thurot

of nature. Consequently, it is in view of these that the generation and exercising of habits must be managed.

1334b17 Next, just as body and soul are two, so we see that the soul is two as well: the part without reason and the part with reason. The dispositions of these two parts are also two, one of which is appetite and the other intellect. But just as the body is prior in generation to the soul, so is the part without reason prior in generation to the part that has reason. This fact too is manifest. For spirit and wish, and desire also, are found in children as soon as they are born, but reasoning and intellect naturally develop in them as they grow older. Consequently, care of the body must come first before care of the soul, and then must come care of the appetite. But care of the appetite must be for the sake of the intellect, and care of the body for the sake of the soul.

CHAPTER 16

Preliminary Stages

Childbirth. *Ensuring that the young have the best bodies requires legislation of the parental union. The parents should unite so that (i) they both reach the age of sterility together; (ii) the children are of age to inherit when the parents are neither too young nor too old; (iii) the bodies of the young conform to what the legislator needs. These results will follow mainly from legislating the time of union: (a) the male should be about thirty-seven and the female about eighteen; (b) the season of union should be winter; (c) the parents' bodies should not be those of athletes or of the pampered; (d) pregnant women should take daily but moderate exercise; (e) defective infants should not be nourished, but abortion should not take place after quickening; (f) men should stop begetting children at about age fifty-five; (g) adultery should be considered ignoble and punished with dishonor.*

1334b29 Since, then, the legislator must see to it from the beginning that those being reared develop the best bodies possible, he must first take care of the parental union—that is, what sort of persons should establish marital relations with each other and when.

1334b32 His legislation for this community must keep in view the spouses

---

and read *all' ou telous* ("but is not from an end"), instead of *allou telous* ("is related to another end") with Dreizehnter and most manuscripts, and have the sense "and that the end is from some beginning but [neither] is from an end." If read in this way, the sense is that the process of generation is unidirectional, so that it goes from the beginning to the end but never back from the end to the beginning. Hence, everything else is for the end of reason, but reason and the training of reason are not for the beginning, or anything prior, but for their own sake. Perhaps not much hangs on the difference, as the same conclusion (that education in habits must be for the end of intelligence and reason, and not the other way round) follows in either case.

themselves and the expanse of their life so that, in terms of their ages, the spouses arrive together at the same point and so that their powers are not discrepant (he still able to generate and she not, or she still able and he not). For these things produce faction and difference between them.

1334b38 Next, his legislation should also keep in view the time of the children's succession. For children should not be too distant from their fathers in age, as older fathers do not receive the benefit of their children's gratitude and children do not receive the benefit of their fathers' help; nor should they be too close, as that causes much trouble, since under such conditions children, being like contemporaries, have less shame, and the closeness leads to quarrels in managing the household.

1335a4 Further, to return whence we began digressing, his legislation should be such that the bodies of those who are born are adapted to the legislator's will.

1335a6 All these three things, pretty much, will result if attention is paid to one particular thing.[79] For since generation comes to an end, to speak of the majority of cases, at an upper limit of seventy years for men and fifty for women, union should begin at such an age that these limits are reached simultaneously. But, on the other hand, the coupling of the young is a base thing from the point of view of getting children, for in all animals the offspring of the young are imperfect, likely to produce females, and small of figure, so the same must happen in the case of human beings too. An indication is that in all cities where the union of young men and women is the norm, the people are imperfect and have small bodies. Further, young women labor more in childbirth and more of them perish. That is why some say that such was the reason for the oracle given to the people of Troezen, that many of their children were dying because the women were being married off too young, and not because of anything to do with the harvesting of crops.[80] Again, being given in marriage at an older age helps women toward moderation, for they seem to be more licentious if they have engaged in sexual intercourse when young. Also, the bodies of males seem to get damaged if they have sexual intercourse while their seed is still increasing (seed too seems to have its defined time, beyond which it no longer gets more plenteous). Hence, women are fittingly united in marriage about the age of eighteen and men about thirty-seven or a little before.[81] For when union occurs at such an age, their bodies will be at their peak and the time when they can no longer produce children will be reached, opportunely, by both together. Further, if generation occurs at once, as can reasonably be

79. That is, as becomes clear, to the time of getting married.
80. The oracle they received said: "Do not plough the young furrow."
81. Reading *ē mikron* ("or a little [before]") with the manuscripts, not *hēlikian* ("age of" thirty-seven) with Dreizehnter.

expected, the children will succeed when at their peak and when the period of their father's vigor is, at about the age of seventy, already over.

1335a35 We have spoken, then, about when union should take place. As regards the season of year, the practice of most people, who set winter as the time for making a home together, is still a noble one. But the couple also should now be studying for themselves what doctors and natural scientists have said about the getting of children. For doctors give adequate information about what the suitable periods for the body are, and natural scientists do the same for winds (they praise northerly rather than southerly ones).

1335b2 As regards what condition of body would be of most profit to the offspring in the process of generation, we must stop to say more in our discussions about child management,[82] but we should also say enough now in outline. For neither is the condition of athletes useful for the physical fitness of a citizen or for health and the getting of children, nor is that condition useful that needs too much attention and is too ill-suited to toil. Something between the two is needed. So the condition must be one that has been hardened by toil but not, as in the case of athletes, by violent toil or by toil directed to one object, but by toil directed to the activities of free persons.

1335b11 These requirements must hold for men and women alike. Even pregnant women must take care of their bodies and not remain idle or follow a meager diet. The legislator could easily achieve this by ordering them to take a walk each day for the purpose of worshiping the deities to whom is allotted the honor of presiding over generation.[83] Their thought, however, in opposition to their bodies, can suitably be employed in more relaxed fashion. For offspring in the process of generation manifestly indulge themselves on her who is carrying them in the same way that plants do on the earth.

1335b19 As regards whether to expose or nourish what is born, let the law be to nourish nothing that is defective but not to expose anything born, where the arrangement of customs forbids [more than a certain number of children],[84] merely because of numbers. For there should be a limit[85] to the amount of child-getting, but if some couple together and get offspring contrary to this, abortion should be procured before perception and life appear (what is and is not holy will be defined by perception and life).

1335b26 Since we have defined the beginning of the age when a man and a

82. A reference either to 5(8).4 or to lost chapters at the end of that book.

83. By tradition, these were in particular the goddesses Artemis and Eileithuia.

84. The Greek simply says "if the arrangement of custom forbids." Some expand this by adding "exposure of children," but I prefer the addition, suggested by others, of "more than a certain number of children" since this seems a bit more consistent with the order of words in the text and with what follows.

85. Reading *hōristhai gar dei* ("for there should be a limit") with some manuscripts, rather than *hōristhō dē* ("let there be a limit"), adopted by Dreizehnter.

woman are to commence their union, let us define also the length of time that it is fitting for them to perform the public service of getting children. For the offspring of older persons, like that of younger ones, is born imperfect in body and thought, while that of the aged is weak. Hence, the time should be defined by reference to when thought is at its peak. This point comes, in the case of most people, at the age mentioned by some poets who measure life by periods of sevens[86]—that is, about fifty years old. Consequently, anyone who has passed this age by four or five years should cease bringing children into the light. After that, it should be manifest that they are having sexual relations for the sake of health or for some other such purpose. And with respect to having sexual relations with another woman or man, let it simply not be noble at all to be found in intimacy of any such kind while one is and is addressed as spouse. But if anyone is found doing anything like this during the period for getting children, let him be punished with the dishonor befitting the crime.

CHAPTER 17

Infancy to Age Seven. *Proper nourishment for infant bodies, as experience shows, is rich in milk but not in wine. Any movements they can perform and habituation to cold are also useful. To age five they should do no hard toil nor any learning; their play should be of a liberal sort and, along with the stories they hear, should imitate their serious activities later; they should be allowed to shout and cry; they should spend little time with slaves and should hear and see nothing illiberal or shameful. The legislator should, for this purpose, banish shameful stories and sights, punishing those who disobey, and allowing such things only for adults and in association with the worship of certain gods. From ages five to seven, children should watch others learning what they themselves will have to learn.*

1336a3 The kind of nourishment children get once they are born must be supposed to make a considerable difference to their bodily ability. It is evident from investigation of other animals and of those nations whose care it is to develop a warlike habit, that what is most proper for bodies is nourishment rich in milk and pretty free of wine (because of the diseases wine causes). Of advantage too are all movements that can be performed at such an age. To prevent the limbs from getting distorted due to their softness, certain mechanical instruments exist, still in use among some nations, to keep such bodies straight. It is beneficial also to accustom children to the cold right from the time they are small, for this is most useful for health

86. For example, Solon frag. 19 Diehl.

and the activities of war. That is why many barbarians are in the habit either of plunging the newborn into cold rivers or of wrapping them, as the Celts do, in scanty clothing. For in the case of anything capable of habituation, it is better to get it habituated, though gradually, right from the start; and the condition of children, because of its warmth, is naturally well suited for training to cold. Concerning the first age, then, this is the sort of care, or any care similar to it, that it is beneficial to give.

1336a23 As regards the following age up to five, an age whose condition is not yet a noble one for learning anything nor for necessary toil (lest this impede growth), there is need of sufficient movement to avoid idleness of body. Such movement is to be secured through their other activities as well as play, and the play must be neither unfree nor toilsome nor lax. As for the sort of stories and tales those of such an age should hear, let the officials called child managers take care of this, for all these kinds of things should be preparing the way for children's later pursuits. That is why most of their play should be imitations of what they will later be doing seriously. Those who, in their laws,[87] prevent children from stretching their lungs and crying are not correct in their prohibition. These things are beneficial to growth, since they are, in a way, gymnastic exercises for the body. The holding in of breath gives strength to those engaged in toil, and that happens to children when they stretch their lungs.

1336a39 The child managers must examine all the children's cultured pursuits and in particular see to it that they spend as little time as possible in the company of slaves. For those of this age and of the age up to seven must necessarily be brought up at home, so they are likely, even when so young, to pick up some illiberality from what they see and hear. The legislator should, more than anything, banish shameful speech altogether from the city, since giving ready expression to something shameful is followed closely by doing it. He should particularly banish such speech from the young, so that they neither say nor hear anything of the sort. If, nevertheless, anyone is found saying or doing something forbidden, let him, if free but not yet deserving to recline at the common messes, be punished with dishonors and a beating; but if he is older than this, let him be punished, for the sake of his slavishness, with dishonors unbecoming a free person.

1336b12 Since we are banishing the speaking of such things, we must manifestly also banish looking at unseemly pictures and stories. Let the rulers then make it their care that there be no statue or painting or imitation of such acts, except in the presence of such gods as also have scurrility assigned

---

87. Perhaps a reference to Plato *Laws* 791e4–792a6, but the reference may be a more general one and directed at all those who have laws forbidding such things.

to them by law.[88] The law will in addition allow those who have reached the appropriate age to do honor to the gods on behalf of their wives and children as well as themselves. But there must be legislation that the younger not be spectators at recitals of iambic lampoons and comedies until they reach the age[89] at which they can already join in the reclining and drinking at table and at which their education will make them all immune to the harm that comes from such spectacles.

1336b24 This subject we have discussed now in passing, but later[90] we must stop to determine it more at length, examining the difficulties about whether there should be such legislation or not and how it should be done. It is because it is something necessary that we have touched on it in the present context. For perhaps the sort of thing Theodorus, the tragic actor,[91] used to say was not bad. He never allowed anyone else, not even a poor actor, to go out on the stage before him, because spectators make their own what they hear first. The same thing happens in the case of our intercourse with human beings and with things: whatever we have to do with first we love more. Consequently anything base, especially if it contains depravity or malice, must be made alien to the young.

1336b35 When the first five years are past, children must then, in the next two years up to seven, become spectators of those kinds of learning that they themselves will have to learn.

Education Proper

The Division of Education and Questions to Examine. *The order of education must be determined by reference to the periods that follow seven to puberty and that follow puberty to twenty-one. The questions are whether care must be taken over education, whether it should be common, and what it should be like.*

1336b37 There are two ages in view of which education must be divided: the one after the age from seven to puberty and again the one after the age from puberty to twenty-one.[92] For those who divide ages into sevens are not, for the most part, speaking nobly;[93] nature's division should be fol-

---

88. Probably Dionysus, but also Demeter and Core.

89. Probably twenty-one.

90. Probably in the lost chapters at the end of book 5(8).

91. A famous actor of the fourth century.

92. Aristotle means that education must be carried out with a view to the ages that follow the education in question. So the education between seven and puberty must be carried out with a view to what the educated will do from puberty to twenty-one; the education between puberty and twenty-one must be carried out with a view to what the educated will do after twenty-one.

93. Reading *kalōs* ("nobly") with the manuscripts, not *kakōs* ("badly") with Dreizehnter

lowed. For all art and education aim to fill up what nature has left wanting. What needs to be examined, then, is first, whether some arrangement must be made about children; next, whether it is better that taking care of them be done in common or in some private way (as happens still in most cities); and third, of what sort the care should be.[94]

and most others, who think that because Aristotle is using the ages of seven and twenty-one as division points, he is approving of the general practice of dividing by sevens. I take Aristotle's point to be instead that whatever may be true of seven and twenty-one, education should not be schematically divided at fourteen but at the natural division of puberty, whenever that happens to occur. Hence, children will pass on to the next stage at younger and older ages according to the natural pace of their own development and will not all be forced on, or kept back, by the number fourteen.

94. The first two questions are dealt with in 5(8).1, and the third occupies the rest of book 5, from 5(8).2 onward.

Book 5

Education in

the Best Regime

CHAPTER 1

That Education Is Necessary and Must Be Common. *Education is necessary because (i) without it, regimes are damaged and (ii) the practice of virtue needs prior learning and habituation. Education must be common because (iii) the city has a single end that needs to be pursued by everyone together and (iv) each citizen belongs to the city as part to whole.*

1337a11 That the legislator should especially busy himself about the education of the young would be disputed by no one, as the regime is damaged in cities where this is not done. For the young need to be educated to the regime, since the character proper to each regime is what customarily preserves it and establishes it to begin with. The democratic character, for instance, preserves and establishes democracy; the oligarchic, oligarchy. And, in every case, the best character is cause of a better regime.

1337a18 Moreover, in order to put any art or ability into practice, there are things one has to learn and get accustomed to first. So clearly the same must also hold of the activities of virtue.

1337a21 But since the whole city has one end, it is manifest that everyone must also have one and the same education and that taking care of this education must be a common matter. It must not be private in the way it is now, when everyone takes care of their own children privately and teaches them whatever private learning they think best. Of common things, the training too must be common.

1337a27 At the same time, no citizen should even think that he belongs to himself but instead that each belongs to the city, for each is part of the city. The care of each part, however, naturally looks to the care of the whole, and to this extent praise might be due to the Spartans, for they devote the most serious attention to their children and do so in common.

CHAPTER 2

The Content and Manner of Education

Review of Difficulties. *There is dispute about what the work of education is and about what should be taught—whether things useful or things virtuous or things extraordinary, and whether thought or character is more important. Existing practice makes nothing clearer.*

1337a33 It is manifest, then, that there must be legislation about education and that this education must be made a common matter. But what the education is and how it should be carried out are questions not to be ignored, for there is dispute about what work it performs. Not everyone thinks the young should learn the same things, either with respect to virtue or with respect to the best life; nor is it manifest whether having thought in view, rather than the character of the soul, is what is appropriate.

1337a39 An investigation based on the education actually to hand proves confusing. There is no clarity about whether training is to be in things useful for life or in things leading to virtue or in things extraordinary[1] (for all of these have got some judges on their side). As regards what leads to virtue, nothing is agreed about it. For indeed, right from the start, the virtue that everyone holds in honor is not the same, so the fact that they differ about the training of it is reasonable enough.

Solution to the Difficulties

Education Must Be Liberal. *Of things useful and necessary only those that are free should be taught, and the young should partake in nothing of a vulgar, mechanical sort or that will render body, soul, or thought unfit for virtue. For the same reason, things free should not be pursued in an unfree or illiberal way, while things unfree may be pursued in a free way if pursued for their own sake, or for friends or for virtue.*

1337b4 Now, there is no doubt that those useful things that are necessary should be taught. On the other hand, it is manifest, since there is a division of works into the free and unfree, that not all of them should be, because the young must partake only in such useful works as will not make the participant a vulgar mechanic.[2] Any work or art or learning must be consid-

---

1. The Greek is *peritta*, which means "what goes beyond the average or the ordinary." I take Aristotle to be referring ahead to the next chapter, where he resolves this question. For there, the third category of things to be taught is things for leisure, and the activities of leisure —in particular philosophy (as in 4(7).15.1334a23, 31–33)—may indeed seem extraordinary in comparison with the ordinary and necessary things that are useful and belong to occupation.
2. Cf. 4(7).9.1328b37–1329a2.

ered vulgarly mechanical if it renders the body of the free, or their soul or thought, useless for the practices and deeds of virtue. Hence, all such arts as put the body into a worse condition we call mechanical, as well as wage-earning labor. For they deprive thought of leisure and make it abject.

1337b15 As regards the free kinds of knowledge, it is not unfree to take part in some of them up to a point, but to get too much involved in the accuracy of the details is to become subject to harm of the sort just mentioned. A great deal of difference is also made by the purpose for which one learns or does something. Doing it for its own sake or for friends or because of virtue is not unfree, while anyone who did the very same thing at the behest of others would often seem to be doing something characteristic of a laborer or a slave.[3]

CHAPTER 3

Education Must Be for Noble Leisure. *Existing educational practice teaches subjects useful for life (as letters and drawing) and subjects tending to virtue (namely courage through gymnastics), but difficulties arise about music. Most think it is for pleasure but it was first introduced for noble leisure, since nature aims at leisure as well as occupation, and leisure is more choiceworthy. The activity of leisure is not play but something proper to leisure itself and of the noblest kind; so there is need for subjects to be taught with a view to leisure spent in cultured pursuits, and taught for their own sake. That is why the ancients introduced music into education. Hence, even useful things should be taught with leisure also in view.*

1337b21 Now, as was earlier remarked, the kinds of learning that are currently in fashion look in two directions.[4] There are four things, pretty much, that are customarily taught: letters, gymnastics, music, and (some add) drawing. Letters and drawing are taught as being in many ways useful for life; gymnastics is taught as tending toward courage; and as for music,[5] one might already be in difficulty. As things stand, most people participate in it as something for the sake of pleasure. But those at the beginning assigned it a place in education because our very nature, as has often been said,[6] seeks to be capable not only of a right occupation but also of a noble leisure (for

3. Cf. 4(7).14.1333a6–11.

4. The reference would seem to be to the previous chapter, at 1337a39–42; the two directions referred to are virtue and the useful.

5. The Greek is *mousikē* and means "the art of the muses" and hence refers to artistic and literary accomplishments generally, not only to what we now call music. Nevertheless, *mousikē* does also mean music in our sense, and Aristotle's attention is focused mainly on this sense of music in what follows, as is shown particularly by the last chapter.

6. Cf. 4(7).13–15 and 2.9.1271a41–b10.

nature, to speak about it once again,[7] is the beginning of everything). For if both are needed and if leisure is more choiceworthy than occupation and is its end, then what we must look for is something in the doing of which we can spend our leisure.

1337b35 For we are not, indeed, to spend it in playing. Otherwise play would necessarily be for us the end of life. But if that is impossible and if play is to be resorted to more during occupation (for anyone engaged in toil needs rest, and play is for the sake of rest, and occupation is accompanied by toil and strain), then we must, for this reason, introduce play keeping a watchful eye on the opportune moment for using it, as if applying it for medicinal purposes. For this sort of movement of soul is a relaxation and a rest on account of the pleasure.

1337b39 Leisure activity seems itself to contain pleasure and happiness and blest living, and these are not the possession of those who are occupied but only of those who are at leisure. For he who is occupied is occupied for the sake of some end that he regards as not yet present to him, but happiness is an end that everyone supposes to be accompanied by pleasure and not by pain.

1338a7 They do not, however, all set down the same pleasure as this pleasure, but each sets down the one that is agreeable to himself and to his own disposition, and it is the best person who sets down the best pleasure, that is, the pleasure that comes from the most noble sources. Consequently, it is manifest that some things must be learned and taught with a view to leisure spent in cultured pursuits,[8] and that these subjects of education and learning must be for their own sake, while those with a view to occupation are things necessary and for the sake of something else.

1338a13 That in fact is why those of former times gave a place to music in education—not because it was something necessary (for there is nothing of that sort in it); nor because it was useful, in the way letters are, for business and household management and learning and a host of political activities (drawing too seems to be useful for making a nobler judgment about the works of artisans); nor again because it was useful, like gymnastics, for health and military prowess (for neither of these do we see resulting from music). What is left, then, is that music is for the cultured pursuits of leisure.

1338a22 And that is the object for which they manifestly do introduce it, for they give it a place in the cultured pursuits that they suppose belong to the

---

7. The Greek is ambiguous at this point. Instead of "nature," one could read "leisure" (the Greek is an indeterminate *hautē*, "this"). If the latter, "to speak about it again" refers to 4(7).13–15; if the former, then the reference is to these same chapters and also, perhaps, generally to the first book in both the *Politics* and the *Ethics*.

8. Reading *tēn en tēi diagōgē scholēn* with the manuscripts, not, in imitation of lines 1338a21–22 below, *tēn en tēi scholēi diagōgēn* ("the cultured pursuits of leisure") with Dreizehnter.

free. Hence, Homer thus composed the line "but such a one is it needful to summon to the bounteous feast," and so continuing he speaks of certain others "who summon a bard to give delight to all."[9] In another place, Odysseus says the best cultured pursuit is when humans are glad of heart and "the feasters, seated in order up and down the hall, listen to a bard."[10]

1338a30 Manifestly then, there is an education that sons must be educated in, not because it is something useful or necessary but because it is something free and noble. Whether it encompasses one or more parts, and what these parts are and how they are to be taught, must be spoken of later.[11] But for the present we have managed to get thus far along the way: that we have evidence for our conclusion also from the ancients and from the subjects of education established among them (for music makes the fact clear). We have also managed to get so far as to see that children should be educated in some of the useful subjects not only because they are useful—as, for instance, the learning of letters—but also because through them many other kinds of learning become possible; likewise, we have also managed to see that children should be taught drawing not so that in their own purchasing they may avoid mistakes and not be taken in when buying and selling wares, but rather because it makes them contemplative of the beauty that belongs to bodies. To be looking everywhere for what is useful is least becoming in the magnanimous and the free.

Treatment of Particular Subjects

Gymnastics. *Education in habits should precede education in reason, and education of body precede education of thought. Hence, one first needs education in gymnastics. Children should not be trained to be athletes, as this damages the body, nor to be wild beasts (like the Spartans), as courage is not the only virtue to aim at. Besides, courage is not achieved in this way, as is shown (i) by other animals and nations and (ii) by the Spartans themselves, who excelled before only because they alone trained, but now that others are doing so as well, they are regularly surpassed. Gymnastic exercises should therefore be light before puberty as well as during the three succeeding years devoted to other learning, and only made more toilsome thereafter.*

1338b4 Since it is manifest that education is to be in habits before it is in reason and is to concern the body before it concerns the soul,[12] it clearly follows that children are to be given over to gymnastics and physical training,

---

9. The reference is to *Odyssey* 17.382–85, but Aristotle's first quotation does not appear in our texts of the *Odyssey*.

10. *Odyssey* 9.5–6.

11. Apparently in a part of this book that is missing.

12. Cf. 4(7).15.1224b5–28.

for the body is put into a certain condition by the first, and its actions are by the second.

Chapter 4: 1338b9 Now, as things stand at present, some of the cities that seem to give most care to children impose on them the condition of athletes and thereby damage shape and growth of body alike, while the Spartans, though they have not made this mistake, nevertheless turn their children into wild beasts by the toil they impose, because this is, so they think, most beneficial for courage. Yet, as has often been said,[13] the care of the young must not be carried out with one virtue as the aim, nor with this one most of all; and even if this virtue were the aim, still the Spartans are not finding the way to it.

1338b17 For neither among the other animals nor among the nations do we see courage accompanying those of them that are wildest but rather those of them that are tamer and more lionlike in character. In addition, many nations, as Achaeans and Heniochi among those about the Black Sea, have a ready disposition to kill and eat human flesh, and others among mainland nations are like them or even worse, and while these nations may be expert brigands, courage is not something they have any share in. Moreover, the Spartans were, we know, superior to others when they alone were persisting in their fondness for toil, but now others surpass them in gymnastic and military contests. For it was not because the Spartans exercised the young in the way they did that they achieved superiority, but only because they were training while their opponents were not.

1338b29 So it is nobility, not bestiality, that should take first place. For it is neither the wolf nor any other wild beast but rather the good man that would enter the lists in the case of a noble danger. Those who give up their boys too much to such exercises and leave them uninstructed in what is necessary turn out vulgar mechanics, to tell the truth, and make them useful to political science for one work only and for this work, as our argument shows, worse than others do. It is not on the basis of former works that judgment must be made but on the basis of present ones, for now the Spartans have competitors in the field of education whereas before they did not.

1338b38 That gymnastics is to be employed, therefore, and how it is to be employed is agreed: up to puberty the young must be put to lighter gymnastic exercises and be kept away from forced diets and constrained toil, so that nothing impedes growth. That growth can be thus impeded is indicated by no small sign, for one could find but two or three who have won victories both as men and as boys in the Olympic games, because the constrained gymnastic exercises of their training in youth took away their strength. But when, for the three years after puberty, they have spent time on other sub-

---

13. Cf. 2.9.1271b3–10 and 4(7).14–15.

jects of learning, then the age following can fittingly be taken up with toils and constrained dieting. For one should not impose toil at the same time on both thought and body, as each naturally works the opposite effect: toil of the body impedes thought and that of thought impedes the body.

CHAPTER 5

Music

Preliminary Discussion. Is music for play and rest, for virtue and character, or for cultured pursuits? If for play, the young should not be taught it, since education is painful, nor if it is for cultured activities, since the young are still too immature. To suppose music is for play when older raises the question of why children should learn music themselves instead of listening to others, and this same question arises if music is for virtue or for cultured activities later.

1339a11 As regards music, we have already raised some difficulties in our earlier discussion,[14] but it is a noble thing also to take them up again now and pursue them further so that they might serve, as it were, for a prelude to the arguments one might use in stating a position about music. For it is not easy to determine what is its power or for what purpose one should participate in it.

1339a16 Is music for the sake of play and rest, as sleep and drinking are? For these are, as such, not included among things serious, though they are pleasant and, as Euripides says, "put a stop to care."[15] That is in fact why people give a like place to, and make a like use of, all of these things: sleep, drinking, and music (and dancing too is added to them). Or must we suppose that music contributes something to virtue, because it can induce in the character, as gymnastics does in the body, a certain sort of quality and make it able, through habituation, to delight in the right things? Or does music contribute something to cultured pursuits and prudence? For, of the things mentioned, this was set down third.[16]

1339a26 Now, there is no doubt that educating the young should not be for the sake of play, for, since learning is painful, they are not playing when they learn. Nor yet are cultured pursuits fit to be given to children and those of that age, since the end is not appropriate to what is incomplete.[17]

14. 5(8).3 above.
15. *Bacchae* 381.
16. 5(8).3.1337b25–1338a22.
17. There is a play on words in the Greek here, for "end" is *telos* and "incomplete" is *atelēs*, which literally means "lacking its end" (*a-telos*).

1339a31 Perhaps, however, it might be thought that the serious activities of children are for the sake of their play when they have become men and are complete. But if that were so, why should they learn music themselves and not, like the kings of the Medes and Persians, take part in the enjoyment and learning of it while others do the performing? Besides, those who have made performance their work and art must necessarily carry it out better than those who have devoted attention to music only long enough to learn it. On the other hand, if children must toil over such things themselves, then they should also be involved in the activity of cooking delicacies, which is absurd. **1339a41** The same difficulty also arises if music has the ability to make character better, for why should children learn it themselves and not, like the Spartans, become capable of right enjoyment and judgment by listening to others? For though the Spartans do not learn music, they are still able, so they say, to judge correctly which tunes are wholesome and which not. **1339b4** The argument is also the same if music is to be used to gladden the heart and for the cultured activities of the free. Why should children learn it themselves instead of getting the enjoyment from others who practice it? We can also look at the supposition we hold about the gods, for Zeus does not himself sing nor accompany poets on the cithara;[18] on the contrary, we even call such persons vulgar mechanics and say that their behavior is not becoming for a man (unless he is drinking or playing).

The Purposes of Music and Education in Music

For Play and Cultured Pursuits. *Music is effective for play and cultured pursuits because both these include pleasure, and music is one of the pleasantest things. Hence music should be taught to the young both for the end of cultured pursuits and for play, because it gives rest and, through a likeness with the end (a likeness that causes confusion between the end and play), it makes up for the fact that the end is seldom enjoyed.*

1339b10 But perhaps these matters must be investigated later;[19] what comes first for investigation is whether music is to be given a place in education or not, and which of the three things we raised difficulties about it has the power to effect—whether education[20] or play or cultured pursuits. It is, reasonably enough, ranked under, and appears to have a part in, all three. For play has rest as its purpose, and rest must be pleasant since it is a cure for the pain arising from toil; cultured pursuits too, it is agreed, must possess not only nobility but also pleasure, since being happy is composed of

18. A kind of stringed instrument, like a lute.
19. The matters about whether the young should learn to play music themselves, discussed in the next chapter.
20. That is, education of character.

both; and music, we all say, is one of the pleasantest things, both by itself and when combined with singing. At any rate, Musaeus says that "singing is most sweet for mortals."[21] Hence the introduction of it into social gatherings and cultured pursuits, on the ground that it can bring gladness to the heart, is reasonable.

1339b24 Consequently, one might also suppose from this that the younger ones should be educated in music. For all pleasures that are harmless are not only appropriate in view of the end but also in view of rest, and since human beings happen seldom to be in possession of their end but are often at rest and use play for the pleasure it gives and not only with some other purpose in view, taking rest in the pleasures of music would also be a useful thing.

1339b31 And it has turned out that human beings make their play into an end—for the end too has perhaps a certain pleasure to it, though not just any pleasure—and in their pursuit of the former pleasure, they identify it with the latter, on account of its likeness to the end of action. For the end is not to be chosen for the sake of what will come later, nor are the pleasures of play for the sake of what will come later, but for the sake of what has passed by—I mean toil and pain. One might plausibly suppose, then, that this is the reason people look for happiness in these pleasures, but that they participate in music not only for this reason but also because, as it seems, music is useful for rest.

For Contributing to Character. *Music also has a nobler power than providing pleasure, namely it contributes to character. The proof is that music makes us take on certain qualities of character. For music excites passions (as the tunes of Olympus and imitations show) and is something pleasant; virtue is a matter of taking pleasure aright, and requires getting used to judging correctly and enjoying decent characters; music contains likenesses of the passions and characters it excites, and getting used to enjoying likenesses is close to getting used to enjoying realities. Hence, getting used to enjoying decent music is a way of getting used to enjoying decent characters and of becoming virtuous. The other senses do not contain likenesses of character (though objects of sight contain signs of character), but music does; that fact is made manifest by the way the different modes put us into different states. Consequently, music must also be used to educate the character of the young, which conclusion is reinforced by the fact (i) that the young need things to be sweetened for them (and music is naturally such) and (ii) that the soul has an affinity for modes and rhythms.*

1339b42 Yet we must also investigate whether this effect might not be incidental to music and whether its nature is in fact more honorable than what

---

21. Musaeus was probably a mythical figure, but certain poems and sayings were attributed to him, one of which Aristotle is evidently quoting.

satisfies the need just mentioned and whether one should not merely partake of the common pleasure it affords and of which all have perception (for music contains a pleasure that is natural, which is why all ages and all characters love to avail themselves of it), but see if it also contributes in any way to character and the soul.

1340a7 The answer would be clear if, because of music, we come to be of a certain quality in our character. But that we do indeed come to be of a certain quality is manifest both from many other things and not least from the tunes composed by Olympus,[22] since these confessedly make our souls enthused, and enthusiasm is a passion of character in the soul. In addition, everyone is moved in passion along with the imitations to which they are listening, even in the absence of rhythms and tunes.[23]

1340a14 But since music happens to be something pleasant, and since virtue concerns taking pleasure aright and liking and disliking, then it is clear that:[24] there is need of nothing so much as learning and getting habituated to judging aright and taking pleasure in decent characters and noble deeds; there are likenesses to be found in rhythms and tunes that are very close to real natures—likenesses of anger and mildness, of courage too and moderation, of all their opposites as well, and of the other qualities of character (the facts themselves make the matter clear, for we undergo changes in soul when we listen to such rhythms and tunes); and getting used to taking pain and pleasure in likenesses is close to being in the same state with respect to the reality (for instance, if someone takes pleasure in seeing another's image for no other reason than that the form is the same, then he must also find pleasant the view of that very thing whose image he is viewing).

1340a28 In the other objects of perception, as it happens (I mean in touch and taste), there exists no likeness to characters, though there does, to a slight extent, in sight. For there are shapes of this sort, if only minimally, and everyone has some perception of them. But they are not likenesses of character; rather the colors and shapes that develop are instead indications of character and are found in bodies in states of passion. Nevertheless, to the extent that the viewing of these things makes a difference, the young

---

22. Another probably mythical figure. He was supposed to have lived in Phrygia in the eighth or seventh century and to have composed music for the pipes.

23. There is dispute about the meaning and even the translation here, but one option is that, since ancient Greek was spoken with a pitch accent, a poetic imitation or drama would, when recited, have a marked musical or singsong quality to it, and so have some of the effects of music, even without the addition of musical accompaniment.

24. Reading *dēlon hoti dei* ("it is clear that: there is need of . . .") with some manuscripts, instead of *dei dēlonhoti* ("there is need clearly of . . .") with Dreizehnter and other manuscripts.

should not view the works of Pauson but those of Polygnotus,[25] or of any other painter and sculptor skilled in character.

1340a38 But in tunes by themselves[26] there do exist imitations of characters, as is in fact manifest. For modes were divergent in nature from the very beginning, and the result is that hearers are put into a different state with respect to each of them and do not stay in the same condition. They are in a condition more of grief and apprehension with respect to some, as the so-called Mixed Lydian; they are in a softer condition of thought with respect to others, as the relaxed modes; they are in a middling and settled condition above all with respect to a different one—I mean the Dorian, which alone among modes seems capable of having this effect; Phrygian makes them enthused.[27] Such is what those who have philosophized about music education say, and rightly, since they give proofs of their words from the facts themselves. The same points hold of rhythms as well, some of which have a more steady character while others are full of movement; and among the latter, the movements are in some cases of a cruder, and in others of a more liberal, sort.

1340b10 From these considerations, then, it is manifest that music is able to endow the character of the soul with a certain quality. But if music can do this, then clearly use must be made of it and the young must be educated in it. And the teaching of music fits the nature of that time of life, for the young, because of their age, put up willingly with nothing that has not been sweetened, and music is by its nature among things sweetened. Also, there seems to be some sort of affinity for modes and rhythms, which is why many among the wise say that the soul is a mode or possesses mode.[28]

25. Not much is known of these two artists from the fifth century, nor of their works, but Aristotle does elsewhere say that Pauson portrayed people worse, and Polygnotus better, than they were, and that Polygnotus was good at portraying character whereas another artist, Zeuxis, failed to do so at all (*Poetics* 2.1448a5-6 and 6.1450a27-29).

26. Reading *autois* with the manuscripts, not *autōn* with Dreizehnter, who would thus have "themselves" going with "characters."

27. The most obvious modern analogy for these modes is our major and minor modes of a scale (which certainly affect hearers in different emotional ways). The ancient Greek modes were, by contrast, more numerous and more richly differentiated.

28. Cf. Aristotle *De Anima* 407b27-30.

CHAPTER 6

The Music the Young Should Be Taught

As Regards Performance. *Performance should be taught because becoming a serious judge and so developing character is otherwise impossible or difficult and because it functions like a rattle in keeping the young diverted. But to avoid becoming vulgarly mechanical, the young (i) should stop performing when they get older and have acquired judgment; (ii) should not learn skills for competitions or for exciting astonishment; (iii) should not learn instruments requiring such skills, in particular the pipes, which anyway are for purification rather than learning and also prevent speech (thus they and several other instruments were rightly rejected by the ancients, and the story of Athena throwing the pipes away makes the same point). Skills designed for competitions are to be rejected as not being for the sake of virtue and as making the performer base by getting him to pander to a base audience.*

1340b20 Whether or not the young should themselves learn to sing and perform with their hands must now be addressed, following the way we raised difficulties about it earlier.[29] There is in fact no doubt that if one does share in the actual doing, it makes a great deal of difference to coming to be of a certain character, since it is something impossible or difficult for those who did not share in the actual doing to have become serious judges.

1340b25 Also children must, at the same time, have something to divert them, and Archytas' rattle,[30] which small children are given to use so that they will not break things about the house, is to be considered a noble invention, for youth cannot keep still. So while this is the rattle that suits infant children, education is the rattle that suits the young when they are bigger.

1340b31 These considerations, then, make it manifest that the young should be taught music in a way that includes taking part in performance. But as regards what is appropriate and inappropriate for the different age groups, it is not hard to determine this and to answer those who say that the concern with music is a vulgarly mechanical one. For, to begin with, since the point of taking part in performance is the formation of judgment, that is why they should engage in doing it when young but should stop performing when they are older and be able, from what they learned in their youth, to judge noble pieces and enjoy them properly.

1340b40 As for the charge, leveled by some, that music makes people vulgar mechanics, the answer is not hard if one investigates to what extent those

29. 5(8).5.1339a33–b11 above.
30. Probably Archytas of Tarentum in Sicily, a Pythagorean philosopher and friend of Plato.

receiving education with a view to political virtue should take part in performance, what tunes and rhythms they should participate in, and, further, what instruments they should learn (for this too is likely to make a difference).[31] It is here that the answer to the charge lies (for nothing prevents its being the case that some ways of doing music have the ill effect mentioned).

1341a5 It is manifest, then, that learning music must not be an impediment to later activities, nor must it make the body that of a mechanic and useless for training in war and politics—that is, for exertions now and for studies later. One could achieve this result as regards learning music if the young toil over such works as are neither aimed at artistic competitions nor excite astonishment and are extraordinary (these have now come into competitions and from competitions into education), and should even toil over these only to the point of being able to take delight in noble tunes and rhythms and not merely in the common element of music which even some animals, as well as the mass of slaves and small children, are capable of.

1341a17 These facts also make it clear what sort of instruments should be used, for neither should the pipes be introduced into education nor any other instrument that requires artistic skill (such as the cithara and anything else of the sort), but only those that will make the young good listeners of musical and other education. The pipes, in addition, are not an instrument that involves character but rather religious frenzy. Consequently, their use is for those occasions when viewing has more the effect of purification[32] than of learning. Let us add further that the fact that playing the pipes prevents one using reasoned speech is also against their use for education.

1341a26 Hence, those of former times nobly rejected their use among the young and the free, even though, initially, they did employ them. For prosperity was providing them more leisure and giving them more magnanimity toward virtue; in addition, their deeds both before and after the Persian Wars filled them with high thoughts. So they seized on every sort of learning, not drawing distinctions but putting it all to the test. Hence they also introduced pipe playing into what they learned. In fact, even in Sparta one chorus leader piped for the chorus himself, and in Athens playing the pipes was so much the fashion that most of the free, pretty well, took part in it, as is made clear by the tablet that Thrasippus set up after leading the chorus for Ecphantides.[33] But later, when they were better able to judge what contributed to virtue and what did not, experience itself made them reject the

31. The first and third of these questions are dealt with in this chapter, the second in the next chapter.

32. The Greek is *katharsis*. Aristotle says more on this topic in the next chapter.

33. Chorus leaders for victorious playwrights sometimes set up tablets recording the victory, as in this case for Ecphantides, who was a comic dramatist of the early fifth century. The tablet presumably said something about pipe playing.

pipes. The same thing happened also in the case of many ancient instruments, like the pectis and barbitos; those that contribute, in the playing, to the listener's pleasure (the heptagon, the trigon, the sambuca);[34] as well as all those that require one to know how to be dexterous with the hands. The story the ancients have told about the pipes — that Athena threw them away after inventing them — is also a reasonable one; and while it is not bad to say that the goddess did so because she was annoyed at the way they distorted her face, it is more likely that it was because education in the pipes does nothing for thought (we associate knowledge and art with Athena).

1341b8 Since we reject education involving artistic expertise when it comes to instruments and performance, we set it down that by artistic expertise is meant expertise for competitions. For in these cases the practitioner is not undertaking the performance for his own virtue but for the pleasure of his listeners, and that a crude pleasure. Hence, it is our judgment that this activity does not belong to the free but is characteristic rather of the laborer. And performers do indeed become vulgar mechanics, since the goal in view of which they fashion their end is an evil one. For the spectator, being crude, is wont to introduce changes in the music, and the result is that he imposes a certain character both on the artists themselves as they perform in front of him and, because of the way they move about, on their bodies too.

CHAPTER 7

As Regards Modes and Rhythms. *There are three questions: (i) whether all modes and rhythms should be used or distinctions made; (ii) whether the modes and rhythms the young are taught to perform should be divided in the same way; (iii) whether some other division is necessary. With respect to modes, and as regards the first question, modes and tunes are distinguished into those of character, of action, and of enthusiasm. All should be used, since music is for several purposes, but the last two are only for listening to. Those of enthusiasm are to be used because, through purification, they provide rest and harmless pleasure. But vulgar modes and tunes should be used only for vulgar audiences. As regards the second question, only modes and tunes of character should be taught for performance, notably the Dorian, which lies in the mean; but, as regards the third question, these modes and tunes need to be further distinguished into the possible and proper according to the different ages.*

1341b19 Investigation must also be made, from the point of view of education, of modes and rhythms: whether all modes and rhythms are to be used or distinctions made; next, whether we must lay down the same division for

---

34. All these were kinds of stringed instruments.

those engaged in toil with a view to education;[35] or whether, third, it is necessary to lay down some other one.[36]

1341b23 Since music, as we see, consists in the making of tunes and in rhythm, we must not fail to note what effect each of these has on education and whether music with a good tune is to be chosen rather than music with a good rhythm. As we hold, therefore, that some modern experts in music, as well as those in philosophy who happen to have experience of music education, say much that is noble on these matters, we will refer any who want an accurate account of each particular to get it from them. For the present, we will draw our distinctions after the manner of law, speaking about these things only in outline.

1341b32 Since we accept the distinction among tunes which certain of those engaged in philosophy draw and set down some as tunes of character, others of action, and others of enthusiasm (the nature of modes they also set down as akin to each of these, one to one sort and another to another), and since we assert that music must not be used for the sake of one kind of help but for several—for it is for the sake of education, and of purification[37] (what we mean by purification will be described simply now, but a clearer explanation will be given in our discussion of poetry),[38] and third for cultured pursuits, for both relaxation and rest from strain—it is manifest that all modes must be used, but not all in the same way. Rather, those most to do with character are to be used for education and those of action and enthusiasm for listening to while other people do the manual work of performing.

1342a4 For any passion that falls with force upon some souls is found in all of them to a greater or lesser extent—as, for instance, pity and fear, and also enthusiasm. For there are some people who become possessed by this movement in them, and we see from the sacred tunes[39] that these people, when they have used the tunes that put the soul into an excited frenzy, calm down as if receiving a cure and purification. The same effect must be ex-

---

35. The young, that is, who are still working hard on learning to perform.

36. This last phrase might also be translated "or whether some third division is required." But this generates a difficulty because only one division has been mentioned so far, not two. Consequently, it becomes necessary to emend the text. But the text admits of an acceptable interpretation as it now stands: the first question is about which modes and rhythms are to be used in education generally (and not only with a view to performance), whether all indiscriminately or with distinctions; the second about whether, as regards those specifically for performance, the same way of dividing is to be used; the third about whether there is need for some other division as well.

37. The Greek word is *katharsis*.

38. The discussion of poetry could be a reference to the *Poetics*, but there is no treatment of purification to be found there (only a brief mention at 6.1449b27-28). Perhaps it is more likely a reference to some later discussion in the *Politics*, which however has not survived.

39. Possibly the same as the tunes of Olympus mentioned earlier, in 5(8).5.1340a9-12.

perienced also by those who are prone to pity and fear, by passionate types in general, and by others insofar as they each share such passions; all receive a certain purification and relief along with pleasure. In like manner, purificatory tunes also afford human beings harmless pleasure. That is why contestants who are undertaking music for the theater should be assigned to⁴⁰ such modes and tunes.

1342a18 On the other hand, since there are two kinds of spectators—one free and educated, the other crude and made up of vulgar mechanics, laborers, and the like—these latter sorts too, for the purposes of rest, should be given contests and spectacles. Just as their souls are twisted from the natural condition, so there exist modes that are deviant and tunes that are strained and highly colored, and what gives pleasure to each is what is akin to his nature. Hence, those who perform in contests in front of such spectators should be conceded the right to use some such type of music.

1342a28 With respect to education, tunes to do with character should be used, as was said, and modes of the same sort. The Dorian is of that kind, as was said before.⁴¹ We should also accept any other mode that is approved for us by those who share in the pursuit of philosophy and in music education.

1342a32 But in the *Republic*, Socrates does not do nobly in leaving only the Phrygian mode along with the Dorian, and that despite the fact he rejects the pipes among the instruments.⁴² For Phrygian has the same force among modes as the pipes have among instruments: both are frenzied and passionate, as poetry shows. For all Bacchic excitement and all movement of this sort are found, among instruments, in the pipes above all and get what befits them, among modes, from Phrygian tunes. Dithyramb, for instance, seems by general agreement to be Phrygian.⁴³ Those conversant with the understanding of it allege many examples, principally the fact that Philoxenus tried to compose his dithyramb *The Mysians* in Dorian but could not.⁴⁴ Instead, nature herself made him fall back again into the appropriate mode of Phrygian.

1342b12 As for Dorian, all agree that it is the most steady and the mode that most has a courageous character. Further, since we praise the mean

---

40. Reading *theteon* with the manuscripts, not the *eateon chrēsthai* ("should be allowed to use") adopted by Dreizehnter.

41. 5(8).5.1340b3–4.

42. Plato *Republic* 399a3–c6.

43. A dithyramb was a song in honor of the god Dionysus or Bacchus.

44. Dithyrambs were choral songs, initially in honor of the god Dionysus. Philoxenus was a dithyrambic poet of the late fifth and early fourth centuries. The manuscripts actually have *muthous* ("stories"), not *Mousous* ("Mysians"), which is a widely accepted scholarly emendation, so the title of the dithyramb might be "The Stories" instead. But nothing seems to hang on this.

between extremes and say it should be pursued,[45] and since Dorian has this nature with respect to the other modes, manifestly it is proper for the young to be educated more in Dorian tunes.

1342b17 But there are two goals, the possible as well as the proper, for everyone should put their hand rather to what is both possible and proper. These features are in fact distinguished by ages. Those exhausted by time,[46] for instance, cannot easily sing the strained modes; it is the relaxed ones that nature suggests for that age. This is why some of those conversant with music do nobly in criticizing Socrates for this too, that he rejected the relaxed modes for education, supposing them to have the character of drink — not in the sense of being able to intoxicate (intoxication is rather cause of Bacchic excitement) but in the sense of being exhausting.[47] Consequently, in view also of the period of older age to come, these sorts of modes and tunes should be taken up as well, along with any other such mode that, because of its ability to combine adornment at the same time as education, is proper for a child's time of life (as seems to be the case with Lydian most of all among the modes). Clearly, these three are the limits to set down for education: the mean, the possible, and the proper.

---

45. Possibly a reference to the *Ethics* (2.5–6), but perhaps a more general remark about what sort of characters people praise.

46. Aristotle could be referring to the old or, perhaps better in this context, to the age after puberty, when the voice has broken.

47. Plato *Republic* 398e6–399a3.

Book 6

Division and
Description of the
Other Regimes

CHAPTER 1

The Questions Political Science Must Study. *Any complete science or art studies the whole of what falls under it, as gymnastics studies the several sorts of training suitable or best for different bodies. So politics likewise must study (i) the best regime simply, (ii) the best regime in the circumstances, (iii) the best regime on the supposition of what people want, (iv) the regime that suits most cities. To fail to study all these, as some thinkers do, is to fail of usefulness. But to undertake this study and to be able to set up each regime, it is necessary also to know (v) how many kinds of regime there are. Knowing (vi) which laws suit which regime also requires knowledge of how many regimes there are.*

1288b10 Among all arts and sciences that are not partial in their development but are complete with respect to some one class of things, it belongs to a single art or science to study what is suitable in the case of each class. For instance, it is the work of gymnastics to study what sort of training benefits what sort of body; what training is best (for what suits the body noblest in nature and equipment must necessarily be best); and what single training, in the case of most bodies, suits all of them (for this too is a work of gymnastics). Further, if anyone desires neither the condition nor the knowledge required of those engaged in competition, it belongs no less to the physical and gymnastic trainer to provide this level of ability too. We see the like happening also in medicine, shipbuilding, clothing, and any other art.
1288b21 So it also clearly belongs to the same science to study the best regime and what it is and must be like if it is most to agree with our prayer and suffer no external impediments, and also, since getting the best regime is perhaps impossible for most people, what regime suits what cities. Con-

sequently, the good legislator and true politician must neglect neither the regime that is simply best nor the regime that is best under the circumstances. Nor, third, must he neglect the regime that is best given a certain supposition. For he must also study how any given regime might come into existence to begin with and how, once in existence, it might be longest preserved—I mean, for instance, when some city happens to be governed neither by the best regime (and happens even to lack the necessary equipment) nor by the best possible under the circumstances, but by some baser one. And he needs, besides all these, to get acquainted with the regime that is most in harmony with every city.

1288b35 So even if the majority of those who have made pronouncements about regimes are speaking nobly in other respects, they are at any rate entirely missing what is useful. For they should not study merely the regime that is best but also the regime that is possible, and likewise also the regime that all cities find easier and have more in common with. As it is, however, some of them seek out only the highest regime or the one that requires much equipment, while others do speak of a regime that has more of what is common about it but remove those that are in place and praise the Spartan or some other regime. But what should be done is to introduce the sort of arrangement that, given what people already have, they will easily consent to or could easily participate in, as it is no less a work to put a regime right than to establish one in the first place, just as it is no less a work to unlearn something than to learn it in the first place. Hence, in addition to what has just been said, the politician must also be able to come to the aid of regimes that already exist, as was in fact stated before.[1]

1289a7 That, however, cannot be done if one does not know how many kinds of regimes there are. The opinion nowadays is that there is one kind of democracy and one kind of oligarchy, but this is not true. Consequently, one must not remain ignorant of the differences between regimes and of how many there are and of the number of ways these differences can be put together.

1289a11 Along with this same prudence goes also the seeing of what the best laws are and which ones suit each regime. For laws must be laid down, and all do lay them down, with a view to the regimes and not the regimes with a view to the laws.[2] For a regime is the way cities arrange their offices, how the offices are distributed, what is the controlling element in the regime, and what is the end of each community. But among the things that show what the regime is, laws hold a distinct place, being what the rulers must rule by and defend against transgressors. So it is clear that, in order to lay

1. Earlier in this chapter, at 1288b24-35.
2. Cf. 3.11.1282b10-11.

down laws as well, one needs to have a grasp of the differences between regimes and of their number. For the same laws cannot be of benefit to all oligarchies nor to all democracies if there is not one democracy nor one oligarchy but rather several kinds of each.

CHAPTER 2

The Questions Remaining to Be Studied and Their Order. *Of the six questions listed in chapter 1, question (i), the best regime (kingship and aristocracy), has been dealt with. It remains to discuss the other regimes, of which tyranny is furthest removed from polity, oligarchy second, and democracy third. So the questions left to discuss are: first, question (v), the several kinds of these regimes; second, question (iv), which of them is most common and most worth choosing; third, questions (ii) and (iii), which regime is preferable for whom; fourth, question (vi), how to set up regimes; and, finally, how they are destroyed and preserved.*

1289a26 In our first enquiry about regimes we distinguished three correct ones (kingship, aristocracy, and polity) and the three deviations from them (tyranny from kingship, oligarchy from aristocracy, and democracy from polity).[3] We have also discussed aristocracy and kingship, for to study the best regime is the same as to speak about these designations, since the aim of each of them is a foundation based on fully equipped virtue.[4] Further, the difference between aristocracy and kingship, as well as when it is necessary to adopt a kingship, was determined earlier.[5] What remains, therefore, is to treat of the regime that has the common name as its designation,[6] and also of the other regimes—oligarchy, democracy, and tyranny.

1289a38 Now, it is clear which of these deviations is worst and which second worst, since the deviation from the first and most divine regime must be worst. But kingship must either have the name only without the reality or have the reality because of the great superiority of the one who is king. So tyranny, being the worst, must be furthest removed from polity,[7] olig-

---

3. 3.6–7.

4. Some hold the view that the reference here is to 3.14–17, but it would seem rather to be to books 4(7) and 5(8).

5. 3.17 and 4(7).14.1332b16–32.

6. That is, polity (*politeia*); so 3.7.1279a37–39.

7. Or "from being a regime," as some suggest. But since Aristotle is now intending to talk only about regimes other than kingship and aristocracy, his interest must primarily be on how these regimes rank among themselves. Hence, it seems to make more sense to suppose that he is here intending to conclude how the other regimes rank in relation to polity, this being the only one among them that is correct.

archy must be second (for aristocracy stands at the opposite extreme to this regime), and democracy must keep most to the measure.

1289b5 Now, this view has also been expressed by one of our predecessors,[8] though he did not look to the same thing we are. For he judged that when all these regimes are decent (as, for instance, when there is a wholesome oligarchy, and so on with the others), democracy is the worst of them, but that when they are base, it is the best. But our position is that these regimes are altogether defective and that it is not a noble thing to say that one oligarchy is better than another but rather that it is less base.

1289b11 But let us leave aside deciding about such matters for the present. What we must distinguish is, first, how many differences of regimes there are, if indeed there are several kinds of oligarchy and democracy;[9] then, which regime has the most of what is common about it and which is the most choiceworthy after the best regime or, if there is another regime that is aristocratic and nobly constituted but is suitable for most cities, which this regime is;[10] then, also, which of the other regimes is preferable for whom (for perhaps democracy rather than oligarchy is a necessity for some, while for others oligarchy rather than democracy is);[11] after this, how anyone who wants to do so should set up these regimes—I mean each of the kinds of democracy and each of those of oligarchy.[12] Finally, when we have, in succinct manner, given a treatment of all these things, we must try to go through, both in common for all regimes and separately for each, the ways in which regimes are destroyed and preserved, and what the causes are by which these results most naturally occur.[13]

CHAPTER 3

First Question: The Differences among Regimes

That There Are Several Kinds of Regime. Every city is divided into many parts—as into the well-off, the needy, and those in the middle; into the several sorts of populace and notables; and according to family and virtue. Regimes vary as the distribution of offices among the parts of the city varies. Consequently, there must be as many regimes as there are ways of distributing the offices among these parts.

8. Probably a reference to Plato's *Statesman* 302e4–303a5.
9. 6(4).3–10.
10. 6(4).11.
11. 6(4).12–13.
12. 6(4).14–16.
13. Book 7(5).

1289b27 The reason there are several regimes is that there are numerically several parts to any city. For, to begin with, we see that every city is made up of households;[14] next, that of this multitude in turn some must be well-off, others needy, and others in the middle; and that the part composed of the well-off has the heavy arms, while the part composed of the needy is without them. Also, we see that the populace is part farmers, part dealers in the market, and part vulgar mechanics. There are also differences among the notables according to their wealth and the amount of their substance—as, for instance, in the rearing of horses (which is a thing not easy to do for those without wealth). That is why in ancient times there were oligarchies among those whose cities had their power in horses, and they used their horses for wars against neighbors—as, for instance, did the Eretrians and the Chalcians, and the Magnesians on the river Maeander, and many of the others in Asia.[15] Further, in addition to differences of wealth, there are also differences of family and of virtue, and also whatever else there may be of the sort said to be a part of the city in our discussion of aristocracy. For there we distinguished the number of parts necessary to the composition of any city, for sometimes all of these parts share in the regime, sometimes fewer of them, and sometimes more.[16]

1290a5 Manifestly, then, there must be several regimes different in kind from each other, since these parts are, among themselves, different in kind. For a regime is the way the offices are arranged, and everyone distributes this arrangement either according to the power of the participants or according to some equality common to them—I mean, for instance, according to the power of the needy and well-off or some equality common to them both.[17] So there must be as many regimes as there are ways of doing this arrangement according to the superiorities and differences of the parts.

Restatement of the Correct View against the Common View. A common view is that there are just two regimes, democracy and oligarchy, from which the others are

---

14. Cf. 1.2.1252b27–28, 1.3.1253b1–3.

15. Eretria and Chalcis were neighboring cities on the island of Euboea; Magnesia was just north of Miletus on the coast of Asia Minor.

16. A reference to 4(7).8–9, especially 1328b2–33, though some want to suggest 3.12.1283a14–22 instead.

17. The Greek of this clause is a bit ambiguous since it contains no word for "power" or "equality" so these have to be supplied from the previous clause. One could accordingly put "power" in both places or "equality" instead, or again one could put "equality" first and "power" second. However, since the equality being talked of seems clearly to be equality in power, the verbal variants perhaps make no great difference to the sense. For in any case the point will be that offices are distributed to the powerful group or, if there are several powerful groups, to some combination of them that balances out their powers or equalizes them, whether with absolute or proportional equality; cf. 6(4).12 below.

deviations, just as there are supposed to be two winds and two harmonies from which all others are deviations. But our view, stated before, is better: there are two nobly constituted regimes, the best and the well mixed, from which the others, including oligarchies and democracies, are deviations.

1290a13 But there seem to be two regimes above all, and just as there are said to be two winds, the northerly and the southerly, with the others as deviations from them, so there are also said to be two regimes, the populace and oligarchy. For aristocracy is set down as a kind of oligarchy, on the grounds it is oligarchy of a sort;[18] and polity, so called, is set down as democracy, just as, in the case of winds, the westerly is set down as a kind of northerly wind and the easterly as a kind of southerly one. The like holds, according to some, also in the case of musical modes, for there also two kinds are set down, Dorian and Phrygian, and the other combinations are called either Doric or Phrygic.

1290a22 That, then, is what people are particularly accustomed to suppose about regimes. But it is truer and better to distinguish them as we have: that there are one or two nobly constituted regimes from which the others are deviations, some from the well-blended mode and others from the best regime,[19] with the tighter and more despotic being oligarchic and the more relaxed and softer being popular.

CHAPTER 4

Falsity of the Common View. It is false to regard democracy as rule by the many and oligarchy as rule by the few, since this way of distinguishing them fails if the many happen to be rich and the few poor. It is better to distinguish by reference to the free and the rich; but even so, if the free are few or the many rich, there is still no democracy. Democracy and oligarchy are determined rather by reference to poverty and wealth.

1290a30 One should not regard democracy, in the way some are now accustomed to do, as being simply where the multitude is in control (for, in fact, both in oligarchies and everywhere else, the greater part is in control), nor should one regard oligarchy as being where few have control over the

---

18. It is a case of rule by a few (the literal meaning of the Greek *oligarchia*).

19. The reference is to 3.7 and 6(4).2.1289a26–b5. There is no conflict between these and the present passage. The one or two nobly constituted regimes are, first, kingship and aristocracy together as the one (for these two together are the simply best regime), and, second, these plus polity as the two (for polity is also a correct regime but falls short of what is simply best). Accordingly, the well-blended mode and the best regime will be polity on the one hand (from which democracy is a deviation) and kingship and aristocracy on the other (from which tyranny and oligarchy are deviations).

regime. For if the whole number were 1,300, and 1,000 of these were rich but gave no share in rule to the 300 who, though free and similar in other respects, were poor, no one would say that they were running a democracy. Likewise too, if the poor were few but stronger than the well-off, who were more numerous, no one would call such a regime an oligarchy if the others, though wealthy, had no share in the honors. It should, then, rather be said that popular rule is when the free are in control and oligarchy is when the rich are; but it happens that the first are many and the second few, since many are free and few are rich. For otherwise there would be an oligarchy if offices were distributed according to size, as some say is the case in Ethiopia, or according to beauty, because the beautiful and the tall are few in number. **1290b7** Yet it is not even enough to distinguish these regimes by these criteria alone. Rather, since there are several parts to the populace and to oligarchy, it is necessary to grasp further that neither would there be popular rule if the free who were few were ruling over those who were a majority and not free (as, for example, in Apollonia on the Ionian Gulf and in Thera, for in each of these cities the honors belonged to those who, though few among many, were superior in good birth and had got first possession of the colonies), nor would there be popular rule if the rich were superior in numbers (as, for example, in Colophon long ago, for there the majority had acquired much substance before the war against the Lydians).[20] But it is democracy when the free and needy who are the majority have control of rule, and it is oligarchy when the rich and better born who are few have control.

Proof of the Correct View and Reason for the Common View. Just as there are different classes and kinds of animals according to the differences among their necessary parts (mouth, stomach, sense organs, limbs), so also with regimes. The necessary parts of regimes are the parts of the city: (i) farmers, (ii) artisans, (iii) dealers in the market, (iv) laborers, (v) fighters, (vi) judges and counsellors, (vii) the well-off, (viii) magistrates. Parts (vi) and (viii) require there to be some in the city with the virtue of politicians. Many suppose that all of these parts can be combined in the same persons. Wealth and poverty, however, cannot be. Hence, they suppose these parts to be the parts above all of cities and also to be—because the wealthy are few and the poor many—the opposed parts. So regimes based on these parts are the ones they set up, and there appear to be only two regimes: oligarchy and democracy.

1290b21 So then, it has been stated that there are several regimes and for what reasons. But that there are more regimes than those mentioned,[21] and

---

20. The war took place in the first half of the seventh century.
21. More, that is, than the democracy and oligarchy of the common view.

which they are and why, let us speak of this next, taking as our beginning principle the one stated earlier.[22] For we agree that every city has not one but several parts.

1290b25 So then, if we were choosing to get hold of the kinds of animal, the first thing we would do would be to mark off what every animal must necessarily possess—as, for instance, certain sense organs, something to work on food and take it in (as mouth and stomach), and, in addition, parts by which each animal moves. If there were only so many kinds,[23] but there were differences to these—I mean, for instance, if there were some several classes of mouth and stomach and sense organs and further also of locomotive parts—then the number of ways of combining these will necessarily make several classes of animals, for the same animal could not have several differences of mouth nor likewise of ears. Consequently, when these have been got hold of, all the ways of pairing them together that are possible will produce kinds of animal and as many kinds of animal as there are combinations of the necessary parts.

1290b37 The same method will hold of what we have been talking about, regimes. For, as has often been said,[24] cities too are made up of many parts and not one. Now, one part is the multitude who are concerned with food, the farmers as they are called. Second is the part called vulgar mechanics. This is the part concerned with the arts without which a city cannot be inhabited (though of these arts, some must be present of necessity, while others are for luxury and living nobly). Third is the part of dealers in the market—I mean those who spend their time buying and selling and in imports and retail trade. Fourth is the part of laborers.

1291a6 A fifth class is the part that goes to war, which must be present no less than the others if they are not to be slaves to attackers, for is it not something impossible that a city which is by nature a slave should deserve to be called a city? For a city is self-sufficient, but that which is a slave is not. Hence, though what is said in the *Republic*[25] is clever, it is not sufficient. For Socrates says there are four parts most necessary to the composition of a city and asserts these to be a weaver, a farmer, a shoemaker, and a builder. He then adds, on the grounds these are not sufficient, a smith and those who tend the needed livestock, and further a merchant and a retailer. All these become the complement of the first city—as if the whole city were put together for the sake of what is necessary and not rather for what is

22. In 6(4).3.
23. That is, kinds of necessary parts, reading *eidē* ("kinds") with the manuscripts, not the *eiē* ("there would be") adopted by Dreizehnter.
24. Twice each in 6(4).3 and 4 above, and also in 2.2, 3.1 and 12, and 4(7).8.
25. Plato *Republic* 369d1–371e11.

noble, and as if there were equal need of shoemakers and of farmers. The warrior part he does not grant as a part until an increase in territory, and territory touching on neighbors, sets them up for war.

1291a22 But yet, even among the four (or however many the participants are), there must be someone to dispense and assess justice. So if one would set down the soul as more a part of an animal than the body, then in the case of cities too such things as these should, more than what promotes necessary needs, be set down as parts, namely the warring part, the part that shares in the virtue of justice involved in settling court cases, and, in addition, the part that deliberates (which is the work of political understanding). It makes no difference to the argument whether these parts are separated out among certain people or belong to the same ones, for in fact it often happens that the same people bear arms and farm. So clearly, if these latter must be set down as parts of the city, then the former should be as well,[26] because the armed part at any rate is a necessary part of the city.[27]

1291a33 Seventh is the part that uses its substance in public service, whom we call the well-off. Eighth is the part of magistrates or those who perform public service in the offices, if indeed there cannot be a city without rulers. There must therefore be some who can rule and perform this public service for the city, either continually or in part, and there must be the rest,[28] which we happened just now to mark off, the part that deliberates and that passes judgment between litigants about what is just. If, therefore, these things must exist in cities and must exist in a noble and just way, then there must also be some who share the virtue of politicians.

1291b2 Now, many think that the other powers can belong to the same

---

26. "These latter" refers to those who bear arms and farm, and "the former" refers to those who judge and deliberate.

27. This sentence is normally translated more after this fashion: "So if both these and those must be set down as parts of the city, then it is clear that the armed part at any rate is a necessary part of the city." In that case, "these" and "those" refer to parts dealing with the political functions of the city on the one hand (fighting, justice, deliberation) and to parts dealing with necessities on the other (food and the arts). The Greek *hoti* can mean either "that" or "because." But such a translation produces a circular argument, since the conclusion is included in the premise: "if the armed part etc. must be parts of the city, then clearly the armed part is a necessary part of the city." It also means that the sixth part in the list is missing. The translation I offer is meant to produce a noncircular argument and to provide a sixth part, namely the judges and deliberators.

28. The Greek here simply says "the rest" (*loipa de*), without a verb, and most translate along the lines of "there remain the things we happened just now to mark off . . ." as if Aristotle were listing another (and ninth) part. The translation I offer aims to connect this sentence immediately with the preceding one and to give it the same verb. For I suppose Aristotle not to be listing a new part here but to be arguing that, since (as was just shown) these parts of judges and deliberators, along with that of the magistrates, are also necessary, there is need of some in the city who have the virtue to discharge these functions well and justly.

persons—for instance, that the same persons can be warriors, farmers, and artisans, and in addition deliberators and judges. Everyone also makes claim to virtue and supposes himself capable of most of the offices. But it is impossible for the same persons to be poor and wealthy. Hence, it is these above all that seem to be parts of the city, namely the well-off and the needy. Further, on account of the fact that the former are generally few and the latter many, these seem to be the parts of the city that are opposites. Consequently, the regimes that are based on the superiorities of these parts are the ones people also set up, and there seem to be two regimes: democracy and oligarchy.[29]

That There Are Also Several Kinds of Democracy and Oligarchy. There are several kinds of democracy and oligarchy because there are several kinds of populace and notables.

1291b14 That, then, there are more regimes[30] and for what reasons was said earlier,[31] but that there are more kinds of democracy and of oligarchy let us now proceed to discuss. This fact too is manifest from what has been said. For there are several kinds both of the populace and of the notables, as they are called. Kinds of populace are, for example: one, the farmers; a second, the kind involved in the arts; another, the kind that deals in the market and spends its time in selling and buying; another, the kind engaged with the sea—and this includes the kinds involved in war, in business, in ferrying, and in fishing. In many places each of these is a large crowd—as, for instance, the fishermen in Tarentum and Byzantium, the trireme[32] kind in Athens, the merchant kind in Aegina and Chios, and the ferrying kind in Tenedos. In addition to these there is the laboring kind and the kind that has little substance, so that it cannot be at leisure. Further, there is the kind that is not free by citizen parents on both sides, and any other kind of multitude that there may be.

1291b28 Among the notables there are kinds according to wealth, good birth, virtue, education, and things that are described with the same differentiating quality as these.[33]

Kinds of Democracy. The kinds of democracy are these: (i) what is said to be most in accord with equality, though it is really domination by the populace; (ii) when offices

29. Though in fact there are others, specifically (since not everyone has the virtue they claim) regimes based not on wealth or poverty but on genuine virtue.

30. That is, than democracy and oligarchy.

31. In 6(4).3 above and also 3.7–13.

32. The trireme was the standard Greek warship and was so called because it had three banks of oars.

33. Things similarly expressive of privilege and advantage, as number and power of friends (cf. 6(4).6.1293a30–31 below).

are filled from low property qualifications; (iii) when all whose citizen descent is un-
questionable share the regime, but law rules; (iv) when all citizens share, but law rules;
(v) when things are the same in other respects, but the multitude and not law rules.
This last is analogous to tyranny: the populace, flattered by demagogues like a mon-
arch, rules all things by decree. It is not really a regime or even a democracy at all.

1291b30 Now, a first democracy is the one that is said to be most in accord
with equality. For equality, says the law of such a democracy, is when the
needy are no more superior than the well-off and when neither of the two is
in control but both are alike. For if freedom does indeed, as some suppose,
exist most of all in democracy, and equality too, then this would most of all
be the case if everyone most of all has a like share in the regime. But since
the populace is the majority, and what the majority think right is what has
the control, this regime is necessarily a democracy.[34] This, then, is one kind
of democracy.

1291b39 Another kind is that in which the offices are filled on the basis of
property qualifications, though these are low, and it is necessary that any
who possess the amount be entitled to take part but not any who lose it.
Another kind of democracy is that in which all the citizens take part whose
descent is unquestionable,[35] but the law rules. Another kind of democracy
is that in which all have a share in the offices provided only that they are
citizens, but the law rules.

1292a4 Another kind of democracy is that in which everything is the same
in other respects but the multitude is in control, not the law. This happens
when decrees, but not the law, are in control, and this is a result of demagogues. For in cities run democratically according to law the demagogue
does not arise, but the best of the citizens occupy the first place. However,
where the laws are not in control, there demagogues arise. For the populace, compounded into one out of many—for the many exercise control as
a whole and not as individuals—becomes a monarch (what kind of "many-
headed" rule Homer says is "not good"[36] is unclear, whether this sort or
one where there are several ruling individually). So such a populace, being
a monarch, seeks to rule as a monarch, because it is not ruled by law, and
becomes despotic. The consequence is that flatterers are held in honor, and
a populace like this is analogous to what tyranny is among monarchies.
Hence, it also has the same character: both rule despotically over their bet-

34. This regime is therefore only rhetorically one of equality and is really domination by
the populace (cf. 8(6).3). It collapses in effect into one or other form of democracy and perhaps most of all the last. At any rate it is not listed separately later in 6(4).6.

35. The word translated "unquestionable" is of the same root as the word used elsewhere
for the giving of accounts by outgoing officeholders (*euthunai*).

36. *Iliad* 2.204.

ters; its decrees are like the tyrant's edicts; the demagogue is the same as the flatterer or analogous and, in particular, both prevail with their own audience, flatterers with tyrants and demagogues with this sort of populace. Demagogues, by bringing everything before the populace, are responsible for decrees and not laws being in control, for they become great as a result, since the populace is in control of everything and they are in control of what the populace thinks (the multitude believes them). Moreover, they bring accusations against the offices and say the populace should do the deciding. The populace gladly accepts the challenge, and consequently all the offices are overthrown.

1292a30 Anyone who said that such a democracy was not a regime[37] would seem to be making a reasonable censure, for where the laws do not rule there is no regime.[38] For the law ought to rule over everything, but it is of particulars that the offices and the regime ought to judge. Consequently, if democracy is one of the regimes, then clearly the sort of establishment where everything is managed by decrees is not even a democracy in the authoritative sense. For no decree can be universal.

1292a37 Let the kinds of democracy, then, be distinguished in this way.

CHAPTER 5

Kinds of Oligarchy. *The kinds of oligarchy are: (i) where property qualifications exclude the poor, but all who meet these qualifications are included; (ii) where property qualifications are high, and officeholders elect whom to include and exclude; (iii) where son succeeds father; (iv) where son succeeds father, but rulers, and not law, rule—this is dynasty, the counterpart to tyranny and extreme democracy.*

1292a39 Kinds of oligarchy are, one, that in which the offices are filled on the basis of property qualifications of such a size that the poor, although a majority, take no part in the regime but anyone who has the qualification is entitled to do so. Another is that in which the offices are filled on the basis of high property qualifications, and they themselves[39] choose those who are left out. If they make the choice from all of these, the practice is held to be more aristocratic, but if from certain determinate ones, more oligarchic. Another kind of oligarchy is that in which son succeeds to father. A fourth is that in which what was just said obtains and law does not rule but the rulers do. This is among oligarchies what tyranny is among monarchies and what

37. Possibly a reference to Plato *Republic* 557c1–558c7.
38. Cf. 3.11.1282b1–6 and 3.13.1284a10–14.
39. A reference either to those who meet the property qualification or to the existing officeholders.

the democracy we spoke of last is among democracies. Such an oligarchy is called a dynasty.

Reason for These Kinds of Democracy and Oligarchy

Preliminary Clarification. *Sometimes, especially after a revolution, a regime is of one kind in its laws and of another kind in the habits and training of those who run it. It is the latter who determine what kind of regime it is.*

1292b11 So many, then, are the kinds of oligarchy and democracy. But one must not fail to notice that it has happened in many places that while the regime by its laws is not popular, it is—because of its habits and training—popularly governed. Similarly again, it has so happened in other places that by its laws the regime is of a more popular sort but in its training and habits is governed in a rather oligarchical way. This result comes about principally after there has been a change in regimes. For the shift is not immediate, but people are content at the beginning to take advantage of each other in small ways. Consequently, the preceding laws continue in existence, but it is those changing the regime who dominate.

CHAPTER 6

Relation to the Kinds of Populace and Notables. *Kinds of democracy arise when those in control are (i) the farmers and those of a measured amount of substance, but without leisure; (ii) those with unquestionable family descent, but without leisure; (iii) all who are free, but without leisure; (iv) the multitude that has leisure to manage everything. Kinds of oligarchy arise when those in control are (i) many and lack excessive property or much leisure; (ii) few and with greater properties and strong enough to choose who is to enter the regime from the outside; (iii) fewer still and with greater properties and strong enough to confine office to themselves and their sons; (iv) those with an excess in properties and close friendships, ruling without law.*

1292b22 That there are this many kinds of democracy and oligarchy is manifest from precisely what we said.[40] For either all the stated parts of the populace must share in the regime or some must and others not. So when the element of farmers or those with a measured amount of substance are in control of the regime, they run it according to laws. For they keep alive by working and cannot be at leisure. Consequently, they put the law in charge and have only necessary meetings of the assembly. And it is open to others,

40. The several parts of the city and specifically of the populace and notables, as discussed above, chapter 4 at 1290b38–1291b30.

when they have acquired the property qualification determined by the laws, to take part. Hence, all those who have acquired this qualification are entitled to take part. For, generally, if all these are not so entitled, the situation is oligarchic, though what makes it impossible for them to be able to be at leisure is the absence of revenues.[41] So this then, for these reasons, is one kind of democracy.

1292b34 Another kind arises from the following division. For all whose family descent is unquestionable are also [42] entitled to take part, though it is those capable of leisure who do take part. Hence, in such a democracy the laws rule because there is no revenue. A third kind arises when all who are free are entitled to share in the regime but they do not take part for the aforementioned reason. Consequently, the law must rule in this democracy too.

1292b41 A fourth kind of democracy is the last in point of time to have arisen in cities. As cities have become much larger than they were originally and as they have an abundance of revenues, everyone takes part in the regime on account of the preponderance of the multitude; also, they all share in the governing together because even the needy, through receiving pay, can be at leisure. In fact, such a multitude is most of all at leisure. For care of their own affairs does not hold them back, but it does hold back the rich who, as a result, often do not take part in the assembly or in judging court cases. Hence, the multitude of the needy, and not the laws, come to be in control of the regime.

1293a10 On account of these necessities, then, the kinds of democracy are of this number and of this sort.

1293a12 As for the kinds of oligarchy, when several have substance, though of a lesser amount and not excessively great, there is the first kind of oligarchy. For they make taking part open to anyone who possesses the amount and, because of the multitude of those who do share in the ruling body, the law and not the human beings is necessarily in control. For the more distant they are from monarchy and the more they have neither so much property that they can be at leisure without worry nor so little that the city looks after them, they must necessarily judge that it is law that deserves to rule and not they themselves.

1293a21 But if those with property are fewer in number and their properties greater than in the previous case, the second kind of oligarchy arises. For, being stronger, they suppose they deserve to have more to themselves. Hence, they themselves choose who from the others are to enter the ruling

---

41. That is, public revenues to pay them to leave their work and spend time attending assemblies.

42. That is, in addition to those with a measured amount of property, who constituted the previous kind of democracy.

body, but because they are not strong enough to rule without law, what they lay down is a law of this sort.

1293a26 But if they draw things tighter by being fewer in number and having greater properties, the third advance of oligarchy comes about, namely their keeping the offices among themselves and in accordance with a law that bids sons succeed to the deceased. But when they are already going far to excess in tightening things in property and many friendships, this sort of dynasty is near to monarchy, and it is human beings who are in control and not the law. This is the fourth kind of oligarchy, the counterpart to the last kind of democracy.

CHAPTER 7

That There Are Also Several Kinds of Aristocracy, Polity, and Tyranny

Kinds of So-called Aristocracy. *Besides democracy and oligarchy, there are also the regimes of so-called aristocracy and of polity. Only the simply best regime is properly called aristocracy, but others are so called in comparison with oligarchy and polity, namely: (i) those that look to wealth, virtue, and populace, as in Carthage; (ii) those that look to virtue and populace, as in Sparta; (iii) those that incline from polity toward oligarchy.*

1293a35 There are, further, two regimes besides democracy and oligarchy, one of which[43] all speak of and is said to be one of the four regimes. The four, they say, are monarchy, oligarchy, democracy, and, fourth, the one called aristocracy. But there is a fifth, which is addressed by the name common to all regimes, for they call it polity. Because, however, it does not often arise, it has escaped the notice of those who try to enumerate the kinds of regimes, and they use only the four in their treatment of regimes, as Plato does.[44]

1293b1 Now it is noble to call aristocracy that regime which we went through in our first discussions.[45] For the only regime it is just to address as aristocracy is the one composed of men who, in respect of virtue, are simply best and not of men who are good by reference to some supposition.

43. That is, so-called aristocracy. The other one is polity, which Aristotle comes to shortly.

44. Probably a reference to *Republic* 8 and 9, where—with the simply best regime of philosopher rulers set to one side—the other regimes of timocracy (i.e., so-called aristocracy), oligarchy, democracy, and tyranny (i.e., monarchy) are discussed. Who the other writers were that Aristotle had in mind is not clear.

45. A reference that could be to 3.7.1279a34–b1 but must be much more to 4(7) and 5(8) (for aristocracy is mentioned in book 3 but not gone through in any detail there). There is also a strong verbal similarity in the next sentence to 4(7).9.1328b37–39.

For here alone is it simply true that the same person is good as a man and as a citizen,[46] whereas in the others they are good with reference to their own regime. Nevertheless, there are some regimes that are different from regimes run oligarchically and from so-called polity and which are called aristocracies. For a regime where offices are chosen not only on the basis of wealth but also on the basis of virtue must differ from both of these and be called aristocratic (for even in regimes that do not make a common care of virtue, there are nevertheless some who are of good repute and are held to be decent).

1293b14 So where the regime looks to wealth, virtue, and populace, as in Carthage,[47] it must be aristocratic, as also must regimes which look to two alone, as Sparta[48] looks to virtue and the populace and is a mixture of these two, democracy and virtue. These, then, are two kinds of aristocracy after the first, the best regime. There are also, third, all those regimes that incline from so-called polity more toward oligarchy.

CHAPTER 8

Kinds of Polity. *Polity is to be treated here, even though neither it nor so-called aristocracies are deviations, because it and they fall short of the best regime, and the deviations are numbered along with them. Polity is a mixture of democracy and oligarchy, and among its kinds the custom is to call those that incline toward democracy polities and those that incline toward oligarchy aristocracies. But the latter are not correctly so called. Only regimes aiming at virtue, the defining mark of aristocracy, in addition to wealth or freedom are to be called aristocracies. Those that aim at freedom and wealth alone are to be called polities.*

1293b22 It remains for us to speak about polity, as it is termed, and about tyranny. We have placed polity here, although neither it nor the aristocracies just mentioned are deviations, because in truth they have all fallen short of the most correct regime and because, next, enumerated along with them and belonging to them are these deviations, as we said in our opening discussion.[49] It is reasonable to make mention of tyranny last because it is least of all a regime, and our inquiry is about regimes. The reason, then, for our ordering things in this way has been stated.

46. Cf. 3.4–5 and 3.18.
47. Cf. 2.11.1273a4–b21.
48. Cf. 2.9.1270b6–26.
49. Or, as is more usually translated: "because they [polity and so-called aristocracy] are enumerated along with these deviations and these deviations are deviations from them." The reference is also usually said to be to 3.7.1279b4–6, but 6(4).2.1289a26–b5 seems to fit better.

1293b31 But we must now explain polity, for its power is more manifest now that we have determined oligarchy and democracy. Polity is, to speak simply, a mixture of oligarchy and democracy. But the custom is to call polities those mixtures that incline toward democracy and to call aristocracies those that incline more toward oligarchy on account of the fact that education and good birth go along more with those who are better off; in addition, the well-off seem to have what wrongdoers do wrong for. Hence, the well-off are addressed as gentlemen and as notables. So since aristocracy wishes to distribute superiority to the best of the citizens, people say oligarchies too are composed rather of gentlemen. And it seems a thing impossible for a city that is not run by aristocrats but by the wicked to be under good laws, and it seems likewise impossible for a city that is not under good laws to be an aristocracy.

1294a3 But there is no good state of law if the laws, though well laid down, are not obeyed. So one must suppose there is a good state of law in one way when the laws laid down are obeyed and in another when the laws that are kept to are nobly laid down (for even badly made laws can be obeyed). This can happen in two ways: either people obey the best laws they can or the best laws simply. Aristocracy seems, above all, to exist when honors are distributed according to virtue, for virtue is the defining mark of aristocracy, while wealth is the defining mark of oligarchy and freedom of the populace. What seems good to the majority, however, is found in all of them. For in oligarchy and aristocracy and rule of the populace, what is in control is that which seems good to the greater part of those who share in the regime.

1294a15 Now, in most cities the kind is the kind that is called polity, for its mixture aims only at the well-off and the needy, at wealth and freedom. For among most people, so to say, the well-off seem to be occupying the place of the gentlemen. But since there are three things that dispute over equality in the regime—freedom, wealth, and virtue (the fourth, which they call good birth, follows the last two since good birth is ancient wealth plus virtue)—it is manifest that the mixture of two of them, the well-off and needy, should be called polity, while the mixture of the three should, most of all among the others, be called aristocracy, after the true and first kind.

1294a25 We have stated, then, that there are other kinds of regime besides monarchy, democracy, and oligarchy. Of what sort these are, how aristocracies differ from each other and polities from aristocracy, and that they are not far from each other, is also manifest.

CHAPTER 9

Reason for These Kinds of Aristocracy and Polity. *Polities arise from the putting together of features of democracy and oligarchy, as when (i) the opposite legislation of both is combined; (ii) the mean between the two is adopted; (iii) one element is taken from one and another from the other. A mark of a nobly mixed regime is that it can be called both oligarchy and democracy, as in the case of Sparta. Another is that no part of the city should want a different regime.*

1294a30 Let us, after what has been said, discuss next in order how so-called polity comes about alongside democracy and oligarchy and how it should be established. The answer will become clear as the defining marks of democracy and oligarchy also become clear. For what must be done is to take the lists[50] of these marks and then make a combination by picking a tally,[51] as it were, from each list.

1294a35 There are three defining principles for the combination or mixture. A first is to take the legislation of both, as in the deciding of court cases. For in oligarchies a fine is imposed on the well-off if they do not take part in deciding cases, but there is no payment made to the needy. In democracies, by contrast, payment is made to the needy, but no fine is imposed on the well-off. To take both is to take something common and a mean between them, and hence something that, as mixed from the two, is proper to polity.

1294b1 This, then, is one way of doing the coupling. Another is to take the mean position between the arrangements of each. For instance, democracies arrange for membership of the assembly to be based on no property qualification or on a thoroughly low one; oligarchies arrange for it to be based on a high one. What is common is to have neither property qualification but instead the mean between the two of them.

1294b6 A third is to select from both arrangements, taking some from oligarchic law and others from democratic law. I mean, for instance, that it seems democratic to have the offices chosen by lot and oligarchic to have them chosen by election; and it seems democratic to have no property qualification and oligarchic to have a qualification. So it is aristocratic, then, and proper to polity, to take one from one and another from the other: from oligarchy that the offices are elected and from democracy that there is no property qualification.

---

50. The Greek is *dihairesis*, literally "division," but it refers here to a division of contrasting features into parallel lists.

51. A tally (*sumbolon*) was a half of a coin, which, along with its mate, was used for identification purposes between contracting parties. So Aristotle is saying that one must take the two columns—of democratic marks on the one hand and of oligarchic marks on the other—and combine marks from each column, rather like combining two tallies.

1294b13 This then is how to make the mixture. But a defining principle that the mixture of democracy and oligarchy has been done well is when the same regime can be said to be both democracy and oligarchy. For it is manifest that those who speak of it thus are getting this impression from the nobility of the mixing. The same impression is also given by the mean, for in the mean each of the two extremes appears.

1294b18 That is indeed how things are with the Spartan regime. For many try to speak of it as if it were a democracy, because the way it is arranged has many democratic features. First, for instance, is the upbringing of the children, since those of the rich are brought up like those of the poor and since they are educated in a way that the children of the poor can also manage. The like holds also of the succeeding age, and when they are men it is the same, for the rich and the poor are not distinct from each other. In similar fashion, the sustenance in the messes is the same for all, and the rich wear clothing that anyone, even from among the poor, might be able to get hold of. Further, the regime is democratic in that, of the two greatest offices, the populace elect the one and take part in the other, since they elect the senators and take part in the ephorate. Others try to say the regime is an oligarchy on account of its having many oligarchic features, as that all the offices are elected and none chosen by lot, that a few have control over penalties of death and exile, and many other such things.

1294b34 In the nobly mixed regime both and neither of the elements must appear to exist, and it must be preserved through itself and not from outside — through itself not in the sense that the majority wish it to exist (for that might be the case even in an evil regime) but in the sense that none of the parts of the city as a whole would even want a different regime.

1294b40 How polity must be established, then, and likewise how the so-called aristocracies also must be, has now been stated.

CHAPTER 10

Kinds of Tyranny. *Two kinds of tyranny are the same as two of the kinds of kingship: (i) barbarian kingship and (ii) Greek dictatorship. A last kind (iii) is most of all tyranny: unaccountable rule over unwilling and better or equal subjects for the ruler's own advantage.*

1295a1 Tyranny is what was left for us to speak of, not as if there is much to say about it, but so that it can take its part in our inquiry, since we lay down that it too is a part of regimes. Now, we determined about kingship in our first discussions (where we conducted an investigation into what is most of all referred to as kingship: whether it is a disadvantage or an advantage to cities, who is to be established as king, and from what source and how).[52] But we distinguished two kinds of tyranny in our examination of kingship, because the power of these tyrannies also overlaps in a way with kingship, since both of them are sorts of rule in accordance with law. For among certain of the barbarians, monarchs with autocratic power are chosen, and in ancient times among the Greeks certain monarchs arose in this way, whom they call dictators.[53] There are differences between them, but both were kingly, because they were according to law and exercised sole rule over willing subjects, while also tyrannical, because they ruled like despots after their own judgment.

1295a17 There is a third kind of tyranny which, being counterpart to total kingship, seems to be tyranny most of all. This is the kind of tyranny that any monarchy must necessarily be that rules without being accountable, over subjects who are all similar or better, and for its own advantage, not that of the ruled. Hence, it is a coercive monarchy, for no one who is free can willingly abide such rule.

1295a23 These and so many, then, are, for the aforesaid reasons, the kinds of tyranny.

CHAPTER 11

Second Question: The Most Common and Most Choiceworthy Regime after the Best

That This Regime Is the Middle Sort of Regime. The best life for human beings and cities is to live according to the mean of virtue. Among the parts of every city, the middle part—between the extremes of wealth and poverty—lives in this way and must be best, for (i) they more readily obey reason; (ii) they covet power least; (iii) they are, unlike those at the extremes, equal and similar, and a city wishes to be composed of such; (iv) they are most likely to survive. The regime based on the middle is therefore best, for (i) the middle are best, as just proved; (ii) the middle, if large, prevents the regime from deviating into the extremes; (iii) the middle regime is free of faction; (iv) the best legislators have come from the middle.

52. This is discussed in 3.14–18, but also 4(7) and 5(8) generally (since the best regime can be either kingship or aristocracy; see 3.18.1288a39–b2 and 4(7).14.1332b16–25).

53. Aristotle is referring to the second and third kinds of kingship mentioned in 3.14.1285a16–b3.

1295a25 If we judge neither by a virtue that is beyond the reach of private individuals,[54] nor by an education requiring a nature and equipment dependent on chance, nor again by a regime that is as one would pray for, but by a way of life that most can share in common together and by a regime that most cities can participate in, what is the best regime and the best way of life for most cities and most human beings? For as regards the regimes called aristocracies, of which we have just spoken, in some of their features they fall rather outside the reach of most cities, while in others they come close to so-called polity; hence, both kinds are to be spoken of as one regime.

1295a34 Decision about all these questions depends on the same elements. For if it was nobly said in the *Ethics* that the happy way of life is unimpeded life in accordance with virtue and that virtue is a mean,[55] then necessarily the middle way of life, the life of a mean that everyone can attain, must be best. The same definitions must hold also for the virtue and vice of city and regime,[56] since the regime is a certain way of life of a city.

1295b1 In all cities there are in fact three parts: those who are exceedingly well-off, those who are exceedingly needy, and the third who are in the middle of these two. So, since it is agreed that the mean and middle is best, then it is manifest that a middling possession also of the goods of fortune must be best of all. For the middle most easily obeys reason, whereas whatever is excessively beautiful or strong or well-born or wealthy, or whatever is the opposite, extremely wretched or weak, and has an exceeding lack of honor, finds it hard to follow reason (for the first become insolent and rather wicked in great things, while the second become villains and too much involved in petty wickedness; and injustices are committed partly out of insolence and partly out of villainy).[57]

1295b12 Further, love of ruling and desire to rule,[58] both of which are harmful to cities, exist least among those in the middle.

1295b13 In addition, those who are surrounded by an excess of good fortune (strength, wealth, friends, and other things of the sort) neither wish nor know how to be ruled, and this is something that begins immediately at home when they are still children. For, because of the luxury they live in, being ruled is not something they get used to, even at school. Those,

---

54. The sort of virtue, presumably, that must be brought about by common care; see 5(8).1.

55. *Ethics* 1.10.1101a14–21, 7.13.1153b9–21, and 2.8.1108b11–13, among other places.

56. Cf. 4(7).1.1323b33–36.

57. Cf. 2.7.1267a2–17.

58. There is some difficulty about the Greek at this point, and several emendations have been proposed. I translate what is contained in most manuscripts and understand the meaning to be that the middle are not moved to act against reason by the love of office when they are ruling nor by the desire to get office when they are not ruling.

on the other hand, who are in excessive need of these things are too abject. The result is that the latter do not know how to rule but only how to be ruled like slaves, and the former do not know how to be ruled in any way at all but only how to rule as masters. So a city of slaves and masters arises, not a city of the free, and the first are full of envy while the second are full of contempt. These things are at the furthest remove from friendship and political community, for community is a thing of friendship (people do not want to share even the road in common with enemies). The city aims at any rate to be composed as much as possible of equals and similars, and this is true above all of those in the middle. Consequently, this city—composed of those elements from which we say the city is naturally made up—must be best governed.

1295b28 Also, those in the middle are, most of all among the citizens, the ones who survive in cities. For neither do they themselves desire the possessions of others, as the poor do, nor do others desire theirs, as the poor desire the property of the wealthy. Also, because they neither plot nor are plotted against, they live out their lives in security. That is why Phocylides did nobly to pray: "Many things are best for those in the middle. To be middle in the city is my wish." [59]

1295b34 So it is clear that in the case of the political community too the one that is based on those in the middle is best, and that cities capable of being well governed are those sorts where the middle is large and, in particular, stronger than both extremes or, otherwise, than either one of them. For the middle will tip the balance when added to either side and prevent the emergence of an excess at the opposite extremes. Hence, the greatest good fortune is for those involved in the regime to have a middle and sufficient property, because where some possess a great deal and others nothing, either ultimate rule of the populace arises or unmixed oligarchy does or, because of the excess on both sides, tyranny. For it is from democracy and oligarchy of the most recent kind that tyranny arises, but very seldom from the middle and those close to each other (we will state the reason later in our discussion of changes in regimes). [60]

1296a7 But that the middle regime is best is manifest. For it alone is free of faction since, where the element based on the middle is large, there factions and dissensions over the regime arise least. Big cities are also free of faction for the same reason: that their middle is large. But in small cities it is easy to separate everyone into two groups, and the result is that no middle is left and pretty well everyone is either needy or well-off. Democracies are also more stable and longer lasting than oligarchies because of those in the middle, for

59. Frag. 12 Diehl. Phocylides was a sixth-century poet from Miletus.
60. In 7(5).8.1308a20–24 in particular.

the middle are more numerous in democracies than in oligarchies and have a greater share of honors. But when the needy, without the addition of the middle, are predominant in numbers, they act badly and are swiftly ruined. **1296a18** One must take as a sign also the fact that the best legislators come from the middle citizens. For Solon belonged to them (he shows it in his poetry), as did Lycurgus (for he was not king), and Charondas, and pretty well most of the rest.[61]

Why Most Regimes Are Not of the Middle Sort. Most regimes are not of the middle sort because (i) the middle in most cities is small; (ii) the extremes, because of their factions and fights, use victory to set up an extreme instead of a middle regime; (iii) those who were leaders in Greece looked to their own advantage and set up democracies and oligarchies in cities; (iv) the custom prevails of wanting either to dominate or to be dominated.

1296a22 It is also manifest from these facts why most regimes are either democracies or oligarchies. For because the middle in them is often small, one or the other side (whether those with property or the populace) are always in excess and, abandoning the middle, they conduct the regime to suit themselves, and so it becomes either a populace or an oligarchy.

1296a27 Add to this the fact that, because there are factions and fights between the populace and the well-off against each other, whenever one side or the other happens to be more dominant than the opposite, they do not establish a common regime, nor even an equal one, but take their superiority in the regime as the reward of victory and make a democracy in one case and an oligarchy in the other.

1296a32 Further, each of those who came to leadership in Greece kept their eyes on their own regime and established either democracies or oligarchies in cities, not having in view the advantage of these cities but their own.[62]

1296a36 Consequently, for these reasons, the middle regime has come about either never or seldom and in few places. For one man alone from among those who formerly came to leadership was persuaded to give this arrangement to cities,[63] but now even among those in the cities the custom is established not to want what is equal but either to seek rule or to put up with being dominated.

61. Cf. 2.12.

62. Aristotle is doubtless thinking in particular of the Athenians who, during their periods of naval empire in fifth- and fourth-century Greece, set up democracies, and of the Spartans who set up oligarchies instead, especially after their defeat of Athens in the Peloponnesian War.

63. The identity of this individual is disputed but seems most likely to be Philip II of Macedon, father of Alexander the Great, who no doubt was persuaded to this course of action by Aristotle himself.

That Other Regimes Are Better or Worse by Reference to the Middle. As the middle is best, so the kinds of the other regimes—democracies and oligarchies—must be better or worse as they are closer to or further from it.

1296b2 Which is the best regime, then, and why, is manifest from these considerations. But as for the other regimes (since we say there are several kinds of democracy and oligarchy), which of them is to be put first, which second, and so on, according as one is better and another worse, is easy to see now that the best has been defined. For the one nearest to this must always be better and the one that is most removed from the middle worse—unless one is making one's judgment on the basis of a supposition. By "on the basis of a supposition" I mean that, though some other regime is more worth choosing, nothing prevents a different regime from being more advantageous to some.

CHAPTER 12

Third Question: Which Regime Is Preferable for Whom

Democracies and Oligarchies. *Regimes must be based on the part of the city that, on the basis of both quantity and quality, is stronger. The several kinds of democracy are preferable in cities where the several kinds of populace are in this way stronger, and oligarchies where the kinds of well-off and notables are. But the legislator should always involve the middle as well in these regimes.*

1296b13 Which and what sort of regime is of advantage to which and what sort of persons is the next thing to go through after what has been said. But first something must be grasped that is universally the same about all of them. For the part of the city that wishes the regime to continue must be stronger than the part that does not. But every city is made up of a certain quality and a certain quantity. By quality, I mean freedom, wealth, education, and good birth; and by quantity I mean superiority in multitude. It is possible that, among the parts of which the city is composed, one of them has the quality and another the quantity. For instance, it is possible that the low-born are greater in numbers than the high-born, or the needy than the wealthy, but yet that they do not exceed in quantity as much as they are exceeded in quality. Hence, quantity and quality have to be assessed together against each other.

1296b24 Now where the multitude of the needy is superior according to the aforesaid proportion,[64] there it is natural for a democracy to exist and each

64. That is, where their quantity outweighs any defect they may have in quality.

kind of democracy according to the superiority of each kind of populace—the first democracy, for instance, if the multitude of farmers is predominant; the last, if the multitude of vulgar mechanics and wage earners are; and similarly also with the other democracies lying between them. But where the multitude of the well-off and notables exceeds more in quality than it is exceeded in quantity, there it is natural for oligarchy to exist, and each kind of oligarchy in the same way according to superiority of oligarchic multitude. But the legislator should always take up the middle sort into the regime:[65] if he is laying down oligarchic laws, he must aim at the middle; if democratic ones, he must bring over the middle to the laws as well.

Mixed Regimes

The General Case. Lasting polities can exist wherever the middle are stronger than both or either extreme, for the extremes could never unite against them. But, in order to make polity last, as well as so-called aristocracy, the mixing must be done well and should not favor the well-off at the expense of the populace.

1296b38 Where the multitude of the middle sort exceeds both extremes or only either one of them, there a lasting polity can exist. For there is no fear that the rich will conspire with the poor against them, since neither rich nor poor will want to serve as slave to the other, and, should they look for a regime that is more common, they will not find any besides this one. For their distrust of each other would prevent them putting up with rule by turns, and it is the arbitrator who is everywhere most trusted, and the middle is an arbitrator.

1297a6 The better mixed the polity is, the more lasting it is. But many also among those who wish to produce aristocratic regimes make the mistake not only of assigning more to the well-off but also of deceiving the populace. For from things falsely good there must in time eventually result a true evil. For the graspings of the rich destroy the regime more than those of the populace.

CHAPTER 13

Particular Applications. Sophistries favoring the well-off against the populace, of which there are five sorts, aim in each case to ensure the participation of the well-off in rule and discourage that of the populace. These oligarchic sophistries can be countered

---

65. Presumably to strengthen further those who support the regime as well as to moderate excesses.

by the opposing democratic ones in order to get the mixture right. Mixed regimes are made up of those who bear arms, and the needed property qualifications must ensure that those who meet the qualifications are more numerous than those who do not (the poor and excluded will not complain if otherwise well treated). Earlier polities were based on the cavalry, but present ones are based on the heavy armed infantry. These earlier ones also inclined, though reasonably enough in the circumstances, toward oligarchy and kingship.

1297a14 The sophistries in regimes[66] devised by way of pretext against the populace are five in number, and concern the assembly, the offices, the law courts, bearing arms, and physical training. As regards the assembly, the sophistry is that attendance at its meetings is open to all, but a fine for non-attendance is imposed only on the well-off, or the fine on them is much heavier. As regards the offices, the sophistry is that those with a property qualification are not permitted to abjure but the needy are. As regards jury courts, the sophistry is that a fine is imposed on the well-off if they do not sit on juries, but the needy are let off with impunity, or, as in Charondas' laws,[67] the fine on the former is heavy but on the latter light. In some places, enrolling for the assembly and juries is open to all, but heavy fines are imposed on those who enroll but fail to attend the assembly or sit on juries, the aim being to get people to avoid enrolling because of the fine and, because of not enrolling, neither to sit on juries nor to attend the assembly. Legislation is passed in the same way about acquiring arms and physical training. For the needy are allowed not to acquire arms, but a fine is imposed on the well-off if they do not. And should they not train, no fine is imposed on the former, but one is imposed on the latter so that the latter will, because of the fine, take part while the former, having nothing to fear, will not.

1297a34 Now these sophistries in legislation are oligarchic, but in democracies there are sophistries counter to them. For pay is provided to the needy if they attend the assembly and sit on juries, but no fine is set down for the well-off. It is consequently manifest that if one wants to get a just mixture, one should draw together sophistries from either side and provide pay for the first and fines for the second, since in this way all would share together, whereas in the other way one side alone gets to possess the regime.

1297b1 The regime must consist only of those who possess arms. But it is not possible to define the property qualification in a simple manner and say that it must be so much. Instead, one should examine what amount will make for the highest qualification while still having the result that those

66. Aristotle means mixed regimes (polities and so-called aristocracies), as a later reference to this passage makes clear (see 7(5).8.1307b30–1308a3).

67. Cf. 2.12.1274a23–25, 1274b5–8.

who share in the regime are more numerous than those who do not. One should then set the qualification at that.

1297b6 For the poor prefer to keep quiet, even when not included in the regime, provided no one treats them insolently or takes away any of their substance (something that is not easy, because it is not always the case that those who participate in the ruling body are refined). They are also in the habit of shirking in time of war if they are not fed and are left in need; yet, if food is provided, they are willing to go to war.[68]

1297b12 In some places the polity[69] is composed not only of those under arms but also of those who used to be so. Among the Malians, the polity was made up of both sorts, but they made appointments to office from among those still soldiering. Also, the first polity among the Greeks came about, after kingships,[70] from those involved in war, and the polity at the very beginning from the cavalry. For strength and superiority in war used to belong to the cavalry, since heavy armed infantry[71] is useless in the absence of tight formations, and experience in such things and regular battle lines did not exist among the ancients. As a result, their strength lay in the cavalry. But when cities increased in size and those possessed of heavy arms grew stronger, more people came to share in the polity. That is why what we now call polities our predecessors used to call democracies. But the ancient polities were oligarchic and kingly,[72] as was reasonable enough, because on account of the lack of human beings, the middle was not large and so, being weak in numbers and in military formation, they were more ready to put up with being ruled.

1297b28 We have stated, then, for what reason there are several regimes and why there are others besides those spoken of (for democracy is not one in number, and likewise with the others); further, what their differences are and why it happens so; in addition, which regime, speaking for the majority of cases, is best, and what sort of regime fits what sort of people.

68. That is, presumably, as auxiliary forces, as oarsmen on ships, and so on, not in the regular battle line (since they are not well-off enough to afford their own heavy arms).

69. Here, and in the rest of this paragraph, *politeia* seems to have its specific sense of polity (or at least mixed regime), not its generic one of regime.

70. Cf. 3.15.1286b11–13.

71. The Greek word is *hoplitikon* (from *hopla* or "arms"), which here must have its precise sense of the hoplite force, the standard, heavy armed infantry of ancient Greece. Elsewhere, the sense is usually less specific and means the armed force in general.

72. That is, the way they were mixed inclined in these directions.

CHAPTER 14

Fourth Question: How to Set Up These Regimes

By Means of the Deliberative Body. Regimes have three parts: the deliberative, the offices, and the law courts. The deliberative has control over the major matters, and either (i) all these things must be decided by all, or (ii) by some, or (iii) some of them by some and others by others, or (iv) some of them by all and others by some. Type (i) is democracy, and its several modes accord with the several kinds of democracy; type (ii) is oligarchy, and its several modes also accord with the several kinds of oligarchy; types (iii) and (iv) are, depending on the mode, aristocracy or polity. In setting up the deliberative body in democracies, it is advantageous to adopt ways of compelling the notables to take part and of preventing the populace from greatly outbalancing them. In setting up the deliberative in oligarchies, it is advantageous to adopt ways of involving the populace in the process of deliberation.

1297b35 Let us, with regard to what comes next, discuss each regime again both together and separately, taking as our beginning what is appropriate to the subject. All regimes have three parts, and the serious legislator must study by reference to them what is of advantage to each regime. As long as these parts are in a noble condition, the regime must necessarily be in a noble condition, and regimes differ from each other by the way each of these differs. One of the three is what deliberates about common matters, a second is what concerns the offices (that is to say, which offices there should be, with control over what things, and in what way they should be chosen), and a third is what decides law suits.

1298a3 The deliberative body has control over war and peace, alliances and their dissolution; over laws; over death, exile, and confiscation; over the selection and auditing of offices. All these matters for decision must either be given to all the citizens, or to some of them (for instance, to a single office or to several), or some matters to some and others to others, or some matters to all and others to some.

1298a9 For all to decide about all matters is popular (for such equality is what the populace seek), but there are several ways in which all can decide. One is for them to do so by turns and not all together in a group, as in the regime of Telecles of Miletus[73] (there are also other regimes where deliberation is done by joint boards meeting together, and all enter upon these boards by turns, beginning from the tribes and the divisions that are altogether the smallest, until all are gone through), and for them to meet

73. Not otherwise known.

together only about the passage of laws and about matters to do with the regime and to hear announcements from the rulers.

1298a19 Another way is for all as a group to decide but to meet together only for the selection of officeholders, passing laws, matters of war and peace, and taking audits, and for the other things to be deliberated on by the offices deputed to each matter, these offices being either elected from all or chosen by lot.

1298a24 Another way is for the citizens to meet about the offices and the audits and to deliberate concerning war and alliances, and for the other things to be managed by offices of which as few as possible (such being those few that require knowledge in the rulers) are elected.

1298a28 A fourth way is for all to come together to deliberate about everything while the offices decide nothing but only reach preliminary determinations. This is the way in which the last democracy is actually managed, the democracy we say is analogous to dynastic oligarchy and tyrannical monarchy.

1298a33 These ways, then, are all democratic. But for some to decide about everything is oligarchic, and there are several differences here too. For when they are chosen on the basis of more measured property qualifications and are, because of this measure in the qualifications, several in number, and do not make changes where the law forbids but keep to it, and permit anyone with the qualification to participate, then such an oligarchy is, because of its measured quality, a political one.[74]

1298a40 When not all[75] but those elected participate in deliberation, and they rule according to law as in the previous case, then this way is oligarchic.

1298b2 When those in control of deliberation also elect themselves, and when son succeeds to father and they have control of the laws, then this arrangement too must be oligarchic.

1298b5 When some have control over some things and others over others—as when war and peace and audits are in the control of everyone but the rest is in the control of the rulers, and these rulers are elected or chosen by lot—then there is an aristocracy or a polity. And if some things are in the control of those elected and others in the control of those chosen by lot, either simply so or from a preelected pool, or if the elected and those chosen by lot act in common, then some of these features are the mark of an aristocratic regime and others of polity itself.

1298b11 Such, then, is how the deliberative body is divided in relation to the regimes, and the way each regime manages things accords with the above determinations.

74. That is, of the character of a polity.
75. That is, not all those who meet the property qualification.

1298b13 In democracy of the sort that now seems most of all to be democracy (I mean the sort where the populace has control even over the laws), it is of advantage, from the point of view of better deliberation, to do the same as is done in jury courts in oligarchies: they arrange for the imposition of fines on those they want to have serve on juries in order to make them do so (whereas the popular sort, by contrast, arrange for pay to the needy). The same should be done also in the case of assemblies, for they will deliberate better when they all deliberate in common, the populace with the notables and these with the multitude. It is of advantage too if those who do the deliberating are elected, or chosen by lot, in equal numbers from these parts.[76] And if those of the citizens[77] who are of the popular sort are greatly superior in numbers, it is of advantage either not to give pay to all of them but only to as many as will be commensurate with the notables, or to exclude the excess by lot.

1298b26 In oligarchies it is of advantage either to co-opt from among the multitude or to set up the sort of board of officials (called precouncillors or guardians of the law) that exists in some regimes, and conduct only that business[78] which this board has already deliberated about. For in this way the populace will have a part in deliberation but will not be able to undermine anything that affects the regime. Further, it is of advantage if the populace vote the same resolutions as, or none contrary to, those laid before them; or if they are all allowed a part in giving advice but the deliberating rests with the rulers. And it is necessary to do the opposite of what happens in polities. The multitude should have the control when vetoing a proposal and not when voting for one; have the latter case referred back to the rulers instead. The reverse is done in polities: the few have the control when they veto and not when they approve, but the proposal is always referred to the majority.

1299a1 This, then, is how the deliberative body, or the part that has control over the regime, should be determined.

CHAPTER 15

By Means of the Offices

The Differences among Offices. *Offices differ in number, kinds, duration, tenure, and appointment. By office is meant that which has assigned to it deliberation, judg-*

---

76. That is, the parts of the populace and the notables.

77. Reading *politōn* ("citizens") with one of the manuscripts, rather than *politikōn* ("the politicians" or "the politically active") with other manuscripts and with Dreizehnter.

78. That is, before the popular assembly.

ment, and command over certain matters. The number and variety of offices in big cities can be large, but in small cities many of them must be combined into one. Which should be combined with which depends on how many offices any city needs, and on questions of location, function, and difference of regime. Some offices are peculiar to certain regimes, as are precouncillors to oligarchy, a council to democracy, and managers of children and women to aristocracy.

1299a3 Next in turn comes the dividing of the offices. For there are many differences in this part of the regime also: how many offices there are and with control over what things; how long, as regards time, each office lasts (for some people make offices to be for six months, others for a shorter time, others for a year, others for longer periods), and whether the offices should be perpetual or have long terms or whether they should not but instead an office may be held many times by the same person or may not be held by him twice but only once; further, as regards the appointment of offices, from whom the appointment should be made and by whom and how. In respect of all these questions one must be able to distinguish how many modes there can be and, after that, to match up which sorts of office benefit which sorts of regime.

1299a14 But even determining what should be called offices is not easy. For the political community is in need of many supervisors, so one must not lay down that all those elected or chosen by lot are rulers or officers—as, for instance, to begin with, the priests, for priesthood must be regarded as something different and extra to the political offices, and further chorus masters and heralds; and even ambassadors are elected. Political sorts of care either concern all the citizens in the doing of some action (as a general in the case of soldiers on campaign) or some part of them (as managers of women and managers of children), while other sorts of care belong to household management (for often there is election of corn measurers), and others are for giving assistance or are of the sort that, if people are well-off, they arrange to use slaves for. To speak simply, those are principally to be called offices which are assigned certain matters for deliberation, judgment, and the issuing of commands—the last in particular, since issuing commands is more characteristic of rule. However, for practical purposes, this makes hardly any difference, as there has never yet been a decision, the dispute being merely about the name; but for thought there is some matter provided.

1299a31 One might raise more of a difficulty about what sort of offices, and how many, are necessary for the existence of a city, and which, while not necessary, are useful for a regime that is serious—and raise it in respect of any regime, and especially of cities that are small. For in large cities one can, and should, arrange one office for one work. For the fact that there are many citizens makes it possible for many to enter upon the boards of offices, and consequently some offices they hold after long intervals while others they exercise once. Each work is also better cared for when it is a single concern than when it is one among many concerns. In small cities, by contrast, it is necessary to bring many offices together into a few hands, since through lack of human beings, there cannot easily be many in office—for who will there be to take over from them? Small cities do sometimes need the same offices and laws as large ones, save that the latter need the same office or law frequently while the latter need it only after long intervals. That is why nothing prevents arranging for many things to be cared for together, since these cares will not get in each other's way, and why boards of offices must, because of lack of human beings, be made like multipurpose lamp holders.[79]

1299b10 If, then, we can say how many offices must be present in any city and how many need not, but should,[80] be present, one could easily combine these facts and know which offices are appropriately combined into a single office. It is appropriate also to pay attention to what sort of things must be cared for by a multitude of boards that are local, and what sort a single office must everywhere have control over. For instance, whether the market manager is to look after well-ordered adornment[81] in the marketplace and others are in other places, or whether the same person is to do it everywhere. Also, whether the offices are to be distinguished according to what they do or according to the human beings they do it for—I mean, for instance, whether there is to be a single office to look after well-ordered adornment in the case of children and women or a different one in the case of each.

1299b20 And according to the regimes too, whether the kinds of offices differ according to each regime or not. For instance, whether in democracy, oligarchy, aristocracy, and monarchy the same offices have control save that they are not composed of equal or similar persons but of different ones in different regimes (as of the educated in aristocracies, of the rich in oligarchies, of the free in democracies), or whether some offices happen to exist because of these very differences and the same offices are in place in some cases but out of place in others (for it is appropriate that the same offices be here great but there minor).

1299b30 There are, to be sure, some offices that are peculiar to certain regimes, as the office of precouncillors. For this is not a democratic office, but what is popular is a council. For there must be some such body whose

79. The Greek is *obelischolychnia* and refers to a kind of roasting spit that could also serve as a lamp holder.

80. Reading *dei* ("should") with the manuscripts, not *lusitelei* ("would usefully") with Dreizehnter.

81. The Greek word for "well-ordered adornment" here, and again in the next few lines, is *eukosmia*, from *kosmos*.

care it is to do the initial deliberating for the populace so that they can attend to their affairs. A council is oligarchic if its members are numerically few. But precouncillors must be few in number, so they are an oligarchic body. Where, however, both these offices exist, the precouncillors stand as a check on the councillors, for the councillor is popular but the precouncillor oligarchic. The power of the council is also abolished in those sort of democracies where the populace itself comes together and conducts all the business, which is a usual result when those attending the assembly are well-off or get pay.[82] For, being at leisure, they can both meet together often and decide everything themselves.

1300a4 A manager of children and of women, and any other office that has control over this sort of care, is aristocratic and not democratic, for how is it possible to stop the women of the needy from going out and about? Nor is it an oligarchic office, for the women of oligarchs live in luxury. But about these matters let so much be said for now.

The Appointment of Offices. *The kind and number of modes of appointment depend on a threefold difference in three terms: who appoints (all, some, both), from whom they appoint (from all, from some, from both), and how they appoint (by election, by lot, by both). Each of the three differences in each term can be combined in four ways with the differences in the other two terms (excluding the paired difference, the "both," in these other terms), to give twelve modes. Democratic modes are when all appoint from all; modes proper to polity are when all by turns appoint from all or from some or from all and some; modes proper to polities leaning toward oligarchy are when some appoint from all, and when some appoint from all and some; oligarchic modes are when some appoint from some; aristocratic modes are when some appoint from all and all from some by election. Which are advantageous to whom with respect to which offices will be manifest from the powers of the offices.*

1300a9 As regards the appointment of offices, we must try to go through things from the beginning. The differences, which when put together must encompass all the modes, are found in three terms. One of these three is who appoint the offices, second is from whom they appoint, and last is the way in which they appoint. Of each of these three there are three[83] differentiations. For either all the citizens appoint or some do, and they appoint either from all or from some demarcated group (demarcated, for instance, by a property qualification, or by family, or by virtue, or by something else

---

82. Reading *euporia ēi ē misthos* ("are well-off or get pay") with the manuscripts, rather than *euporia ēi misthou* ("are well-off through pay") with Dreizehnter.

83. Reading *treis* ("three") with the manuscripts, not the *duo* ("two") adopted by Dreizehnter. There are, in each case, two simple differences (i.e., all, some), and the third, as Aristotle notes shortly, is their combination (i.e., both all and some together).

of the sort—as in Megara where they appointed from those who came back from exile together and fought against the populace),⁸⁴ and they do this either by election or by lot; again, these are paired—I mean, some offices are appointed by some and others by all, some are appointed from all and others from some, and some are appointed by election and others by lot.

1300a22 In the case of each differentiation of these terms, there will be four modes. For either all appoint from all by election or all appoint from all by lot (and from all either in sections—for example, from all according to their tribes and wards and clans until all the citizens are gone through⁸⁵—or from all every time), [or all appoint from some by election or all appoint from some by lot], or they appoint partly in this way and partly in that. Again, if it is some who do the appointing, they do it either from all by election or from all by lot, or from some by election or from some by lot, or they do it partly in this way and partly in that (such as⁸⁶ partly from all by election and partly by lot). Consequently, there arise twelve modes (without reckoning the two pairings).⁸⁷

1300a31 Of these modes, the two appointments when all appoint from all by election or by lot or by both means (some offices being appointed by lot and others by election) are popular.⁸⁸ But when they do not all appoint at

---

84. Possibly a reference to the overthrow of the democracy at Megara in 424.

85. Aristotle is presumably thinking of the sort of thing that happens in the democracy of Telecles of Miletus, and other democracies, where all are eligible for office but by turns and not all at once, 6(4).14.1298a11–19.

86. The Greek literally says "I mean" (*legō*), but here it is introducing an instance only, for the other instance (some appointing from some, partly by election and partly by lot) is not stated, being left to be supplied from the context.

87. The Greek of this passage is notoriously controversial. I follow the manuscript readings as given by Newman and abandon Dreizehnter but insert, with many editors, the words marked by square brackets (the only addition that seems necessary for the sense). Aristotle's meaning is that we take each of the three differences in the third term and combine them one after the other with the four combinations formed by the first two differences in the other two terms (omitting the third difference, the "two pairings," in these other two terms). Thus, the three differences (election, lot, election and lot) are combined in turn, first with the combination of all appointing from all, second with the combination of all appointing from some, third with the combination of some appointing from all, fourth with the combination of some appointing from some. There are thus twelve modes (three differences times four combinations). If the omitted pairings are then introduced (which Aristotle does not do, leaving us to do it for ourselves), we will get a combination of each of the three differences with another five combinations: first with all appointing from all and some, second with some appointing from all and some, third with all and some appointing from all, fourth with all and some appointing from some, fifth with all and some appointing from all and some. This will give another fifteen modes (three differences times five combinations), producing a total of twenty-seven modes (these fifteen plus the original twelve), which is the necessary mathematical result of combining three groups of three (three times three times three).

88. The two appointments are the two ways of all appointing from all mentioned just above (1300a24–26), when the appointment is made from all the citizens in sections and when it is made from all the citizens together.

the same time but do appoint from all or when they appoint from some, by lot or election or both, or when they appoint some offices from all and others from some by both (by "both" I mean that some are appointed by lot and others by election), it is proper to polity. Also, when some appoint from all, some offices by election and others by lot, or from both,[89] some offices by lot and others by election, it is oligarchic;[90] and it is also more oligarchic when appointment is from both (the practice of aristocratic polity, some offices appointed from all and others from some) than[91] when some offices are appointed by election and others by lot. When some appoint from some, it is oligarchic, and likewise when some appoint from some by lot (though it does not occur) and when some appoint from some by both means. When some appoint from all and when all appoint from some by election, it is aristocratic.[92]

1300b5 So many in number, then, are the modes of appointing the offices, and this is how they are divided in relation to the regimes. Which are of advantage to whom or how the appointments should be made will become manifest along with the powers of the offices and what these powers are.[93] By "power of an office" I mean, for instance, the power of control over revenues and the power of control over defense, because there is, for example, a different kind of power involved in generalship and in control over agreements in the market.

CHAPTER 16

By Means of the Law Courts. *Differences in law courts depend on from whom they are appointed (all, some), over what they have jurisdiction, and by what means they are appointed (election, lot). Courts divide into those having jurisdiction over (i) audits, (ii) crimes involving common matters, (iii) matters affecting the regime, (iv) disputes between rulers and private persons, (v) private transactions of some magnitude, (vi) homicides (four kinds), (vii) foreigners (two kinds), (viii) small claims. There are four modes of all deciding all cases, four of some deciding all cases, and four of all*

89. The Greek is ambiguous. The word "both" (*amphoin*) could be genitive, as I take it, and meant to be read with "from" (*ek*) supplied from the "from all" just mentioned, so as to mean "from both" (that is, from both all and some); or it could be dative, as others take it, and meant to be read by itself, so as to mean "by both" (that is, by both means, lot and election). But this second way makes little sense in the context and forces emendations on the text.

90. That is, it makes the polity oligarchic or inclines it toward oligarchy.

91. Many suppose the Greek *ē* here means "or" and not "than" (it can mean both); but this makes little sense in the context and also forces emendations on the text.

92. In this paragraph too I follow the manuscript readings as given by Newman, abandoning Dreizehnter.

93. A topic taken up in 8(6).8.

and some deciding all cases. The first are democratic, the second oligarchic, the third aristocratic and proper to polity.

1300b13 Of the three parts, it remains to speak of the judicial. We must grasp the modes of this too following the same supposition. The differentiation of law courts is found in three terms: from whom they are appointed, about what things they judge, and how they are appointed. I mean, in the case of from whom, whether they are appointed from all or from some; in the case of about what things, how many kinds of courts there are; in the case of how, whether by lot or election.

1300b19 First, then, let a division be made of how many kinds of courts there are. They are eight in number. One is the court of audits; another is concerned with anyone who commits wrong in any common matter; another with whatever bears on the regime; a fourth is for rulers and private persons with respect to their disputes over imposition of fines; a fifth is concerned with private transactions that have some magnitude; and, in addition to these, there are the courts of homicide and of foreigners. Now, kinds of homicide court (whether involving the same or different jurors) are that concerned with premeditated homicide, that concerned with involuntary homicide, that concerned with cases where the fact is admitted but the justice of it disputed, and a fourth concerned with cases brought against fugitives for murder on their return (as the court at Phreatto in Athens is said in fact to be).[94] But such cases are few at any time, even in large cities. Of the foreigners' court, one kind is for foreigners against foreigners, another for foreigners against townspeople. Further, in addition to all these courts, there is one concerned with small transactions, those involving a drachma or five drachmas or a little more (for judgment must be given in these cases too, but there is no need for a multitude of jurors). But let these courts that have to do with homicides and foreigners be set to one side, and let us speak about the political courts, which, when not managed nobly, occasion factional conflict and changes of regimes.

1300b38 It is necessary either that all decide all the cases just distinguished, being appointed either by election, or by lot, or that all decide all cases but some courts are appointed by lot and others by election, or that those who decide certain of the same cases are appointed by lot while others of them are appointed by election. These modes, then, are four in number. There are as many others as well when a part does the deciding. For, again, the jurors also can be appointed from some by election and decide all cases, or they can be appointed from some by lot and decide all cases, or some

---

94. These four kinds of homicide reflect Athenian practice. In the court at Phreatto the defendant had to argue his case from a boat (*Athenaiōn Politeia* 57).

courts can be appointed by lot and others by election, or some courts deciding the same cases can be composed of those appointed by lot and of those
appointed by election. These, then, in the way they have been stated, are
the modes for the above mentioned alternatives.[95] But there are, further, the
same courts when paired — I mean, for instance, when some courts are appointed from all and some from some and others from both (as when some
in the same court are appointed from all and others from some), and appointment is either by lot or election or both.

1301a10 How many modes there are for courts, then, has been stated. The
first of these courts, those appointed from all deciding all cases, are popular;
the second, those appointed from some deciding all cases, are oligarchic;
the third, some courts appointed from all and others from some, are aristocratic and proper to polity.

95. That is, the alternatives, mentioned at the beginning of the chapter, of whether the
courts are appointed from all or from some. I translate the manuscript readings omitting
Dreizehnter's addition (*heteroi para*), which would give the sense: ". . . are the other modes
additional to those mentioned," where "those mentioned" means the modes for when all decide all matters. But the Greek makes sense as it stands and no addition is necessary.

Book 7

Destruction and
Preservation of the
Other Regimes

CHAPTER 1

Fifth Question: Destruction and Preservation of Regimes

Destruction of Regimes in General

The Starting Point of Change. *Regimes can change because there is not one regime but several, based on the several understandings of justice—as, notably, democracy and oligarchy. These understandings are partly true and partly false, but it is on their basis that the adherents of each, when they do not think they have the share they believe they should, start factions to change the regime. The virtuous would be most justified if they started faction, but they do it least.*

1301a19 The other things we chose to treat of have pretty well all been discussed. What next in order requires investigation are the things that originate change in regimes, how many of these there are and of what sort, and what are the ways in which each regime is destroyed and from what regimes into what regimes they alter most; further, how regimes are preserved, both in the case of all generally and of each in particular, and what, in addition, are the means whereby each regime can most especially be preserved.

1301a25 What must be assumed first as starting point is that many regimes have come into being because, though everyone agrees about the just and the proportionally equal, they err, as was in fact said before,[1] about what this equality is. For rule of the populace came into being because those equal in one respect suppose themselves to be equal simply (since, being all in like manner free, they think themselves equal simply), while oligarchy came into

---

1. 3.9, 12, and 13.

being because those unequal in one respect take themselves to be unequal simply (being unequal in substance, they take themselves to be unequal simply). The former then claim, on the ground of being equal, that they deserve equal shares in everything, while the latter, on the ground of being unequal, seek to gain more for themselves (since what is more is unequal).

1301a35 Now all these regimes are in a way just, though, simply speaking, they are mistaken, and that is why, when the share that each side has in the regime does not accord with what they happen to believe, they start factions. Those who are superior in virtue, however, would be most just of all in starting faction, though they do it least, for it is they alone who, in the most reasonable sense, are simply unequal. There are also some who are surpassing in family and, because of this inequality (for those who have the virtue and wealth of their ancestors seem to be well-born), do not think they deserve equality.

Kinds of Change and Which Regimes Suffer Them. *Change occurs in two ways: either (i) from one regime to another or (ii) within the same regime (a) when control of it changes hands, (b) when it is made more or less strict, or (c) when a part of it is changed. Factions arise where there is inequality, for people start factions when they are seeking equality, the equality determined by their understanding of justice. So since equality is twofold, regimes based on only one form of equality, oligarchy and democracy, suffer most from faction and change, while middle regimes that are based on both are most stable.*

1301b4 These are, so to say, the first beginnings and springs from which factions originate. Hence, there are two ways in which regimes undergo change. In one way the change is directed against the regime, so as to alter it from the established one into another—as, for instance, from democracy to oligarchy, or from oligarchy to democracy, or from these to polity and aristocracy, or from the latter two to the former. In the other way, the change is not directed against the established regime; instead, the choice is for the same setup, but people want to have control of it in their own hands, as with oligarchy and monarchy. The change can also be about the more or less— as, for instance, to make an existing oligarchy more or less oligarchical, or to make an existing democracy more or less democratic, and likewise with the remaining regimes, to tighten or relax them. Further, the change can be against a part of the regime, as in setting up or abolishing a certain office. So Lysander, as some say, undertook to destroy the kingship in Sparta, and King Pausanias the ephorate.[2] In Epidamnus too the regime was partially

---

2. Lysander was Spartan admiral at the end of the Peloponnesian War. Pausanias, king or rather regent after the Persian Wars, was mentioned earlier, in 4(7).14.1333b29–35, and is mentioned later, in 7(5).7.1307a2–5.

changed, for instead of tribal magistrates they set up a council, although the officeholders among those in the ruling body are still required to enter the tribal hall whenever an office is voted on;[3] the single magistrate was also an oligarchical element in this regime.

1301b26 For wherever there is no proportion among those who are unequal, faction arises because of the inequality (for a perpetual kingship is unequal if it exists among equals), since people generally start factions when they are seeking equality. But equality is twofold, and one is numerical and the other according to merit. By numerical equality I mean what is the same and equal in amount and size, and by equality according to merit I mean what is the same and equal in ratio. For instance, three exceeds two and two exceeds one by an equal amount numerically, while four exceeds two and two exceeds one by an equal amount in ratio (for both are halves). But though people agree that equality according to merit is what is simply just, they differ, as was said before,[4] in that some think that they are altogether equal if they are equal in one respect while others think that they deserve to be unequal in every respect if they are unequal in one.

1301b39 That is also why two regimes in particular arise, rule of the populace and oligarchy, for few possess good birth and virtue but more possess these things[5] (for nowhere are there a hundred well-born and virtuous, but everywhere the well-off are many).[6] To have an arrangement that accords in every respect simply with one or the other equality is base, as the results make manifest, for none of these sorts of regimes is lasting. The reason is that it is impossible for the initial error, and one in the first principle, not to end up eventually in something evil. Hence, it is necessary to use numerical equality in some things and equality according to merit in others.[7] Still, democracy is more stable and more free of faction than oligarchy. For in oligarchies two kinds of faction arise, one between the oligarchs themselves and another against the populace, while in democracies there is only faction against the oligarchy and no faction of the populace against itself arises that is worth speaking of. Further, the regime based on the middle, which

3. Nothing further is known about these events at Epidamnus, and the precise significance of the change is unclear too. One suggestion is that, despite the changes in the regime, only existing officeholders were obliged to take part when elections were held. This would have the oligarchical effect of tending to keep the regime in the hands of these officeholders, since they alone, as being obliged to attend elections, would always be present in large enough numbers to be able to sway the result.

4. 3.9, 12, and 13, and also earlier in this chapter, at 1301a25–39.

5. That is, freedom and wealth, the bases on which democrats and oligarchs make claims to rule.

6. The well-off are many, that is, in comparison with the virtuous, though few, of course, in comparison with the needy.

7. An allusion to well-mixed polity; 6(4).9, 12, and 13.

is the most stable among these kinds of regimes, is closer to rule based on the populace than to rule based on the few.

CHAPTER 2

Beginnings and Causes of Change

Their Kinds and Number. *The beginnings and causes of change are: (i) the disposition people are in when they start factions, that they do not think they have the equality they deserve; (ii) what they start factions for, honors and profit; (iii) the beginnings that incite them to action—that is, (a) others getting more profit, (b) others getting more honor, (c) insolence, (d) fear, (e) sense of superiority, (f) contempt, (g) disproportionate increase; in addition, there are (h) campaigning for votes, (i) disregard, (j) small things, and (k) dissimilarity.*

1302a16 Since we are investigating what originates factions and changes in regimes, we must first grasp in general their first beginnings and causes. These are, roughly speaking, three in number and they must first be defined in outline by themselves. For it is necessary to grasp what condition people are in when they start factions, what they start factions for, and, third, what beginnings of political disturbances and mutually opposing factions there are.

1302a22 The cause of people being in some way conditioned for change must, in its most general terms, be set down as the one about which we have already had occasion to speak. For some, if they think they are getting less despite being the equals of those who are getting more, start factions from the desire of equality, while others, if they suppose they are not getting more, but equal or less, despite being unequal, start factions from the desire of inequality and superiority. It can be just to have these desires but it can also be unjust, since the lesser can start factions in order to be equal and the equal in order to be greater.

1302a31 We have stated, then, what disposition people are in when they start factions. But what they start factions about are profit and honor and their opposites (for people also start factions in cities to avoid dishonor and fines, whether on their own account or on that of friends).

1302a34 The causes and beginnings of change, which get people into the disposition stated and about the things stated, are in one way seven in number but in another way more than seven. Two are the same as those just mentioned, though not after the same manner. For people are incited against each other on account of profit and honor—not, as was stated before, in order to get these for themselves, but because they see others, whether justly or unjustly, getting more of them. They are also incited against each other because of insolence, fear, superiority, contempt, disproportionate increase, and further, in a different way, because of campaigning for votes, disregard, small things, and dissimilarity.

CHAPTER 3

The Power of Their Operation. *Faction and change are incited by (c) insolence and (a) profit when people see the rulers behaving insolently and getting more for themselves; by (b) honor when they see others honored or themselves dishonored; by (e) superiority when one or more individuals have too great power; by (d) fear when people are afraid of being punished for doing wrong or of suffering wrong from others; by (f) contempt when they think themselves stronger than the rulers or despise the way the rulers are behaving; by (g) disproportionate increase when some part of the city grows far beyond the others. Change can occur without faction by (h) campaigning for votes, when to prevent this, people change the manner of appointment; by (i) disregard, when they allow hostile persons into the regime; by (j) small things, when overlooking something small introduces a large change in customary behavior; by (k) dissimilarity, when difference of tribe or of location or of character or other things splits the city into parts.*

1302b5 What the power of insolence and profit is among these causes and how they are causes is pretty well manifest. For when those in office are insolent and are increasing their gains, people start factions both against each other and against the regimes that gave the rulers power. Sometimes the gains are at the expense of private properties and sometimes at the expense of common funds.

1302b10 It is also clear what the power of honor is and how it is a cause of faction. For people start factions when they themselves are dishonored or when they see others being honored (which honoring and dishonoring happen unjustly if done contrary to merit but justly if done according to merit).

1302b15 Factions arise because of superiority when there is some single person, or several persons, whose power is too great for the city or too great for the power of the ruling body. People like this usually bring about monarchy or dynasty. That is why the habit of ostracism exists in some places, as in Athens and Argos. Yet it is better to see to it from the start that no one with a superiority so great can emerge than to let things go and apply a remedy afterwards.[8]

1302b21 Factions are started because of fear both when people have committed wrong and are afraid to pay the penalty and when they are about to

8. Cf. 3.13.1284b17–20.

suffer wrong and wish to anticipate the infliction of it—as in Rhodes where, because of the lawsuits brought against them, the notables banded together against the populace.[9]

1302b25 Factions are also started and attacks launched because of contempt —as in oligarchies, for instance, when those who do not partake in the regime are more numerous (for this makes them think they are stronger) and in democracies when the well-off are contemptuous of the disorder and anarchy. In Thebes, for example, the democracy was destroyed when it was being badly governed after the battle of Oenophyta, as was the democracy of the Megarians after they suffered a defeat through disorder and anarchy. The same was true also of the populace in Syracuse before the tyranny of Gelon and of that in Rhodes before the uprising.[10]

1302b33 Changes in regimes also occur because of disproportionate in-crease. Just as a body is made up of parts and must grow proportionately in order to retain its symmetry (since it will otherwise be destroyed, as when the foot is four yards long and the rest of the body two feet high, or might sometimes, if the disproportionate increase is not only in quantity but also in quality, change into the form of another animal), so a city is made up of parts as well, and one of them can often increase undetected—as, for instance, the multitude of the needy in democracies and polities. This can sometimes happen by chance as well—as in Tarentum, for example, when many notables were defeated and slain by the Iapygians shortly after the Persian Wars and a democracy took the place of a polity.[11] In Argos too, after those of the seventh were destroyed by the Spartan Cleomenes, they were compelled to accept some of their serfs into the regime;[12] and in Athens, at the time of their reverses by land, the notables were reduced in numbers be-cause service in the army during the Spartan War was based on the citizen rolls.[13] The same also happens, though less often, in democracies, for when the well-off grow in numbers or properties increase, change into oligarchies and dynasties occurs.

1303a13 Regimes also undergo change without faction, both, as in Heraia, because of vote-getting (for elections were being won by those campaign-

9. Perhaps a reference to events in 390.

10. The particulars of all these events are obscure. The battle of Oenophyta happened in 457, and Gelon took power in Syracuse in 485. The events in Rhodes are probably the same as those just mentioned.

11. In the year 473.

12. In the year 494. Those of the seventh were so called, apparently, because the battle was fought on the seventh day of the month; or the phrase may mean that they belonged to the seventh tribe.

13. The Spartan War is probably the Peloponnesian War of 431–03, or its first stage, the Archidamian War of 431–21. Citizens then served as soldiers, whereas in Aristotle's day sol-diers were predominantly mercenaries.

ing for votes and so they had the officials chosen by lot instead),[14] and, as in Oreus, because of disregard, when they allow those who are not friendly to the regime to enter the controlling offices (the oligarchy was dissolved there when Heracleodorus became one of the rulers and established a polity and democracy in place of the oligarchy).[15]

1303a20 Change also occurs because of small differences. By small differences I mean that when a small thing is overlooked, a large shift in customs can often take place without notice. So in Ambracia the property qualification was low, and in the end, on the grounds that a low qualification was close to or no different from none, the offices were filled without any property qualification at all.

1303a25 Not being of the same tribe is also a cause of faction, until people breathe as one. For just as a city is not generated from any chance multitude, so it is not generated in any chance period of time. Hence, most of those who take in joint or later settlers split into factions. Sybaris, for instance, was settled by Achaeans along with Troezenians, and when the Achaeans became more numerous, they threw the Troezenians out. That was the origin of the curse that fell on the Sybarites. In Thurii also, the Sybarites fell out with their fellow settlers, for when they supposed they deserved more because the land was theirs, they were expelled.[16] At Byzantium, the later settlers were discovered in a conspiracy and were driven out in a battle. The Antissaeans took in the fugitives from Chios and then expelled them in a battle. The Zancleans who took in the Samians were themselves driven out. The Apollonians on the Black Sea, after taking in later settlers, fell into factions. The Syracusans, when they made citizens of foreigners and mercenaries after the period of the tyrants, started factions and fell to fighting. The Amphipolitans, after they took in latter settlers from the Chalcidians, were for the most part driven out by them.[17] In the oligarchies it is the many who, on the grounds of being wronged, start factions because, as was said before,[18] though equal, they do not share things equally; in the democracies it is the notables who start factions because, though unequal, they do share things equally.

1303b7 Cities sometimes also fall into factions because of their location, when the territory is not naturally well suited for unity of city. In Clazo-

14. An event about which nothing further is known.

15. Oreus in Euboea, also known as Hestiaea, revolted from Sparta in 377, and Heracleodorus may be associated with this event.

16. Sybaris was settled about 720. The nature of the curse is unknown. Thurii was settled near the ruins of Sybaris in 444.

17. Nothing further is known of the events at Byzantium, Antissa, and Apollonia; those at Amphipolis probably took place in 370; at Zancle in 497; at Syracuse in 467.

18. 7(5).1.1301a25–35 and 1301b35–40.

menae, for instance, those on Chytrus started faction against those on the island, and so also did the Colophonians and Notians. People are not alike at Athens either, but those in the Peiraeus are more popularly inclined than those in the town.[19] For as the crossing of ditches, even very small ones, causes battle ranks to split, so every difference, it seems, makes for factional divisions. The greatest factional division, perhaps, is virtue and depravity, then wealth and poverty, and so on as one is more of a division than another (and the division just mentioned is one such).

CHAPTER 4

Occasions and Means of Their Operation. Factions are (i) about great things but can arise from small things; and (ii) even small factions can wax strong when they concern (a) those in control, for then the faction is in the principle and the principle is half the whole, or (b) the notables, for then the whole city can be dragged into the quarrel. Changes can also arise when (iii) some part of the regime increases in reputation or power, or when (iv) the parts are roughly equal and balanced. The means used to effect and sustain change are force and deceit.

1303b17 Factions originate, then, from small things and not about small things, but it is about great things that people start factions. Even small factions wax especially strong when they occur among those in positions of control. This happened, for instance, in Syracuse in ancient times. For the regime underwent change because two young men in office started factions about a matter of love. While one was away from home, his lover was seduced by a certain messmate of his, and on his return he became enraged and prevailed on the other's wife to commit adultery with him. Thence they began bringing over to their respective sides those in the ruling body and split them all up into factions.[20] So it is necessary to be on guard against such things in their origins and to bring factions among the leaders and the powerful to an end. For the fault is in the principle and the principle is said to be half the whole,[21] and that is also why a small fault there is equivalent to faults throughout the remaining parts.

1303b31 As a general rule, factions among the notables cause the whole city to join in, as happened in Hestiaea, for example, after the Persian Wars,

19. Clazomenae was an island off the Ionian coast and Chytrus close by on the mainland; Notium was the port of Colophon, the Peiraeus the port of Athens.

20. This event is usually placed just before the tyrant Gelon seized power in 485.

21. There is a play on words here, since the word translated "principle" (*archē*) also means both "beginning" and "rule."

when two brothers quarreled over the distribution of their inheritance. For the one who was more needy accused the other of not revealing the property nor the treasure their father had found and brought the popular party over to his side while the other, who had much property, brought the well-off over to his.[22] In Delphi too, the beginning of all the later factions arose from a quarrel over a marriage alliance. For when the bridegroom came for the bride, he interpreted an accident as an ill omen and went off without her. The bride's family, thinking themselves the victims of insolence, cast some sacred objects into a sacrifice he was making and then slew him for sacrilege. In Mytilene, faction arose over heiresses and was the beginning of many evils and also of the war against the Athenians during which Paches took their city. For Timophanes, one of the well-off, left two daughters, and Dexander, who was rejected and did not get them for his sons, began factional strife and incited the Athenians, being, as he was, their vice-consul.[23] Among the Phocians, faction arose about an heiress and concerned Mnaseas, the father of Mnason, and Euthycrates, the father of Onomarchus. This same faction was for the Phocians the beginning of their Sacred War.[24] The regime in Epidamnus underwent change because of a marriage. For a certain man had betrothed his daughter, and when the father of the one to whom he had betrothed her became one of the rulers and imposed a fine on him, he felt himself insulted and brought those outside the regime over to his side.

1304a17 Regimes also undergo change into oligarchy or rule of the populace or polity when an official board or part of the city wins some repute or becomes greater. The council of the Areopagus, for instance, won repute during the Persian Wars and was considered to have made the regime more strict; and again, when the crowd of sailors became responsible for the victory at Salamis and, as a result, for hegemony based on sea power, they made the democracy stronger.[25] In Argos, when the notables there acquired repute in the battle of Mantinea against the Spartans, they tried to destroy the rule of the populace.[26] In Syracuse, the populace, after becoming responsible for the victory against the Athenians, brought about change from polity to democracy.[27] In Chalcis, the populace, along with the notables, got rid of the tyrant Phoxus and then immediately took over the regime. In Ambracia,

22. An event about which nothing further is known.
23. In the year 428. The Greek for vice-consul is *proxenos*, a technical term for someone who undertook to represent in his own city the interests of a foreign city, and received in return privileges for himself in that foreign city.
24. This war broke out in 356. Mnason is said to have been a friend of Aristotle.
25. The battle of Salamis occurred in 480; cf. 2.12.1274a3–21 and *Athēnaiōn Politeia* 23.
26. The battle of Mantinea occurred in 418.
27. The victory occurred in 413.

things were again similar. The populace threw out the tyrant Periander with the aid of his assailants and then turned the regime in their own direction.²⁸ One should, in fact, as a general rule not neglect the fact that those who are causes of power, whether as private individuals or as offices or tribes or any part generally or any multitude whatever, are a stimulus to faction. For either those who envy their honor initiate factions or they themselves, because of their superiority, do not wish to remain on a level of equality.

1304a38 Regimes also change when the parts that seem to be opposites in the city, as the rich and the populace,²⁹ are equal with each other and when the middle is either nonexistent or altogether tiny.³⁰ For wherever one or the other of the parts is greatly superior, the rest are not willing to take any risks against their manifestly superior strength. That is also why those who are superior in virtue do not create any faction worth speaking of, for they are few against many.

1304b5 Such, then, is how matters stand with respect to beginnings and causes of faction and change in all regimes generally.

1304b7 But people change regimes sometimes by force and sometimes by deceit. They use force to compel either right at the beginning or afterwards, for deceit is also twofold. Sometimes they use deceit at the beginning and effect a change in the regime when people are willing, but afterwards, when people are unwilling, they retain control by force. For instance, during the 400 they deceived the populace by saying the Persian king would provide money for the war against the Spartans, and then tried, after putting about this lie, to keep their grip on the regime.³¹ At other times they use persuasion at the beginning, and afterwards, when people are again persuaded, rule them willingly.

1304b17 Concerning all regimes simply, then, the origins above stated are those from which changes come about.

CHAPTER 5

Destruction of Regimes in Particular

Destruction of Democracies. *Democracies undergo change principally because of the license of demagogues. These attack the notables and stir up the populace and*

28. Nothing else is known of Chalcis. Events in Ambracia took place in 580; cf. 7(5).10.1311a39–b1.

29. Cf. 6(4).4.1291b9–13.

30. Cf. 6(4).11.1296a23–27.

31. These events took place in Athens in 411 during the oligarchy of the so-called 400.

either (i) the notables effect change to oligarchy or (ii) the demagogue becomes a tyrant (which happened more in the past than now). Change can also occur (iii) from moderate to extreme democracy, when those eager for office play the demagogue and set the populace in control even of the laws.

1304b19 But it is necessary to divide and study, from these origins, what happens in the case of each kind of regime. Democracies, then, undergo change principally because of the licentious behavior of demagogues, who in some respects force the owners of property to combine by bringing false accusations against them individually (for common fear brings together the worst of enemies), and in other respects act against them in common by egging on the multitude.

1304b24 One can see this happening in fact in many cases. For the democracy in Cos underwent change after the rise of wicked demagogues, because the notables united. In Rhodes, the demagogues provided for distribution of pay and prevented reimbursement to the trireme captains of expenses incurred and they, because of the lawsuits brought against them,[32] were compelled to combine and destroy the populace. In Heraclea too, immediately after the founding of the colony, the populace was destroyed because of demagogues. For the notables were wronged by them and went into exile. Then, after gathering together, these exiles returned and destroyed the populace. Rather similar also was the way the democracy was destroyed in Megara. For the demagogues, in order to have money to confiscate, drove out many of the notables until they multiplied the number of exiles. These then returned, defeated the populace in a battle, and established the oligarchy. The same thing also happened at Cyme under the democracy that Thrasymachus destroyed.[33] In the other cases too, pretty much, one would see, upon study, that this is how changes occur. For sometimes demagogues wrong the notables in order to win public favor, forcing them to combine — they either redistribute their properties or, through public service, their revenues — and sometimes they slander the wealthy in order to have their money to confiscate.

1305a7 In ancient times, when the same man was both a demagogue and a general, democracies changed into tyranny, for pretty well most of the ancient tyrants came from demagogues. The reason this happened then but not now is that then demagogues came from serving generals (for no one was yet clever at speaking), but now with the advance of rhetorical skill,

---

32. Presumably by the contractors who had refurbished the ships at the command of the captains and who, because of the refusal of the demagogues to reimburse expenses, had not been paid by them.

33. Little further is known of any of these events. Those at Rhodes and Megara were also referred to in 7(5).3.1302b21–24, 30–33.

able speakers are the demagogues who, however, through their lack of military experience, launch no attacks—unless some rare case of the sort has occurred somewhere.

1305a15 Tyrannies arose more in the past than now because great offices used to be in the hands of particular individuals—as in Miletus, where a tyranny arose out of the presidency since the president was in control over many great matters.[34] A further reason is that cities were not large then and the populace dwelt in the countryside busy with their work, so when the patrons of the populace became skilled in war, they used to make attempts at tyranny. But they all did this with the trust of the populace and this trust was their hostility to the rich. Peisistratus, for instance, laid claim to tyranny at Athens after starting faction against the men of the plain; Theagenes did so in Megara after slaughtering the cattle of the well-off, whom he caught pasturing these cattle beyond their own land beside the river; Dionysius did so after bringing accusations against Daphnaeus and the wealthy. All of them were trusted as belonging, because of this enmity, to the popular party.[35]

1305a28 Democracies also undergo change from the ancestral kind to the newest kind. For where the offices are elected, but not on the basis of property qualifications, and the populace do the electing, those eager for office engage in demagogy to get elected and set the populace in control even of the laws. A cure to prevent this happening, or to make it less frequent, is to have rulers elected by the tribes and not by the populace en masse.

1305a34 Changes in democracies, then, pretty well all occur for these reasons.

CHAPTER 6

Destruction of Oligarchies. Oligarchies undergo change (i) from without (a) when their mistreatment of the multitude stirs up a popular leader against them or (b) when the oligarchy is narrow and those excluded revolt; (ii) from within (a) through the rivalry of demagogues working either on the oligarchs themselves or on the populace, (b) through oligarchs who squander their substance in riotous living, (c) through an oligarchy arising within the oligarchy, (d) in war or peace when military necessities require the employment either of mercenaries and a military leader who becomes tyrant or of the populace who have to be given a share in the regime, (e) through factions over marriages and lawsuits, or (f) through the despotic behavior of some in the regime;

34. Possibly a reference to the tyrant Thrasybulus, but the matter is not certain.

35. Peisistratus became tyrant of Athens in 560, being the leader of the popular faction against the rich (the men of the plain). Theagenes was tyrant of Megara in the seventh century, and Dionysius I became tyrant of Syracuse in 405.

(iii) by accident, when existing property qualifications are inappropriate to changed conditions.

1305a37 There are two very evident ways in particular in which oligarchies undergo change. One way is if they wrong the multitude, for then anyone will do as their patron, especially if he happens to come from the oligarchy itself, as in the case of Lygdamis at Naxos, who also became tyrant of the Naxians later.[36] There are also differences to the faction that takes its origin from others.[37] For sometimes, when those with the honors are especially few, dissolution comes about from the well-off themselves but from the well-off who are not in office. This has happened, for instance, in Massilia, Istrus, Heraclea, and other cities. For those with no part in the offices began to initiate change until first older brothers took part and then younger brothers too (for in some places father and son, and in others older and younger brother, do not rule at the same time). In Massilia, the oligarchy became more like a polity; in Istrus, it ended in rule of the populace; in Heraclea, it passed from the hands of rather few into those of 600.[38] The oligarchy underwent change also in Cnidus when, because few had a share and the son, as was said, did not share if the father did, nor the brothers if there were several, but only the eldest, the notables fell into factions among themselves. For while they were engaged in factions, the populace seized the opportunity and, choosing a patron from among the notables, launched an attack and were victorious (for what is split by faction is weak). In Erythrae in ancient times, even though during the oligarchy of the Basilidae those in the ruling body took noble care of things, the populace was angered nevertheless, because rule was in few hands, and effected change in the regime.[39]

1305b22 Oligarchies are, alternatively, changed from within, as through the rivalry of demagogues. For demagogy is twofold, and one sort of it exists among the few themselves (for a demagogue can arise even when there are very few). At Athens, for instance, Charicles and his friends became strong among the Thirty by playing the demagogue to them, and similarly Phrynichus and his friends among the 400.[40] Another sort is when those in the oligarchy are demagogues to the crowd, as the regime guardians were in Larissa, for instance, because it was the crowd that elected them. The same is true of all oligarchies where those who provide the rulers are not those who

36. Lygdamis became tyrant in 540.
37. That is, those outside the regime.
38. For Massilia (modern Marseilles), see 8(6).7.1321a29–31. Istrus and Heraclea were both on the Black Sea, but nothing further is known of events there.
39. These events in Cnidus and Erythrae are not otherwise known.
40. The thirty tyrants, as they were called, ruled Athens at the end of the Peloponnesian War in 404–3, and the oligarchy of the 400 ruled there in 411.

elect to office, but the offices are filled from high property qualifications or from political clubs and those possessed of heavy arms[41] or the populace do the electing (this happened in Abydus). It also occurs where the law courts are not drawn from the ruling body, for judicial decisions become objects of demagogy and so change is effected in the regime, something that happened in fact in Heraclea on the Black Sea.[42] It occurs, further, when some are drawing the oligarchy into fewer hands, for those who want equality are compelled to call on the populace for help.

1305b39 Changes in oligarchy also occur when they squander their private property in riotous living, for such people strive for innovations and either make a bid for tyranny themselves or secure it for someone else. This is what Hipparinus did for Dionysius in Syracuse; and in Amphipolis someone named Cleotimus brought in later settlers from Chalcis and, after their arrival, stirred them up in factional division against the well-off. In Aegina it was for this sort of reason that the one who struck the bargain with Chares undertook to effect a change of the regime.[43] Sometimes, then, such people try at once to bring about some change. But sometimes they steal common funds and thence either they themselves or those who are fighting against their thieving start factions against the oligarchs, something that happened in Apollonia on the Black Sea.[44] But an oligarchy that is of like mind is not easily destroyed from within. A sign is the regime in Pharsalus, where, though few, they are in charge of many because they treat each other nobly.[45]

1306a12 Oligarchies are also overthrown when another oligarchy arises within the oligarchy. This is the case when, though the whole ruling body is small, not all of these few share the greatest offices. Such happened once at Elis, for the regime was in the hands of a few elders and these became exceedingly few because they were ninety in number, held office for life, and were elected in dynastic fashion and after the manner of the senators at Sparta.[46]

1306a19 Change in oligarchies can happen both in war and in peace. In war it happens because the oligarchs are compelled, from their distrust of the

41. Here the reference is to the hoplites.

42. The events at Abydus may have occurred in 411 when Lysander the Spartan was setting up regimes based on oligarchical clubs. The events at Heraclea are otherwise unknown.

43. For Amphipolis, see earlier remarks at 7(5).3.1303b2–3; of events at Aegina nothing further is known save that Chares was an Athenian mercenary commander stationed in Corinth, not far from the island of Aegina, in 367.

44. An event about which nothing further is known.

45. Nothing much is known of Pharsalus in Aristotle's time, but earlier it had been racked by faction and was dependent on Macedon from 350 onward.

46. Nothing further is known of Elis; for the election of senators at Sparta, see 2.9.1270b35–1271a18.

populace, to hire mercenaries. For he who is put in charge of them often becomes tyrant, as Timophanes did in Corinth.[47] Or, if several are put in charge, these encompass a dynasty for themselves. Sometimes fear of these results compels the oligarchs to have recourse to the populace, and so they hand over a share in the regime to the multitude. In peace, through distrust of each other, they hand over their defense to mercenaries and to a ruler who is neutral, and he sometimes gets control over both sides. This happened in Larissa under the rule of Simus and his followers among the Aleuadae, and in Abydus under the rule of the political clubs, one of which was that of Iphiades.[48]

1306a31 Factions also arise because some within the oligarchy are pushed around by others within it and are driven into factional strife over marriages and lawsuits. The factions mentioned earlier,[49] for instance, arose from marital causes; and Diagoras overthrew the oligarchy of the knights in Eretria because of a marriage. The factions in Heraclea and Thebes arose from a judgment in court when Euetion in Heraclea and Archias in Thebes were justly punished for adultery but in a factious way. Their enemies were so bitter against them they had them bound in the stocks in the public square.[50]

1306b3 Many oligarchies, being too despotic, have also been overthrown by those in the regime who resented it, as in the case of the oligarchies in Cnidus and Chios.[51]

1306b6 Changes also occur as a result of accident, and in so-called polity as well as in oligarchies, when a property qualification is required for exercising deliberation and judgment and for the other offices. For often the qualification first laid down is relative to existing circumstances and ensures that a few have shares in the oligarchy and that the middle do in the polity. But when peace or some other stroke of fortune brings prosperity, the same properties turn out to be worth an assessment that is many times greater, and the result is that everyone shares everything. Sometimes the change occurs little by little and without being noticed, and at other times it happens quickly.

1306b16 Oligarchies, then, undergo change and fall into factions for these sorts of reasons. But generally both democracies and oligarchies can also sometimes shift, not into opposing regimes, but into those of the same

47. Timophanes became tyrant in 350 during Corinth's war with Argos.

48. The Aleuadae were one of the chief clans of Thessaly, and Simus is probably the Simus who brought Thessaly into subjection to Philip of Macedon in 342. Nothing further is known of Iphiades.

49. 7(5).4.303b37–1304a17.

50. Nothing further is known of these events in Eretria, Heraclea, or Thebes.

51. Events not further known, unless those at Cnidus are the same as were mentioned above at 1305b12–18.

class—as, for instance, from democracies and oligarchies under law to those that are in control by themselves, and vice versa.

CHAPTER 7

Destruction of Mixed Regimes. *Factions arise in aristocracies because (i) as in oligarchies, few share in the honors and (a) the multitude is composed of those who think highly of themselves, or (b) someone of equal virtue is deprived of honor by those with greater honors, or (c) someone of spirit lacks honor, or (d) some are excessively needy and others well-off, or (e) some individual already great is capable and ready to become greater. Both aristocracies and polities undergo change, but aristocracies more so, because (ii) they deviate from justice through being badly mixed, and they change (a) toward or (b) against the direction they are already leaning in. Aristocracies change without notice most when (iii) they are destroyed little by little, and an initial small concession by those in the regime leads to greater ones. All regimes, however, can be destroyed by an opposing regime that is nearby or powerful.*

1306b22 In aristocracies, factions arise because few share the honors, a fact which, indeed, was said to change oligarchies as well, because aristocracy is oligarchy of a sort since in both the rulers are few, though not few for the same reason. At any rate that is why aristocracy is held to be oligarchy.[52] Such faction must of necessity happen in particular: when the multitude is composed of those who have a high opinion of themselves as being similar in virtue, like the so-called Partheniae, for instance, in Sparta (for they were born from the Peers), who were discovered in a plot and sent out as colonists to Tarentum; or when some who are great and second to none in virtue are deprived of honor by those held in greater honor, as Lysander was by the kings; or when someone of a manly sort does not share in honors, like Cinadon who put together the attack on the Spartiates in the reign of Agesilaus;[53] or, further, when some people are excessively needy and others well-off, a thing that comes about especially during wars and also happened in Sparta at the time of the Messenian War (the fact is clear from the poem of Tyrtaeus called *Eunomia*), for when some were hard-pressed because of the war, they claimed they deserved a redistribution of the land;[54] or, in addition, if

52. Cf. 6(4).3.1290a13–29.

53. The Partheniae were illegitimate sons of Spartan fathers or mothers or disenfranchised citizens at the time of the First Messenian War (eighth century). The Peers, or more literally the Similars (*homoioi*), were the Spartiates, the full Spartan citizens. Lysander was Spartan admiral toward the end of and after the Peloponnesian War. Cinadon's conspiracy at Sparta was in 398.

54. The reference is to the Second Messenian War (seventh century); Tyrtaeus' *Eunomia* ("Good State of Law") is still extant (frags. 2–5 Diehl).

there is someone great and capable of being greater, who starts the faction in order to be monarch, as Pausanias seems to have done in Sparta (the one who was general during the Persian Wars) and Hanno in Carthage.[55]

1307a5 But polities and aristocracies are destroyed mainly because of deviation from justice within the regime. What begins it is the failure to get a noble mixture, in polity a mixture of democracy and oligarchy and in aristocracy of these and virtue as well, though in particular of the two—I mean the two of rule of the populace and oligarchy, since it is these that polities and most so-called aristocracies try to mix. For it is by their mixture that aristocracies differ from polities as they are called, and it is for this reason that the former are less and the latter more lasting. For people call aristocracies those that incline more toward oligarchy, and polities those that incline toward the multitude. Hence it is that these latter sort are more stable than the former, because the majority are stronger and are more content when they have equality, but those who are in conditions of prosperity try, if the regime gives them the superiority, to act insolently and get more for themselves.

1307a20 As a general rule, whichever side the regime inclines toward is the side that, as either group strengthens its own position, it changes into—for example, polity into rule of the populace and aristocracy into oligarchy. Or it can change into the opposite—as aristocracy, for instance, into rule of the populace (because those who are rather needy, on the ground of being wronged, bring the regime round to the opposite side), and polities into oligarchies. For the only lasting thing is equality according to merit and each having his own. What has been said took place in Thurii, for because, on the one hand, the offices were based on a rather high property qualification, a change was made to a smaller one and to more official boards, but because, on the other hand, the notables bought up the whole of the land contrary to law (for the regime was too oligarchical), they were able as a result to get more for themselves. The populace, however, were physically trained by the war and proved stronger than the garrisons, until all those who had more than their share of the land voluntarily gave it up.[56] Moreover, because all aristocratic regimes are oligarchic, the notables can do more to increase their share. Even in Sparta, for instance, properties keep coming into few hands.[57] The notables are also more able to do whatever they wish and to contract marriage alliances with whomever they wish. That, in fact, is why

---

55. The incident concerning Pausanias was mentioned in 7(5).1.1301b17–21 and 4(7).14. 1333b29–35. Hanno may be the Carthaginian general who fought against Dionysius I of Syracuse in about 400.

56. These events at Thurii seem unrelated to those recorded in 7(5).3.1303a31–33 above, but little is known for certain.

57. Cf. 2.9.1270a11–b6.

the city of the Locrians was destroyed, because of a marriage alliance with Dionysius, which would not have happened in a democracy or in an aristocracy that was well mixed.[58]

1307a40 Aristocracies change without notice most when the destruction happens little by little. This fact was mentioned in the earlier general discussion about all regimes, that changes are also caused by small things.[59] For once anything pertaining to the regime is let go, people can more readily change something else afterwards that is slightly greater, until they change the whole orderly array of things.[60] This also happened in the regime at Thurii. For there was a law that one could be general only at five-year intervals, but when some of the younger men became skilled in war and won reputation among the mass of the garrisons, they developed contempt for those in charge of affairs and supposed it easy to get the upper hand. They first undertook to annul this law, so that it would be possible for the same persons to be generals continuously (they saw that the populace would eagerly vote for them). Those of the rulers who had responsibility for the matter, the so-called joint councillors, bestirred themselves at first to oppose the change but were jointly won over because they took the view that once this law had been changed, the rest of the regime would be left alone. Later on, however, when other things were being changed and they wanted to prevent it, they could no longer do anything, but the whole arrangement of the regime underwent change into a dynasty of those who had put their hand to introducing the innovations.[61]

1307b19 But while all regimes can sometimes be destroyed from within, they can also sometimes be destroyed from without, when an opposite regime is nearby or, though far off, powerful, as happened under the Athenians and the Spartans. For the Athenians destroyed oligarchies everywhere, and the Spartans destroyed rule of the populace.[62]

1307b24 What are the origins, then, of changes and factions in regimes have been pretty well discussed.

---

58. In the 350s Locris was under the tyranny of Dionysius II, son of Dionysius I by a Locrian woman.

59. 7(5).3.1303a20–25.

60. The Greek is *kosmos*.

61. Of these events, and how they do or do not tie in with the other events reported about Thurii, nothing further is known.

62. The Athenians did this during their naval empires in the fifth and fourth centuries, and the Spartans did it during their empire after the Peloponnesian War.

CHAPTER 8

Preservation of Regimes in Particular. *The things that preserve regimes are the opposite of those that destroy them. Thus, to preserve regimes, (i) guard against small changes that introduce the habit of transgressing the law; (ii) do not trust to political sophistries against the multitude; (iii) treat well both those in and those outside the regime; (iv) induce fears, so that people's vigilance over the regime does not slacken; (v) guard, through the laws, against the factions and rivalries of the notables; (vi) have a law requiring property qualifications to change with changing prosperity; (vii) make no one overly great but give small and long-lasting honors, or take away great honors only gradually, or have the great spend time abroad; (viii) have an office to watch over those whose lives are contrary to the regime; (ix) guard against any part of the city becoming too successful by dividing actions and offices between opposed parts and mixing these parts or strengthening the middle; (x) arrange things so that it is impossible to make a profit from office; (xi) spare the wealthy and take special care of the needy; (xii) give those with lesser shares in the regime equality or precedence in everything save the controlling offices.*

1307b26 The next thing to speak of, both in common and separately for each regime, is how to preserve them. Now, it is clear to begin with that if we have what destroys regimes, we also have what preserves them. For opposites are productive of opposites, and destruction is opposite to preservation. **1307b30** In well-mixed regimes, then, if one needs to be alert against people breaking the law in any other respect, one must above all guard against small changes. For a state of law-breaking can insinuate itself unawares; it is like small expenditures which, when often repeated, consume one's property, for as they do not happen all at once, the total expense goes unnoticed. Thought commits a fallacy as a result, as in the sophistical argument that if each is small then all are, which is true in one way but not in another. For the whole and all things are not small, but they are made up of small things. One kind of guard, then, must be kept against this beginning of change. **1307b40** Next is not to trust to things constructed for the purpose of sophistry against the multitude, since these have been refuted by the facts. What sort of things we mean by sophisms in regimes was stated earlier.[63] **1308a3** Further, it is necessary to note that not only do some aristocracies endure, but some oligarchies too, not because the regimes are stable, but because those who are in office treat well both those outside the regime and those in the ruling body. They do this as regards those who have no share in the regime by not wronging them, by bringing those with the quality of leaders into the regime, and by not wronging the ambitious with respect to

---

dishonor or the many with respect to profit. They do it as regards themselves or those who do have a share by treating each other in a popular spirit. For what the popular party seeks for the multitude, equality, is not only just for those who are similar but advantageous as well. Hence, if there are several in the ruling body, many pieces of popular legislation are advantageous— as, for instance, having the offices last six months so that all who are similar may take part (for the similar are already, as it were, a populace, and that is why demagogues often arise among them, as was said earlier).[64] Oligarchies and aristocracies, then, fall less frequently into dynasties because criminal activity is not as easy for those who rule a short time as it is for those who rule a long time. For this is why tyrannies arise in oligarchies and democracies since either the greatest persons in each regime, the demagogues here and the dynasts there, make attempts at tyranny, or those in the greatest offices do, if they are in office a long time.

1308a24 Regimes are preserved not only because of being far away from what destroys them but sometimes also because of being close by, for fear makes people hold onto the regime more. Consequently, in order to keep people on their guard and, like a night watch, not relax their vigilance over the regime, those whose care is for the regime must procure fears and also bring the faraway near to hand.

1308a31 Further, one must also try by means of the laws to guard against the rivalries and factions of the notables and to prevent those outside the rivalry from also getting caught up in it, for it is not the part of anyone to recognize an evil in its beginnings but only of a man who is a politician.

1308a35 As regards change away from oligarchy and polity because of property qualifications, when this happens because the qualifications remain the same but money becomes abundant, it is advantageous to examine the amount of the common[65] assessment with respect to what it was previously (either every year, in the case of all cities that make an assessment every year, or, in the case of larger ones, every three or five years), and if it is many times more or less than before, when the valuations for the regime were established, to have a law that the property qualifications should also be tightened up or relaxed: tightening them up if it is in excess, according to how many times more the excess is, and relaxing them and making the valuation less if it falls short. For in oligarchies and polities where this is not done, what happens is that, in the second case,[66] an oligarchy emerges from the polity and

---

64. 7(5).6.1305b22–27.

65. Reading *koinou* ("common") with the manuscripts, not *kainou* ("new") with Dreizehnter. Aristotle's point is that, in order to ensure that neither too few nor too many come to share in the offices, periodic adjustments to the qualifications must be made relative to the overall wealth of the city.

66. That is, when values decline but qualifications for office do not.

a dynasty from the oligarchy, and that, in the first,[67] a democracy emerges from the polity and a polity or rule of the populace from the oligarchy.

1308b10 It is something common to rule of the populace and to oligarchy,[68] and to any regime, to make no one too great beyond proportion but to try to give honors that are small and last a long time rather than great ones quickly; for people can become corrupted, and it is not any man who can handle good fortune. Or, failing this, one should at least not give honors all at once and take them back again all at once, but gradually, and above all try so to proportion things by the laws that no one arises who is far superior in power either of friends or money, or, if this does not succeed, to have these persons removed abroad.[69]

1308b20 But since people make innovations because of their private lives too, it is necessary to introduce an office that will watch over those who are living in a way disadvantageous to the regime, whether to the democracy in a democracy or to the oligarchy in an oligarchy or likewise in the case of each of the other regimes.

1308b24 For the same reasons it is necessary also to guard against the city becoming prosperous part by part. A cure for this is always to have actions and offices carried out by opposed parts (I mean the opposed parts of the decent and the multitude and also of the needy and the well-off), and to try either to mix together the multitude of the needy and of the well-off or to increase the middle, for this dissolves factions that are caused by inequality.

1308b31 A very great thing in any regime is to have things so arranged both by the laws and by the rest of household management that it is not possible to make a profit from office. One must especially watch against this in oligarchies, for the many are not as annoyed at being barred from ruling (on the contrary they are even glad if someone allows them leisure for their own affairs) as they are if they think the rulers are stealing common funds. Then it pains them both not to share in the honors and not to share in the profits. It would in fact be possible for there to be a democracy and an aristocracy at the same time only if this arrangement were instituted by someone, as it would be possible for both the notables and the multitude to get what they each want. For it is democratic to have rule open to everyone but aristocratic to have the notables occupying the offices, and this will be the result when a profit cannot be made from office. For the needy will not want to rule, because it brings no profit, but will prefer to be engaged in their own affairs; and the well-off will be able to rule because not in need of anything from the common funds. So the result will be that the needy become

67. That is, when values rise but qualifications for office do not.
68. Some manuscripts add "and to monarchy" here.
69. Presumably either by ostracism or by sending them on embassies and the like.

well-off through spending time on their work, and that the notables are not ruled over by any chance person. But, to ensure there is no theft of common funds, let the handing over of monies be done in the presence of all the citizens and let records be filed with clans, companies, and tribes; and, to ensure that rule brings no profit, legislation has to have been passed giving honors to those of good repute.

1309a14 In democracies it is necessary to be sparing of the well-off by refraining from redistributions not only of their properties but also of their incomes (a thing that can pass unnoticed in some regimes). It is also better to prevent the well-off, even when willing, from taking on expensive but useless public services, as leading choruses, officiating at torch races, and anything else of the sort. But in oligarchy it is necessary to take much care of the needy, to distribute to them those offices that generate an income, and if any of the well-off treats them insolently to impose on him a greater penalty than if he thus treated one of his own. Inheritances should not be passed on by bequest but by family, and the same person should not receive more than one inheritance. For in this way properties would be more on a level, and more of the needy would establish themselves among the well-off.

1309a27 It is an advantage in both democracy and oligarchy to distribute to those who have a lesser share in the regime (to the well-off in rule of the populace and to the needy in oligarchy) an equality or a precedence in all things save the offices that have control over the regime. These offices should be undertaken, either solely or for the most part, by those who belong to the regime.

CHAPTER 9

Preservation of Regimes in General. *As regards preserving regimes in general: (i) rulers should be friendly to the regime, able, and possessed of the virtue relative to the regime; (ii) whatever in laws benefits regimes preserves them, as does also ensuring that the regime is favored by the stronger part; (iii) do not neglect the middle, especially in deviant regimes, nor push things to either extreme but instead take special care of the excluded or opposing part; (iv) above all, educate citizens to the regime, not by indulging them but by enabling them to continue ruling.*

1309a33 As for those who are going to rule in the controlling offices, they should possess three things: first, friendliness toward the established regime; second, very great ability for carrying out the work of the office; and third, the virtue and justice in each regime that is relative to that regime (for if what is just is not the same thing in each regime, then there must be differences in the virtue of justice as well). But a difficulty arises. If these three things are not all present in the same person—as, for instance, if someone is a skilled general but he is evil and not friendly to the regime, and someone else is just and friendly—how is the choice to be made? It seems one must keep an eye on two things: which quality everyone has more a share of and which they have less a share of. Hence, in the case of generalship, one must look to experience rather than virtue, for everyone shares in generalship less and in decency more. But in the case of guarding property and of the treasury it is the opposite, for here there is need of more virtue than the many have, whereas the knowledge is common to everyone. One might also raise the difficulty, supposing that ability and friendliness to the regime already exist, whether there is any need of virtue, for beneficial results will come just from the first two. Or could it not happen that those who have these two qualities are weak-willed,[70] and just as people can fail to serve their own interests even though they have the knowledge and the self-love, so nothing prevents them being the same way in respect of common affairs as well?

1309b14 Simply speaking, everything in laws[71] that we say is of advantage to regimes preserves them, and also that very great principle, often mentioned, of keeping watch that the multitude that wants the regime is stronger than the multitude that does not.[72]

1309b18 In addition to all these, the mean must not be neglected, as it is now by the deviant regimes. For democracies are destroyed by many things that seem popular and oligarchies by many things that seem oligarchic. For those who think that this is the only virtue push things to excess. They do not recognize that the same thing happens in the case of regimes as in the case of noses, and that though a nose that has deviated from the straightness that is most beautiful toward being hooked or snub can yet still be beautiful and favorable to look at, nevertheless if it gets pushed further toward the extreme, it will lose the measure proper to it as the part it is, and in the end, because of the excess and deficiency of the opposites, be such as no longer to be a nose (and the same is true of the other parts too). For both oligarchy and democracy can be in an adequate condition even though they have departed from the best arrangement, but if one extends either of them any further, one will first produce a worse regime and in the end no regime at all. Hence, the legislator and politician must not overlook which of the popular features preserve democracy and which of them destroy it and which of the oligarchic ones preserve and destroy oligarchy. For neither regime can exist and last without the well-off and the multitude, but when

---

70. The Greek is *akrateis*, from *akrasia*, which is the condition of knowing what to do but failing to do it; see *Ethics* 7.1–10 and cf. especially 7.10.1152a19–24.
71. The reference seems to be to laws determining the distribution of rule, in 6(4).14–16.
72. 6(4).9.1294b34–40 and 12.1296b14–16.

a leveling of substance occurs, the regime in question must necessarily be different. The result is that by destroying things with laws carried to excess, they destroy their regimes.

1310a2 Errors are committed in the case of both democracies and oligarchies. In democracies the demagogues go wrong where the multitude has control over the laws, for they split the city into two by always fighting against the well-off. But they should, on the contrary, always seem to be speaking on behalf of the well-off. In oligarchies the oligarchs should always seem to be speaking on behalf of the populace and should swear oaths the opposite of those they swear now. For in some cities now they swear "and I will be evil-minded to the populace and I will advise whatever evil I can." But they should adopt and act on the opposite supposition and declare in their oaths "I will not wrong the populace."

1310a12 But of all the things mentioned for maintaining regimes, the greatest is what is now slighted by everyone, namely getting an education relative to the regime. For the most beneficial of laws are of no help, even when approved by everyone engaged in politics,[73] if people are not going to have been accustomed and educated in the regime—in a popular manner if the laws are popular and in an oligarchic one if they are oligarchic. For since there can be weakness of will in the case of a single individual, so can there also be in the case of a city.

1310a19 But to have been educated relative to the regime is not a matter of doing whatever gratifies those who are oligarchs or whatever gratifies those who want a democracy, but of doing what will enable the first to rule oligarchically and the second to rule democratically. But as it is, in oligarchies the sons of the rulers live in luxury while those of the needy get exercised in toil and so are more willing and able to introduce innovations. In those democracies that seem to be the most democratic what has become established is the opposite of beneficial. The reason for this is that they define badly what it is to be free. For there are two things by which democracy seems in particular to be defined: by the majority being in control and by freedom. For justice seems to be equality, and equality is that whatever seems right to the multitude is in control, and freedom and equality are doing whatever one wants. Consequently, in such democracies each lives as he wishes and, as Euripides says, "with a view to what he craves."[74] But this is base. For one ought not to think it slavery but safety to live relative to the regime.

1310a36 So many, then, in number, to speak generally, are the origins of

---

73. By the citizens, in other words, or those who share in rule.
74. Frag. 891 Nauck.

change and destruction in regimes and the means whereby they are preserved and endure.

CHAPTER 10

Destruction of Monarchies

How Kingships and Tyrannies Are Like Regimes. *Kingship accords with aristocracy and tyranny with ultimate democracy and oligarchy. They each have a different
genesis, as the facts manifest: kingship coming from the decent to unite the populace
with them, tyranny coming from the populace to oppose the notables; and they each
have different features: kingship being based on virtue and looking to the common good
and nobility, tyranny looking to wealth and making war on populace and notables alike.*

1310a39 It remains to go through a discussion of monarchy too, both the
origins of its destruction and the means whereby it is naturally preserved.
What happens in the case of kingships and tyrannies is pretty similar to what
has been said about regimes. For kingship accords with aristocracy while
tyranny is constituted from ultimate oligarchy and ultimate democracy
(which is why indeed it is the most hurtful to the ruled, being composed of
two evils and possessing the deviations and errors present in both regimes).
1310b8 Each monarchy gets its genesis directly from opposites. For kingship came into being to provide help from the populace for the decent,[75]
and a king is established from the decent on the basis of excess of virtue or
of deeds proceeding from virtue or on the basis of a family of the sort. But
the tyrant is established from the populace and the multitude against the
notables, to prevent the populace suffering wrong from them.
1310b14 This is manifest from events. For pretty well most tyrants have
arisen out of demagogues, so to speak, winning trust because of their slander of the notables. Some tyrannies were established in this way when cities
had already increased in size; others arose earlier out of kings who were
deviating from ancestral traditions and were desiring a more despotic rule;
others from those elected to the controlling offices (for in ancient times,
magistrates and ambassadorships of long duration were set up by the popu-

---

75. I translate the manuscripts literally here, though most commentators and translators
wish to adapt them to read "to provide help for the decent *against* the populace." But this
reading makes of the king a tyrant in reverse and conflicts with what is said later in this chapter (at 1310b40–1311a4): that the king acts as a guardian for both the decent and the populace,
while the tyrant has no common good in view. I take Aristotle's meaning to be that the difference between kingship and tyranny is that the first aims at reconciliation and unity and
the second at division and mutual hatred.

lace); and others from oligarchies that used to choose some one individual with control in the greatest offices. For, provided only they had the desire, they could easily accomplish tyranny in all these ways because of the power they already possessed, either through kingly office or positions of honor. So Pheidon in Argos, for instance, and other tyrants got established from an existing kingship; Phalaris and those in Ionia from their positions of honor; and Panaetius in Leontini, Cypselus in Corinth, Peisistratus in Athens, Dionysius in Syracuse, and others similarly from being demagogues.[76]

1310b31 As we said then, kingship is arranged on the basis of aristocracy, for it accords with merit, whether the king's own virtue or his family's, whether his deeds of beneficence or these together with ability. For all kings attained this honor because they performed, or were capable of performing, deeds of beneficence for their cities or nations. Some, like Codrus, prevented them being enslaved in war; others, like Cyrus, liberated them, or, like the kings of the Spartans, Macedonians, and Molossians, were founders or acquired territory.[77]

1310b40 The king wishes to be a guardian, to prevent those who possess substance from suffering any wrong and the populace from suffering any insolence. Tyranny, as has often been said,[78] looks to nothing common, except for the sake of its own advantage. The goal of tyranny is pleasure and of kingship nobility, and that is why, of the things people take more of, those to do with money are characteristic of tyrants and those to do with honor characteristic rather of kings. Also, a king's guard is taken from citizens but a tyrant's from foreigners. That tyranny possesses the evils both of democracy and of oligarchy is manifest. From oligarchy comes its having its end in wealth (since, of necessity, defense and luxury can only be secured in this way), and also its not putting any trust in the multitude (which is why tyrants also confiscate arms). Common to both oligarchy and tyranny is ill treatment of the crowd, expelling them from the city, and dispersing them about the countryside. From democracy comes tyranny's war on the notables, its destruction of them both in secret and openly, and its exiling them as rivals in skill and as impediments to rule. For it is these who generate conspiracies, some of them wishing to exercise rule themselves and others not wishing to serve as slaves. Hence Periander's piece of advice to

76. Pheidon was tyrant of Argos in the mid-seventh century; Thrasybulus, one of the best known of the Ionian tyrants, rose from general, as did Phalaris of Agrigentum; for Peisistratus and Dionysius I among the demagogues, see 7(5).5.1305a21–28.

77. Codrus was a legendary king at Athens who saved it from a Dorian invasion; Cyrus liberated the Persians from the Medes in the sixth century; the first and sometimes also succeeding kings in the other cases led campaigns of acquisition.

78. 3.6, 3.7, and 6(4).10.

Thrasybulus, to lop off the preeminent ears of grain, his idea being that it is always necessary to do away with the preeminent citizens.[79]

That They Are Destroyed in Similar Ways

In General. Monarchies, like regimes, are attacked because of injustice, mainly the injustice of insolence but also of theft, and because of fear and because of contempt. The goods aimed at are again wealth and honor. Attacks against the monarch's body are because of insolence, against his rule because of other reasons. Examples illustrate these points.

1311a22 One must suppose, then, according to what has been more or less said, that the beginnings of changes are the same in both regimes and monarchies. For it is on account of injustice and fear and contempt that many of the ruled make attempts on monarchies, and, in the case of injustice, on account of insolence above all, but sometimes on account of the seizure of private possessions as well. Their goals in the case of tyrannies and kingships are also the same as they were there, for wealth and honor, which everyone desires, exist in abundance in monarchies.

1311a31 Of attacks, some are against the rulers' body and some against their rule. Those made because of insolence are against the body, and though insolence is manifold, each form of it is a cause of anger and pretty well most of those who are angry attack to get revenge, not to get superiority. For example, the attack on the Peisistratids happened because of the indignity suffered by Harmodius' sister and the insult to Harmodius (for Harmodius attacked because of his sister, and Aristogeiton because of Harmodius).[80] The plot against Periander, tyrant of Ambracia, happened because, when drinking with his boy lover, he asked if he was yet pregnant by him. The attack by Pausanias on Philip happened because Philip let him be insulted by Attalus and his friends, the attack by Derdas on Amyntas the Small happened because Amyntas vaunted over the boy's youth, the attack by the eunuch on Evagoras of Cyprus happened because Evagoras' son seduced the eunuch's wife (the eunuch killed him on the grounds he had been treated insolently).[81]

1311b6 Many attacks have happened also because of the shameful treat-

---

79. Cf. 3.13.1284a28–33.

80. In the year 514. Aristotle says the Peisistratids were attacked, not overthrown, by Harmodius and Aristogeiton. In fact, only Hipparchus among Peisistratus' sons was killed, and the older brother, Hippias, continued ruling until expelled four years later with the help of the Spartans.

81. Periander was mentioned earlier, in 7(5).4.1304a31–33; Philip, Alexander's father, was slain in 336; nothing further is known of Amyntas the Small; Evagoras was slain in 374.

ment of others' bodies by certain monarchs—as, for example, the attack by Crataeus against Archelaus.[82] For Crataeus always took their sexual relationship ill, so that it would have been enough for him to have even a lesser excuse than the fact that Archelaus did not give him either of his daughters despite agreeing to (instead he gave the elder to the king of Elimaea, being pressed in the war against Sirras and Arrabaeus, and the younger to his son Amyntas, supposing that in this way he would reduce to a minimum the quarreling between Amyntas and his son by Cleopatra). Nevertheless, the beginning of the alienation was that Crataeus took ill the sexual favors[83] he was doing him. Hellanocrates of Larissa also joined him in the attack for the same reason. For when Archelaus took advantage of Hellanocrates' youth and yet did not restore him to his home despite promising to, Hellanocrates supposed that their relationship was a result of insolence[84] and not erotic desire. Python and Heracleides from Aenus slew Cotys in revenge for their father, and Adamas revolted from Cotys on the grounds of insolence because he had been castrated by him as a child.[85]

1311b23 Many have been angered because they suffered outrage from blows to their bodies and, on the grounds of being insolently treated, have slain or attempted to slay those associated with offices and royal dynasties. For example, when in Mytilene the Penthilids went about beating people with clubs, Megacles along with his friends attacked and destroyed them, and later Smerdes, who had been beaten with blows and dragged away from his wife, slew Penthilus.[86] Decamnichus was leader of the assault on Archelaus and the first to stir up the attackers, and the reason for his anger was that Archelaus had given him over to the poet Euripides to be whipped (Euripides was angered by something he said about the foul smell from his mouth). Many others have also been done away with or plotted against for such reasons.

1311b36 The like has happened also because of fear (which was one of the causes in the case of monarchies, just as in the case of regimes). For instance, Artapanes slew Xerxes from fear of being accused in the matter of Darius (he had hanged Darius without order from Xerxes and had supposed he would be forgiven when Xerxes was carousing and would not remember).[87]

1311b40 Other attacks are because of contempt, as that against Sardana-

---

82. Archelaus was king of Macedonia from 413 to 399.

83. Literally, "favors to do with Aphrodite" (*aphrodisiastikēn charin*).

84. The Greek for "insolence" here (*hubris*) can also carry the connotation of rape.

85. Cotys was king of Thrace and was murdered in 359. Nothing is known of what happened to Python's and Heracleides' father.

86. Mytilene was under an oligarchy in the seventh century, and the Penthilids seem to have been a leading family within it.

87. Xerxes was king of Persia in 485–465. Darius was Xerxes' son, Artapanes the chief bodyguard.

palus when, if the storytellers speak true, someone saw him carding wool with the women (though if this is not true of him, it might well be true of another). And Dion attacked the younger Dionysius out of contempt when he saw that the citizens were likewise contemptuous and that Dionysius himself was always drunk.[88] Even some friends launch attacks out of contempt, for the fact that they are trusted makes them contemptuous and confident of not being found out. Also those who think they are capable of securing rule attack in a way out of contempt, since it is because of their ability and the contempt of danger their ability gives them that they are ready to undertake something, as in the case of generals against monarchs. Cyrus, for instance, attacked Astyages, despising both Astyages' way of life and his power because his power lay unused and his life was one of luxury. Seuthes the Thracian also, while general, attacked Amadocus.[89] Some even launch attacks for several of these reasons—for example, both out of contempt and for profit, as Mithridates did against Ariobarzanes.[90] Attempts for this reason are principally made by those who are bold in their nature and possess military honor at the hands of their monarch. For courage possessed of power is boldness, and both of them together induce people to attack on the ground that conquest will be easy.

1312a21 When attacks are launched from love of honor, the cause operates in a manner different from what has been mentioned above. For in the case of those who attack out of love of honor it is not true that they each choose to run the risk for the same reason that some others do when making attempts against tyrants, namely that they see themselves winning great profits and great honors. But while these others act for this reason, the former make attempts against monarchs for the same reason that they would undertake any other action that was extraordinary and brought name and renown before others—because they wish to win, not a monarchy, but glory. Nevertheless, those driven by this sort of reason are very few in number, for one has to presume in them a lack of concern for personal safety should the deed miscarry. They must take with them the view of Dion (a view not easily generated in many people): Dion marched against Dionysius with a few men, saying he was so minded that he would be satisfied with his share in the action however far he was able to get with it, as that, for instance, if he died as soon as he had advanced a few steps on land, he would hold such a death to be a noble one.

88. Sardanapalus was king of Assyria in 668–626. Dionysius was expelled from Syracuse by Dion in 357.

89. Astyages, king of Media, was overthrown by Cyrus in 559; Seuthes was a local ruler in Thrace in the early fourth century and Amadocus was a neighboring king.

90. Probably the Ariobarzanes who was satrap of Pontus in the mid-fourth century.

In Particular. Tyranny is (i) destroyed from without by an opposite and stronger regime or from within when the ruler's family falls to faction; (ii) most attacks on tyrannies are inspired by hatred or contempt; (iii) whatever destroys extreme oligarchy and democracy also destroys tyranny. Kingship is mainly destroyed (i) from within when those associated with the kingship fall to faction or when the king becomes more tyrannical; (ii) in the case of kingships based on family, when the king becomes easy to despise and acts insolently.

1312a39 One way in which tyranny, like each of the other regimes, is destroyed is from without, if some opposing regime is stronger. The desire to destroy will certainly be present because of opposing intentions, and everyone does what they want when they can. Regimes opposed to tyranny are rule of the populace, because of Hesiod's "potter against potter," [91] since the last kind of democracy is a tyranny; and kingship and aristocracy, because of opposition of regime. That is why Spartans destroyed many tyrannies, as did Syracusans during the time they were nobly ruled.

1312b9 Another way in which tyranny is destroyed is from within, when those who share in it start factions, as with the tyranny of Gelon and his associates and as, in our day, with that of Dionysius and his. The tyranny of Gelon was destroyed when Thrasybulus, brother of Hiero, played the demagogue to Gelon's son and urged him on to pleasures so that he himself could rule. The family relatives got a band together to destroy Thrasybulus, though not the tyranny, but those in the band seized their opportunity and threw out the lot of them. Dion, who was related by marriage to Dionysius, marched against him and won over the populace, and then, after throwing him out, was himself killed. [92]

1312b17 Attacks on tyranny are made principally for two reasons, hatred and contempt, and though one of them, hatred, is always present, many tyrants are overthrown because they are despised. A sign is that most of those who won tyrannies also maintained their rule to the end, but their successors all pretty much perished at once. For since they live in an indulgent manner, they become easy to despise and offer assailants many opportunities. Anger must also be set down as part of hatred, since in a way it causes the same deeds. It is often in fact more a cause of action than hatred is. For the angry attack in a more impetuous way because their passion does not pause to calculate (they follow their spiritedness principally on account of insolent treatment, and insolence is why the tyrannies of the Peisistratids and of many others were destroyed). But hatred makes more use of calcu-

91. *Works and Days* 22, a proverbial expression of the strife of like with like.
92. The tyranny founded by Gelon in Syracuse (Hiero, his immediate successor, was his brother) was overthrown in 466. Dion expelled Dionysius II in 357 and was himself assassinated four years later.

lation. For anger is accompanied by pain, so that calculating is not easy, but hatred is without pain.

1312b34 To speak summarily, however, all the causes we stated in the case of the unmixed and last oligarchy and in the case of ultimate democracy must be set down as causes in the case of tyranny too. For these regimes are, in fact, tyrannies divided among many.

1312b38 Kingship is destroyed least by what comes from without, which is also why it is longer lasting. Destruction mostly comes from within itself. There are two ways in which it is destroyed, one when those who share in the kingship start factions and another when the kings try to manage things more tyrannically and claim they deserve to control more matters and contrary to the law. Kingships no longer arise nowadays, but if there are any monarchies that do arise, they are more like tyrannies. The reason is that kingship is voluntary rule and with control over rather great matters, but now those who are similar are many and no one is so superior as to measure up to the greatness and dignity of the office. Consequently, for this reason people do not put up with it willingly, and if someone is using deceit and force to rule, this already seems to be tyranny.

1313a10 In kingships based on family one should also set down, in addition to causes of destruction already mentioned, the fact that many kings become easy to despise and that though what they have is royal honor and not tyrannical power, they engage in insolent behavior. For then overthrow is easy since, as soon as the subjects are no longer willing, he will no longer be king; to rule also over the unwilling is to be tyrant.

1313a16 Monarchies then are destroyed for these and other like reasons.

CHAPTER 11

Preservation of Monarchies

Kingships. *Kingships are preserved above all by being made more measured.*

1313a18 Monarchies, it is clear, are preserved, to speak simply, by what comes from the contrary sources but, in the case of kingships in particular, by being drawn toward something more measured. For the fewer the things over which kings have control, the longer must their entire rule last; they become less despotic themselves, more equal in their character, and less envied by those they rule over. That is also why the kingship of the Molossians lasted a long time and why that of the Spartans has lasted, both because the office was divided from the beginning into two parts and again because Theopompus, besides making it more measured in other ways, set up in addition the office of the ephors. By diminishing the power of the kingship, he increased it in duration so that, in a way, he made it not less but greater. That is also what they say he replied to his wife when she asked him if he was not ashamed to be handing over a lesser kingship to his sons than he had received from his father. "Not at all," he said, "because what I am handing over is more lasting."[93]

Tyrannies. Tyrannies are preserved in two opposite ways: (i) the traditional way of making them more tyrannical by the use of a multitude of devices, which leave nothing out in point of wickedness, for securing among the subjects (a) thinking small, (b) mutual distrust, (c) weakness; (ii) the opposite way of making tyrannies more kingly, so that the tyrant (a) appears a steward and trustee of the city's wealth; (b) appears dignified and venerable through military virtue, measured behavior, stewardship, and piety; (c) distributes honors justly and carefully and refrains from, or covers up, acts of insolence; (d) appears a friend to both notables and populace alike. This second way will make the tyranny better and longer lasting and the tyrant himself a better man.

1313a34 Tyrannies are preserved in two ways that are most opposed to each other. One of them is the traditional one, the one in accordance with which most tyrants manage their rule. Periander the Corinthian is alleged to have established most of these devices, but it is possible also to gather many things of like sort from the rule of the Persians. Besides the things mentioned some time ago for the preservation—to the extent that that is possible—of tyranny, namely cutting down the superior and doing away with those of high thoughts,[94] there are also: not allowing common messes nor clubs nor education nor anything else of the sort but guarding against everything from which are wont to arise two things, high thoughts and trust; not permitting schools[95] nor other leisurely gatherings to take place and doing everything that will make everyone as much as possible ignorant of each another, for knowledge makes for more mutual trust among people; in addition, keeping the residents always in view and having them wait at the tyrant's doors, for what they are doing will in this way least escape notice and by always serving as slaves they will get used to thinking small. Other things of like sort found among Persians and barbarians are tyrannical, for they all have the same effect.

1313b11 There is also trying to let nothing that any of the subjects happens

93. Not much is known of the kingdom of the Molossians; as for the founding of the ephorate at Sparta by King Theopompus (eighth or seventh century), see 2.9.1270b17–26.

94. 3.13.1284a26–b3 and 7(5).10.1311a8–22.

95. The Greek is *scholas* (the origin of our word "school"), or literally "places of leisure," the reference being presumably to the sort of schools founded by Plato, Isocrates, and Aristotle himself at Athens.

to say or do go unnoticed, but to have spies like the so-called women in-ducers among the Syracusans and the eavesdroppers Hiero[96] sent out wher-ever there was some meeting or gathering, for people speak less freely when they fear such spies and if they do speak freely, they escape notice less. There is also slandering people to each other and setting friends against friends, the populace against the notables, the wealthy against themselves. Tyranni-cal also is making the ruled poor, so that they can provide themselves no defense and, being taken up with daily needs, have no leisure for plotting. As examples of this are the pyramids in Egypt, the votive monuments of the Cypselids, the building of the temple of Olympian Zeus by the Peisistratids, and the works of Polycrates on the temples at Samos. For all these things have the same effect: lack of leisure and poverty for the subjects. There is also paying of taxes, as in Syracuse where in the time of Dionysius their total substance was paid over in five years. A tyrant is also a maker of war, so that the ruled may have no leisure and be continually in need of a leader. Fur-ther, while kingship is preserved by friends, it is a mark of tyranny to distrust friends most of all because, though everyone wants to attempt something, these are most able to do it.

1313b32 Everything that happens in ultimate democracy is also typical of tyranny: dominance of women about the house so that they can inform on their husbands, and, for the same reason, the license of slaves. For slaves and women do not plot against tyrants and, because they are having a good time, are of necessity kindly disposed to tyrannies and democracies. For the populace too wants to be a monarch. That is also why both hold the flatterer in honor—the populace the demagogue (for the demagogue is the flatterer of the populace) and the tyrant fawning hangers-on (for fawning is the work of flattery). For this reason too tyranny is dear to the wicked, for tyrants are glad to be flattered, but no one possessed of freedom of thought would do this. On the contrary, the decent can be friends, but they are no flatterers. The wicked are also useful for wicked things; "nail for nail," as the proverb says. It is also a mark of tyranny not to take delight in anyone who is dignified or free, for the tyrant supposes he alone deserves to be like that. But one who is a rival in dignity and asserts his freedom deprives tyranny of its superiority and of its character of despotism, and so tyrants hate such people as being destroyers of their rule. It is, further, a mark of tyranny to use foreigners rather than people of the city for companions at dinner and for spending time with, because the latter are his enemies while the former are not going to assert rival claims.

1314a12 These and the like things are marks of tyranny and preserve its rule, and in respect of depravity they leave nothing out. All of them, more or

---

96. Tyrant in Syracuse from 478 to 467 after his brother Gelon.

less, can be embraced under three heads. For tyranny aims at three things: first, the ruled thinking small, for someone small-souled would plot against no one; second, the ruled not trusting each other, for a tyranny cannot be overthrown until some start trusting each other (which is why tyrants in fact wage war on the decent sort as being harmful to their rule, not only on the ground that the decent do not think they deserve to be ruled despotically, but also on they ground that they are faithful both to themselves and to others and accuse neither themselves nor others); third, powerlessness to do anything, for no one will put his hand to what is impossible and so not to overthrowing a tyranny either if he has no power. The heads, then, to which all the wishes of tyrants can be reduced turn out to be these three, for one may reduce all marks of tyranny to these suppositions: some of them are for making subjects not trust each other; others for making them powerless; others for making them think small.

1314a29 One way, then, by which to preserve tyrannies is like this. A second devotes its care to virtually the opposite of what has just been said. One can get an understanding of it from the way kingship is destroyed. For as one way of destroying kingship is to make rule more tyrannical, so a way of saving tyranny is to make it more kingly, keeping watch over one thing only, the tyrant's power, so he can rule his subjects not only when they are willing but also when they are unwilling. For if he lets go of this, he lets go also of his tyranny. Instead this must remain as a presupposition, and he must either do or seem to do everything else acting out in noble manner the part of king.

1314a40 First, then, he must seem to be taking care of the common funds not only by not spending money on such gifts as enrage the multitude (when he takes from their grinding work and toil and gives lavishly to mistresses, foreigners, and artisans), but also by rendering account of the revenues he received and the expenses he paid (as some tyrants have in fact done in the past). For in this way he would seem a householder in his management of things and not a tyrant. He has no need to fear, having control of the city as he does, that he will ever run out of money; but for those tyrants, at any rate, who go abroad from their own territory, this practice is of more advantage than collecting a great hoard and leaving it behind. For then those guarding it would make fewer attempts against the tyrant's position, and a tyrant is more afraid when traveling abroad of those left to do the guarding than of citizens, since the citizens go with him but the former stay behind. Next, he should conspicuously impose taxes and public service for the purpose of household management and for occasions of war, if there should ever be need. And generally he should present himself as a guardian and steward of common and not of private funds.

1314b18 Also, he must appear not harsh but dignified, and such, further, as to inspire not fear but reverence in those who come upon him. It is, however, not easy for one who is readily despised to achieve this, so even if he gives no care to other virtues, he should to warlike[97] virtue and create about himself a reputation for being such. Further, he should not only be conspicuous himself in not treating any of his subjects insolently, whether youth or maiden, but so should everyone else among his entourage. The womenfolk too should behave similarly toward other women because many tyrannies have also been destroyed by the insolent behavior of women. As regards bodily indulgences, he should do the opposite of what some tyrants do now. For not only do they engage in this indulgence as soon as it is dawn and continue for many days, but also, in order to be admired as happy and blessed, they wish their doing so to be conspicuous in the sight of others. Yet in such things they ought to be most measured, or if not, they should at least avoid being seen by others. For it is not someone sober who is easily attacked and despised but the drunkard, not he who is alert but he who dozes. And the opposite of pretty much everything said before must be done. For he must furnish and adorn the city as if he were a steward and not a tyrant. Further, with respect to what concerns the gods, he must be conspicuous in being always exceptionally serious. For if people think the ruler stands in awe of the divine and takes thought for the gods, they have less fear that they will suffer something illegal at such hands as his. They also plot less against him believing he has the gods as well on his side. But the way he displays himself as such must be without any silliness.

1315a4 As regards those who are good in any respect, he must give them such honor that they do not think they would receive more honor at the hands of citizens living under their own laws. Also, he should distribute such honors himself, but punishments he should have dispensed by others, whether officials or law courts. But it is a defense common to any monarchy not to make anyone great, or if need be to make several so (for they will watch each other). If, however, there is need to make some one person great, let him at any rate not be bold in character. For a character of this sort is most impetuous whatever the action. And if it should seem good to remove someone from power, it must be done gradually, and all his ability must not be taken away at once.

1315a14 Further, he should refrain from every sort of insolence, and from two above all: punishment directed against a person's body and against his youth. Especially must this care be taken in the case of those who love honor. For while those who love money take it ill when they are slighted in regard to their money, those who love honor and are the decent among

---

97. The manuscripts have "political" (*politikē*) not "warlike" (*polemikē*), but the emendation seems supported by later remarks (7(5).12.1315b16–17, 28–29) and to make more sense in the context.

human beings take it ill when they are slighted in regard to their honor. Hence, either he should not engage in such acts or he should inflict punishments in a manifestly fatherly spirit, not out of slight, and should engage in sexual relations with youth for reasons of love, not because he has the power to. And as a general rule he should compensate apparent losses of honor with grants of greater honors. Of those who attempt assassination, most to be feared and most in need of watching are those who are not planning to save their life after they have destroyed his. Hence, it is necessary to take especial care with respect to those who think that either they or their loved ones have been treated insolently.[98] For they who are driven to their attempts by spiritedness are not sparing of themselves. As even Heracleitus said: "to fight with spiritedness is hard, for it buys with its soul."[99]

1315a31 Since there are two parts that make up cities, needy human beings and prosperous ones, what would be best is if both of them supposed that it was because of the tyrant's rule that they were being preserved and that neither of them was being wronged by the other. But whichever side is the stronger, these above all the tyrant should make privy to his rule since, with these supporting his interests, there will be no necessity for him to engage in freeing slaves or confiscating arms. For the addition of one or the other part to his power will be enough to make them stronger than attackers.

1315a40 But it is superfluous to speak about such things in detail. The goal is manifest, that the tyrant must seem to his subjects not tyrannical but a household manager and a king, not an embezzler but a trustee. He must also pursue measure in his way of life, not excess, and must keep company with the notables while being a demagogue to the many. For as a result, not only will his rule be more noble and more enviable because exercised over better people instead of over those who have been rendered abject, and not only will he not end up being hated and feared, but his rule will also be longer lasting and, in addition, he himself will, in his character, either be nobly disposed for virtue or half serviceable for the purpose, and not wicked but half wicked.

CHAPTER 12

Durability of Tyrannies. *Tyrannies are short-lived, the longest lasting only a hundred years and others about seventy years or thirty or much fewer.*

1315b11 Yet of all regimes, oligarchy and tyranny are rather short-lived. For the tyranny at Sicyon, that of Orthagoras' sons and of Orthagoras himself,

98. Here again insolence might carry the connotation of rape.
99. Frag. 85 Diels-Kranz.

was in being for the longest time. It lasted a hundred years.[100] The reason for this was that they treated their subjects in measured fashion and were, in many respects, slaves to the laws; Cleisthenes was also, because of his warlike character, not easy to despise; and they acted the demagogue by acts of care in many matters. At any rate, Cleisthenes is said to have crowned the one who decided a victory against him, and some allege that the statue seated in the marketplace is an image of the person who gave this decision (they also say that Peisistratus once put up with being summoned to court in the Areopagus).

1315b22 Second is that of the Cypselids in Corinth, for it lasted seventy-three years and six months. Cypselus was tyrant for thirty years, Periander for forty and a half, Psammetichus the son of Gorgus for three.[101] The reasons are the same here as before. For Cypselus was a demagogue and had no armed guard throughout his reign, and Periander, though he became tyrannical, was warlike.

1315b29 Third is the tyranny of the Peisistratids at Athens. It was not, however, continuous. For Peisistratus twice went into exile while tyrant, so that in thirty-three years he was tyrant for seventeen of them. His sons ruled for eighteen years. Consequently their total years were thirty-five.

1315b34 Among the remaining tyrannies there was that associated with Hiero and Gelon in Syracuse. Yet not even this lasted long, and its total years are eighteen. For Gelon, after ruling seven years, died in the eighth, Hiero ruled for ten, and Thrasybulus was expelled in his eleventh month.[102] Most tyrannies have lasted an altogether short time.

1315b40 The things, then, in regimes and monarchies out of which come their destructions and also their preservations have pretty well all been discussed.

Refutation of the Rival Views of Socrates. *In the* Republic, *Socrates' discussion of changes is deficient because (i) with respect to the best regime (a) no explanation proper to it is given, (b) the explanation given creates a problem about time and (c) supposes falsely that the change must always be to the neighboring regime; (ii) with respect to the whole progress of change, there can be changes opposite to those it posits; (iii) with respect to tyranny, no account of change is or could be given; (iv) with respect to oligarchy, (a) change can be directly from oligarchy into tyranny, (b) change into oligarchy does not happen because the rulers become lovers of money, (c) oligarchy is no more two cities than some other regimes are, (d) change can occur for reasons other than the one alleged, (e) this reason anyway makes several false assumptions; (v) with*

100. This tyranny was founded in about 670. Cleisthenes was Orthagoras' great-grandson.
101. Cypselus ruled from about 657 to 627, Periander from 627 to 586, and Psammetichus from 586 to 583.
102. Cf. 7(5).10.1312b9–16.

respect to oligarchy and democracy, Socrates speaks as if there were only one kind of each regime.

1316a1 There is in the *Republic* a discussion by Socrates about changes,[103] but it is not nobly done. For he posits no change proper to his first and best regime. The reason he gives is that nothing endures but undergoes change within a certain cycle, and that the beginning lies in those things in which "a basic ratio of four to three, joined to five, produces two harmonies" (he means by this when the number on this diagram is cubed), his idea being that nature sometimes produces base persons who cannot be mastered by education.[104] Now as regards this fact itself, he has perhaps not spoken badly, for people can exist who are incapable of being educated and of becoming serious men, but how could this be a change peculiar to the regime he calls best, instead of to any regime and to anyone who is born? Yes, and as regards the time during which he says everything undergoes change, does this time also cause things that did not begin to be simultaneously to undergo change simultaneously? For instance, if something came to be on the day before the turning point, will it also undergo change at the same time? In addition, why does change in this regime lead to the Spartan regime? For it is often the case that every regime undergoes change into its opposite rather than into its neighbor.

1316a20 The same argument applies also to the other changes. For he says that change from the Spartan regime is into oligarchy and from oligarchy into democracy and from democracy into tyranny. Yet changes can also be the other way around, as from rule of the populace to oligarchy, and to this more than to monarchy.

1316a25 Further, in the case of tyranny, he does not say whether it will or will not undergo change, nor why, nor into what regime. The reason is that he would not have found it easy to say. For the thing is indeterminate, since, according to him, it ought to change into the first and the best regime (for then the process would be continuous and circular).[105] But there can also be change of tyranny into tyranny, as at Sicyon from that of Myron to that of Cleisthenes; or into oligarchy, as that of Antileon in Chalcis; or into democracy, as that of the sons of Gelon at Syracuse; or into aristocracy, as that of Charilaus at Sparta, and at Carthage.[106]

---

103. *Republic* 545a2–580a8.

104. 546c1–d2. How to interpret the mathematics of this passage properly is a matter of much controversy.

105. Apparently a reference to Socrates' remarks at 546a1–7.

106. Myron was Cleisthenes' brother; Antileon is not otherwise known; the regime that followed tyranny at Syracuse is called a democracy here (though earlier it was implied to be a polity or aristocracy; see 7(5).4.1304a27–29 and 10.1312b6–9), presumably because Aristotle is now using Socrates' categories, not his own (for Socrates is his target), and Socrates does

1316a34 There is also change into tyranny from oligarchy, as was the case with pretty well most of the ancient oligarchies in Sicily (the change in Leontini was to the tyranny of Panaetius, in Gela to that of Cleandrus, in Rhegium to that of Anaxilaus, and so on in many others). It is also strange to suppose that change into oligarchy happens because those in office become money-lovers and businessmen,[107] and not because those far superior in possessions do not think it just that those who do not have property should have equal shares in the city with those who do. Also, in many oligarchies it is not possible to engage in business but there are laws to prevent it; and in Carthage, which is run timocratically,[108] they engage in business and the regime has not yet undergone change.

1316b6 Strange too is saying that oligarchy is two cities, one of the rich and another of the poor.[109] For why is oligarchy more like this than the Spartan or any other regime where it is not the case that all have equal possessions or that all are equally good men? And, even when no one has become poorer than before, changes from oligarchy to rule of the populace happen no less if the needy become more numerous, and from rule of the populace to oligarchy if the part that is well-off is stronger than the multitude and the latter are careless but the former alert. Also, though there are many reasons that changes occur, Socrates alleges but one: that by living profligately and having to pay out interest on loans, they become poor[110] — as if everyone or almost everyone were rich to begin with. But this is false. Rather, innovations are made when some of the leaders have ruined their substance, but nothing terrible happens when some others have done so. Also, not even then is change more into rule of the populace than into any other regime. Further, people start factions and effect change in regimes if they do not share in honors or if they are wronged and insolently treated, even though they have not, through being able to do whatever they wish, squandered their substance (the cause of which, he says, is too much freedom).[111]

1316b25 Though there are several oligarchies and democracies, Socrates speaks of their changes as if there were only one of each.

---

not distinguish polity from democracy; Charilaus was mentioned earlier, in 2.10.1271b24–26; the tyranny at Carthage presumably preceded the establishment there of the regime praised in 2.11 (cf. 1272b30–33), just as the tyranny of Charilaus is thought to have preceded the final establishment in Sparta of Lycurgus' aristocracy.

107. 550e4–551b7.

108. The manuscripts say "democratically," but the change to "timocratically" seems required because Carthage is elsewhere said to be an aristocracy (6(4).7.1293b14–16) and Socrates' word for Aristotle's so-called aristocracy is timocracy.

109. 551d5–7.

110. 555c1–e1.

111. 555c2–4, d3–5; 556a4–9.

Book 8

Addendum on

Setting Up the

Other Regimes

CHAPTER 1

Reason and Order of the Addendum. *An addendum is necessary because (i) there are kinds of the kinds of regimes, as kinds of democracy, and anything left about them and what modes fit each would best be set forth; and (ii) there are combinations of these modes that make mixed regimes overlap with oligarchies and democracies and which have not been examined. Democracies are to be treated first, followed by oligarchies.*

1316b31 We have spoken already about the number and sorts of differences there are in the deliberative or controlling part of the regime, and also in the arrangement of the offices and of the law courts, and about which arrangement corresponds to which regime;[1] we have, in addition, spoken about the destruction and preservation of regimes and what are their origins and causes.[2] But since it turned out that there were several kinds of democracy and of the other regimes likewise, it will not be a bad idea to examine anything that remains to be said about them and to set forth at the same time the mode that is proper and beneficial for each of them.

1316b39 In addition, the combinations of all the aforesaid modes need to be examined, since these, when paired, make regimes overlap, and the result is that there are oligarchic aristocracies and polities of a more democratic sort. I mean by these pairings that need to be examined, though now they are not examined, such cases as when, for instance, the deliberative body and the choosing of offices are arranged in oligarchic fashion but the jury

1. 6(4).14–16.
2. 7(5).

courts in aristocratic fashion, or when these last and the deliberative body are arranged in oligarchic fashion but the choosing of offices in an aristocratic one, or when in some other way not everything that is proper to the regime is combined together.

1317a10 Now it was stated before which sort of democracy suits which sort of city and likewise which sort of oligarchy suits which sort of multitude, and also which of the remaining regimes is of benefit to whom.[3] Nevertheless, since it must not merely be made clear which of these regimes is best for cities but also how these and the others are to be set up, let us briefly go through this, and first let us speak about democracy, since its contrasting regime, the one some call oligarchy, will become manifest at the same time.

The Setting Up of Democracies. *Democracies come in several kinds because of the several ways the features typical of democracy are put together, as well as because of the different kinds of populace. So in order to set up and correct each kind of democracy, it is necessary to grasp all these features.*

1317a18 With respect to this investigation, all those features must be grasped that are characteristically popular and that seem to accompany democracies, because it is as a result of the way these are put together that the kinds of democracies arise and that there are more democracies than one and democracies of different sorts. For there are two reasons for the existence of several democracies. The first was mentioned before, that there are different sorts of populace, one of which is the multitude of farmers, another of vulgar mechanics, and another of laborers. When the first of these multitudes is taken along with the second or the third again with both, the difference in the democracy is not merely that it becomes better or worse but also that it is not the same democracy.[4] The second reason is the one we just stated: democracies are made different when the features that accompany democracies and that seem to be proper to this regime are put together, since fewer of them accompany one democracy, more another, and all of them a third. It is useful to be able to recognize each of these features, both for establishing whichever democracy one may happen to want and for making corrections. For those who set up regimes seek to put everything together that corresponds to the supposition of the regime, but they err in doing so, as was said earlier in our discussions of the preservation and destruction of regimes.[5] But now let us speak of the claims and character of democracies and what are the objects they desire.

3. 6(4).12–13.
4. Cf. 6(4).4 and 6.
5. 7(5).9.1309b18–1310a12.

CHAPTER 2

Features of Democracy. *The supposition or aim of democracy is freedom, both in the sense of each ruling and being ruled in turn on the basis of numerical equality and in the sense, which leads to the first, of living as one likes. From this aim come the following features of democracy: (i) choosing all offices from all; (ii) rule by turns; (iii) all or most offices chosen by lot; (iv) no or a low property qualification; (v) no repeated holding of the same office; (vi) offices of short tenure; (vii) court cases decided by everyone; (viii) control by the popular assembly and no office having a final say in anything; (ix) payment for assembly, courts, and offices; (x) citizens of no family, wealth, or education; (xi) no offices held for life.*

1317a40 Freedom is the supposition of the democratic regime, for it is the usual thing to say that only in this regime do people partake of freedom, since freedom, they say, is what every democracy aims at. One sort of freedom is to rule and to be ruled in turn, for popular justice is numerical equality and not equality according to merit.[6] But if this is what justice is, then the multitude must necessarily be in control, and whatever seems good to the majority must be what the end is and what is just (for they assert that each citizen must have equality). Consequently, in democracies the needy must have more control than the well-off, since they are the majority, and what seems good to the majority has the control. So one sign of freedom is this, and it is what the whole popular party lays down as the defining mark of the regime.

1317b11 Another sort of freedom is to live as one likes, for they say this is the work of freedom since to live as one does not like is characteristic of the slave. This, then, is the second defining mark of democracy. From it has come the feature of not being ruled, by anyone at all preferably, but, failing that, of being ruled only by turns; and that is how this defining mark contributes to freedom based on equality.

1317b17 From these suppositions and from this sort of principle come the following features of popular rule: choosing all the offices from everyone; everyone ruling each and each ruling everyone in turn; having all the offices chosen by lot, or as many as do not need experience and skill; having no property qualification for any office or the smallest qualification possible; having no one occupy the same office twice or rarely or only in the case of few offices (excepting those related to war); having all the offices, or as many as possible, of short duration; having everyone, or those chosen from everyone, decide all court cases, or most of them and those that are most important and have most control, such as those to do with the giving of ac-

---

6. Cf. 7(5).1.1301b29–40.

counts and with the regime and private contracts; having the assembly in control of everything or the most important things and no office in control of anything or as few things as possible (among offices the council is the most characteristic of popular rule when there is no ready supply of funds to give payments to everyone, but when there is, even this office is deprived of its power, for a populace that has an abundance of pay has all decisions referred to itself, as was said earlier in the preceding enquiry);[7] next, having pay provided for everyone, for the assembly, the law courts, and the offices if possible, or if not, for the offices, the law courts, the council, and those meetings of the assembly invested with most control or for those offices where common messes are a necessity; further, since oligarchy has the defining marks of family, wealth, and education, their opposites seem to be marks of popular rule—no family, poverty, and vulgarity; in the matter of offices, having none of them perpetual but if one might be left over from an ancient revolution, stripping it of its power and having it chosen by lot and not by election. These, then, are the things common to democracies.

How to Set Up the Kinds of Democracy

The First or Rhetorical Democracy. From what is agreed on to be democratic justice, namely everyone being numerically equal, results the democracy that is most of all held to be democracy, where they say everyone is in control and the needy rule no more than the wealthy. But the question is how to secure such equality, whether by dividing control between a smaller number of the rich and a larger number of the poor whose wealth is equal or by giving total control to the numerical majority. The second way is manifestly unequal and unjust since it will justify robbery of the rich, as the opposing oligarchic view will justify tyranny. The first way does secure equality, since it combines the views of poor and rich and gives control in the regime to the separate majorities of both, or to some balance between them. But discovering this equality is easier than persuading either side to accept it.

1318a3 From the justice that is agreed on to be democratic, namely everyone having numerical equality, results the democracy that seems most of all to be democracy and rule of the populace. For they say equality is when the needy are in office no more than the well-off nor are alone in control but everyone is so on the basis of numerical equality.[8] For thus, they say, everyone would believe there was equality and freedom in the regime.

Chapter 3: 1318a11 But the difficulty that comes next is how to get the equality. Must the property qualifications of the 500 be divided through 1,000 and the 1,000 have equal power with the 500, or must this sort of equality not

7. 6(4).15.1299b38–1300a4.
8. Cf. 6(4).4.1291b30–39.

be established after such a manner but instead the division be made in this way and then an equal number taken from the 500 and the 1,000 and these be the ones who will have control over elections and law courts? Would this regime, therefore, be the most just according to popular justice? Or would it rather be the one that was according to quantity? For the popular party say that whatever seems good to the greater number is just, but the oligarchs say that whatever seems good to the greater property is so, for they say the decision must be made according to quantity of property.

1318a21 Both views, however, are unequal and unjust. For if that is just which the few decide, there will be tyranny, since if one of the well-off has more than the rest, then, by the standard of oligarchic justice, it will be just for him to rule alone. But if that is just which the numerical majority decide, they will do wrong and confiscate the possessions of the minority and the wealthy, as was said before.[9]

1318a27 To find out what equality they will both agree to, one must begin from the definitions they both give of justice. For they assert that the view of the greater part of the citizens should be in control. So let this stand, though not in every respect. Rather, since two parts happen to compose the city, rich and poor, let the view of both or of the majority of both be in control. Or if they hold opposing views, let that view be in control which is held by the majority, that is, by those whose property assessment is greater. For example, if there are ten rich and twenty poor, and a conflicting view was reached by six of the rich and by fifteen of the needier, and four of the rich have gone along with the poor and five of the poor with the rich, then the side with the superior assessment when both groups on either side are added up has the control. If the sides happen to be equal, one must consider it a difficulty common to what happens now when the assembly or the jury court is split in two: recourse must either be had to lot or something similar must be done.

1318b1 But even if finding out the truth where equality and justice are concerned is very difficult, achieving this is still easier than convincing those people of it who have the power to gain more for themselves. For the inferior always seek equality and justice, but the dominant care nothing for them.

CHAPTER 4

The Other Democracies. *As regards the first of the four democracies, that based on an agrarian populace of farmers or herdsmen, this is best, because it has the best character as being without leisure for frequent attendance at the assembly and as preferring*

9. 3.10.1281a14–28.

work to holding office, and because, combining fewer of the democratic features, it is nobly governed. To set up such a democracy, one needs laws to preserve and limit property and to encourage farming, though herdsmen too, as next best after farmers and similar to them, can be included, but not any of the other populaces, which are all more base. As regards the remaining democracies, these are worse, and to set them up one must mark off each time a slightly worse multitude. But, as regards the last democracy, one must avoid the demagogues' habit of extending the franchise as far as possible but instead extend it no further than is necessary to give a predominance to the multitude, mix up the new citizens with the older ones by dissolving previous groupings, and copy some of the institutions of tyranny, such as the license of women, children, and slaves.

1318b6 There are four democracies and the best is that which is first in order, as was said in the preceding discussion,[10] and it is also the oldest of them all. It is first in the sense of the rankings one might draw between kinds of populace, for the best populace is an agrarian one. Consequently, it is also possible to set up a democracy where the multitude lives from farming or herding. For since, on the one hand, the populace do not have much property, they are not at leisure and so cannot often attend the assembly, and since, on the other hand, they do not have the necessities of life, they spend their time at their work and have no longing for others' possessions; instead, where there are no great spoils to be had from office, they find it more pleasant to work than to engage in politics and exercise rule. For the many desire profit rather than honor. An indication of this is that they even tolerated the tyrannies of the old days and tolerate oligarchies now if no one prevents them working or robs them of anything. For it is not long before some of them become rich and before others cease to be needy. Moreover, if they do have any spark of ambition, control over elections and audits would give them what they need, since there are populaces where the many are satisfied even if they do not take part in elections but, as in Mantinea, some of them are chosen from all by turns and have control over deliberation, which, in the way it once was in Mantinea, must be considered a sort of pattern of democracy.[11]

1318b27 That is why, indeed, it is both an advantage and a customary practice in the aforementioned democracy for everyone to elect and audit the offices and to sit on juries, but for the greatest offices to be elected and on the basis of a property qualification, greater offices having greater property qualifications; or even for no office to be held on the basis of a property qualification but rather by those with ability. Those who govern themselves in this way must necessarily have a government that is run nobly, for the

---

10. 6(4).4.1291b39–1292a39 and 6.1292b22–1293a12.
11. Not much further is known about this regime in Mantinea.

offices will always be in the hands of the best while the populace consent and do not envy the decent, and this arrangement must necessarily be enough for the decent and notables, since they will not be subject to the rule of others who are worse and they will rule justly because others are in control of the audits. For it is an advantage to be responsible to others and not be able to do whatever one thinks good. The license to do whatever one wishes is incapable of providing defense against the base element in each human being. So the necessary result, and a result of very great help in regimes, is that the decent rule without falling into error and the populace are oppressed in nothing. It is manifest, then, that this is the best of the democracies and it is also manifest why: because the populace is of a certain kind of character.

1319a6 As regards establishing the populace as a farming one, useful in every respect are some of the laws that used to be laid down in ancient times, which either wholly banned the right to acquire more than a certain measure of land or banned the acquisition of it between a given location and the town or city. And there used to be a law in many cities, at any rate in ancient times, denying a right even to sell the original allotment. The so-called law of Oxylus[12] had this sort of effect. It forbade borrowing against a certain portion of the land belonging to each individual. But given the way things are now, it is necessary to make corrections by also using the law of the Aphytaeans, since it is useful for what we are talking about. For although the Aphytaeans are many and occupy little land, they are all nevertheless farmers. The reason is that they do not go by the values of entire properties but make divisions into parts of such an amount that even the poor can surpass the property qualification.[13]

1319a19 The next best populace after the multitude of farmers is where they are herdsmen and live from flocks, for herding has much in common with farming and, as regards the activities of war, herdsmen above all are trained in their habits, useful in their bodies, and capable of living outdoors. The other multitudes that make up the remaining democracies are pretty well all more base, for their way of life is a base one, and no work to which the multitude of vulgar mechanics, traders in the market, and laborers puts its hand involves virtue. Further, because they wander about the public square and the town, all folk of this class, so to say, find it easy to attend the assembly. But farmers are scattered about the country and accordingly do not come together nor have the like demand for these meetings, and where it is further the case that the countryside is so placed that it lies a great distance from the city, one can easily construct a serviceable democracy or polity,

---

12. An ancient lawgiver in Elis.
13. Nothing further is known of these arrangements at Aphytis.

for the multitude must have its lodgings in the fields. Consequently, if there also exists a crowd of traders, one should not in democracies have meetings of the assembly without the multitude from the country.

1319a38 How, then, the first and best kind of democracy should be set up has been stated. But how to set up the other ones is also manifest, for it is necessary to make progressive deviations and to keep on separating out a worse multitude.

1319b1 The last kind of democracy, however, because it is one that all take part in, cannot be borne by every city, nor can it easily endure when it is not well put together in its laws and customs (most of what destroys it and other regimes was pretty much stated earlier).[14] For the purposes of setting up this kind of democracy and of making the populace strong, those in power are wont to get hold of as many people as possible and to make citizens not only of the legitimate but of bastards too and of those who are citizens by a parent on one side, whether the father's or mother's, for all these types have more of an affinity with a populace of this sort. This, then, is how demagogues are in the habit of setting up democracy. But one should make additions only up to the point where the multitude outweigh the notables and the middle and not go beyond this limit. For when this limit is overstepped, the regime is made pretty disorderly and the notables are more provoked and can barely tolerate the democracy. This in fact was the cause of faction in Cyrene,[15] for a little evil can be overlooked, but when it becomes sizable it is more in the eye.

1319b19 Further, the sorts of institutions used by Cleisthenes at Athens,[16] when he wanted to enlarge the democracy, and by those who set up the democracy in Cyrene[17] are useful for this sort of democracy. For one should make more and different tribes, combine private rites into a few common ones, and use every sophism to mix people up as much as possible with each other and dissolve previous bonds of familiarity. In addition, the institutions of tyranny all seem to have a popular character—I mean, for instance, not imposing any rule on slaves (which is of advantage up to a point) or on women and children and ignoring the fact that people are living as they wish. For those who support such a regime will prove considerable, since the many find it pleasanter to live a life of disorder than of moderation.

14. 7(5).
15. Perhaps a reference to disturbances there in 401.
16. Cf. 3.2.1257b34–39.
17. Probably in 462.

CHAPTER 5

How to Make the Kinds of Democracy Endure. *To ensure duration, (i) guard against the causes of destruction studied earlier and include in the laws the causes of preservation; (ii) have the property that has been confiscated in cases involving common matters declared sacred instead of public, and use heavy penalties to reduce the number and arbitrariness of prosecutions; (iii) to enable the populace to attend assembly and law courts where there are no revenues, have few meetings of the assembly and have jury courts of large competence but short duration; (iv) where there are revenues, do not dissipate them in doles but give occasional large sums, sufficient to enable the poor to acquire property or set up in trade or farming, and in the meantime tax the rich for necessary assemblies but impose no pointless public service; (v) have the rich make the poor their protégés or have them open up their land for common use; (vi) make offices double, one chosen by lot and one elected, or combine election and lot for the same office.*

1319b33 But for the legislator and those who want to establish some such regime, setting it up is not the greatest nor even the only work. Rather their work is to ensure that it is preserved, for it is not hard for people to continue governing themselves in any way whatever for one or two or three days. Hence, it is necessary to take what was studied earlier, the ways of preserving and destroying regimes, and try, from these, to procure stability, exercising caution against causes of destruction and laying down such laws, both written and unwritten, as will include within them what in particular preserves regimes. And one must not suppose that what is popular or oligarchic is that which will make the regime as democratic or oligarchic as possible but rather that what will make it last the longest period of time is.

1320a4 Demagogues nowadays curry the favor of the populace and use the law courts for many acts of confiscation. So it is necessary for those who care about the regime to act in contrary fashion and pass laws requiring that nothing forfeit in a case involving common matters be common property but rather be sacred property. For wrongdoers will be no less careful, since they will be fined just the same, while the crowd will vote less against those on trial since they are not going to get anything from it. Further, it is necessary always to have as few public lawsuits as possible and to use large penalties to curb random prosecutions. For such prosecutions are not usually brought against the popular party but against the notables, and it is also necessary for all the citizens to be most kindly disposed to the regime or, if not, at least for them not to think of those in control as their enemies.

1320a17 Since in democracies of the last kind the numbers are large and it is hard for them to attend the assembly without pay, this makes them, if they have no revenue, hostile to the notables, for they must get funds through taxation, confiscation, and corrupt juries, things that have already overturned many democracies. So when there happen to be no revenues, there must be few meetings of the assembly and jury courts must have cognizance over many matters[18] but sit on few days. For this leads both to removing from the rich any fear of the expense if the well-off do not receive jury pay but the needy do, and also to the making of much better verdicts. For the well-off do not want to be away from their private affairs for many days but are willing to be so for short periods.

1320a29 But when, on the other hand, there do happen to be revenues, one must not do what demagogues do nowadays. They distribute the surplus and people both take it and immediately demand the same all over again. Such a way of helping the needy is the proverbial "leaking jar."[19] He who is truly of the popular sort should see to it instead that the multitude is not excessively needy (for this makes the democracy a depraved one), and so should devise ways for making abundance lasting, and, since this also benefits the well-off, should collect together the proceeds from the revenues and distribute them to the needy in lump sums, especially when enough can be accumulated for the purchase of a plot of land or, if not, for making a start in trade or farming. And if this cannot be done for all, distribution must instead be made tribe by tribe or by some other part in turn. In the meantime the well-off must be taxed for the payments of necessary meetings and be released from pointless public services. It is by governing in this sort of way that the Carthaginians have secured the friendliness of the populace, for they are always sending out some of them to subject cities and making them prosperous.[20]

1320b7 It is also a mark of the refined and of notables who have sense to divide up the needy among themselves and, by giving them a start, turn them to industrious work. A noble thing too is to imitate what the Tarentines do, for by opening up their properties for the common use of the needy they secure the kindliness of the multitude.[21]

1320b11 In addition, they have made all their offices double, one set is elected and the other chosen by lot, so that by means of the latter the populace get a share and by means of the former government is carried on in a

---

18. The meaning could also be that jury courts should have "many members" (the Greek is an indeterminate *pollōn* or "many").

19. An illusion to the daughters of Danaus, whose punishment in Hades for murdering their husbands was to keep on pouring water into a leaking jar; cf. also 2.8.1267a41–5.

20. Cf. 2.11.1273b18–21.

21. Nothing is known of the details of this arrangement at Tarentum, but as Tarentum was a colony of Sparta, its practices may have been similar; cf. 2.5.1263a30–37.

better way. But it is also possible to do this by dividing up the selfsame office and having some of the members elected and others chosen by lot.

1320b17 How democracies, then, should be set up has been stated.

CHAPTER 6

The Setting Up of Oligarchies

How to Set Up the Kinds of Oligarchy. Oligarchies are to be constructed from the contrary features using the corresponding democracy as analogue. So in a well-mixed oligarchy, (i) have low property qualifications for the necessary offices and high ones for those that are more in control, (ii) allow anyone with the qualification to share in the regime, (iii) make the qualifications such that those who share are stronger and better than those who do not. In the next oligarchies, just tighten the qualifications a little, but as these oligarchies, especially the last and tyrannical one, are the worst or most sickly, they need the most looking after.

1320b18 How oligarchies must be constructed is also pretty well manifest from these considerations. For each oligarchy must be brought together from the contrary features, with the democracy opposed to it used as the analogue, as in the case of the most well mixed and first of the oligarchies. This is the one that is akin to so-called polity. Here the property qualifications should be distinguished from each other, and some must be set lower and some higher; the lower will be the basis on which people share in the necessary offices and the higher the basis on which they share in those that are more in control. Anyone who acquires the qualification must have the right to take part in the regime, the qualification must be used to include a large enough multitude from the populace so that those who share in the regime will be stronger than those who do not, and those who do share must always be taken from the better part of the populace.

1320b29 The next oligarchy following must also be constructed in like manner by slightly tightening the qualification. But as for the oligarchy opposite to the last democracy, which is the most dynastic and tyrannical of oligarchies, the worse it is the more guarding it needs. For just as bodies in good condition for health or ships with crews in noble condition for a voyage can have more things go wrong without thereby being destroyed, and just as bodies in a sickly condition or ships with loose timbers and a base lot for their crew cannot even put up with small things going wrong, so too in the case of regimes the worst ones need the most guarding. Now democracies on the whole are preserved by their great numbers (for this is the justice opposed to justice based on merit), but it is clear that oligarchy must, on the contrary, get its preservation from how well it is arranged.

CHAPTER 7

How to Make the Kinds of Oligarchy Endure. *As there are four kinds of military forces, oligarchies can be made strong and lasting where defense depends on the more expensive arms. So an oligarchy of the very rich can so survive where the land is best suited to the cavalry, or an oligarchy of the moderately rich can so survive where the land is suitable for heavy armed infantry. In either circumstance, to counter the threat from a large populace equipped with the light arms they can afford, have a corps of light armed troops drawn from the young oligarchs. Further, a share in the regime should be given to any of the excluded who acquire the property qualification or give up their former ways or are adjudged worthy of rule. Also, the offices that must be in the hands of oligarchs should be burdened with public service, and upon entry into office magnificent sacrifices should be held or the city adorned with buildings and statues.*

1321a5 There are four parts in particular to the multitude—the farmers, the vulgar mechanics, the merchants, and the laborers—and there are four parts useful for war: the cavalry, the heavy infantry, the light infantry, and the sailors. So where the land happens to be suitable for horses, there things are naturally well adapted to making the oligarchy strong, for preservation of the inhabitants rests on the power of the cavalry, and the rearing of horses belongs to those who have large properties. But where the land is suitable for heavy armed infantry, things are adapted to the next kind of oligarchy, for heavy armed infantry come from the well-off rather than the needy.

1321a13 Light armed forces and naval forces, however, are entirely popular, so as things stand now, where there is a large multitude of this type and there are factional divisions, the oligarchs often come out worse in the contest. A cure for the problem is to be taken from generals expert in war who couple to the forces of the cavalry and the heavy armed troops a suitable force of the lightly armed. In this manner the populace prevail over the well-off during factional strife, since being lightly armed they can easily contend against the cavalry and the heavy armed infantry. So if oligarchs set up this lightly armed force with recruits from the populace, they are setting it up against themselves; but since there is a distinction between ages and there are some who are older and others younger, oligarchs must have their sons taught auxiliary and light armed work when they are still young, and these must then be athletes in doing this work when they have passed out of the ranks of boyhood.

1321a26 A share in the ruling body must be given to the multitude, either, in the way said before,[22] to those who have acquired the property qualification or, as in Thebes, to those of them who have kept away from the work of vulgar mechanics for a certain period of time[23] or, as in Massilia, by making a judgment about who, both from within and without the ruling body, is worthy of office.

1321a31 Further, the offices with most control, which must be kept in the hands of those in the ruling body, should have imposed on them acts of public service so that the populace will be willing not to have a share in them and will be forgiving to the rulers as to those who have paid a heavy fee for office. Also appropriate is to make magnificent sacrifices and undertake some public project upon entry into office, so that when the populace take part in the events associated with the festivities and see the city adorned with votive statues here and buildings there they will be glad to see the regime continue. It will also be the case that the notables have memorials of their expenditure. Nowadays, however, those associated with oligarchies do not do this but the opposite, since they seek profits no less than honor. So it is well to call them small democracies.

1321b1 Let these, then, be our distinctions about how to set up democracies and oligarchies.

CHAPTER 8

The Setting Up of the Combinations of Regimes

The Elements of Rule Available for Combining. *The offices necessary to a city are: (i) care of the market; (ii) care of the public and private spaces; (iii) care of the countryside; (iv) the receipt and disbursement of revenues; (v) registration of contracts and lawsuits; (vi) the carrying out of sentences passed down by the courts (which because of its odium must be divided up in a variety of ways); (vii) affairs of war; (viii) accounts and audits; (ix) deciding and introducing measures for decision or presiding over the assembly; (x) priests and other sacred ministers; (xi) management of women and of children, guardianship of the laws, presidency of the gymnasium, and public spectacles, which are peculiar to more leisurely regimes.*

1321b4 The next thing after the above discussion is, as was stated earlier,[24] to divide up in noble fashion what concerns the offices, how many there are

22. 8(6).6.1320b25–26.
23. Cf. 3.5.1278a21–26.
24. Usually understood as a reference back to 6(4).15, in particular to 1300b7–12, but perhaps better, or also, regarded as a reference to the program of study proposed for the present book, in 1.1316b39–1317a10.

of them, which they are and with control over what matters. For without the necessary offices a city cannot exist, while without those that concern its good arrangement and ordered adornment²⁵ it cannot be managed nobly. Furthermore, in small cities there must be fewer offices and in large ones more, as was said earlier.²⁶ What offices, therefore, are suitable for being combined and what for keeping separate must not be overlooked.

1321b12 First, then, there is among the necessary offices the care of the public square, where there must be some office to oversee contracts and the well-ordered adornment of things. For pretty well all cities have to buy some things and sell others for their mutual necessities, and buying and selling is the handiest way to get the self-sufficiency that seems to be what draws people into one regime.

1321b18 A second care, following on from the first and close to it, is the care of public and private spaces in the town, so that things might be in well-ordered adornment, preserving and repairing collapsing buildings and roads, ensuring that people have no complaints about their mutual boundaries, and for all the other similar things that are part of the same care. Most people call this sort of office town management, and it has numerically many parts and in rather populous cities different persons are set up over the different parts —as, for instance, wall builders, supervisors of wells, and harbor guards.

1321b27 There is another office that is necessary and rather similar to this one, for it is about the same things but with respect to the country and what lies outside the town. Some call these officials field managers and others forest rangers.

1321b30 These cares, then, concerned with these matters, are three. Another office is that to which the revenues from common sources are given and by which they are guarded and distributed to each part of administration. They are called receivers and treasurers.

1321b34 Another office is that with which private contracts and decisions from the jury courts must be registered. Before the same officials must also come indictments and the initiation of lawsuits. Now, in some places this office is divided among many persons, but all these matters fall under the control of a single office.²⁷ They are called sacred recorders or presidents or recorders or other similar names.

1321b40 The next office after this, but pretty well the most necessary and most difficult among them, is concerned with actions against those who

25. The Greek for "ordered adornment" here and in the rest of chapter is *kosmos*, or a cognate thereof.

26. 6(4).15.1299a31–b30.

27. Reading *esti de mia kyria* ("fall under the control of a single office") with the manuscripts, rather than *esti d' hou mia kyria* ("in other places fall under the control of a single office") with Dreizehnter.

have been convicted in court or whose names are posted for fines and debts, and with guarding the bodies of prisoners. It is a difficult office because of the great odium attached to it, and consequently, where there are no great profits to be made from it, people cannot endure to undertake it or, if they do, they do not want to act in accordance with the laws. It is a necessary office because having court cases about matters of justice is no use if these cases do not realize their end. Consequently, if people cannot live in community with each other unless cases about justice are heard, neither can they do so unless the decisions are acted upon. Hence, it is better for this office not to be a single one but rather for some to come from one court and others from another. An attempt at a similar distinction must also be made in the case of the posting of notices. Further, some actions must be taken by the offices; in particular, suits decided by outgoing offices must be acted on by incoming offices and, in the case of sitting offices, one of them must pass judgment and another must act on it—as, for instance, town managers might act on cases decided by managers of the public square and others might act on cases decided by the former. For the less odium attached to those who take the action the more the actions will be completely carried out. Thus, to have those who pass judgment on a case be the same as those who act on it involves a double odium, but to have the same persons act on all cases makes them everyone's enemies.[28]

1322a19 In many places the office that does the guarding is distinguished from that which carries out the sentence, as with the Eleven at Athens.[29] Hence, it is better also to make this separate and to apply the sophistry in its case too. For it is no less necessary than the office just mentioned, but the decent have a particular aversion to it, and putting the depraved in control of it is not safe as they are more in need of being guarded than capable of guarding others. That is why there must not be a single office deputed to these matters, nor must the same office continually be so, but this care must be undertaken by different persons in turn, both from among the young, where there is a detachment of cadets or garrison troops, and from the offices.

1322a29 These offices, then, are to be put first as being most necessary. Next must be put those that are no less necessary but are arranged at a higher rank, for they require much experience and trust. Of such a sort would be

28. Reading *polemious pasin* with the manuscripts, not *polemian pasan* (involves an odium that is "wholly hostile") with Dreizehnter.

29. Reading *dihēirētai* ("is distinguished from") with the manuscripts, rather than *sunhēktai* ("is joined to") with Dreizehnter. The reason for suggesting an emendation is that the Eleven at Athens (the officials in charge of prisons) do not seem to be an instance of the separation of guarding prisoners from carrying out a sentence, since the Eleven did also carry out executions and had some role in collecting debts. Still, the collectors of debts were a distinct office from the Eleven, and that may be all Aristotle has in mind here.

those that concern the protection of the city and all those that are arranged for its needs in time of war. There is need both in peace and war of people to look after the defense of gates and walls and to inspect and marshall the citizens. In some places many offices are in charge of all these things, but in others fewer are (in small cities, for instance, one office deals with all of them). They are called generals and war leaders. In addition there is sometimes an office each set in charge of cavalry, light armed troops, archers, and sailors (where these exist). They are called admirals, cavalry commanders, and regimental commanders, and under these in turn are trireme captains, company commanders, tribal commanders, and all their subordinates. But these things constitute a single whole kind, that of taking care of the affairs of war. That then is how things stand with this office.

1322b7 But since some offices, though not all, handle considerable quantities of common funds, there must be some other office to do the accounts and receive the audits but which does not undertake any other office. Some call these auditors, others accountants, others examiners, others advocates.

1322b12 Besides all these offices there is the one that has the most control over everything. For often the same office makes the final decision about a proposal as well as introduces it, or it presides over the multitude where the populace is in control (for there must be something to convene the body that controls the regime). Sometimes they are called precouncillors because they deliberate beforehand, but where the multitude is in control they are instead called a council.

1322b17 These, then, are the number of the political offices. Another kind of care is about the gods—as the priests, for instance, and the supervisors of things to do with the sacred places (both preservation of existing buildings and restoration of those that are falling down) and of anything else arranged for the gods. It is sometimes the case that this care is a single one, as in small cities, whereas elsewhere it is many, and all are distinct from the priesthood—as, for instance, sacrificers, temple guards, and treasurers of sacred monies. Next after this is the office that is specifically devoted to the common sacrifices, those that are by law not entrusted to priests but get their position of honor from the common hearth. These officials are called kings by some and presidents by others.

1322b29 The necessary cares, then, to speak summarily, are concerned with these matters: with things both spiritual and military, with revenues and with expenses, with the public square and with the town, the harbors, and the country; further, with what concerns the jury courts, registering of contracts, exacting penalties, guarding prisoners, accounts and examinations, auditing of officials; and lastly, offices to do with deliberation on common affairs.

1322b37 Peculiar to cities that have more leisure and enjoy more prosperity and which, in addition, take thought for the well-ordered adornment of things, are the offices of manager of women, guardian of the law, manager of children, president of the gymnasium, and also taking care of gymnastic and Dionysiac contests and of any other spectacles there may be. Of these offices some are manifestly not popular, as the manager of women and of children, for the needy, lacking slaves, must use their wives and children as attendants. Of the three offices under which election to the controlling offices are sometimes made—law guardians, precouncil, and council—law guardians are an aristocratic feature, precouncillors an oligarchic one, and a council a popular one.

1323a9 Concerning the offices, then, pretty much everything has been said in outline.[30]

---

30. This concluding sentence may be incomplete since, in the Greek, it has a solitary *men* ("on the one hand"), which normally would be followed by a corresponding *de* ("on the other hand").

Index